DATE			

WE ASK ONLY A FAIR TRIAL

BLACKS IN THE DIASPORA SERIES
Darlene Clark Hine and John McCluskey, Jr.
General Editors

MIDWESTERN HISTORY AND CULTURAL SERIES
James H. Madison and Thomas J. Schlereth
General Editors

WE ASK ONLY A
Fair Trial

A HISTORY OF
THE BLACK COMMUNITY
OF
EVANSVILLE, INDIANA

DARREL E. BIGHAM

INDIANA UNIVERSITY PRESS

Bloomington & Indianapolis

Published in association with the

UNIVERSITY OF SOUTHERN INDIANA

Library of Congress Cataloging-in-Publication Data

Bigham, Darrel E.
We ask only a fair trial.

(Blacks in the diaspora) (Midwestern history and
culture)
"Published in association with the University of
Southern Indiana."
Bibliography: p.
Includes index.
1. Afro-Americans—Indiana—Evansville—History.
2. Evansville (Ind.)—Race relations. I. Title.
II. Series. III. Series: Midwestern history and
culture.
F534.E9B58   1987   977.2'33   86-45892
ISBN 0-253-36326-8

1 2 3 4 5 91 90 89 88 87

To the memory of
Elizabeth F. Hitchcock
and
John McDill

CONTENTS

ILLUSTRATIONS

MAPS

TABLES

PREFACE

With few exceptions, studies of urban black communities published in the past twenty years have treated large American metropolises and ignored the experiences of blacks in towns and small to middle-sized cities. That, and the paucity of literature on blacks in Indiana (and the virtual exclusion of blacks from histories of Evansville), prompted the author to commence research on the Evansville black community in the early 1970s. Out of that emerged several articles on the 1865–1900 period which appeared in the *Indiana Magazine of History* between 1979 and 1982.[1]

Further research on the history of Evansville blacks and additional reading in secondary literature led the author to conclude that a book-length study was necessary.[2] In part, that was due to his realization that Afro-American history in urban settings is best understood by attempting to explain the development of a subculture and the interrelationships among its members as well as between it and the majority community. The progress of members of that community must also be compared with that of whites, native and foreign-born, as well as with other black communities throughout the nation. The countless offenses against Evansville blacks need to be described, to be sure, but they form only the backdrop for the story. From the initial settlement of the river city in the summer of 1812 to the end of the Second World War, during which faint signs of a new era in race relations emerged, black Evansville offers a rich and variegated history.

Evansville is intriguing not only because of the ways in which its history corroborates the patterns of ghetto life present in other cities, but also due to the unique factors which shaped it. Black population development, for one, is distinctive, for unlike most Northern cities it grew rapidly between 1865 and 1900, attaining a proportion of total population (13 percent), which was one of the highest in the Midwest. Thereafter, it declined and then leveled off until the Second World War, when it grew modestly. In the meantime, the urban black population in the North expanded substantially. The relatively small size and the lack of growth of black Evansville meant, among other things, that the development of a middle and an upper class was more difficult than in many Northern cities.

Geography and culture also shaped the course of black Evansville. A Northern border city, the second most southerly in the Old Northwest (after Cairo, Illinois), Evansville was heavily influenced by its economic and demographic ties to the South. Because of its distance from the capital city (and most other cities in Indiana) and its poor inland transportation connections to most of the state, it was often referred to as the "pocket city," an epithet which connoted insularity and even parochialism. Added to that was the fact that the culture of the city was shaped by its connections to the South, particularly its many Upper Southern settlers. Also important in the formation of Evansville culture was the coming of Germans—mostly from Bavaria, Hesse, Württemberg, and Baden—beginning in the late 1830s. Primarily members of the Missouri Synod Lutheran Church, the Evangelical Synod of North America, and the Roman Catholic Church, they represented almost half of the city's population by 1900. Mostly blue-collar workers, they shared the Upper Southerners' negative attitudes and values about black Americans.

Evansville's economy was also a factor. The city did not develop the level of heavy industry and the requisite number of semiskilled mass production jobs which attracted black population growth in such cities as Chicago, Gary, Detroit, and Indianapolis after 1900. A large proportion of the white work force was employed in firms requiring a relatively high degree of skill—furniture and stove manufacturing, for example—before the 1930s. Employment opportunities for blacks remained limited to domestic and public service and to unskilled labor.

The virulent form of racism which resulted thrived not only because of American attitudes and values of the time but also certain local traits: the small size of the black community, the homogeneous, traditional culture of the region, and the extremely limited opportunity for black social and economic advancement. It created an environment which from the earliest days made for continuity, not change, in the quality of race relations. Nevertheless, out of this evolved a plethora of efforts by black Evansvillians to obtain a fair chance to realize the American dream. Their pursuit of that dream was unyielding, despite frequent setbacks and shifts in tactics, and out of that emerged a subculture which, by the 1930s, was able, in modest ways, to begin challenging the premises on which the segregated city had functioned since its founding.

This study comprises four chronological divisions: before 1865, when black Evansville was a small part of the city populace; 1865–1900, years of rapid expansion in the black population and of the formation of an incipient ghetto society; and 1900–1930, a period of consolidation of the racial ghetto; and the years of the Great Depression and the Second World War. An epilogue dealing with the immediate postwar years is also provided. Within parts II and III are topical chapters treating population and residential patterns, economic opportunity, race relations, class and culture, and politics and leadership.

The historical resources available for a study of black Americans in a medium-sized city in which there was a low degree of residential persistence are limited. Few records of black institutions survive, and because of white racism local blacks are virtually ignored and treated stereotypically in primary and secondary sources. There are, nevertheless, other resources—the federal population schedules from 1820 to 1910, the aggregate census records printed decennially, city directories (first published in 1858), and a wealth of public materials, such as deeds, articles of association, trustees' elections, school board and city council minutes, police arrest records, and cemetery records—which allow a substantial amount of insight into the lives of ordinary people. Also valuable are interviews conducted by the author between 1972 and 1985 with scores of black Evansvillians.[3]

In addition, newspaper sources are plentiful, although they must be used with care. Particularly valuable is the *Evansville Journal* (later *Journal-News*), a Whig-Republican daily which prior to its demise in the mid-1930s provided much information about black Evansville, due to the special relationship that Republicans of the era felt toward blacks. During the decade prior to 1909, the paper also published regularly a column for blacks, which is a rich lode of details about black society in the most difficult years of black-white relations in American history. The *Courier*, a Democratic daily, is also a useful source after the 1890s, when its extreme anti-black rhetoric began to diminish. Probably the most sympathetic—relatively speaking—was the *Evansville Press*, a Scripps daily begun in the summer of 1906, which afforded a balanced view of the way local Democrats and Republicans sought to manipulate black voters. Although black newspapers in Indiana are few and far between, *The* (Indianapolis) *Freeman* and the *Indianapolis Recorder* for ca. 1893–1945 provide valuable perspectives of black Evansville, as does Evansville's short-lived *Argus*, published between 1938 and 1943.

The author wishes to thank the staffs of Willard Library, the Indiana Historical Society Library, the Indiana State Library, and especially the Media Services Department and the Special Collections Department, University Archives, of the University of Southern Indiana Library for their assistance. Joan Catapano and Jane Rodman of Indiana University Press nurtured the development of the manuscript. The author is deeply indebted to Josephine Elliott of New Harmony, USI archivist emeritus, who provided substantial guidance in the collection and interpretation of historical resources relating to the black community of Evansville, and to Joan Marchand, Director of the Historic Preservation Office of the City of Evansville, who generously shared the fruits of her labors. He is also grateful for the exemplary scholarship of Professors C. S. Griffin, John G. Clark, David Katzman, Donald McCoy, and William Tuttle of the University of Kansas. James Madison of Indiana University, Thomas Schlereth of Notre Dame University, Darlene Clark Hine of Purdue University, and Kenneth Kusmer of Temple University read the entire manuscript and offered valuable advice. The late Professor Elliott Rudwick's comments on the section dealing with the Second World War—a paper delivered at the 1984 meeting of the Southern Historical Association—were most useful. He is especially appreciative of Professor Emma Lou Thornbrough of Butler University, the pioneer in the study of black Hoosiers, who has offered encouragement and assistance at several stages of his research. He wishes to thank Drs. David L. Rice and Robert L. Reid of USI, who have been supportive of this project since its inception, and to recognize the assistance provided by the USI Foundation in publishing this work.

Finally, he acknowledges the insights and the assistance provided by three persons—Alberta and Solomon Stevenson, and Charles Rochelle—whose quiet and firm resolve and wealth of contributions to Evansville's development distinguish them as remarkable citizens who happen to be black.

WE ASK ONLY A FAIR TRIAL

PART I

Faint Beginnings,
1812–1865

From the Founding of the City to the End of the Civil War

The first deed record book of Vanderburgh County contains an unusual entry for December 26, 1822. Identified as part of the Montgomery County (Indiana) records for 1818, it described one George Washington, twenty-six, as being about five feet, ten inches in height and having three scars. It certified that he had been born and raised of free parents in Rockville. Aside from its legal significance, this appears to be the first occasion in which an Evansville black was identified by a name. It also reveals much about the history of blacks in the river city before 1865, for life was neither profitable nor secure for those residing on the north shore of the Ohio River, ostensibly the border between freedom and slavery. At the first meeting of the trustees of the town of Evansville on March 20, 1819, officials recognized the uniqueness of the black presence by subjecting to taxation "bound or hired servants of color."[1]

By traditional measurements, the Afro-American role in antebellum Evansville would seem to be minor. The number of Afro-Americans in Vanderburgh County slowly grew from the handful (twelve) identified in the federal census enumeration of 1820 to the antebellum high of 230 in the census of 1850, about 2 percent of the population. Ten years later, it had declined to 128, less than 1 percent of the total. The number in Evansville and its sister town of Lamasco, annexed in 1857, rose slightly—to ninety-six in 1860.[2] Compared with the black experience in Boston, Philadelphia, or even Indianapolis, and especially among the millions of enslaved Afro-Americans residing to the south of the Ohio, this was perhaps an insignificant number of people in an insignificant part of the United States. Yet even this modest development vividly illustrated the plight of freed blacks in Indiana, and particularly its southern region, and the foundation of postwar black society and black-white relations in Evansville was partially laid before the end of the Civil War.

The small number of blacks in the region reflected decisions which were largely external to Evansville. Not only were most Afro-Americans enslaved, but their status was reinforced by state and federal law. The stringent fugitive slave law of 1850, for instance, "protected slaveholders in their efforts to capture alleged fugitives and enormously increased the power of the federal government to assist them in the process. The law also provided for stringent penalties for anyone assisting a fugitive. . . ." Those unfortunate enough to be apprehended were brought before special federal commissioners, where they were presumed to be runaways, and their alleged masters did not need to be present to present evidence of ownership. The law, which applied *ex post facto*, "denied [blacks] the right of trial by jury . . . [and] the right to confront witnesses as well as [the] right of habeas corpus." Federal commissioners were also rewarded if they decided in favor of the purported master.[3]

Despite misgivings that many Hoosiers harbored about the morality of slavery, there was little doubt that blacks were unwelcome in the state. Blacks could not vote, serve in the state militia, attend public school, or testify in court except in cases in which blacks, mulattoes, or Indians were indicted, or in civil actions in which Afro-Americans alone were parties. The dominant attitude was "neither proslavery nor antislavery but anti-Negro."[4] A vivid expression of that was Article XIII of the Constitution of 1851, which provided that "[n]o negro or mulatto shall come into or settle in the state after the adoption of this Constitution." The article voided "contracts made with any Negro or Mulatto coming into the state" and fined "any person who shall employ such Negro or Mulatto , or otherwise encourage him to remain in the state." The fines were to be applied to "the colonization of such Negroes and Mulattoes and their descendants, as may be in the state at the adoption of the Constitution, and may be willing to migrate."[5]

By 1860, Indiana's black population was only 11,428, less than 1 percent of the total population and a net increase of 166 persons in the preceding decade. More than half resided in ten counties, some of which contained a large Quaker population. Many lived in Marion County and in Clark and Floyd counties, adjoining Louisville. Except for the 449 blacks in Knox County, few were present in the southwestern part of the state.[6]

Location, local culture, and state customs and laws combined to make Evansville and Vanderburgh County especially inhospitable to Afro-Americans. In Vanderburgh County slightly over 87 percent of the electorate—more than the average percentage for the statewide vote—endorsed Article XIII, which was submitted to the electorate separately from the Constitution. In the largest township, Pigeon, the article received slightly over 88 percent of the vote.[7]

Such restrictions notwithstanding, some Afro-Americans settled in Evansville and Vanderburgh County. Blacks enumerated in the 1820 census were unnamed, but beginning in 1830 free black heads of household were identified. One of the five was George Washington, aged between twenty-four and thirty-five. Washington must have resided in the town for at least eight years, given his testimony before the county recorder in 1822 and the fact that years later an old resident of Evansville recalled that when he arrived in the town in 1823 there was only one black resident, a blacksmith named Washington.[8] Many black newcomers were natives of the South, and especially Kentucky and Tennessee. According to the federal census enumeration of 1850, the first to offer information about birthplace, about 34 percent of the county's blacks had been born in those two states, and another 16 percent were natives of the lower South. Sixty-seven, or 30 percent, were native Hoosiers. Similar patterns would persist for years to come. It should also be noted that the population was largely illiterate. In 1850, thirty-one black Evansvillians, or 75 percent of those not of school age, could neither read nor write.[9]

TABLE 1:   Black Population of Vanderburgh County, 1820-1860

Region	Year				
	1820	1830	1840	1850	1860
Evansville	10			89	96
Other Pigeon	1		83	31	0
Center Twp.				0	3
Knight Twp.				36	23
Perry Twp.				25	0
Union Twp.	1		28	42	0
Armstrong Twp.			1	0	0
German Twp.				1	0
Scott Twp.				6	6
Total black	12	48	112	230	128
Total population	1,787	2,610	6,136	11,414	20,552
Percent black	0.7	1.8	1.8	2.0	0.6

Sources: U.S. Fourth Census, Population Schedules of Vanderburgh County, 1820, National Archives Microfilm Publications No. M33, Roll 14, Indiana, pp. 179–183; U.S. Fifth Census, Population Schedules of Vanderburgh County, 1830, National Archives Microfilm Publications No. M19, Roll 32, Indiana, pp. 386–422; U.S. Sixth Census, Population Schedules of Vanderburgh County, 1840, National Archives Microfilm Publications No. M704, Roll 96, Indiana, volume 10: 321–60; U.S. Seventh Census, Population Schedules of Vanderburgh County, 1850, National Archives Microfilm Publications No. 432, Roll 176, Indiana, pp. 727–1008; U.S. Eighth Census, Population Schedules of Vanderburgh County, 1860, National Archives Publications No. M653, Roll 302, Indiana, volume 32: 399–926. See also Department of State, *Compendium of the Enumeration of the Inhabitants and Statistics of the United States* .... (Washington, D.C., 1841), pp. 80–3; J. D. B. De Bow, Superintendent of the United States Census, *Statistical View of the United States.* ...(Washington, D.C., 1854), 230–35; Department of the Census, Department of the Interior, *Population of the United States in 1860, Compiled from the Original Returns of the Eighth Census* .... (Washington, D.C., 1864), 112–13. Hereafter the population schedules will be referred to in abbreviated form (e.g., Eighth Census, Population Schedules of Vanderburgh County), as will the aggregate statistics (e.g., Eighth Census, 1850, *Compendium*, p. 230). Because population statistics in the population schedules and the printed censuses were provided in irregular and incomplete form, the following must be noted: numbers are listed only in cases in which township statistics were given; in some cases the figures are composites, as in 1840, when the totals for Pigeon Township only were listed and the data for Perry and Union were combined; and the 1850 totals for Evansville include 10 blacks residing in Lamasco.

Distinctive patterns of settlement began to appear in the antebellum era (Table 1). Most blacks resided in Pigeon Township—Evansville and its immediate environs. From the outset, the number of black residents was small, as was the rate of growth of the black community. The stricter enforcement of the fugitive slave law and the enactment of Article XIII made the rate of growth in the 1850s particularly low. By contrast, the more northerly Midwestern cities of Cleveland and Detroit experienced significant increases in the number of free blacks during that decade. Like most Southern and Eastern cities, moreover, there was a consistently higher proportion of females to males. The ratio of males to females was .78 in 1830, .89 in 1840, .82 in 1850, and .92 in 1860. The percentage of persons aged twenty-three or less, moreover, was nearly 75 percent in 1830 and 70 percent in 1840; it declined to 57 percent in 1850 and 51 percent in 1860. The rise in the share of the black population over that age was due in part to the increase in the number of childless adults who settled in the 1840s and the 1850s.[10]

Since census data did not identify residence by ward until 1850 and by street until 1880, and since city directories of Evansville did not appear until 1858, it is difficult to pinpoint the residences of Evansville's black population in this era. One settlement was in the northeastern part of Union Township, in the bottomland near the southwest boundary of the town. Most Pigeon Township blacks in 1850 resided in Evansville, although some were residents of Lamasco, between town limits and Pigeon Creek to the northwest. Occupational patterns and other clues, notably the location of the first black church in Evansville, suggest that for the most part antebellum Afro-Americans dwelled near the waterfront, between the mouth of Pigeon Creek and Main Street in the town of Evansville.[11] A cross-check of the black household heads enumerated in the 1860 census with the list of black residents in the 1860 city directory lends support to this view, although it must also be observed that neither the size nor the racial density of that area would allow it to be pictured as black ghetto.[12]

Occupation and residence were closely related, and the patterns commenced in this period persisted after the Civil War. The earliest record of occupation was provided in the federal census enumeration of 1820, in which all were residents of white households, probably as servants. Half of them were slaves—residents of Matthew Lane's household—who found their status reinforced by the first town ordinance. In spite of the provisions of the Northwest Ordinance of 1787 and the Indiana constitution of 1816, both of which forbade slavery and involuntary servitude, the Indiana Supreme Court's ruling in 1820 interpreting the constitution as having abolished slavery was silent on indentures made before 1810, when Indiana Territory had for a time permitted slavery under the guise of indentured servitude. Although the Indiana Supreme Court outlawed involuntary servitude in 1821, instances of dubious legality recurred through the remainder of the decade. The fate of Matthew Lane's slaves is unclear, as Lane was not enumerated in the federal census of 1830.[13]

Evansville experienced an economic "takeoff" in the 1840s and 1850s, largely due to the commerce encouraged by steamboats and railroads, to the arrival of businessmen hoping to take advantage of the proposed Wabash and Erie Canal, and to the exploitation of the natural resources of the region, primarily coal and hardwood. That in turn contributed to a population explosion, as thousands of newcomers arrived from rural parts of the Midwest and the Upper South and from southern and central portions of Germany.

TABLE 2:   Occupations of Evansville Blacks, 1850 and 1860

	Year			
	1850		1860	
Occupation	Number	Percent	Number	Percent
High White Collar				
Professional	0	0	1	2.2
Major Proprietor,				
Manager, Official	0	0	0	0
Low White Collar				
Petty Proprietor,				
Manager, Official	1	3.3	1	2.2
Semiprofessional	0	0	0	0
Clerical/Sales	0	0	0	0
Blue Collar				
Skilled	5	16.7	5	11.4
Semiskilled/				
Service	15	50	23	52.3
Unskilled	9	30	14	31.8
TOTAL	30	100	44	100

Sources: Seventh and Eighth Censuses, Population Schedules for Vanderburgh County, 1850 and 1860, *passim.* The occupational categories are based on the suggestions of two authors whose analysis of occupation is especially persuasive: Kathleen Neils Conzen, *Immigrant Milwaukee, 1836–1860: Accommodation and Community in a Frontier City* (Cambridge, Mass., 1976), pp. 234–39, and Stephan Thernstrom, *The Other Bostonians: Poverty and Progress in the American Metropolis, 1880–1970* (Cambridge, Mass., 1973), pp. 289–302.

Blacks also participated in this process. Their share of the economic pie, as shown by Table 2, was meager. Most of the workers were semiskilled and unskilled workers—servants, cooks, washwomen, and laborers. Some were skilled artisans—bakers and carpenters. One, James Carter, ran a coffee house. Kentucky-born, Carter arrived in Evansville about 1840 and established what was probably the city's first black-owned business. The only professionals prior to 1860 were clergymen. The names of most of the AME pastors of the 1840s and the 1850s are not known, although a clergyman named S. W. Bath [Bass?]

was listed in the 1860 census and a Rev. Black was included in the 1863 city directory. Ordinary workers in 1850 were such men as Joseph Trimmer, a forty-year-old Virginian who worked and resided in the livery stable of James White, and Alexander Jones, a forty-year-old cook and also a native of Virginia. In 1860, typical workers included Aaron Flowers, a twenty-eight-year-old Mississippian employed as a steamboat hand, and Charlotte, his wife, who was a washwoman.[14]

It should also be noted that in 1850 and 1860, a substantial proportion of black workers (27 percent and 36 percent, respectively) were women. Most were domestics and washwomen, and one may infer from the enumerations that they were either single or widowed. In addition, a number of black workers were young. In 1850, for example, seven of the thirty workers were aged eighteen or less. All but one were servants.[15]

Despite menial status and the transience associated with river town society, especially during an era of such blatant racism, some blacks did remain in the city, and with that came property-holding and the rudiments of social order. James Carter was one of the most notable Evansville blacks prior to 1860. Enumerated in the censuses of 1840, 1850, and 1860, he was in his early thirties when he arrived in the town with his children. In 1850, he owned real and personal property worth $1,500 and was head of a household of six—his mother, four children, of whom three had been born in Indiana, and a mulatto servant. Ten years later, Carter was enumerated as a hotel keeper with personal property worth $560. (The value of his real property was not given.) The city directory of 1860 associated him with the National Hotel on Water Street, between Pine and Leet. Apparently Carter had remarried, as there was in his household a thirty-seven-year-old woman named Mary and a child, aged one. Two of the children listed in 1850 were also present.[16]

Another prominent family prior to 1860 was that of Kentucky-born Sina [Lena?] McDaniel. (A Thomas McDaniel was enumerated in 1830, but his relationship to her is unclear.) In 1850 her household numbered ten persons, and she possessed property worth a thousand dollars. A widow, she had three daughters as well as four other children with a different surname living with her. Ten years later her real and personal property amounted to slightly over $4,000, by far the greatest amount for any Afro-American in Evansville. Her household also included two boarders: a barber and the Methodist clergyman.[17]

Still another eminent family was that of Joseph Smith, a carpenter. Born about 1800 in Virginia, he resided in Lamasco with his wife, also a Virginian, and their sixteen-year-old son in 1850. The household also included another adolescent with a different surname. The family probably migrated to the town in the 1840s. By 1850 the Smiths had accumulated property worth $1,400, and ten years later that amount had nearly doubled.[18]

Several other important Afro-American households had been established near the town limits, in the northeast corner of Union Township, and they also helped form the nucleus of the antebellum and postbellum black community in

Evansville. The oldest was that of Henry Beatty, recorded in the 1830, 1840, and 1850 censuses. From a small household of four, recorded in 1830, Beatty, a native of Tennessee, built a farm which was worth $700.00 in 1850, when he was in his forties. Arriving in the late 1830s from Tennessee with his wife and nine children was Daniel Lyles. In 1850 Lyles possessed a farm worth $600.[19]

In both census years, 1850 and 1860, the value of black-owned real property amounted to about 0.3 percent of the total for the county, but the amount of property held by these few families was, under the circumstances, remarkable. In 1850, only twelve heads of Afro-American households owned real estate, and that was valued at $8,900. Three persons accounted for nearly half of the total. Ten years later, the total value of black-owned real estate was $11,760, and personal property was worth another $4,500. Only nine household heads owned real estate, and Mrs. McDaniel's share was one-third of the total. The ownership of property was an important aspect of free society, and black property owners provided models for their peers. The influence of this small group was undoubtedly much greater than the numbers would indicate.[20]

Even more important to the incipient community was the family, the core of social organization. Despite the vicissitudes produced by slavery, the vitality of the family was evident in several ways. A number of marriages—illegal across the river—were recorded by the county clerk, perhaps the earliest being that of John Lile [sic] and Minerva McDaniel in Union Township on July 28, 1836. Between March, 1839, and August, 1843, another twelve marriages were entered in county records. Most blacks in Evansville and Vanderburgh County, moreover, resided in households headed by blacks. In 1850 and 1860, only about one in five dwelled with whites, who employed them chiefly as servants. In 1850, for example, Louisa Simmes, aged fifteen, was part of the household of the wealthy physician Daniel Morgan, and Ann Sanderlin, sixteen, lived in the home of the prominent attorney, Thomas Garvin. The average size of the black household in the town was 4.3 in 1850 and 4.5 in 1860. As in slave society, black households included not only members of the immediate family but also more distant blood relatives and other persons adopted by the family heads. That was illustrated by the household of Sarah Gover [Glover?], a washwoman who in 1860 headed a seven-person household which included John Gover, seventeen; Aaron and Charlotte Flowers (he was a steamboat hand and she was a washwoman), and their two small children; and a waiter named George Caldwell who was twenty-two. Perhaps the household had migrated to Evansville together, as all but the children had been born in Mississippi. Such patterns of nurture, commenced in slave society, established important means whereby blacks learned to cope with the rigors of life in Northern urban society.[21]

Also vital was the black church. Although a handful attended white churches ("Aunt Judy Duprey, colored" was admitted to the Evansville Presbyterian Church in April, 1858), most, as in other free states, worshiped at their own institution, the African Methodist Episcopal Church. The AME Church became "a potent force not only in the religious life but also in education and in the development of race pride and unity." Barred from equal opportunity, blacks looked to their church as "a symbol of the ability of members of their race to elevate themselves through their own efforts."[22] By 1858 there were seven annual conferences of the denomination in the United States, including one in Indiana. Circuit preachers and missionaries organized congregations in Terre Haute in 1839 and nearby Mt. Vernon in 1842. By 1860 the Indiana Conference had a membership of 1,386, one-fifth of the Afro-American population of the state.[23]

The "Evansville African Methodist Church" was organized sometime before June 5, 1843, when four trustees of the congregation—Joseph Turner, Paul Henderson, Primas Lofton, and George Johnston, who was probably the first pastor—leased a quarter of an acre from Henry Harper for $1. Located in the Fourth Enlargement (Lamasco), the land was on the northeast corner of lot seventeen, and was twenty-two feet wide and thirty feet long. Granting the lease for five years, Harper allowed the trustees to build and subsequently remove a meeting house or any improvements they had made on the lot.[24]

The first city directory of 1858 listed an "African Church" on Leet Street which held two Sunday services and a Sunday School. The pastor was identified as Abram Hill. Because of Methodist policy, pastors were changed about every two years. Census records and city directories list three AME ministers between 1858 and 1865. The clergyman was the town's only black professional and among the few who were literate, and as such was the social as well as spiritual leader of Evansville's blacks. Trustees of the congregation, who were elected annually, were also prominent members of the small black community. The earliest extant records of elections in that era show that in July 1860 Lewis Jackson, James Amos, and James Goins became trustees. Amos, the only one identifiable in the federal census enumeration of 1860, was a Pennsylvania-born farmer who resided in nearby Knight Township with his wife and four children. He had property worth $500 and employed several farm laborers. He died in 1864 and was replaced by Israel Glenn. In 1865, two new trustees replaced Glenn and Goins.[25]

Another AME congregation held services during the 1850s in the northeastern part of Union Township, about two miles from the present southwestern boundary of the city of Evansville. A "Bayou Society" of the AME Church was organized sometime before August 1850 when five trustees—Henry Beatty, Trimers Rawlins, William Bug, Henry Jackson, and Ezekiel Gillespie—purchased a quarter-acre of land for $1 from John Shanklin and Samuel Lister for the purpose of building a place of worship. Given the absence of other records and the departure of most blacks from Union Township in the late 1850s, it is not known whether a building was erected or how long that congregation survived. The return of blacks to that region after the Civil War, however, led to the establishment of another church near that site in the 1880s.[26]

Custom and law dictated that blacks be excluded from white schools, which were inferior to begin with. Indiana's illiteracy rate was the highest in the North. Consequently, the only opportunities open to Negroes before 1869 were those afforded by private schools and teachers. Most of these educational efforts were carried on by religious groups, in some instances by Negroes themselves, in others with the assistance of white persons.[27]

No black schools can be located in city directories or census records prior to 1869, but evidence that schooling was occurring does exist. The federal census enumeration of 1850, which recorded school attendance, reveals that nine black children in Evansville, aged six to fourteen, had attended school in the previous year. (No rural black youths, however, had gone to school.) Where the nine went to school and what they learned remains a mystery. Prior to state school laws passed in 1852 and 1855, some black youths in Indiana attended public schools, but whether that was the case in Evansville is unlikely. In February 1856 a Mr. Green, who was probably black, requested that the City Council allocate funds for the support of his school for black children. Although his petition was supported by prominent white businessmen Samuel Orr and John Shanklin, it was tabled indefinitely. The precise fate of the school—and its location, size, and sponsorship—is unclear. Some years later the *Journal* reported that a prominent black had attended school with a member of the eminent Reitz family in the 1850s, but since the family was German Catholic, it is probable that the black student studied in a parochial school. Published reports of public school activities between 1860 and 1869 reveal no trace of Afro-American students, and school board records for the period do not exist.[28]

In 1860, census enumerators recorded thirteen black youth in the town as having gone to school the previous year. In the fall of 1859 a young woman opened a black school under the auspices of the American Missionary Association, founded by antislavery leaders in 1846 as a nonsectarian antislavery missionary organization. The society was most renowned for the schools it established for freedmen. In the fall of 1863, the Republican daily newspaper reported that the young woman, whose race and name were not given, was seeking contributions from white citizens in the amount of $1,200 to purchase a lot and a building. The teacher was encouraged by the progress of the youthful scholars, but reported that "the tenement" in which they were taught was in poor condition. The editor observed that since the state had done nothing to provide for these children, Evansvillians should at least give them a chance for a common school education through their philanthropy. He commented that blacks were denied formal education and yet blamed for being stupid and ignorant. The effort to secure a new facility was apparently unsuccessful. As the civil conflict wore on, the editor reminded his readers that the education of the black soldier would be the best guarantee that slavery would not be reinstated. His observation that education and slavery were inherently antagonistic was an article of faith among Evansville's blacks, who despite formidable obstacles—including a double tax, being forced to support a private school while being denied access to public school—thirsted after whatever formal education they could obtain.[29]

The small black community in the river city could not be separated from the slave society which literally began at the water's edge on the waterfront. Unlike white newcomers the foothold that blacks had on the new land was extremely precarious. Evansville was one of several major points of entry in Indiana for fugitives, but its Southern roots were deep. The earliest newspaper account of blacks in the town was an advertisement placed in the May 4, 1822, issue of the *Evansville Gazette* by Elijah King, a Kentuckian. King offered a reward of $5 for his slave, Jesse, who was twenty-two and "rather knock-kneed," had rheumatism in his ankles and walked stiffly, but otherwise was "a pretty good fellow, speaks fast, his voice fine like a woman's."[30]

Similar pleas for assistance appeared in Evansville newspapers during the next four decades. Life for free blacks was insecure, as slavecatchers were a constant threat. Interviewed by a Federal Writers' Project researcher in the late 1930s, Hattie McLain, the daughter of a slave woman and her white master, recalled how her father had brought the mother and daughter out of Henderson County, Kentucky, to Evansville and presented them with certificates of freedom. Despite this gesture, slave catchers abducted them and took them back to Henderson County, where they were re-enslaved. Records of Vanderburgh County show that another master—a Louisianian in 1851—brought his slave to Evansville and freed him, but the fate of that manumitted black is unknown. Proving their free status was a fact of life for Evansville's blacks. As in the case of George Washington in 1822, Ezekiel Gillespie—one of the founders of the Bayou Society—had the County Recorder in 1842 document the fact that he had been purchased by a Mississippian in Carroll County, Tennessee, in 1839 and freed there. The presence of slave catchers and the widespread sympathy for the South in Evansville—including officials like the sheriff in the 1850s who assisted slave catchers—made freedom extremely tenuous. One local historian, who otherwise ignored Afro-Americans in his writings, described this situation as the most exciting and disturbing aspect of life in antebellum Evansville.[31]

Evansville was, nonetheless, in free territory, and it lay on one of the major routes of the Underground Railroad. Many fugitives crossed the river near the Henderson Ferry and entered Indiana via the southern tip of Union Township. Others crossed at Diamond Island near Posey County, and some fled thence to Union Township. Fugitives traveled north from Vanderburgh County to Terre Haute and Lafayette, whence many proceeded to Canada. After the passage of the Fugitive Slave Act of 1850, slaves had to have written permission from their masters to cross the Ohio, and local and federal authorities made escaping from slavery more difficult.[32]

A hardy band of antislavery men and women of both races, however, stepped up their efforts to assist fugitives. "Fishermen" ferried hundreds acoss the Ohio at night. According to William Cockrum, some of them were men of "literary achievement" who had come from the East and received assistance from antislavery societies there. Fugitives were hidden in the homes of Afro-Americans and even in coal mines on the west side of the city. Given its location and size, it is likely that the Lyles settlement in Union Township was a haven for runaways. The identities of agents of the Underground Railroad and the duration of the stays of fugitives are sketchy. One prominent white who was probably an agent was Willard Carpenter, an entrepreneur who had come to Evansville from Vermont in the late 1830s. It is perhaps more than coincidental that many of Evansville's early blacks resided near Carpenter's home in the Lamasco section of town. Another sympathizer was Judge A. L. Robinson, described as a "radical reformer" in temperance and slavery matters. Robinson refused to hold alleged runaways in his court when the owner was not present and the slave catcher presented a letter of request from the owner stating that the black in question was a fugitive. Local historian Frank Gilbert recalled in 1910 that Conrad Baker's most satisfying act prior to becoming Governor of Indiana was his liberation of "Old Tom," a servant Gilbert's father had brought with him from the South when he settled in Evansville about thirty years before the Civil War. After Gilbert's father died, an uncle residing in the South claimed an indenture on Tom, but Baker prevented him from succeeding. Several other eminent whites may also have assisted the runaways, but records of their efforts are undocumented. One suspects, however, that, as elsewhere in the North, the bulk of the effort was expended by the free black community.

Whatever their race, those who helped runaways took great risks. Armed guards patrolled the river banks at night, and those like the unfortunate Thomas Brown, a white peddler from Kentucky who transported runaways in his spring wagon, stood to lose much if they were apprehended. Arrested in Evansville by the Democratic sheriff in May 1854, he was convicted in a Kentucky court and spent three years in a miserable prison in Morganfield. Brown lived to write of his tale, but one of his fellow prisoners—an Evansville black—was not so lucky, as he was abused by his jailer and died in prison.[33]

For the most part, local whites were either indifferent or unsympathetic where such matters were concerned. Stealing a horse, wrote Frank Gilbert, was considered a more serious crime than stealing a slave. Few were troubled until the latter part of the 1850s, when law and order seemed threatened by the South. Most local residents treated Afro-Americans with contempt and ridicule, whatever their views of slavery: The local Whig (later Republican) newspaper, for instance, portrayed them as shiftless, irresponsible, and unreliable.[34] The lower section of the city—from Main Street downriver to Pigeon Creek—was regularly described as an abode of noisy and treacherous black rowdies. On April 15, 1853, the *Journal* reported that on the night before a crowd of "big and little buck negroes kept up a riotous scene the whole night through" on High Street, intermingling "entertainments" with fisticuffs. Another story, "How to Get a Hat," explained how one black, Pomp, had obtained his new hat—"at the shop, ob course." When asked the price of the hat, Pomp explained, "I don't know nigger . . . de shopkeeper wasn't dar."[35]

Like many Indiana politicians, Evansville leaders advocated colonization. The editor of the *Journal* insisted it was the only means whereby the slave's freedom was "made compatible with his happiness and best interests." Abolitionists and the "more intelligent class" of freed blacks would find this attractive, he argued, because it obtained their goals without "dangerous designs." The comparison of the state of the freed black and of the resident of Liberia would demonstrate how much better off the latter was.[36]

One problem with that view was that it neither took into account the sentiments of local blacks nor placed any obligations on the local white population, which on occasion utilized vigilantism as a means of keeping blacks in their place. A serious incidence of this occurred in late July and early August 1857. On July 20, two white farmers—John Edmonds and his son Mike, neighbors of Daniel Lyles—became embroiled in a dispute with Lyles's sons because the whites had taken a pig belonging to their family. The younger Edmonds was badly injured in the fight which ensued. The township constable and his deputies arrived at the Lyles farm the next day to serve warrants and found—to the amazement of the editor of the *Journal*—"*nineteen* [sic] of the family . . . eating breakfast." Five of the brothers were brought to town, charged, and released on bail. The journal openly criticized the judge for releasing them after such a serious crime had been committed.[37]

On the afternoon of July 23, an animated crowd surrounded the crowded courthouse, where the elder Edmonds testified that he had in fact taken the pig, but only because it was a stray, and that he had planned to return it. He asserted that he and his son had been wantonly attacked by the Lyles brothers. (The brothers' testimony went unreported.) The judge fined three of the brothers $25 each and placed bail on John Lyles at $1,000 and Wesley Lyles at $500. The two were ordered to appear in county court for trial two weeks later.[38]

The judge's decision prompted an outcry that even the "most outrageous" crimes were mildly punished in Evansville. Late Friday evening, July 24, a mob of fifty to seventy-five whites marched on the black settlement in Union Township to settle "a long series of offenses which neighbors have been treasuring up against the colony of blacks. . . ." Although the residents were able to repel the attack by the whites, another mob of 150 to 200 marched on the settlement the next day. Sheriff John Gavitt and his deputies averted further bloodshed, however, by persuading many of the black men to place themselves in protective custody.[39]

On Monday, July 27, inflammatory handbills which called for the expulsion of blacks from Perry as well as Union Township were posted in Evansville. The sheriff thwarted the effort to gather an even larger crowd to march on the Lyles settlement. One factor may have been the news that the two white men wounded in earlier clashes were recovering. The editor of the *Journal* also suggested that legal action against white vigilantes would be ill-considered, as it would provoke further violence. He observed that perhaps the most important reason for moderation was the report that "the obnoxious negroes" were leaving the area for Gibson County to the north, where there was a large black settlement (eventually known as Lyles Station).[40]

The *Journal* blamed the Democratic newspaper, the *Enquirer*, for inciting the people of Evansville to riot, and in particular for allowing the incendiary handbills to be published in its office. Its editor also alleged that his Democratic counterpart had declared that "Union Township would do herself credit by ridding herself of a large number of free blacks who now infest it. They are the most troublesome and worthless set of people we have amongst us."[41] He singled out sheriff-elect John B. Hall for special criticism, as Hall had been a leader of the vigilantes. He did not acknowledge that he had contributed to the crisis by his attacks on the justice system or the blacks who had settled in the area affected. (Unfortunately, relevant issues of the *Enquirer* are not extant.)[42]

On August 19, the *Journal* declared that all of the blacks in Union Township had left after having sold or leased their land, but the story did not end there. On the 25th it published the resolutions adopted at a meeting of township residents four days earlier. The township's citizens, English-speaking and Republican in politics (unlike their German, Democratic neighbors in Perry and western Pigeon townships), resented the image that the *Enquirer* had presented of them. In particular, they attacked the notion that they were "so intensely American [Know-Nothing], or anti-Democratic, that they would rather have a free negro for a neighbor or a laborer than a German or an Irishman" and that "they make equals of them—eat at the same table and sleep in the same bed with them, as though they were whites."[43]

The facts surrounding this episode are incomplete and distorted. That the number of blacks in Union Township had been increasing in the 1850s is undeniable, as is the fact that blacks did not settle in regions of the county (Armstrong, German, Perry, and western Pigeon townships) in which there were large numbers of German Americans. The identity of the leaders of the mobs is not clear, although news accounts treated the men as Evansvillians, not residents of Union Township. Undoubtedly there was deep-seated hostility toward the black newcomers, some of whom were fugitive slaves, and the dispute over the pig sparked the ample fuel of hatred. The role of political controversies over the Kansas-Nebraska Act, the Dred Scott decision, and the settlement of Kansas in all of this is not clear, but it is evident that the summer's heat helped to fan the fires of racial animosity. Both editors contributed to the spread of the blaze. The editor of the *Journal* ignored some basic questions—what the Edmonds were doing on the Lyles farm to begin with, what John and Wesley Lyles's crimes were, and why no whites were indicted. Most revealing was his treating the black newcomers as troublemakers whose exit, literally at the point of the gun, was to be welcomed.

Such developments notwithstanding, Evansville could not escape the growing national crisis which led to civil strife in 1861. One aspect of that was a huge influx of fugitive slaves into Indiana, which contributed to a series of nasty incidents in the state between 1861 and 1865. The worst of these was a race riot in New Albany in the summer of 1862, but relatively milder forms of racial strife were commonplace in Evansville during that period.[44] Perhaps the most serious incident occurred on January 3, 1864, when a number of "fast young men on a splurge" stabbed to death the AME pastor, a Rev. Jackson, whom the *Journal* described as quiet and inoffensive. One of the culprits was apprehended by a Union soldier and taken to the provost marshal, who instructed the soldier to take the culprit to a civilian judge for arraignment. The soldier unaccountably released the man, who quickly disappeared. "Nobody feels an interest in the case," admitted the editor of the *Journal*, "because he [the minister] is colored."[45]

Given the fact that Southern and anti-black sympathies were widespread in wartime Evansville, that response was remarkable.[46] Stereotypes of blacks persisted during the war, but the exigencies of war required some rethinking of the validity of slavery, the wanton abuse of Afro-Americans, and the exclusion of blacks from the military. In the early fall of 1863, for example, a black man was robbed of all of his money at the Shamrock Saloon on Water Street. Although the white steamboat hand who committed the crime boasted that the "nagur" had no rights, the town marshal jailed him after the black identified him. In what was probably the first case of its kind in the history of Evansville, the hand was convicted and sentenced to four years in prison, fined, and disfranchised for ten years. That the white was clearly a Democrat may have had an important part to play, for as the *Journal* noted, "we fear that [Clement] Vallandigham will lose one more vote at the coming election."[47]

Local Republicans, moreover, found the emancipation of slaves a just punishment for the Southern rebels. After initial misgivings, the *Journal* came to support emancipation enthusiastically. When the antislavery leader Levi Coffin came to Evansville on June 9, 1863, to solicit money for freedmen's aid, a number of local leaders contributed liberally. On October 15, 1863, after the *Journal* learned that a gang of thirty slaves had been taken through the city the previous night to Henderson, Kentucky, the editor inquired when the "infernal inhumanity" would cease. Contrasting a recent rally for Frederick Douglass in Baltimore with the mobbing of Union troops there in 1861, he warned Kentuckians that they would soon be surrounded by free territory and isolated from the rest of civilization because of their support of slavery. Commenting on a local thanksgiving service in August 1864, he said he had observed with delight the faces of two

> conservative [Evansville] ladies sneering at and evidently dissenting from the sentiments of the prayer offered up by Rev. Mr. [Albion] Fellows [the Methodist clergyman], in which he asked that "if the oppression of an inferior race was our nation's great sin, that the Lord would show it unto us."[48]

The corollary of this was support for the use of black men in the Union army. In July 1862 the *Journal* ridiculed Democrats for opposing the use of blacks in entrenchments and fortifications. Such critics, declared the editor, found no fault with Jefferson Davis, but when it came to the relief of Union troops they had no more regard for the negroes than for the Union soldiers."[49] After President Abraham Lincoln authorized the induction of blacks in the Union army in the summer of 1862, a number of Hoosier blacks enlisted, and many fugitives from Kentucky and other Southern states also joined all-black

Hoosier regiments. Governor Oliver P. Morton was eager to use Afro-Americans to fill enlistment quotas, and few white men—Democrats included—preferred to lose a limb if a black could do that instead. The Republican newspaper carried a number of stories about the enlistment of blacks in the Union army for the remainder of the war, and after the heroism of black troops at Port Royal and Fort Wagner initial skepticism and cynicism subsided.[50]

Evansville's location made it a prime recruiting ground for black troops. Agents from Marion County and Cook County (Illinois) frequented Evansville, much to the chagrin of local officials, who sought to fill draft quotas with Afro-Americans. By August 1864 many black men were being brought into the city via Union Township, and the business of hiring substitutes "had been brisk for some time . . . and as high as $550 has been paid for able-bodied sable sons of Africa."[51] The local provost marshal was busy "trotting 'smoked Yankees' through the examination preliminary to admission to the dignity of soldier of the Republic." All told, by August 1864, 200 had been credited to the city and sent to Indianapolis for assignment,

> all from Tennessee, Alabama, Georgia, and the extreme Southern states. That is, they say so, and of course they never lie! A liberal proportion are substitutes for gentlemen of the Copperhead persuasion who have a great horror of "niggers" . . . except on particular occasions.[52]

The number of Afro-American recruits increased sharply with the expansion of the Union war efforts and the demand for substitutes. In late August 1864 a recruiting station was opened in Henderson, obviously to prevent Evansville from securing all the credit for black enlistments, and 150 to 200 were enrolled in a few days. On August 23 the *Journal* reported that 160 "Ethiopians" had arrived the previous night en route from Henderson to Owensboro for assignment.[53] Two days later, the black unit, the 46th Infantry Regiment, departed the city. Its members, encamped at the waterfront, had been so orderly, according to the editor, that not even the Democrats could find fault with them. Many similar stories appeared over the following eight months. The editor urged the local marshal to continue to fill local draft quotas with the scores of fugitives who had arrived in the city by the early part of 1865. He even proposed the establishment of a special recruiting officer "to gather in the Ethiopians."[54]

The number of blacks recruited in Evansville and sent to Indianapolis is unclear.[55] Equally if not more difficult to determine is the response of local Afro-Americans to the war effort. Some local black barbers helped slaves flee Kentucky and boarded them until they enlisted. A number were housed at the Washington Hotel at Third and Main streets. Some local men like John Carter signed up. Many Kentucky and Tennessee blacks also arrived as fugitives, and their numbers varied according to the course of the war in the west. Nearly 200 arrived on one occasion, and were provided temporary shelter by white citizens in Blackford's Grove before moving north. Local blacks also formed several mutual aid organizations during the war: a Union Aid Society in early 1862, and a chapter of the United Brothers of Friendship in January 1864. Undoubtedly one role which these groups performed was assisting in the burial of dead fugitives and soldiers. The city's public cemetery, Oak Hill, recorded the first burial of a black soldier, John Rudell, in July 1863. Two more blacks—a soldier and a sailor—were buried there in 1864.[56]

The vagaries of war also brought hundreds of blacks to settle in Evansville, and by early 1865 the city's Afro-American population was much higher than it had ever been. Despite their contributions to the war effort, however, blacks were not necessarily welcomed to the river city. The gaining of liberty, moreover, did not also secure equality. In the heat of the 1863 city election, for example, local Democrats charged that the election of Republicans, and especially school board leader Horatio Q. Wheeler, would bring the admission of blacks to the public schools and the attempt to put blacks on an equal footing with whites. Defenders of Wheeler, a partner of A. L. Robinson, were quick to deny both charges. "The unfortunate people have a school of their own," insisted the editor of the Republican daily, "and it is honorable to our city that it is so."[57] Over the next two years Democrats argued vehemently that it was the intention of Republicans and blacks to engage in race-mixing. The Republican editor responded that "the cry of 'nigger equality,' once a rare political trick, has lost its magical influence."[58]

The debate over the proper place of Afro-Americans was only beginning, for by 1870 the number of Afro-Americans had risen to nearly 1,500. Although some social patterns had been established in the antebellum period, the arrival of hundreds of former slaves was bound to affect the structure of the black community as well the relations between blacks and whites.

PART II

Years of Growth,
1865–1900

T W O

Population and Housing Trends to 1900

 On May 13, 1865, Evansville's Afro-American Baptists met at their usual place of worship, the Baptist Lecture Room on Chestnut Street near the Wabash and Erie Canal. The meeting had been called by the deacons of the congregation, Travis Ford and Green McFarland. Along with four others, they were elected trustees of a church organized that day, appropriately named Liberty. Like the black school established in 1859, the church was a symbol of pride to the hundreds of black newcomers and of hope to the thousands of Kentucky slaves. Located at Seventh and Oak streets, the congregation grew rapidly, and in the early 1880s erected a large brick edifice on the site. By 1889 it had 800 members, and the region in which it was situated, the largest black enclave, was known as Baptisttown.[1]

Evansville and its rural environs witnessed a dramatic increase in the number of Afro-Americans from the end of the Civil War to the end of the century. There were nearly 1,400 blacks in the city by 1870 (Table 3), and another 722 blacks resided in rural Vanderburgh County.[2] In the summer following the end of the war, the local black population was a mixture of ex-soldiers, fugitives, and freedmen. As Kate Rose recalled that summer in Henderson County, Kentucky, "After the war was over, the slaves heard the old missus blow the horn for 'em to get to the house. When they got there she said, 'You are all free men and women.'"[3] Some like Kate remained on the plantation for a time, but others left to make a new start in the bustling city on the north shore of the Ohio. Moses Slaughter, who joined the Union army in 1863 at the age of thirty, came to the city in 1867 and "found it a good place to live in."[4] Like George Winlock, another veteran, he remained in the city for over seventy years. Most newcomers, however, were ex-slaves who flooded north when the noise of battle ceased, for Kentucky did not abolish slavery until the ratification of the Thirteenth Amendment in December 1865 forced it to.[5]

The years from the Civil War to the early part of the twentieth century were the formative years of the black ghetto in the United States. In some cities, clearly identifiable black ghettos emerged in this period, but in most "there was a noticeable increase in the residential segregation of blacks in a few fairly

TABLE 3:   Black Population of Evansville, 1860-1900

Date	Total Pop.	Black Pop.	Percent Black	Percent Increase: Total	Black
1860	11,484	96	0.8		
1870	21,830	1,408	6.5	90.1	1466.7
1880	29,280	2,686	9.2	34.1	90.8
1890	50,756	5,553	10.9	73.3	106.7
1900	59,007	7,405	12.5	16.3	33.4

Sources: Ninth Census, Population Schedules for Vanderburgh County, Indiana, 1870, National Archives Microfilm Publications No. M593, Roll 364, frames 89–515a; Tenth Census, Population Schedules for Vanderburgh County, Indiana, 1880, National Archives Microfilm Publications No. T9, Rolls 316–17, frames 88–542; Twelfth Census, Population Schedules for Vanderburgh County, Indiana, 1900, National Archives Microfilm Publications No. T623, Rolls 239–241; Census Office, Department of the Interior, *Statistics of the Population of the United States . . . Ninth Census* (Washington, D.C., 1872), 130; Census Office, Department of the Interior, *Statistics of the Population of the United States at the Tenth Census (June 1, 1880)*, volume I (Washington, D.C., 1883), 155; Census Office, Department of the Interior, *Report on the Population of the United States at the Eleventh Census*, part 1 (Washington, D.C., 1895), 370–75, 456; Census Office, Department of the Interior, *Twelfth Census of the United States Taken in the Year 1900*, volume I: *Population*, part 1 (Washington, D.C., 1901), 446–48, 866–67. The statistics for the black population in 1860-1880 and 1900 were compiled from the federal population schedules and are slightly different from the totals in the printed census. The data for total population in 1890–1910 exclude the town of Howell, incorporated in 1880 and annexed in 1916. In 1900, its population was 1,421.

well defined sections." Intensified racism was one cause, but it was not the sole factor, as it "has always existed in the United States, but black ghettos have not." The context of growing racial hostility "coincided with an era of dramatic change in the patterns of urban life." American urban society grew from about 6,000,000 in 1860 to slightly over 40,000,000 in 1910. Equally important was "the reorganization that accompanied this growth in numbers." Stimulated by new transportation technology, the "walking city" was replaced by "a much more tightly organized urban structure." Expansion promoted racial, ethnic, and socioeconomic concentration as well as corporate bureaucratization and consolidation. The result was "the emergence of huge urban centers tied together by a nexus of economic relationships, but divided geographically into numerous commercial, industrial, and residential districts."[6]

Much has been written about the most vivid example of this shift, Chicago, as well as such cities as Cleveland, Milwaukee, and Detroit.[7] Evansville, Indiana, also was part of this process. The rivertown of 11,484 in 1860 grew 500 percent by 1900. By 1900 the city was not only the economic and cultural hub of a three-state region in the lower Ohio Valley, a wholesale center as well as a manufacturer of flour, stoves, furniture, cigars, and agricultural implements, but also a part of a complex national economy, as evidenced by the

TABLE 4:   Birthplaces of Evansville Blacks, 1870-1900

State or Region	Year			
	1870	1880	1890	1900
Indiana				
Number	224	690	1964	2712
Percentage	15.9	25.7	35.4	36.6
Other Midwest				
Number	62	63	149	193
Percentage	4.4	2.3	2.7	2.6
Northeast				
Number	12	9	15	5
Percentage	0.9	0.3	0.3	0.1
Kentucky				
Number	828	1386	2290	3182
Percentage	58.8	51.6	41.2	43.0
Other Upper South				
Number	210	405	817	956
Percentage	14.9	15.1	14.7	12.9
Lower South				
Number	72	96	202	270
Percentage	5.1	3.6	3.6	3.6
Other				
Number	0	37	116	87
Percentage	0	1.4	2.1	1.2
TOTAL				
Number	1,408	2,686	5,553	7,405
Percentage	100.0	100.0	100.0	100.0

Sources: Ninth Census, Population Schedules for Vanderburgh County, 1870; Tenth Census, Population Schedules for Vanderburgh County, 1880; Twelfth Census, Population Schedules for Vanderburgh County, 1900; Eleventh Census, *Population*, part 1, 580–82, 588–90, 596–98.

introduction of the city's most famous brand-name product, Swans Down Cake Flour, in the early 1890s. Attracted to the city's thriving economy were thousands of newcomers from rural environs of the city, the Upper South, and Europe, especially southern Germany. By the First World War, about 40 percent of the city's people were first or second generation German-Americans. Urban growth was also evident in the development of a central business district, industrial regions, working-class neighborhoods, and affluent subdivisions on the urban fringe on the east side, due to the building of streetcar lines after the early 1890s.[8]

As indicated in Table 3, Afro-Americans also flocked to the city. Between 1870 and 1900 the black population grew from 1,408 to 7,405, or almost 13 percent of the total population. The increase per decade consistently exceeded that of the population at large. By percentage in 1900 the proportion of blacks in Evansville was greater than that of most cities in the Middle West. In addition, black Evansville accounted for 94 percent of the total nonwhite population of Vanderburgh County.[9]

By birthplace, the Afro-American population was rooted in the Upper South (Table 4). The number of Kentucky-born Evansvillians increased to 828 in 1870 and 3,182 in 1900; by percentage, the Kentucky-born population decreased from 59 to 43 percent. The number of those born in other Upper South states, especially Tennessee, was 210 in 1870 and 956 in 1900, and the proportion from this section of the nation remained fairly constant. With growth came a degree of stabilization, as shown by the increasing number and proportion of those born in Indiana, undoubtedly in Vanderburgh County. By 1900 nearly 37 percent were native Hoosiers, and most of them were children of blacks born in the Bluegrass State. The relatively high percentage of native-born blacks was nearly the same as that of Cleveland in 1900 and higher than that of many other Northern cities.[10]

Migration from the South was the chief reason for the growth of black Evansville before 1900—"part of a general drift of rural inhabitants to cities before World War I. Declining or unstable economic conditions in many farming regions, especially the South, caused many to move." Given the choice between stagnation in the South and growth in the North, "the potential migrant had little trouble making a decision." But northward migration was not simple a search for better life chances, in economic terms.

> The desire for better schools, recreational facilities and the need (especially among the younger generation that had grown up since the Civil War) to escape the hard, humdrum conditions and poor accommodations on plantation and farm undoubtedly played an important part in motivating these early migrants.[11]

In 1870 and 1880 there were slightly more females than males, as in many cities to the east and south. The marked shift indicated in the 1890 census (115 males to 100 females) reflected the influx of many young male workers, a phenomenon not limited to Afro-Americans, for in the same census year the ratio of foreign-born men and women was nearly the same as that among blacks. By 1900, however, the distribution of males and females had become fairly even.

The establishment of an approximately equal distribution of the sexes reflected the increased migration of black families as well as of single men, but it belied trends within certain portions of the city. In 1880, for example, Wards 3 and 4, regions with a preponderance of warehouses and steamboat and railroad facilities, contained more men than women. By contrast, black women were more numerous in Ward 1, which comprised hotels, restaurants, and the homes of affluent whites in which black domestics were a common feature. About one-third of Evansville's black women, in fact, lived in this ward. In the other three wards, the ratio of men to women was nearly equal. In addition, there were more black women than men in three age brackets—fifteen to twenty, sixty-one to seventy, and over seventy. The first perhaps reflected the job opportunities for young women as domestics, and the latter two were evidences of the lower life expectancy of black men.[12]

TABLE 5:   Black Population by Ward, 1870-1900

Ward Number

Year	1	2	3	4	5	6	7	8	9
1870									
Total	2,717	2,620	2,207	2,330	2,393	3,229	1,879	1,381	3,074
Black	415	130	257	168	83	118	23	54	160
Percent	15.3	5.0	11.6	7.2	3.5	3.7	1.2	3.9	5.2
1880									
Total	4,696	4,585	5,113	3,979	4,904	5,743			
Black	852	633	314	215	178	494			
Percent	18.1	13.8	6.1	5.4	3.6	8.6			
1890									
Total	9,111	5,778	6,519	9,257	7,973	12,118			
Black	1,894	1,047	588	591	366	1,067			
Percent	20.8	18.1	9.0	6.4	4.6	8.8			
1900									
Total	8,784	4,918	7,028	10,874	9,422	9,968	8,013		
Black	1,023	1,023	938	869	469	427	2,656		
Percent	11.6	20.8	13.3	8.0	5.0	4.3	33.1		

Sources: Ninth Census, Population Schedules for Vanderburgh County, 1870; Tenth Census, Population Schedules for Vanderburgh County, 1880; Twelfth Census, Population Schedules for Vanderburgh County, 1900; Ninth Census, *Population*, I:130; Tenth Census, *Population*, I:155; Eleventh Census, *Population*, part 1, 456; Twelfth Census, *Population*, I: part 1, 645.

By age, most of Evansville's blacks were somewhat younger than those in Cleveland, which had a relatively high proportion of young men between ages fifteen and forty. In 1880 about 30 percent were under age fifteen, and another 40 percent were aged fifteen to thirty. In Cleveland at the turn of the century, two-thirds of the blacks were fifteen to forty-four, and only 17 percent were below age fifteen. In 1890, one in three Evansville blacks was five to seventeen years of age, about five times the proportion of foreign-born whites in this bracket. Another 29 percent were males aged eighteen to forty-four, as compared with 24 percent among native whites and 23 percent among foreign-born whites. All told, Evansville's blacks were younger than those in more northerly industrial cities at the time, where the black population by age was more akin to the immigrant population, which had large numbers of single males in their twenties and thirties. The migration of black families and the demand for young people in service jobs seem to explain the patterns of age among Evansville blacks.[13]

After the Civil War—as in most Northern cities—there emerged one large enclave as well as smaller outlying clusters. The spatial development of Evansville's black neighborhoods was somewhat like those of Southern cities, for they were scattered throughout the city at first and not concentrated in one region. The opening up of residential areas for blacks near the old canal by Willard Carpenter and Thomas Garvin, among others, combined with the proximity of that area to service jobs on or near Main Street and Water Street, explains the shift of the majority of black residences away from the waterfront regions. In 1870 (Table 5) Wards 1 and 3 included well above the citywide proportion of black residents, and between them accounted for nearly half of the city's black population. Ward 1 contained not only the homes of the affluent near the river but also parts of the emerging black enclave near Liberty Baptist Church. Ward 3, the center of the commercial district, comprised hotels and restaurants, residences, and the city wharf. Blacks in Wards 2 and 4, which adjoined it and resembled it in occupational and land use patterns, constituted another third of the city's total. Ward 9, located to the north and east of Eighth Street and to the north and west of the old Wabash and Erie Canal, filled in after its failure as a channel of trade, included another 160 blacks, most of whom resided near the boundaries of Ward 1 and 9. By contrast, relatively few dwelled in the predominantly German Wards 5 and 6, located to the north and west of the older portions of the city. About 200 blacks lived the immediate northwest part of the city, the site of the first black enclave before the war.[14]

Ten years later, blacks were even more concentrated in the largest section, roughly within a four-block radius of Eighth and Canal streets. (See Map 1.) This area, contiguous portions of Wards 1, 2, and 6, represented slightly over 44 percent of the Afro-American population of the city. Of these, three-quarters lived on or adjacent to Canal Street and Fifth Street, the site of the old canal. Another black enclave, situated in Ward 3 on the near northwest side, accounted for approximately 8 percent of the total in the city. This section was bounded by Pearl Street on the west, Pennsylvania Street on the north, Second Avenue on the east, and Water Street on the south. Still another cluster was located immediately to the north of the Evansville and Terre Haute Railroad yards in Ward 6. Defined by Main and Harriet streets on the west, Illinois Street on the north, Lafayette Street on the east, and Eighth Street on the south, this area comprised about 6 percent of the total black population. About the same proportion resided on the far west side, within a block of Twelfth Avenue and West Virginia Street, and another 5 percent were located on the southeast side on portions of Taylor, Judson, and Campbell streets. If one excludes blacks residing in white households and hotels or enumerated on steamboats, these sections accounted for four-fifths of the total Afro-American population of Evansville. (There were also smaller clusters of blacks near the confluence of Columbia, Harriet, and Mary streets on the near north side; on or near north Fulton Avenue and its intersection with Heinlein Avenue and Missouri Street; and on East Division Street, near Kentucky Avenue.)[15]

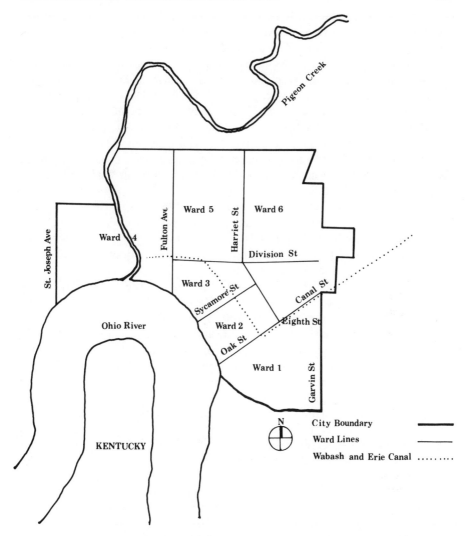

1.   Evansville in 1880. *Indiana Magazine of History*, LXXVI (December 1980), 303.

Although these enclaves were dispersed throughout the city and were racially mixed, there were several indications that by 1880 the residential lines between the races were being clearly drawn. In the first place, few blacks had settled in predominantly German regions. In 1880, Wards 3, 4, and 5, with foreign-born populations ranging from 33 to 40 percent, had proportionately and numerically the fewest blacks in Evansville. A second clue was the fact that certain portions of the city received disproportionately large numbers of the black newcomers. Ward 1, the boundaries of which were similar in 1870 and 1880, nearly doubled its black population; the population of Ward 2, with the same boundaries, quintupled. Slightly over half of the city's black population lived in contiguous parts of Wards 1, 2, and 9 in 1870, and ten years later the same region—now sections of Wards 1, 2, and 6—included about 75 percent. The number of Afro-Americans in that area, 1,979, represented an increase of about 300 percent in ten years. An even more striking fact was that many streets or portions of streets were largely if not totally black: Canal between Fifth and Eleventh, Oak between Sixth and Eighth, Lincoln between Canal, Gordon, Douglas, Bell, Reilly, Mitchell, Church, and Sumner. Blacks were also predominant on Taylor Avenue in Ward 1; Oak Alley in Ward 2; Chestnut Alley in Ward 3; West Virginia Street between Eleventh and St. Joseph in Ward 4; Pearl Street, near the river and the city gas works in Ward 4; and East Nevada Street in Ward 5.[16]

These trends continued into the 1890s. In 1890 the Afro-American population of Wards 1, 2, and 6, which had about the same boundaries as in 1880, was more than double the total of 1880. Four of every five black residents of the city lived here. Of the blacks listed in the Evansville city directory of 1891, half lived near Eighth and Canal streets.[17]

As indicated on Table 5, Wards 1, 2, and 7—the latter combining what ten years earlier had been upper Ward 1 and lower Ward 6—contained 4,702 Afro-Americans in 1900, about 64 percent of the total in the city of Evansville. (See Maps 2, 3, and 4.) Thirteen of the fifty-one census districts—three in Ward 1, two in Ward 2, one in Ward 3, and seven in Ward 7—accounted for nearly two-thirds of Evansville's blacks. In eight of these districts blacks represented at least one-quarter of the population. The Eighth and Canal area, known popularly as Baptisttown by the early 1890s, housed 3,987, or 350 percent more than twenty years before. Fifty-four percent of all Evansville blacks lived there. The other three enclaves of note—First and High, West Virginia Street, and Taylor-Judson (known by 1900 as Oakdale or the Sandpit)—had larger numbers of black residents (418, 229, and 121, respectively), but they represented a smaller proportion of the total (11.3 percent) than they had in 1880. One emerging enclave outside Baptisttown had grown noticeably in the previous decade. Traversing Wards 4 and 5, it lay near several coal mines in the vicinity of north Fulton Avenue, between a railroad track and Pigeon Creek. This region, known as Blankenburg, included about 8 percent of the city's blacks in 1900. Smaller enclaves also persisted. "Newtonville," near Division and Kentucky, had been settled by Morris and Annie Newton in the early 1880s. Newton had a lucrative wood and coal hauling business. Also developed was "Jimtown," on East Missouri, East Louisiana, and East Oregon, between Morton and Garvin. The origins of that enclave are unclear. The nearly 5,500 in Baptisttown and the four major enclaves, however, accounted for well over 80 percent of the city's Afro-Americans if one excludes residents of hotels, steamboats, and white households.[18]

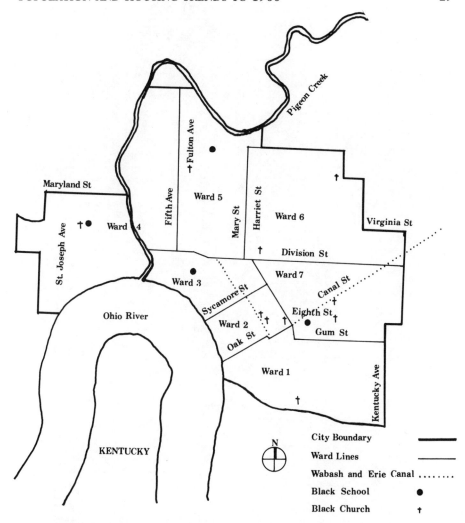

2.   Evansville in 1899, showing the locations of black schools and churches.
Indiana Magazine of History, LXXVI (December 1980), 307.

The federal census enumeration of 1900 and the city directory of the same
year also confirmed that there were more predominantly black streets and that
more blacks resided on them. Twenty streets or significant portions of them
were at least 80 percent black, and another fifteen were between 50 and 79
percent black. All but ten were in Baptisttown. Nearly 800 blacks resided on
Day's Row, Short Eleventh Street, and the 1000 blocks of Cherry and Canal
streets. Almost 700 lived on Ballard, Brower, Douglas, Gordon, Mitchell,
Hogan's Alley, and Rowley—all short streets in Baptisttown. Another 600
dwelled on Oak betweeen Fourth and Eighth, Canal between Seventh and
Eighth, Fifth between Cherry and Oak, and Sumner and Church streets.[19]

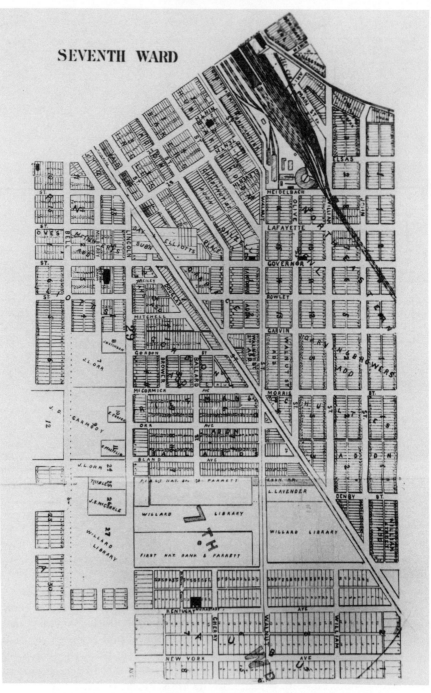

3. The Seventh Ward, 1899. Many blacks resided within the area
bounded by Oak, Walnut, Bland, Bell, and Eighth streets. Tillman
and Fuller, *An Illustrated Plat Book of Vanderburgh and Warrick
Counties, Indiana* (Evansville, 1899; reprinted by the Friends of Willard Library, 1976).

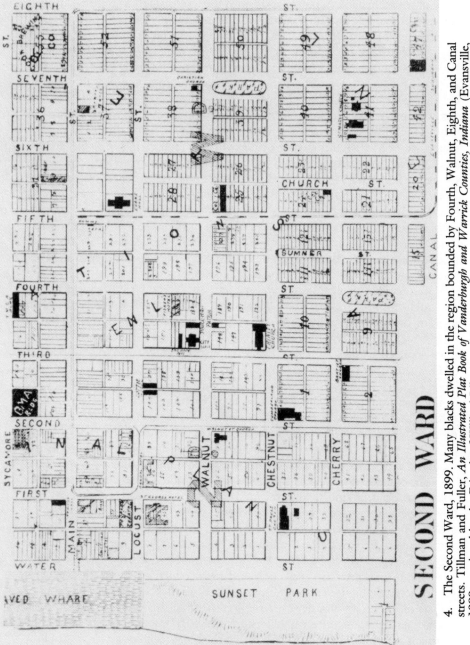

SECOND WARD

4. The Second Ward, 1899. Many blacks dwelled in the region bounded by Fourth, Walnut, Eighth, and Canal streets. Tillman and Fuller, *An Illustrated Plat Book of Vanderburgh and Warrick Counties, Indiana* (Evansville, 1899; reprinted by the Friends of Willard Library, 1976).

Even though there was a large black enclave which claimed an increasing share of the total black populace and which was increasingly segregated, Evansville's black neighborhoods remained racially mixed, like those of other Northern cities in the early industrial era. Examined by the index of dissimilarity, the segregation of any two groups in the population on a scale of 0 to 100 (with 100 being totally segregated), the city's enumeration districts rose from 28 in 1870 to 45 in 1900. Despite the increase, Afro-Americans could be found in all but two of Evansville's fifty-one census districts, and only eight of these had less than a 1 percent black population. (So were fourteen of thirty-five wards in Chicago in 1900.) Thirty-four were at least 5 percent black. Evansville, nonetheless, showed a slightly higher degree of residential exclusion than Chicago and Cleveland, the latter of which had no census district over 25 percent black. Evansville had seven: four in Ward 7 and three adjoining them in Wards 1 and 2. One district, number 126, was 80 percent black. Almost half of the city's blacks lived in these seven districts—about the same proportion as in the heaviest black regions in Chicago. In addition, eight districts, 15 to 24 percent black, claimed 1,898 black residents. Altogether, about 5,300 blacks dwelled in those fifteen districts. Four of them—numbers 89, 92, 126, and 129—included one-third of the 7,405 Afro-Americans in Evansville.[20]

Residential segregation, however, was not limited to Afro-Americans. Although present in every census district, the German-Americans, three-quarters of them first and second-generation Americans, were also clustered in certain regions. In 1880 they dominated Wards 4 and 5 on the north and west sides of the city. In the six census districts constituting that area, the proportion of German-American families ranged from 30 to 65 percent. Like the largely black enclaves, these German sections were not homogeneous, but they were distinctive, as relatively few Germans lived in other sections of the city of Evansville. As in most American cities prior to World War I, the trend toward residential segregation was not limited to blacks. This was "the age of 'the segregated city,' and it would indeed have been surprising if blacks had not shared the same experience that other urban groups were undergoing."[21]

The context of urban change, however, does not "entirely explain the situation that blacks found themselves in. There were some forbidding signs that the black urban experience was destined to be different from all other groups."[22] As in Chicago and Cleveland, the residential experiences of blacks and Germans diverged, even though both began to arrive in the city well before the Civil War. By 1900 German-Americans were found in every part of Evansville, but Afro-Americans were not, and they resided in fewer enclaves with proportionately higher concentrations of black residents. These trends continued despite the fact that newcomers supplemented the ranks of both populations. The divergent patterns of residential distribution between blacks and Germans was not the result of the fact that the black community alone faced the task of coping with hundreds of newcomers, which resulted in greater difficulty in assimilation and thus in greater racial segregation. The 1880s brought a flood of German immigrants to Evansville, so that in 1890 Evansville ranked

1. These homes on Day's Row were typical of black housing in the early twentieth century. Special Collections, University of Southern Indiana.

second in the state in the percentage of foreign-born residents, and its rate exceeded that of Chicago and St. Louis. The rapidly growing city, in which the rates of increase of black and German residents were high, was the scene of increasing assimilation for whites and of increasing segregation for blacks.[23]

As Howard Rabinowitz has noted about five Southern cities in that era, the unique residential patterns of urban blacks reflected, to some extent, voluntary choice. That is, some resided where they did because of proximity to white employers, whether the affluent in the Upper Water Street vicinity or the coal mine operators on the north and west sides. (See chapter 4.) Some, moreover, resided among poor whites, as in the Canal Street neighborhood, because the whites were unable to afford a move elsewhere.[24]

Limited economic opportunity was especially important for blacks. This inhibited the growth of a black middle class and made migration within the city extremely difficult. But this alone does not explain residential patterns. White opposition to the settlement and the mobility of Afro-Americans in Evansville were also important. Animosity to the presence of blacks had been present prior to the Civil War, and the rapid growth of the Evansville black community after emancipation led to the use of violence against Afro-Americans. Although lynchings occurred in the city only in August 1865 (see chapter 3), and the number of large-scale disorders was by Southern standards small, hostility was demonstrated in many other ways. In August 1867 the Evansville City Council received a petition from whites living near Liberty Baptist Church who complained that the church was a nuisance because the members met until late in the evening and "their music was bad." The same session of the council also heard complaints from a Democratic member that pupils at the black school "used such language that no decent lady would pass that way." Another member said that the school was "demoralizing to the white children in the vicinity, that the location was very inconvenient, and that it was very annoying to the people in the neighborhood."[25] Later in the same year, posters erected in the German sections of the city notified Afro-Americans that they were unwanted there, and that any who resided in those sections should leave by New Year's Day. A man who had rented a home to an Afro-American family was warned that his house would be put to the torch if the family were not evicted.[26]

Such factors helped restrict the city's Afro-American population to a limited portion of the town. These regions, especially Baptisttown, were not necessarily all-black, but as in other cities they represented the least desirable segments of low-income areas and often commanded higher rents than comparable shelter for whites. As Rabinowitz has observed, whatever the reasons for settlement patterns, urban blacks resided in the worst areas. The stench and health hazards associated with the old canal were well known, as were similar problems in low-lying, flood-prone areas near Pigeon Creek, either at the Ohio River or in Blankenburg. Blacks also occupied unkempt alleys which, like the other regions, lacked basic city services.[27] Heavily black districts also were among the most crowded in Evansville. District 77, which included Canal beyond Sixth, Douglas, and parts of Lincoln, was the most densely populated in the city: it had 555 blacks and 1800 whites. In the adjoining district, 78, were 2,100 persons, 18.3 percent of whom were black. The number of households per dwelling here (1.25) was 25 percent higher than the city as a whole, and, each dwelling housed an average of six persons, 20 percent above the city average.[28]

In 1900, the most densely populated district housed 1,881 persons, 225 more than the next largest. Located in Baptisttown, it had the largest number of blacks in Evansville (775). Not surprisingly, there were many roomers and boarders here. The three districts with the highest number of blacks contained one-third of all the augmented families in Evansville. Low income and high rents forced families to take in roomers and boarders, who thus found themselves limited to the least attractive quarters of the city, where housing was dilapidated and furnishings were poor. In the late 1890s, a prominent white official, Lee Howell, complained to the Board of Public Safety about the way in which blacks lived in the near downtown region. It was not uncommon, he said, to find fifteen persons dwelling in a single cottage. Such early advocates of urban renewal, as Rabinowitz has argued, were interested in black housing conditions only when they threatened the white property values or when whites were forced to view them as they traveled to work from their new suburban subdivisions.[29]

As in most Northern cities, another obstacle to residential mobility and decent housing was the proximity of black residences to vice districts. Cities like New York, Columbus, Cleveland, and Detroit had vice districts in or near predominantly Negro neighborhoods . . . . [T]he association of blacks with vice amounted to a kind of self-fulfilling prophecy on the part of the white population. In the late nineteenth century, many whites, in accordance with the stereotypes then in vogue, conceived of blacks as prone to loose morals and illicit (if not humorous) behavior. Yet the predominantly white police forces . . . often refused to allow red-light districts to develop anywhere except in or near a black neighborhood.[30]

Evansville's blacks were consistently portrayed as shiftless, unreliable intruders upon an otherwise stable, thriving society. A typical news account of black society appeared in March 1867, when the Republican daily picturesquely recounted a fight between two black women over "a gay and festive negro of the male persuasion."[31] As early as 1870 heavily black sections of Evansville were becoming known for their gambling houses, brothels, and "dives."[32] Newspaper accounts regularly carried stories about black men being arrested and convicted of gambling or being drunk and disorderly. Black women were usually arrested, by contrast, for prostitution. The monthly police report for June 1872, for example, listed 117 arrests during the previous month, and of these fourteen black men and twelve black women—over one-fifth of the total—were involved. The black women represented more than half of the women arrested, and all but three were described as prostitutes.[33]

Police raids on "low negro dens" became commonplace. These places were concentrated near the waterfront in the lower part of the city, especially on High Street, and near the old canal, particularly on Fourth Street between Walnut and Chestnut and in several alleyways nearby. These "dens" were portrayed as being visited by the lowest level of Evansville society and were noted for their "unhallowed jubilees." By the 1890s the section of Fourth Street, popularly known as "the Midway," was especially notorious, although stories of vice among Afro-Americans in other regions regularly appeared in the newspapers.[34]

As in several other Northern cities, "a few civic-minded individuals, white as well as black, attempted to eliminate some of these unsavory aspects of urban life, but the resultant reforms were usually ineffective or short-lived."[35] The first such effort appears to have occurred under the administration of Democratic Mayor William Akin in the spring of 1899, when Councilman John W. Boehne led a fight to clean up Fourth Street. Blacks had allegedly gotten into the habit of "lounging" on the west side of the street between Walnut and Locust and taunting white men and women who dared to pass by. The city police eliminated the saloon music machines and ordered the saloons closed between 11:00 P.M. and 5:00 A.M., but success was short-lived. Politicos apparently preferred to reap the benefits of vice, not to eliminate it. In addition, fears of driving vice into white residential areas, as well as the absence of recreational facilities for blacks outside these sections of Evansville, helped to perpetuate the vice districts. By the early 1900s "Darktown Bohemias" thrived, according to reformers, and a "lower colored world" prospered, especially on Clark, Lower Water,

High, Church, Canal, Fourth, and Fifth streets. The continued presence of these sections reflected the priorities of Evansville's white leaders.[36]

In short, by the turn of the century Evansville's black population was the product of not only rapid urban growth but also experiences which set the Afro-American residents apart from the rest of the citizenry. Although small by comparison with New York's 92,000 blacks or Chicago's 42,000, Evansville's black metropolis of 7,405, about the size of Cleveland's, shared the experiences of urban change, black migration, and residential discrimination which created a black ghetto as well as a handful of smaller enclaves throughout the city.

As Kenneth Kusmer has observed, there was "great variation in the spatial distribution of blacks in American cities." A black ghetto had not yet appeared in Evansville, despite centripetal population trends. Black enclaves remained somewhat more scattered outside the largest black region than in more northerly cities, and to that extent resembled Southern cities. Within these clusters, though, the degree of residential segregation was steadily increasing, especially in Baptisttown. In that respect Evansville had much in common with cities of the Midwest and Northeast. In Western cities, "high levels of geographic mobility, combined with excessive population turnover and unstable housing markets," contributed to the population dispersal of Afro-Americans. In Southern cities, which had high percentages of blacks, slow growth rates helped to keep blacks dispersed in antebellum patterns.[37] When compared with most American cities at the beginning of the twentieth century, Evansville's black community was far along the road to residential segregation by race.

THREE

The Myths and the Realities of Opportunity in a Northern City

 "During the generation following the Compromise of 1877," two noted scholars have observed, blacks "throughout the country found themselves increasingly the victims of discrimination, proscription, and mob violence."[1] Most historians of this tragedy have focused on the South, where the removal of Federal soldiers and the hegemony of conservative white Democrats devastated black Americans. "The betrayal of the Negro" was characterized by the rise of white supremacy, of the disfranchisement of Afro-Americans, and of the segregation of the black populace by law as well as custom. It was aided and abetted by the laissez-faire policies of Republican leadership and the decisions of the Supreme Court, particularly its support of the "separate but equal" doctrine. By 1900 black Americans experienced a degree of racial prejudice which would be unabated until the mid-twentieth century.[2]

Undeniably important, the emphasis on race relations in the South misses the fact that "shifts in public opinion on the race question during this period were actually national rather than sectional in nature." Race relations were "extraordinarily fluid in both sections." In the North, initial postwar patterns were mixed, but as

> memories of the war dimmed, so too did sympathy for the former slaves, and instead the nineteenth century witnessed the growth of racial stereotypes and the emergence of a new "scientific" racism whose appeal transcended sectional boundaries.[3]

The new racism stressed the inferiority of the Afro-American in most respects except for physical endurance and musical ability, and especially noted the moral deficiencies of the former slaves. Whites, in turn, became less favorable to the idea of equality, and by the turn of the century, discrimination in public accommodations and instances of mob violence were present in the North as well as the South.[4]

The development of discrimination varied enormously from city to city in the North. In Cass County, Michigan, "a sizeable group of black settlers shared governmental power and lived in integrated harmony with their white neighbors. . . ." Whites in certain large cities like Boston and Cleveland were less hospitable, but here "the growth of racism . . . was more muted in its effects, and integrationist traditions remained influential much longer than elsewhere." More common were cities like Chicago and Indianapolis, where "[r]acial lines hardened most rapidly. . . . [There] white hostility frequently led to violent clashes between the races." Even more extreme were border towns and cities like Evansville and East St. Louis and Cairo, Illinois, "where the forces of segregation and discrimination were so strong that the pattern of race relations closely resembled that of the South."[5]

Evansville's character was in part the product of Indiana law. Although the exclusion portion of the constitution was nullified by the state's highest court in 1866, it was not until 1881 that a constitutional amendment removed it. In 1885 the state legislature banned discrimination in public accommodations, but the law was ineffective because of the cost of litigation for blacks, the difficulty in proving discrimination, and the frequency with which blacks sought out places patronized by whites. The 1869 legislature provided public education for blacks, but it also required that school trustees organize separate schools for black children if there were sufficient numbers of children of color. (Otherwise, several districts might be consolidated in order to provide public schooling for blacks, or trustees could provide other means of educating black children.) State law also prohibited marriage between a white and a person deemed one-eighth or more Negro. Blacks could testify in court and serve on juries, but Indiana was notorious for lax enforcement of these essential components of the justice system.[6]

Evansville's proximity to the South was also a factor, and as Rabinowitz has observed about the urban South, no matter how whites may have wished the freedmen whom they detested to remain in the countryside, hundreds flocked to the city. Whether whites of Southern extraction who had only the tradition of slavery to fall back upon or of Northern birth who had had little contact with blacks prior to 1865, Evansvillians were thus forced, by their location, to join together to find ways of controlling an ever-growing black populace. Location also meant that the attitudes and values of the white population were heavily influenced by the customs and laws of the South of that era.[7]

The consistently large number of black newcomers, especially in the 1880s and 1890s, not only made assimilation difficult, but also provided a continuous source of interracial friction. German-American residents seemed especially hostile to blacks—due perhaps in part to the fact that German-Americans constituted the bulk of the local working class. (It should be noted, however, that rural areas near Evansville with large numbers of Germans had few if any blacks.) The absence of Puritan and Quaker traditions among the city's white leaders meant that there was one less potential source of assistance to the former slaves. Less than three months after the end of the Civil War, the editor of the *Journal*, presumably a friend of the freedman, declared that "no one but a fool ever did believe that freedom in the case of the negro meant social and political equality. . . ."[8]

A harbinger of future relations between the races occurred on July 30, 1865, when a middle-aged German-American woman, who was visiting the city to attend church, was reportedly "overpowered by [two] brutes" and "outraged" by the two, who subsequently attempted to murder her. Two young black men were subsequently apprehended, and although they professed their innocence, one allegedly possessed some of the woman's belongings and a bloody knife. The Republican newspaper reported the incident under the headline, "A Diabolical Outrage," and urged severe punishment. The next day at noon a crowd broke into the county jail, dragged the two men out, shot and clubbed them, and hanged them from a nearby lamppost. Cigars were stuck in the mouths of the corpses. (A white child molester in the jail, by contrast, was unharmed.) The lieutenant governor, Conrad Baker of Evansville, wrote Governor Oliver P. Morton that as a result many blacks had fled, including the families of men in the Union army. Intoned the Republican editor,

> Everyone execrates the abominable and brutal crime committed by the negroes, but mob law is a dangerous remedy for the evils of this or any kind . . . and we hope that this fearful and summary punishment will present such a warning as that we shall never again hear of such a crime in our midst.[9]

The only lynching in the history of the city, the incident revealed much about the state of race relations in the postwar era. Even the supposedly friendly editor of the Republican newspaper had convicted the two men before a trial. In the wake of the incident, civic leaders James G. Jones and Conrad Baker, both Republicans, wrote the governor that crowds of "Copperheads" and German-Catholic "Butternuts" terrorized many innocent blacks and threatened to burn the tobacco factories which employed them. Local authorities were powerless, however, because of the numbers of rioters and the inability of the governor to send the militia to restore order.[10]

The crisis eventually subsided, and blacks began to return to Evansville, but the fact that whites and blacks would be judged by different rules was inescapable. Three years later a white steamboat fireman, David Crayton, allegedly chased overboard by a group of black deckhands, disappeared beneath the surface of the muddy Ohio. The next day sixteen blacks were tried for murder. The defense for the men was loosely organized, and key witnesses were not called to testify. Eventually four were imprisoned. In 1871 Crayton was discovered living in Paducah, Kentucky, and several affidavits were signed to that effect, including one by a black who had witnessed Crayton's swimming away from the steamer and had been denied the opportunity to testify in 1868. The affidavits were collected by A. L. Robinson, the antislavery attorney, and forwarded to Governor Conrad Baker, who pardoned the one black man whose term had not yet expired. No pardon was granted the three who had served their time, no restitution was made, and Crayton went unpunished, even though he acknowledged he had known of the trial three years before and had seen no reason to come forward with the proof that he was alive.[11]

After 1870 the recurrence of mob violence was rare, but wanton attacks on Afro-Americans were commonplace, especially when insults on white women were alleged. Some of that was politically motivated, as local Democrats were openly critical of the three Reconstruction amendments to the constitution and perceived blacks as the lackeys of the Republicans. But ideology was more often mixed with the vicissitudes of waterfront society. Such was the case of a drunken youth who in February 1868 threatened black hotel employees on Water Street and called for a war to "get the g-- d----- niggers out of here." The *Journal* lamented the fact that "negroes go about the streets attending to their own business . . . [not] protected from the attacks of such characters."[12]

All but a few whites supported the notion that blacks had to occupy a separate and inferior stratum of local society. Little evidence of integration exists for the immediate postwar years. Blacks and whites were housed together, for example, in the County Poor Asylum, and separate asylums were never built. The city's public cemeteries, Oak Hill (1856) and Locust Hill (1867), were open to blacks from the beginning, although separate sections were provided. Some public service occupations (policeman and postman) were initially available to blacks and later closed. Robert Nicholas, a Union army veteran, became a policeman in 1875. Three others were also enumerated in the federal census of 1880 as members of the police force. Only one, however, was so listed in the Evansville city directory of 1891, and no blacks held that position in other directories in the decade or in the federal census enumeration of 1900. No other blacks were appointed to the police force until 1915, although one was named a deputy sheriff in 1903. By the 1890s the highest governmental appointments to which blacks could aspire were custodian of the city hall, county courthouse, or black schools, or fireman in Hose House No. 9, located at Olive and Governor streets, which became an all-black unit in the late 1880s. A few blacks could also become "colored county physician" (after 1900, "colored [Pigeon] township physician"), one of three such positions appointed by county officials to provide medical care for the indigent and to promote public health measures.[13]

Perhaps the most visible sign of racial separation was the city's black schools, which initially depended on white and black philanthropy. Details about events between 1865 and 1869 are sketchy. The first school, formed in the late 1850s, was probably situated in or near the AME church. In mid-April 1865 the City Council received a petition from several citizens identified as "heavy taxpayers" which called for the appropriation of funds for a school building for blacks. A council committee, chaired by Samuel Orr, investigated the request and recommended approval of the petition. It was "a matter of humanity and policy," wrote Orr, and it was also cheaper "to provide a school room for them now, than it would be to provide prison room for them if permitted to grow up among us without proper instruction."[14] The council

2.   The crew of Hose House No. 9, about 1910. Special Collections, University of Southern Indiana.

delayed action on the report until late August, when school board leader H. Q. Wheeler offered to donate the land for a school if the city would provide the building. On October 30 the council authorized the expenditure of $1,000.00 for the construction of a school building.[15]

Records of the location and nature of the new facility are scarce, but there is no doubt that many Evansvillians did not support the project. In the city election of 1866, one Democratic candidate for City Council, Herman Fendrich, a prominent tobacco manufacturer, proposed "to sell the negro school houses [sic] and churches. . . ."[16] Fendrich lost to plow maker William Heilman, later a Congressman. In early 1867, the session of the Evansville Presbyterian Church met at the home of Samuel Orr, an elder of the church, to consider a request from Governor Baker, Judge Asa Igleheart, and several others that until the state legislature authorized public funding of schools for blacks, the congregation take up a collection to support the local black school. Members of the session agreed to do that if other Protestant churches joined them, and ordered the pastor to look into the matter further. Apparently no other churches offered support, as the minutes of the session provide no record of further action. Presumably members of the session, however, contributed on their own.[17]

In August 1867, following complaints from citizens about allegedly bois- terous and lewd conduct of black schoolchildren, the City Council established a committee to consider a new site for the school. The issue dragged on for some time, as the council continued to debate the location of the school in the late summer of 1868. Whether a new building was erected as a result or the build- ing authorized in 1865 remained the main black school is unclear. The city's tax assessment rolls for 1869 listed a "colored school" on a forty-five by seventy- five foot lot in the Donation Plan or Enlargement, at Fifth and Chestnut streets. The older facility in the lower part of the city continued to be used as a black school due to the number of children in that section.[18]

In 1869, the Indiana General Assembly, led by Governor Baker, author- ized the appropriation of tax money for schools for Indiana's blacks. The law was amended in 1877 to allow blacks to attend white schools if separate schools were not provided or if black students were sufficiently advanced to attend white high schools, but it did not guarantee that separate schools would be equal in quality. Local option also meant that most Indiana communities— especially those on the Ohio River—would opt for segregated schools.[19]

The school trustees of Evansville began to provide formal education for black children of the city after June 6, 1869, when a committee of the board was appointed "to investigate and report upon the best way to furnish Negroes of the City and [Pigeon] Township with school privileges." The same board also received a petition from blacks "asking that colored teachers might be appointed to teach the colored children."[20]

Although crowded and understaffed, the schools were strong magnets to the black community.[21] Desperately poor and only recently slaves, the newcom- ers "clutched at any morsel of education." Education, like the cultivation of family life and the accumulation of property, was essential to achieving success. As Booker T. Washington recalled, "There was never a time in my youth, no matter how dark and discouraging . . . when one resolve did not remain with me, and that was a determination to secure an education at any cost."[22]

During the 1869–1870 term two schools enrolled 181 pupils, and there was also a popular night school four days a week at James M. Townsend's schoolroom at Fifth and Chestnut. An Oberlin graduate, Townsend, who also served as the AME pastor, was one of several teachers in the pre-public school era and remained in the city for four years, until about 1873. An Evansville Board of Trade publication in 1880 indicated that he had arrived in 1868 to teach in "the colored school." The school was identified as being partly funded by private subscription. Additional funding came from the Freedmen's Bureau, which may have sent Townsend to Evansville. He may, in fact, have been the first black teacher in the black schools. His contributions were recognized at one of the earliest recorded social events among Evansville blacks, a "Straw- berry Festival" at the home of Mrs. James Carter between Main and Locust streets. Assisting him at the "Upper Colored School" was Evansville native

Lucy Wilson, twenty years old. George Jackson was the teacher at the "Lower Colored School," by now located on Clark Street between Third and Fourth avenues. Three rural schools were opened for blacks in the 1870s—one in the northeastern part of Union Township on Daniel Lyles's land; another in Center Township, near the southeast corner of the intersection of Stringtown and Bergdolt roads, which served a black enclave in Smithland; and a third in Knight Township, which was erected on Green River Road in 1873.[23]

The earliest extant minutes of the school board indicate that in the fall of 1871 there were four black teachers. Appointments were made on a different basis from those of whites, as black teachers were listed simply as first, second, third, and fourth colored. Salaries were also lower than those given whites. Townsend's $700 salary, highest among the four black teachers, was equal to the amount paid the heads of the smallest white schools. The average for the other three teachers was less than $400, substantially lower than that of whites. The number of pupils rose to 348 in 1874, when crowded conditions at the two schools and two additional rented classrooms prompted the board to erect a new building, Governor Street School, at the corner of Governor and Mulberry for nearly $38,000 on a lot purchased from Thomas Garvin. In the same year the board also authorized the opening of a school for blacks in Independence, a semi-autonomous community near the coal mines in the western part of the city. Clark Street School and rented space at St. John's Evangelical Church continued to be used for the 1874–1875 year.[24]

Early on, the local school board faced several problems resulting from the 1869 school law. For one, trustees of adjoining townships sought to send their black pupils to the city schools and pay their tuition, as that was cheaper than providing facilities and staff in the country. The school board initially rejected those petitions due to lack of space. Eventually, however, the requests were honored. By 1897 the city schools enrolled 102 black pupils from rural Pigeon, fifty-seven from Perry, eight from Knight, and five from Center. Apparently two of the three rural black schools ceased to exist, but Union Township's survived. A second problem surfaced in April 1877, when several black parents petitioned the board to admit their children to the eighth grade of the white school nearby "to receive the benefits of public schools in common with others of like grade, there being no adequate provision made for colored children for that grade. . . ."[25] The board did not grant the request.

The rapid growth of the black population required the school board to expand facilities and curricula for black pupils in the late 1870s and early 1880s. Lucy Wilson was named Clark's principal in 1876—the first black woman to direct an Evansville school—and the facilities were expanded in the late summer of 1877. A room for the seventh and eighth grades was also rented at St. John's in the 1878–1879 term. In the same year, a high school for blacks was opened at Seventh and Vine streets. (From the early 1880s until 1897 the high school was located in Governor Street School.) The first graduation of the "Colored High School" occurred on June 14, 1882, at Evans Hall, the largest public meeting hall in the city. Three students graduated, one of whom—Georgia Nance, class valedictorian—later became a teacher at Governor.[26]

The number of black students increased to about 700 in 1889–1890, the first year in which enrollment was systematically recorded. All but a handful were enrolled in primary grades. (White enrollment for the same year was 4,875.) By 1897–1898, the number of black pupils had risen to 1,029, sixty-eight of whom were in the high school. (There were 6,283 white students that year.)[27] Enrollment trends prompted the board to move the high school to Clark Street in 1897, where a new building had been erected eight years earlier. A two-room addition was made to the school when the high school was moved there. Thereafter the high school was known as Clark, and some elementary students also attended school there. A school for Blankenburg students was erected for 1897–1898. The new facility, known as Third Avenue School, was located at the corner of Tennessee Street and Third Avenue.[28]

To assess the quality of this segregated education, one must first acknowledge that, white or black, Evansville's schools were inferior by state and national standards. In 1900, there were 247 Evansvillians for every teacher, as compared with 168 statewide and 174 nationwide. The illiteracy rate in the city was also high (6 percent) in a state with the highest illiteracy rate in the North (4.6 percent). Rapid urban growth and fiscal conservatism meant consistently high student-faculty ratios. In 1880, there were forty-one white students per white teacher, as compared with thirty-seven blacks per black teacher. In 1900 there were, respectively, thirty-five and twenty-nine to one.[29]

Black education fared poorly when compared to that of whites. In 1880 white teachers earned an average of $420, about 9 percent more than blacks; in the 1901–1902 year, the average white teacher earned about $65 more a year than an average black teacher. White high school teachers received an average of $924 , as compared with the mean salary at Clark High School, $580. In 1889 the value of the black school buildings was 9.3 percent of the total value of school property, although black students accounted for 14 percent of school enrollment. In 1897–1898 per capita expenditures for instruction for all students was $24; for blacks it was $13. Given the quality of equipment and facilities for the education of blacks, such differentials in expenditures are even more striking.[30]

Instructional differences were also significant. The first state-licensed black teacher was not hired until 1884, although there were already twelve white teachers with licenses. The vast majority of black students, moreover, were exposed to a maximum of only six years of schooling. None of the black schools had a kindergarten, but five of the nine white schools did. Offerings above the sixth grade were also limited. In 1899, for example, only Governor had a teacher (J. D. Cox) whose sole task was teaching the seventh grade. Third Avenue, Independence, and Governor students wishing the eighth grade had to walk to Clark. High school education was even more a luxury for blacks than it was for whites, for most students desiring it had to travel about a mile and also faced the pressure to enter the work force immediately after grammar school.[31]

It is unsurprising, therefore, that in 1900 44.5 percent of black children aged five to twenty were in school, as compared with 57.9 percent of white children. The illiteracy rate among black residents aged ten or more was 26.6 percent. For native whites, it was 1.7 percent, and for foreign-born whites it was 9.6.[32]

White images of black schools tended to reinforce the the status quo, as newspaper coverage of black school activities was scarce and often devoted to some amusing incident. Evansville High School was described regularly as "the crowning glory of the public schools" or "the public high school."[33] Aside from implying that Clark was not public, such comments suggested that its quality was inferior. That was also evident in coverage of graduation ceremonies at Clark, which consistently received second (and brief) billing, and stressed the crowd's orderliness and love of music. Planning for the introduction of vocational training in the 1890s and early 1900s followed a similar vein, with the attention first given to white students.[34]

Even the efforts of those friendly to the education of blacks seemed governed by a custodial spirit. Samuel Orr's argument for public funds reflected that, as it presumed that blacks were prone to criminal behavior. Black teachers, moreover, were permitted to attend the monthly meetings of all public school teachers, but news accounts of their participation in those meetings suggest that they were invited not as co-workers but as entertainers, singers of spirituals and dancers. A. M. Weil, prominent Jewish businessman and president of the school board, told the graduates of Clark High School in 1899 that the board had spent $20,000 on the education of blacks during the previous year. He proceeded to ask the large black audience for an adequate return on the investment by racial self-help, although he failed to note that the per capita allocations ($13.38) were half that given to white schools.[35]

Such problems notwithstanding, the schools were an object of great pride and a source of encouragement to the black community. The desire for education was omnipresent. Of particular interest to blacks was night school, obviously due to the scores of black workers who desired an education. Such classes were offered as early as 1870. The demand for evening classes was substantial, as evidenced by a successful petition in October 1895 to open a night school at Independence in addition to the one at Governor. By that time, five black teachers had been assigned to these classes. Board records indicate that in January 1898 there were 164 black and 132 white students in evening classes. As Superintendent J. W. Layne observed in 1892,

> For the past two years the Board has maintained evening schools for the benefit of those between 14 and 30 years of age whose necessities compel them to labor during the day. These schools have been largely attended by colored people who, not having had the opportunities to secure an education earlier in life, now eagerly strive to acquire at least the ability to read, write, and spell. For this class of people, the evening schools are accomplishing a noble work.

> The attendance in the evening schools for white pupils has been neither so large nor so regular as in the colored schools; nor has the work been so satisfactory.[36]

The schools met other needs. James Townsend formed the first black literary society in Evansville in early 1872. In June 1896 J. R. Blackburn opened a summer school for the training of younger black teachers at Governor, a service which he offered without pay to the school board. In early 1897, black citizens requested that the board allow them to use Governor for a private school in the evenings, probably the original "industrial school" that Lucy Wilson McFarland, former Clark School principal, headed.[37]

The importance of education was especially evident at the annual high school commencement ceremony, which filled Evans Hall to overflowing. Friends, relatives, and interested citizens joined high school students and graduates to witness what in that era was a rare academic achievement. In the process, the black community united behind its young scholars and put forward an image of orderliness and harmony for white observers. The graduation ceremony included prayers and speeches by clergymen as well as orations from the graduates, vocal and choral music presentations, and the awarding of diplomas by the school board president. The following Sunday morning, graduates attended church services at one of the larger congregations, where an eminent minister presented a graduation sermon.[38]

The black teachers—thirty, by 1900—greatly enriched the life of the black community. Some were local graduates, but others were hired from Indianapolis; Nashville, Tennessee; and Wilberforce, Ohio. Their educational backgrounds were, by white standards, limited, but they made enormous contributions. As the most highly educated members of the community, they not only fostered literacy but also formed the nucleus of the middle class. As the youthful teacher, Edwin F. Horn observed in the dedication ceremony for Governor School in January 1875, education, along with the acquisition of property, were essential to the progress of ex-slaves. Hence they offered a model to youth and encouraged racial pride. In early 1898, for instance, twenty-two of the teachers petitioned the school board to purchase copies of George Washington Williams's *History of the Negro Race in America from 1619 to 1880*, the first historical study by a black to be taken seriously by American scholars. The board permitted classroom use of the book, provided that the teachers raise the money for its purchase.[39]

There were, of course, hazards to being a black teacher. White school board members and school administrators expected exemplary conduct and living proof of the economic value of education. School board records reveal instances of peremptory removal of teachers for insubordination and misconduct, a fate rarely suffered by whites. Occasionally black citizens also brought charges of immorality or excessive corporal punishment. When the aggrieved identified themselves—and that was rare—they were black clergymen, perhaps an evidence of jealousy of a teacher's influence. In only one such case between 1871 and 1900, however, did the board uphold such charges.[40]

3. John R. Blackburn, Sr. (left), a Dartmouth College graduate, and R. L. Yancey (right) a Fisk University graduate, were principals of Clark High School between 1897 and 1913. Special Collections, University of Southern Indiana.

4. Colored Orphan Asylum on West Indiana Street, near Barker. Special Collections, University of Southern Indiana.

These perils notwithstanding, black teachers were in the forefront of black community development. Among the educators hired in this era, aside from those mentioned earlier, were George Washington Buckner, principal of Independence School after 1890; J. R. Blackburn, a Dartmouth graduate who was principal of Governor School from 1890 to 1897, when he became Clark High School's first principal; Pinkney T. Miller, born in Tennessee in 1860, who was hired at Governor in 1884 and served as its principal from 1890 until the late 1920s; Tennessean Fannie Snow, a Fisk graduate hired in 1893, who taught English without missing a day until her retirement in 1939; Hallie Carr, daughter of a local AME pastor, who taught at Governor from the late 1890s until the 1930s; and Sallie Wyatt, born in Tennessee in 1881, who graduated from Clark and shortly thereafter began a fifty-year career in the local schools.[41]

Although education provided the most formal instance of discrimination, it was only one of many forms, some of which were the product of state law and others emanated from local decisions.[42] In 1883, for example, the city and county government decided to build separate orphanage facilities for black children near the existing building on West Indiana Street which had served both races for ten years. In later years it was known as the Booker T. Washington Home. The facility was notoriously inferior in quality, and improvements came slowly.[43]

Evansville's Southern connections reinforced what was generally from the outset a practice of racial exclusion, but the higher degree of residential segregation than in the urban South and the lower proportion of black residents helped to make the formalization of racial separation less necessary. Whites and blacks lived in worlds which rarely touched each other. Except for racial slurs, blacks were rarely mentioned in the newspapers. Regarding public accommodations, the patterns in Evansville were fluid prior to the 1870s, as they were in the urban South. Education and certain other functions were segregated by law, but in other areas the record is unclear. With respect to horse cars, "dummy" lines, and electric streetcars, the absence of records poses a problem, but probably—given the distance of mass transit lines from black enclaves and the income and occupational patterns of blacks—blacks rarely used such transportation, thus obviating the need for Jim Crow cars or sections within cars. The custom of having blacks sit in the rear of streetcars was developed, however, by the turn of the century. Parks present an especially complex problem, as public parks did not exist until late in the century. Blacks used public halls such as Peoples' Theatre and Evans Hall, but whites were rarely present when they did. The Fair Grounds, Barnett's Grove, and Garvin Park were available to blacks, under segregated circumstances. For most events at Garvin Park, recalled Will Lavender, the only blacks present were vendors selling fried fish from booths at the entrance to the park. The records of racial policies are extremely sketchy, but it appears that opportunities for use were broader in the 1870s and 1880s than they were by 1900. In other aspects of social intercourse, the evidences of racial separation are strong—for example, in athletic competition.[44]

The most important public event for the black community was Emancipation Day, commencing in 1865, which drew hundreds from the city and its
environs to daylong festivities at one of the local parks. Held well into the
twentieth century, the event occurred on September 22. Independence Day was
also important, but blacks and whites observed it separately from 1865 onward.
Racially mixed observances were exceedingly rare. Robert Nicholas served as
the sole black member of the city's Centennial Committee in 1876, and in the
massive parade on July 4 there was a single black unit comprised of members of
the Odd Fellows and the Benevolent Aid Society. Some of the earliest Labor
Day celebrations included blacks. In 1892, in fact, a black laborer was a member of a ten-man planning committee for Labor Day activities. Black workers—
Hod Carriers—always marched in the parade, but at the end of the line. Even
these rare instances, however, ceased after the turn of the century.[45]

Dividing lines regarding other aspects of social intercourse emerged,
mostly by custom. Blacks did not frequent the hotels, restaurants, and stores on
Main Street. Saloons and other businesses on the waterfront were less race conscious at first. Interracial sexual relations in the red light region, usually
between white men and black women, were reported in the newspapers. Social
relations were tense there, and reports of fighting between blacks and whites
were often found in the local newspapers. By 1900 racial lines appear to have
been sharpened. This section contained the town's first black businesses—
boarding houses, brothels, and hotels—and in 1900 there were four boarding
houses and a saloon in the neighborhood.[46]

The region near the old canal, between Walnut and Chestnut streets, was
also the scene of some racial intermingling. Several black businesses were situated there. Black travelers were informed by *The Freeman* in 1892, for instance,
that there was a black-owned hotel at 417 Fourth Street. Interracial relations
were also tense in that area, as blacks from the nearby alleys and white workers
and businessmen in that near downtown section competed for territorial
hegemony. During the city's first "Blue and Gray Encampment" in October
1899, for instance, fights between veterans and young blacks on Fourth Street
were reported. It was to that region that early "urban renewal" advocates
turned their attention in the late 1890s.[47]

Access to health and medical care also reflected race consciousness. The
first city hospital, St. Mary's, opened in 1872, provided care for blacks, as did
Dr. Edwin Walker's public dispensary, begun shortly thereafter. The city's later
hospitals, both private (Deaconess and Walker, later known as Welborn), also
cared for blacks. All, however, offered service in a separate ward, usually in the
basement.[48]

The extent to which white physicians cared for blacks is unclear, but soon
after the end of the Civil War there were black physicians in the community.
The first was George Brown, enumerated in 1870 as a sixty-nine year-old Geor-
gian. By 1900 there were six, including S. S. Dupee, born in Kentucky in
1872; Jeremiah Jackson, born in Indiana in 1870; Willis Green, born in Kentucky in 1842; and George Washington Buckner, Tennessee born, who also
taught school. Green, who had the longest tenure of the early generation of

taught school. Green, who had the longest tenure of the early generation of physicians, was known as "the Baptistown surgeon," and for a number of years was "colored county physician" prior to his death in 1908.[49]

Whether due to inferior and limited medical care or to the harshness of life in the river city, or both, the death rate in black Evansville was high. Between 1880 and 1895, for example, the percentage of blacks buried in Oak Hill, a city-owned cemetery, ranged from 18.2 to 22.9 percent annually, although the city's black population was less than 12 percent in the period. In 1900 the death rate for Evansville blacks was 22.6 per 1,000, as compared with 17 per 1,000 among whites. (In Indianapolis the rates were, respectively, 23.8 and 15.9.) Mortality rates for children were especially high—267.6 per 1,000 births, as compared with 167.1 among whites.[50]

The criminal justice system also demonstrated the pervasiveness of race discrimination. One aspect of that was the state's antimiscegenation law. Violators were subject to public ridicule as well as severe punishment, especially when a white woman was involved. In October 1869 a black man was fined $300 and sentenced to three months in prison for having had sexual relations with a white woman who, the *Journal* observed, "the casual observer would suppose would have a more refined and critical taste. . . ."[51] (The woman was fined only $5 but jailed for the same length of time.)

Afro-Americans of lighter complexion were subject, from time to time, to peculiar indignities. In October 1878 the Republican newspaper reported "a strange marriage at Squire Roberts' Court" in which one Charles Hill—"black as black can be"—sought to marry a woman "who would pass for white almost anywhere. . . ." After the judge was convinced she "had colored blood in her veins," the two were married.[52] Four years later, Morton Northington and Georgie Tidrington appeared before a judge to be married. Northington swore he was "a descendant of the Negro race and . . . has a right to be married to a coulared famel [sic] according to the laws of Indiana."[53] It was little wonder that when an Indianapolis pastor, who was white, proposed intermarriage in 1899 as a solution to the race problem, the anger of that city's citizens was reported on the front page of the *Journal*.[54]

Given the ambiguity of the black's status under Indiana law, it is understandable why a double standard prevailed. Violations of the law by blacks against whites were punished more frequently and severely. Although Evansville Republicans were fond of ridiculing Southern Democrats for their support of mob violence against blacks—a practice which was reported with increasing frequency in the newspapers—the uncomfortable truth was that justice was little better in the river city.[55] In one of the earliest reports of arrests, in September 1870, the city disclosed that 258 had been arrested in the previous two months. One-quarter were black. Similar proportions were evident in subsequent reports. During 1883 to 1892, for example, the percentage of blacks arrested annually ranged from 19.7 to 43.3 percent. In 1895 and 1896 the rates were 33.6 and 38.5. As in the urban South, Evansville blacks were not only more likely than whites to be arrested, but they were also usually charged with petty crimes—drunk and disorderly, or petty larceny. An overwhelming number of the men listed their occupation as day laborer, and most of the women said they were prostitutes (although they were arrested for being drunk and disorderly, not for prostitution). Most arrests involved grievances between blacks.[56]

To be sure, the level of arrest was related to the fact that poor people in general tended to suffer at the hands of the law, but race was even more significant. Caprice was at the heart, therefore, of the administration of justice. That is borne out by patterns of not only arrest but conviction. During a typical month in 1883, 26 blacks and 146 whites were arrested and jailed by city police. The conviction rates, however, were, respectively, 61.5 and 43.2. In June 1885 the police locked up 42 blacks and 150 whites. Of these 27 blacks (64.3 percent) were convicted and sent to the county jail, as opposed to 36.3 percent of the whites. The county jail population between June 1893 and March 1894 averaged about 40 percent black. About 10 percent of the inmates were black women—twice the proportion of white women.[57]

Specific cases, beginning with the August, 1865 lynchings, are equally revealing. When blacks committed crimes against each other, as in the frequent newspaper accounts of gambling, knifings, and even murders near the waterfront, on the Midway, or in Baptisttown, white Evansvillians seemed unfazed, because that sort of behavior confirmed racial stereotypes. When a white was involved, the response was different. Like urban white Southerners, Evansvillians failed to appreciate the sources of criminal behavior or to see the travail that black newcomers faced when they confronted the legal system. The chief concern was social control, not justice.[58]

A major reason for discrimination in the administration of justice was the absence of blacks from the police force, the paucity of black attorneys, and the presence of all-white juries. Mixed juries never existed, and the use of all-black juries was so rare that in May 1894 Judge J. P. Elliott caused a major stir at the courthouse when he called one to hear a case involving the theft of a mule. Both the plaintiff and the defendant were black. Touted at the time as the first trial involving an all-black jury, it was actually the second, as one had been used in an election fraud case in 1870. The third would not be called until 1946. Even the most celebrated trial involving a black—the trial of John Temple, an AME pastor who killed a neighbor as a result of a domestic dispute in 1892—had a white jury.[59]

By the late 1890s, when local fears about a rapidly expanding and self-confident black populace were joined with the rise of Jim Crow to the south, the quality of justice deteriorated even more. The racial stereotypes of the era abetted that process. In an ironic twist, the *Journal*, which had once chided its competitor for its intolerance, became especially strident.[60] Stories of lynchings to the south invariably treated the black man as the guilty party, as in the case of a man lynched for allegedly assauting a white woman in nearby Henderson, whom the paper deemed a "lecherous brute." The paper attributed the proliferation of lynchings in April 1899 to "the crimes of negroes. . . . The home must be sacred."[61]

The *Journal* thus found untroubling the wanton arrest, beginning in the early summer of 1895, of loiterers at the corner of Lincoln and Governor, the heart of Baptisttown, because the blacks "blockade the sidewalk, use offensive language, and their conduct was very objectionable to all who were compelled to pass that corner."[62] In fact, the presumed prevalence of crime among Afro-Americans had become such a concern that the Republican editor wrote on "Comparative Race Criminality" on the last day of the century. Citing figures from the chief statistician of the United States Census Office that "conclusively demonstrate . . . the increase of negro criminality . . . exceeded the increase of white criminality more in the north than it did in the south," he noted

> a frightful promise for the future. The lack of moral principle, due partly to the negro's lower animal nature and partly to an inherited degradation derived from his savage ancestors, and but partially modified by centuries of slavery, and exaggerated by the removal of all practical restraints, is at the bottom of the atrocious crimes which are becoming peculiarly characteristic of the race.[63]

Such pronouncements, which ignored the deeper causes of social stress, demonstrated that the custodial approach of some white Republicans immediately after the Civil War had given way to blatant expressions of racial prejudice. Certain forms of racism had always been present, but race consciousness increased in quantity and virulence by the early 1890s. As in the urban South, a tradition of racial exclusion was surpassed by a combination of de facto and de jure segregation, due to white fears of a growing black populace and the concomitant defection of Northern Republicans from the equal rights struggle. Beginning in 1891 (and ending in 1926), city directories identified blacks by either "c" or "col." The *Journal* also began to publish a "Colored Folk" column in the early 1890s. Edited by a prominent black, the brief column—usually printed in small type and located on or near the want ads section—appeared irregularly until 1899, when it appeared several times a week (until 1909). The column contained news about churches, social events, illnesses, and deaths, as well as occasional aphorisms on matters of health and politics. The *Evansville Courier* began a similar column in 1897 which appeared irregularly for a few years. The segregation of news—with the exception of racial slurs and stories about crimes which were printed in other sections of the newspapers—underscored the intense race consciousness of the period.[64]

By 1900, in short, racial discrimination in Evansville was an omnipresent aspect of life. Developed by custom more than law, it was more pernicious than in many cities of the North. Unlike Cleveland, for instance, where initial integrationism had given way to segregationism, Evansville's early practices of racial separation were extended and sometimes formalized. Being a black at the turn of the century in Evansville meant being virtually shut off from white society, except as convenience—especially in matters of employment—allowed.[65]

FOUR

Black Evansville and the Evansville Economy

Although an inhospitable and occasionally dangerous place, Evansville attracted many rural Southern blacks. The tremendous population increase between 1865 and 1900 indicated that, whatever its faults, the river city appeared to offer a better life to ex-slaves and their offspring. As compared with the vagaries of sharecropping, the city on the northern banks of the Ohio seemed to provide a chance to make a new start.

Among other things, Evansville afforded a wider range of employment opportunities than those available in the rural South. Although a segregated city with far fewer jobs and a more limited level of achievement for blacks than cities like Boston or Cleveland, Indiana's second largest city was a mecca to blacks who had only the clay fields of western Kentucky on which to make a living. Spurred by the transportation revolution, Evansville became the world's largest hardwood center and by 1900 had the world's largest furniture factory. Drawing on coal and iron ore from the region, by 1895 it also had thirteen foundries, several machine shops, and a rolling mill. It was, moreover, a wholesale center and the site of one of the nation's biggest tobacco markets as well as one of its largest cotton textile mills.[1]

River traffic accounted for much of the early employment of Evansville's blacks. In 1939 George Taylor Burns, an ex-slave, recalled that the war opened many opportunities for blacks to hire on steamers as roustabouts and deckhands because so many white men had joined the Union army or navy. The first postwar census underscored the river's importance. Of the 553 blacks who had a job, one-fifth worked on the river as cooks, stewards, porters, chambermaids, boatmen, or cabin boys. Between 1863 and 1870, scarcely a day passed without a story in the Evansville newspapers about the lively and often violent world in which black and white boatmen lived. Theodore Dreiser, who resided in the city as a youth, vividly remembered the bustle of commerce at the city's doorstep on the vast, muddy Ohio, where there were "scores of small mule-drawn drays driven by Negroes in sleeveless cotton undershirts and batted trousers gripped tightly about the hips."[2]

The census of 1870 also confirmed that many other employment opportunities existed for blacks. Aside from the 76 men who were enumerated as steamboat laborers, another 283 were common laborerers—mostly day laborers—and nearly 100 were domestics. Of the remainder, 17 were barbers and 10 were cooks; 75 other persons divided another 17 job titles—minister, school teacher, washwoman, plasterer, and the like.[3]

The table of occupations (Table 6) for 1870 reveals not only the kinds of work which blacks found but also provides an index of their socioeconomic status and standard of living. Slightly over 1 percent were professionals (teachers and preachers), and about the same proportion were proprietors (owners of boardinghouses and saloons). None was a semiprofessional (e.g., nurse), clerical or sales worker, or a minor proprietor, manager, or official. A handful were skilled workers. By contrast, nearly 93 percent of the black workers in 1870 were at the lowest end of the occupational spectrum as laborers and service workers.

TABLE 6:   Occupations of Evansville Blacks, 1870-1900

	Year							
	1870		1880		1891		1900	
Occupation	No.	%	No.	%	No.	%	No.	%
High White Collar:								
Professional	7	1.3	27	2.1	35	2.3	61	1.7
Major Proprietors,								
Managers	6	1.1	4	0.3	12	0.8	24	0.7
Low white Collar:								
Semiprofessional	0	0	4	0.3	6	0.4	34	0.9
Clerical/Sales	0	0	7	0.5	15	1.0	10	0.3
Minor Proprietors,								
Managers	0	0	4	0.3	24	1.5	9	0.2
Blue Collar:								
Skilled	29	5.2	72	5.5	93	6.0	119	3.3
Semiskilled/								
Service	132	23.9	483	36.9	627	40.4	1524	42.2
Unskilled	379	68.5	705	53.9	739	47.6	1830	50.7
Total	553	100	1,308	100	1,552	100	3,611	100

Sources: Ninth Census, Population Schedules for Vanderburgh County, 1870; Tenth Census, Population Schedules for Vanderburgh County, 1880; Twelfth Census, Population Schedules for Vanderburgh County, 1900; Bennett and Co. *Evansville Directory for 1891* (Evansville, 1891), 59-592. This table includes all persons aged thirteen or more who listed occupations in the federal census enumerations. Because the 1890 enumeration schedules were destroyed by fire and the printed census data for Evansville in 1890 were insufficiently specific, the author used the 1891 city directory, the first to identify persons by race. Because directories were promotional devices as well as community records, they must be utilized with caution. Probably the data for 1891 undercounted black residents and also recorded occupations more generally than census enumerations.

With minor exceptions, this pattern would remain unchanged during the following thirty years. The number and the proportion of professionals increased slightly. The number of proprietors, managers, and officials also grew somewhat, but the proportion of major proprietors decreased. The percentage of minor proprietors, semiprofessionals, and clerical and sales persons, expanded modestly. The number of skilled workers (which included barbers) grew to 119, but the proportion in this category decreased. At the bottom of the scale, the number of semiskilled and unskilled workers rose substantially; especially notable was the large number of service workers. These two groups of workers accounted for a slightly higher share of the total than they had in 1870. The number of jobs available to blacks between 1870 and 1900, moreover, did increase significantly. In 1870 blacks listed 24 different kinds of employment and 150 in 1900. Most of these, however, were in the two lowest occupational categories.[4]

TABLE 7: Evansville Blacks, Sector of Employment, 1870-1900

	Sector of Economy	Percentage of Blacks Employed			
		1870	1880	1891	1900
I.	Primary				
	Agriculture	0	0.5	0.3	1.6
	Extractive	0	0.2	0.8	3.0
II.	Secondary				
	Manufacturing	1.1	5.4	3.1	3.7
	Construction	1.3	3.4	3.1	2.8
	Labor	50.6	29.8	41.4	23.8
III.	Tertiary				
	Commerce	1.1	1.1	2.4	0.9
	Transportation	17.1	9.7	8.5	17.4
	Public Service	3.8	10.3	9.1	10.5
	Domestic Service	23.1	37.0	29.5	33.5
	Professional	0.9	0.9	0.9	0.8
	Education/government	0.4	1.5	1.5	1.6
	Number	553	1,308	1,552	3,611

Sources: Same as Table 6. This table is based on Theodore Hershberg, et al., "Occupation and Ethnicity in Five Nineteenth-Century Cities: A Collaborative Inquiry," *Historical Methods Newsletter*, VII (June, 1874), 188–89, Table V. The authors of that study place carpenters, painters, and brickmasons in construction. Labor includes only those who listed themselves as day laborer or laborer. Public service comprises such jobs as cook in a hotel, porter, and waiter.

When the sector of the economy in which blacks were employed (Table 7) is examined, one gains additional insight into the manner in which they participated in the economic transformation of Evansville between the Civil War and the turn of the century. In 1870, for example, no blacks were employed in agriculture and mining and only a handful held manufacturing and construction jobs. In the tertiary sector, most worked in transportation—the steamboats and the railroads—or in domestic service. Over the next thirty years, several changes occurred. The hiring of blacks in local coal mines beginning in the late 1880s increased the proportion of blacks in the primary sector. Increases in the share of manufacturing and construction employment occurred in the 1870s, but these were only temporary, for the percentages of Afro-Americans in these two sectors dropped by 1900. Although no changes occurred in commerce and the professions, there was notable growth in the share of public service jobs and a small expansion in the proportion of those in education or government. The percentage of those in transportation remained about the same. For those reasons, the proportion of blacks employed in the tertiary sector increased to nearly two-thirds of the total.[5]

Tables 6 and 7 afford, however, only a partial picture of the employment patterns of the period. For one thing, it appears that being born in the North was not an appreciable factor in determining occupational success. Given the small size of the Evansville black community (and of Indiana-born blacks) prior to 1865, it is unsurprising that in 1870 Kentucky-born blacks were more likely than Indiana-born blacks to be employed in a wider range of occupations. That was probably due to skills learned on the plantation and to the fact that the native-born population was on the average younger than the Southern-born. In 1880 and 1900, however, there was no significant difference between the occupations of natives and nonnatives, especially Kentuckians.[6]

Skin pigmentation, by contrast, was an important factor. Those with lighter complexion—defined as mulattoes by census takers—as a rule held jobs with higher status. In 1870, for instance, about 18 percent of Negro workers were mulattoes, but mulattoes constituted 20 percent of the professionals, 22 percent of the public service workers, and 25 percent of the barbers. By contrast, they represented 14 percent of the common laborers and 7 percent of the domestics. In 1880, the mulatto population accounted for 27 percent of all Negro workers but 29 percent of the preachers, 37 percent of the porters, 31 percent of the cooks, 41 percent of the housekeepers, 38 percent of the stewards, 70 percent of the teachers, and 60 percent of the steamboat engineers. As in 1870, they were underrepresented among common laborers, washwomen, domestics, teamsters, and hostlers. Similar patterns prevailed in 1900. The higher status jobs were by custom defined by the degree of contact with and responsibility granted by whites, and at the turn of the century continued to be associated with those deemed to have mixed blood.[7]

There was also a correlation between work and residence. Evident even before the Civil War, when blacks lived and worked near the waterfront, this aspect became well entrenched by 1900. In 1870, for example, nearly one-third of the city's blacks resided in Ward 1, most of whom resided to the northeast of Fourth Street. Only about one-fifth of the blacks who had a job, however, were located here. A similar pattern existed in Ward 9, located to the east of Ward 1. Conversely, although about 18 percent of the black population lived in Ward 3, one-third of the city's employed blacks were enumerated in this region, center of the business and commercial activities of the city. Most of the Afro-Americans in Wards 1 and 9—405 of 415 in Ward 1, for instance—resided in households headed by blacks, and many of the residents were children. Eight of every ten workers there were day or common laborers who worked in transportation or service, and relatively few were domestics. In Ward 3, 118 of the 257 blacks lived in households headed by whites. This ward had 162 blacks who were employed—as compared with 119 in Ward 1. Ninety-nine were enumerated on the steamboats anchored at the foot of Main Street. The other 63 were laborers and domestics, the latter of whom were employed by wealthy whites who lived near the riverfront. A similar pattern prevailed in Ward 2, situated between Wards 1 and 3, where 38 of the sixty-six who had a job were domestics. All told, in 1870 two-thirds of the domestics lived in Wards 2 and 3. One hundred of those with riverboat jobs were found in Ward 3. Those who worked in public service jobs—cooks, waiters, and porters—resided for the most part in Wards 2 and 3. Eighty percent of those listing a job dwelled in four wards located in or near the downtown.[8]

The relationship between work and residence was even more distinct in 1880, when laborers, domestics, and washwomen constituted 75 percent of the work force. The 509 who described their work as "laborer" were distributed throughout the city, but three-fifths resided in six of the sixteen census districts—77, 78, and 79 (Ward 1), 89 (Ward 2), and 91 (Ward 6)—which adjoined one another and were located on or near the old canal on the near east side. The common laborers who resided there were employed in such nearby places as the Evansville and Terre Haute Railroad yards, the flour mills, the tobacco factories, the foundries, and stove works. Most of the 237 domestics lived in the households of affluent whites in three districts—76, 78, and 79—which constituted the riverfront portions of Wards 1 and 2. The third most numerous occupation—washwoman—was even more concentrated, as 128 of the 176 in the city dwelled in two heavily black census districts—77 and 91. Most of these (103) resided in district 77. This form of employment, which black women performed at home, provided an essential supplement to the household income of the blacks who lived on the streets and alleys within a few blocks' walking distance from the riverside residential region.[9]

Residence and employment were also closely associated among those holding the remaining 25 percent of the jobs. Most of the waiters, cooks, hostlers, porters, and other public service workers lived in either the hotels on or near Main or Water streets, in districts 77 or 78, or in the black sections of several districts near the canal, three or four blocks away. Similar patterns prevailed among the teamsters. Half of the black barbers resided in parts of Wards 1 and 2, for they served a predominantly white clientele in the business district. The other half were located in district 91. Nearly all the clergymen and teachers dwelled in the five districts with most of the black residents of the city. To the north and west, where a few enclaves were located, virtually all the workers were common laborers. As in 1870 black businesses were concentrated near the waterfront in the lower part of the city or the old canal region (Fourth and Fifth streets beyond Walnut).[10]

The coming of black coal miners provides the only significant change in these patterns in the 1890s. Blacks represented about one-fifth of all the miners in Evansville by 1900. Fifty-five of them resided near several coal mines in Wards 4 and 5. Of these, thirty-six lived in two census districts in Ward 4, situated on the west side: district 103, mostly on Decker Road, near the Ingleside Mine; and district 105, residents on Sunnyside Row or West Iowa and West Virginia streets between Tenth and Twelfth avenues, near the Sunnyside Mine. Smaller clusters were found near mines located at the northern boundaries of the city in Wards 4 and 5—on or near north Fulton Avenue between the Beltway and Pigeon Creek, or on or near north First Avenue, adjacent to Pigeon Creek.[11]

In general, however, the patterns established shortly after the end of the Civil War remained. A significant majority of common laborers lived around the old canal region and worked in the nearby railroad yards, factories, and businesses. There were 312 black cooks enumerated in 1900, 169 of whom dwelled in four census districts in Wards 1 and 2, which included downtown hotels and restaurants. Another 52 lived in Ward 7, adjoining these wards and also within easy walking distance of the downtown region. All but 35 of the 265 steamboat laborers either lived in or were enumerated in census district 92, the original site of black settlement which included parts of Lower Water, Lower First, and Lower Second streets. Laundresses and washwomen, who constituted about 10 percent of the black work force, were concentrated in four districts which were parts of Wards 1, 2, and 7. In general, the domestics lived in white homes in a few districts of Ward 1. The largest single category of worker, day laborer, accounted for one-sixth of the city's 3,611 black workers, and about half of them resided in two census districts in Ward 7.[12]

Ironically, unskilled labor and service jobs persisted among blacks while the city, like the northeastern quadrant of the United States, was experiencing vast industrial growth. Evansville's economy was increasingly based on manufacturing and was linked to the national economy by modern transportation and by the revolution in corporate organization. At the turn of the century, Evansville had about 7,300 wage earners, the third highest among Indiana cities. The number of workers, capitalization, and value of products had increased about 250 percent since 1870.[13]

The "proletarianization" of black workers—that is, urbanization and industrialization—which occurred in such other Northern cities as Milwaukee was negligible in Evansville. While the city enjoyed an upsurge of industrial activity, blacks found industrial jobs difficult to obtain. In 1900 (Table 7) less than 4 percent of the black work force was engaged in manufacturing, and, as elsewhere, most were employed at the lowest level—for example, as cleanup workers and porters. Only a handful—twenty at most—held such skilled positions as plow grinder, polisher, or machinist. The industrial jobs were, moreover, concentrated in two industries: brick and tile making, and lumber and

5.   Fourth Street, near Walnut, in the early 1880s. Evansville Museum of Arts and Sciences.

saw mills. Several factors accounted for the absence of blacks from industry: the assumption that blacks were inherently suited to agricultural labor and unfit for industrial work; the absence of economic necessity, prior to the reduction in 1914 of the stream of European immigrants that had provided an abundant supply of cheap labor; and the hostility of trade unions, especially the newer ones, to black membership.[14]

Trade unions affiliated with the American Federation of Labor generally

refused to accept black members. Only nine AFL unions openly prohibited Negro membership through clauses in their constitutions, but others accomplished the same purpose by excluding Negroes from the initiation ritual; still others, although they had no national policy of exclusion, allowed locals to bar Negroes if they saw fit, or to segregate black members in subordinate Jim Crow locals. Since before the 1930s few unskilled workers were unionized, these policies of the AFL did not prevent many blacks from entering industry at the lower occupational levels. They did, however, prevent most blacks from moving into the better paying skilled jobs in factories.[15]

In Evansville, union policies on the national and local levels barred most blacks from the trade union movement. By national policy, the Boilermakers' Union, the International Association of Machinists, and the Plumbers' and Steamfitters' Union excluded blacks. Labor records in Evansville, unfortunately, are extremely limited. Evidently most locals refused to allow blacks to join. One local which apparently had black members was Local No. 15 of the

National Brotherhood of Operative Potters, organized in the late 1890s. The Hod Carriers had an all black local, No. 11, organized about 1890, which was renamed the Building Laborers' International Protective Union of America in 1901. Although little direct evidence survives, one also suspects that the miners' local, as in other parts of the nation, eventually admitted blacks. Excluded from most unions, blacks were also prevented from making local union policy.[16]

As Kenneth Kusmer has observed, the exclusion of blacks from trade unions was on one level the product of the elitism of the AFL in that era. The AFL was uninterested in organizing any unskilled workers. More important than this was the fact that many trade unionists, as members of "the new middle class," were "anxious to gain respectability, and they were eager to dissociate themselves from a racial group that was becoming stereotyped by popular writers and social scientists as ignorant, lazy, and immoral."[17] The pervasive antiblack mood of Evansville reinforced that. When a black leader in a Georgia town wrote the Evansville Business Men's Association in 1890 for assistance in locating homes in Evansville for blacks from that town, an official of the EBMA informed the press that he would not reply, since Evansville already had enough black men without the desire or the means to obtain employment.[18]

The use of blacks as strikebreakers, or "scabs," also guaranteed poor relations between blacks and whites. "Employers who balked at hiring Negroes on a permanent basis were quite willing to use them to break strikes." This created "a peculiar situation" for blacks because they found tempting the "temporary employment at good wages when the opportunity presented itself." That, however, "only confirmed the worst fears of the white unionists: that all blacks were potential scabs who, because of their servile inclinations, would never be able to sympathize with the cause of labor."[19] In Evansville most of these cases involved the coal mines, as a strike in the fall of 1897 illustrated.[20]

Racial animosity was an omnipresent facet of the Evansville workplace, and it consistently transcended class considerations among city workers. Rare was the occasion in which an employer openly recruited workers without racial preference—as in the case of the Indiana Contract Company, which in June 1899 advertised for "100-150 laborers, white or black," to work at $1.50 a day until Christmas. Local newspapers were filled with advertisements for job openings which specified racial as well as age and experience requirements; they also carried many accounts of racial strife among local workers. In September 1897 a fight broke out in a canning factory over the complaints of black workers that they were receiving tomatoes which were smaller and harder to peel. The management fired all the black workers as a result. When a Board of Public Works official sent two teams with black drivers to do street work on the West Side in April 1899, another city official in that part of town sent the blacks home. "If you are going to work niggers," he complained, "we don't want the teams."[21]

It was not surprising that when black roustabouts went on strike for the first time in the spring of 1899, the responses of white leaders were negative, and white unionists did nothing to aid their fellow workers. After the blacks refused to load or ship out on steamboats until their work conditions were improved, the Republican editor praised the decision of the mayor requiring them to go to work or to leave the city. He observed that the charge that the work was difficult was merely an excuse for an essentially unreliable class of persons. The work stoppage lasted several days, nevertheless, and a number of boats had to leave the city without freight. Arrests followed, and white miners—on strike at the time—were invited to show up for work on the riverfront. About forty roustabouts were hired by a foreman of the Baltimore and Ohio Railroad and taken to Vincennes to lay track. The strike was ended shortly thereafter when the remaining roustabouts agreed to return to work. The terms of the agreement were not publicized.[22]

Whether Northern trade unionism was the greatest enemy of Afro-American workers, as one Hoosier black noted in 1899, is debatable, but clearly it was "a major reason for the decline in the number of blacks in the skilled trades, thereby undercutting one of the most important elements of the black middle class of the nineteenth century."[23] As shown on Table 8, the proportion of blacks in the skilled trades declined between 1870 and 1900. That must be qualified in several ways: Due to the rise of manufacturing, the percentage of all workers in skilled jobs was lower by 1900, and the decreases in the percentages of blacks in skilled trades were not uniform. There were, for example, four carpenters in 1870 and five in 1900. The number of plasterers increased from three in 1870 to ten in 1900. Black barbers numbered seventeen in 1870 and thirty-seven in 1900. There were no black bakers, blacksmiths, or machinists in 1870, but thirty years later there were, respectively, one, four, and two. By contrast, among other crafts not represented in 1870, the number of shoemakers decreased between 1880 and 1900 (from eight to two), as did brick molders (eight to six). Among the newer trades there were increases between 1880 and 1900 in the number of painters (one to four) and paperhangers (one to eleven). Although Evansville had a strong heritage of racial discrimination, its relatively smaller size, lower degree of industrialization and specialization, and smaller immigrant population meant that the rate of the decline of the black skilled trades was slower than that in larger cities, especially those on the East Coast.[24]

Despite small numerical increases, the proportion of blacks in the skilled trades in 1900 was, nevertheless, about half of what it had been in 1870. The percentage of black men in skilled trades (Table 8) was one-third that of white men with native-born parents and even less than that of white men who were foreign-born or who had foreign-born parents. In addition, certain of the newer trades—cabinetmakers, typesetters, tinsmiths, electricians, and plumbers, for example—totally excluded blacks. One may also assume that compensation and job security among skilled black workers were lower than among their white counterparts.[25]

In Evansville, as elsewhere, the skilled trades were the primary locus of integrated occupations that receded in importance in this period. Black employment on the police force also disappeared, but unlike Cleveland, the demand for black waiters increased. The number of black barbers decreased somewhat,

TABLE 8:   Occupations of Evansville Males, 1900, by Percent

Occupation	All	Native Whites/ Native Parents	Native Whites/ Foreign Parent(s)	Foreign-Born Whites	Blacks
Professional	4.1	5.7	3.2	3.9	1.9
Proprietor	9.1	7.8	11.2	15.5	1.7
Clerical	13.3	17.6	16.1	7.7	0.3
Skilled	36.8	34.8	44.7	49.5	11.7
Semiskilled/ service	16.2	14.8	13.2	13.9	29.2
Unskilled	20.4	19.3	11.5	9.5	55.1
Total	100.0	100.0	100.0	100.0	100.0
Number	18,222	7,065	6,174	2,402	2,581

Source: Derived from Department of Commerce and Labor, Bureau of the Census, *Special Reports: Occupations at the Twelfth Census* (Washington, D.C., 1904), 556–57. The percentage calculations are mine. Because of the ambiguity surrounding certain occupations listed in that printed report, proprietor represents major and minor entrepreneurs, officials, and managers, and the category of semiprofessional is not included here.

as in other cities, because of the decline in the number of black barbers serving white customers and the increase in the number of immigrant workers who entered barbering. Like other black businessmen, black barbers increasingly served an all-black clientele. The number and the proportion of black barbers (27 percent in 1900), nonetheless, remained high, as compared with larger Eastern cities.[26]

The decline of the black entrepreneurs who served an elite white clientele was in part, as August Meier has stated, the result of "growing antipathy on the part of whites toward trading with black businessmen and of changes in technology and business organization." It was also, as Kusmer has indicated, the product of the changing nature of American urban society, as white elites were "beginning to set themselves apart from the rest of society residentially . . . and institutionally. . . ." Such self-segregation "helped break the paternalistic tie between themselves and the black elite, and it is likely that this break would have eventually occurred even if racial discrimination had not been on the rise at the time." In addition, black entrepreneurs serving a predominantly white clientele "were adversely affected by the status anxieties of nouveau riche whites who, around 1900, were challenging an older, more genteel group of wealthy individuals." In the face of these changes, blacks who sought upward mobility had three options: They could engage in clerical work or in the professions, or begin a small business which served a predominantly black clientele. Each of these choices had its pitfalls.[27]

Although the emergence of white-collar employment in clerical and managerial positions was a feature of the nation's industrial explosion in the nineteenth century, blacks in Evansville, as in most American cities, found few opportunities. By 1900 the number of clerical workers (seven) was unchanged from 1880. One is struck by the extent to which this aspect of industrial change affected Evansville society unevenly (Tables 8 and 9). These limited clerical opportunities, morever, were situated at the lowest levels, as three of the clerks in 1900 worked in grocery stores and one was employed in a drugstore. The other workers were agents—one for a life insurance company. The highest government jobs, as noted in the previous chapter, were held by the firemen of Hose House No. 9, the captaincy of which was a major political plum in the black community. Also important were the positions of township physician and janitor in public buildings. Most blacks employed by government, however, held menial jobs, such as street cleaning, garbage removal, and truck driving.[28]

Several factors accounted for this: status anxieties among whites who had moved up from factory to clerical work; and the preoccupation of American business with public relations and advertising techniques, and thus the exclusion of blacks from jobs involving contact with the public, whether in department stores or the newer communications and transportation industries. There were, for example, no black streetcar conductors in Evansville, and in only a few Northern cities could blacks be found in this position. Similarly, there were no black telephone operators, a situation similar to all but a handful of Northern cities.[29]

Opportunities in the professions provided an easier route to success. Population growth and the refusal of most white professionals to accept Afro-American clients encouraged the expansion of the number of black professionals in Evansville from seven in 1870 to sixty-one in 1900. The proportion of the black work force in the professions increased slightly in this period, but Tables 8 and 9 indicate that the proportion of black men and women in the professions remained below that of both native and foreign-born whites. At the outset, the most prominent black professional was the clergyman, poorly paid and educated, but the mainstay of the black community. By 1900 there were fifteen black clergymen in the city. The most significant change was in the number of teachers, which rose to thirty-nine in 1900.[30]

Blacks also secured employment in medicine and law. By 1900 there was one physician for every 1,234 blacks (as compared with one white physician for every 400 whites). Small by such measurements and by modern-day standards, the number and the proportion of black doctors in Evansville compared favorably to many other black communities in the North. Serving a black clientele and somewhat dubiously educated, black physicians, like black teachers, influenced the growth of the Evansville black community in many ways. The most eminent black doctor in the late nineteenth century was Willis Green, who according to oral tradition learned medicine sitting in the back of a lecture hall at the Evansville Medical College while the person who had employed him as a chauffeur took classes. Green was the first black certified to practice medicine

6. Jeremiah Jackson, the pioneer black graduate of the Indiana University Medical School and an Evansville physician for sixty years.

by the county clerk. Probably the most well qualified was Jeremiah Jackson, the first black to graduate from the Indiana University School of Medicine. There were no black attorneys in Evansville until the early 1890s, when J. H. Lott and Fred Smith established a law practice. The first black to try a case before a federal judge was Lott in May 1892. There was only one black attorney enumerated in the federal census enumeration of 1900, G. W. McMechan, who remained in the city only a few years. Because of the poverty of Evansville's blacks and the racial climate in the city, especially in its legal system (no black, for example, was admitted to the county bar associaion until the mid-1920s), black attorneys found little business upon which to make a living.[31]

The opportunity for mobility by establishing a business also existed, although on a smaller scale than the professions. In the first postwar census, there were only six Afro-American proprietors—three each as keepers of saloons or boardinghouses. The number remained small in 1880, when the city claimed three black saloonkeepers, a grocer, and a keeper of an "eating house." The federal census enumeration of 1900 reported thirty-seven black entrepreneurs, although there was little change in the nature of those enterprises. The most significant change was the emergence of a black insurance agent, Willis Smith, and of a black druggist, John H. Jones. As in the case of black teachers, discrimination—in this case in housing and services to blacks—encouraged the growth of businesses which served the highly concentrated black community, and the black middle class enjoyed an infusion of new members into its modest ranks.[32]

It is difficult to detect much difference between the older group of black entrepreneurs and the newer one which emerged in the 1890s. The absence of a tradition of integration and paternalistic support by much of the white upper class, combined with the limited resources of a small, poor black community, meant that from the outset the establishment of black businesses was extremely rare. These firms were small and, as a rule, ephemeral. Some of the older ones—notably barber shops—catered to whites as well as blacks. Augustus H. Carter, first enumerated as a Kentucky-born barber in 1860, had by the 1880s established a shop of his own on Upper Third Street between Main and Locust streets, but he resided near Fifth and Cherry streets. Shops which served whites continued to exist after Carter's death in the 1890s. Probably the most notable was that of William Glover, born in Kentucky in 1867, whose shop on Upper First between Main and Locust survived into the late 1920s.[33]

The vast majority of black businesses, however, served only the black community, and with the intensification of racial separation the range of these establishments became somewhat broader by the 1890s. A short-lived black hotel was opened at 417 Upper Fourth Street in the early 1890s. (See chapter 3.) Perhaps the owners—like A. G. Smith, who owned a barbershop and who had been described by *The Freeman* in the fall of 1892 as one of the leading businessmen in Evansville—decided to seek their fortunes in Oklahoma Territory, pictured by some publicists as the panacea not only for Southern blacks but also for those in Evansville as well. More long-lived were three businesses established at the turn of the century: two hotels—Bell's, at 318-320 Upper Water, between Main and Locust, and Black's, at 420 Walnut, between Fourth and Fifth—and the life insurance business formed by Logan Stewart, a native of Kentucky who graduated from Clark High School in 1899 at the age of twenty. In general, the rate of growth of Evansville black businesses, however, was slower than that of most Northern black communities, and the types of firms remained marginal.[34]

TABLE 9: Occupations of Evansville Females, 1900, by Percent

Occupation	All	Native Whites/ Native Parents	Native Whites/ Foreign Parent(s)	Foreign-Born Whites	Blacks
Professional	4.5	5.4	4.8	3.5	2.3
Proprietor	1.1	1.6	0.7	2.3	0.7
Semiprof'l	3.1	3.5	0.3	6.6	1.9
Clerical	12.5	15.4	15.9	12.9	0
Skilled	27.1	33.7	35.0	30.9	1.1
Semiskilled/ service	42.4	36.2	37.7	35.9	65.4
Unskilled	9.2	4.2	5.6	7.8	28.6
Total	100.0	100.0	100.0	100.0	100.0
Number	5,988	2,402	2,146	256	1,184

Sources: Derived from the same census data as Table 8.

As in other Northern cities, occupational limitations upon black males were offset somewhat by the expansion of the female work force. From the time the first postwar census was taken, it was obvious that black women did not—and could not—abide by the notion, widely promulgated at the time, that respectable women did not work outside the home. Black women represented 17 percent of the black work force in Evansville in 1870 and nearly 30 percent by 1900. At the turn of the century nearly 45 percent of black women in the city were employed, as compared with 10 percent of foreign-born white women and 25 percent of native-born white women. As shown on Table 9, 1,184 black women were at work in 1900, or one in five of all females at work in Evansville that year and about twice the proportion of black women in the total population of the city.[35]

Black women consistently found work, however, in the most menial service positions. In 1870 seventy-seven of the ninety-four employed black women were domestics, and the remainder were chambermaids, washwomen, cooks, housekeepers, and seamstresses. In 1900 30 percent were washwomen, and an additional two-thirds were in service. The clerical revolution had not touched black women, and only a handful—all teachers—had risen to the ranks of professional occupations. Cooks, laundresses, and washwomen accounted for 568 of the 1,184 black women at work in 1900. As before, moreover, many of these women who worked were married—in 1880, about one-quarter—because of the need to supplement meager family income.[36]

A fuller understanding the socioeconomic status of blacks in Evansville in these years also emerges from a comparison of black and white occupational patterns. One clue is provided in Table 6, which shows little change among black workers in the 1870-1900 era. On an occupational index, black workers moved slightly upward. From an extremely low index of 653 in 1870 (with 700 being lowest), they increased their standing to 632 in 1880 and 613 in 1900. The slight improvement in status applied to men as well as women (Table 10), with black men experiencing a somewhat higher rate of increase.

In spite of these modest increases, significant gaps continued to exist between whites and blacks. Among men, the index for native whites with native-born parents was 490, and for whites with mixed or foreign-born parents it was 473. The index for foreign-born men, 463, was highest. Although black and foreign-born newcomers in 1870 or 1880 may have once been underrepresented in the professions, proprietorships, or clerical work, and overrepresented in semiskilled and unskilled work, the opportunities for occupational mobility were clearly dissimilar. Similar patterns existed among women. The index for foreign-born white women probably reflected cultural influences—in this case southern German—on that part of the work force. The few German women who worked in 1900 were on the whole younger than other white females at work and were likely to be found in domestic service or in the tobacco factories (Table 9).[37]

These measurements of the occupational status of various racial and ethnic groups, of course, do not disclose such differences as the levels of compensation

TABLE 10:   Occupational Index by Race and Ethnicity, Evansville,
1880 and 1900

	1880	1900
Males		
Blacks	656	626
Native Whites/		
Native Parents	n/a	490
Native Whites/		
Foreign Parent(s)	n/a	473
Foreign-Born Whites	n/a	463
All	n/a	500
Females		
Blacks	626	608
Native Whites/		
Native Parents	n/a	496
Native Whites/		
Foreign Parent(s)	n/a	495
Foreign-Born Whites	n/a	504
All	n/a	520

Sources: Derived from the same census data as Table 8.

or the relationship between socioeconomic status and educational achievement.[38] Nor do they indicate the disproportionate distribution of blacks in the
kinds of employment available to men and women at the time. On the one
hand, blacks accounted in 1900 for 73 percent of the boatmen and sailors, 63
percent of the hostlers, 41 percent of the unspecified laborers in domestic and
personal service, 78 percent of the servants and waiters, 43 percent of the janitors and sextons, 55 percent of the porters and helpers, and 53 percent of the
brick and tile workers. On the other hand, they constituted less than 1 percent
of the attorneys, 3 percent of the restaurant proprietors and saloon keepers, 1.3
percent of the merchants and dealers, 6 percent of street railway employees, and
less than 2 percent of the bakers and blacksmiths.[39]

Differentials also existed among white and black women. The latter were
38 percent of the servants and waitresses and 63 percent of the laundresses in
the river city. Only 1.8 percent of factory women were black, and there were no
black bookkeepers, clerks, saleswomen, or stenographers. Blacks and whites
were distributed according to overall population percentages among teachers,
boardinghouse keepers, housekeepers, and nurses.[40]

A similar picture of limited economic opportunity appears through the
case histories of individuals and their families. One of the results of limited
occupational mobility and widespread racial discrimination was a low rate of
residential persistence. Of the 324 heads of household enumerated in the federal census enumeration of 1870, only forty-three, or 13.3 percent, were also

listed in the federal census enumeration of 1880. Of the 2,083 persons recorded in the Evansville city directory of 1891, only 568, or 27.3 percent, could
be located in the 1900 directory. Among those who remained during the
1870s, three-quarters experienced no change in status; all but three of them
were unskilled workers. Five of the forty-three declined in status in the decade,
and about one-fifth gained in status, although modestly. Eli Jackson and Bryant
Goins, laborers in 1870, were members of the police force in 1880, and Zack
Taylor, a laborer, became a church sexton. All three secured jobs which in the
black community represented a significant level of accomplishment. The most
substantial advancement was made by Willis Green, who was first enumerated
in 1870 as a plasterer.[41]

Similar patterns recurred in the 1890s. Of those who remained in Evansville, most stayed at the same socioeconomic level. About an equal number of
persons saw their fortunes improve (twenty-two) as those who declined
(twenty-seven). The most notable cases of advancement involved four barbers
who were able to open their own shops and four laborers who became proprietors of small establishments—a barbershop, a grocery, and two restaurants.[42]

Few blacks can be traced for twenty years or more in that period. For those
listed in the federal census enumeration of 1870, the federal census enumeration of 1880, and the Evansville city directory of 1891, social advancement was
scant. Ten of the twenty-three appeared to experience improvement in their
condition—Alex Sigler and Bryant Goins, engineers by 1891; Willis Green, the
physician; James Amos, Gus Carter, John Grandison, and William Jones, barbershop owners; Zack Taylor, church sexton; Charles Asbury, a foreman at
Igleheart Brothers Mill; and Felix Pryor, who became a custodian at National
City Bank. The rest remained at the same type of employment or declined
somewhat in status.[43]

Another testament to the weak economic position of blacks was the virtual
absence of property ownership. The total amount of property owned by blacks
increased between 1865 and 1900, but the rate of increase, like the total, was
small. The city tax assessments for 1869 included only eleven black taxpayers
whose lots, improvements, and personal property were assessed at $6,600; the
eleven paid a combined tax of $106.47. In the federal census enumeration of
1870, Vanderburgh County's real property was valued at $8.9 million and per-
sonal property at $4.9 million. Blacks in the county possessed real property
worth $42,300 and personal property valued at $10,000, or 0.5 and 0.2 percent, respectively, of the total. One rural black, Daniel Lyles, had property valued at $15,000, more than one-third of the total among blacks in Vanderburgh
County. There were fourteen blacks in the city who, all told, owned real property worth $24,000 and personal property of about $7,000.[44]

Little advancement was evident by the 1890s. In the fifty-eight American
cities—including Evansville—which in 1890 had 50,000 people or more, 24
percent of the heads of household owned their homes and 76 percent were
tenants; for blacks, only 9 percent were homeowners, as compared with 32
percent of the German Americans. In Evansville, the proportion of all home-

owners was slightly higher—25 percent—than the average for the fifty-eight cities. In 1900, 45 percent of Indiana's nonfarm homes were owned and 55 percent rented; among nonfarm blacks the percentages were, in order, 25.4 and 74.6. About 32 percent of Evansville's heads of household owned their own homes. The federal census enumeration of 1900 reveals that only 125 black household heads in Evansville—about 9 percent—owned homes. (In Indianapolis, 21.5 percent did.) What this extremely low figure does not reveal is the value of the homes. (Of the eleven homes listed as owned in census district 101, for example, all but two were houseboats owned by fishermen.) In addition, it does not show how unevenly distributed were the homes that blacks owned. In most districts, home ownership was non-existent. In the three districts with the largest number of blacks—89, 126, and 129, all in Baptisttown—twenty-seven, or only 6.2 percent, of the homes were owned. Thirty-seven household heads in West Side districts 100 and 105, by contrast, owned their homes; most were coal miners near Ingleside or Sunnyside mines. Proportionately large numbers of blacks owned their homes in Jimtown and on East Division Street between Hendricks and Denby streets, and on the 800 block of John and William streets.[45]

To be sure, blacks in some cities in the North and the South had an even worse experience regarding home ownership.[46] Yet the fact remains that less than one in ten household heads in the river city had gained that distinction by 1900. That was substantial evidence of the pervasiveness of discrimination in the workplace. Nevertheless, hundreds continued to flock to Evansville to attempt a new start. That attested to the even greater miseries of life across the Ohio River, where Jim Crow and agricultural depression were omnipresent. It also testified to the hope that even a discriminatory Northern city offered.

Evansville's Black Society, 1865-1900

 Even the most cursory examination of the newspapers of late nineteenth century Evansville reveals the extent to which whites held blacks in low regard. Cartoons in the Republican and Democratic newspapers reinforced the stereotypes of blacks as shiftless and irresponsible or brutal and dangerous. Even well-intentioned gestures, such as the support offered by affluent whites for black migration to Oklahoma Territory in 1892, reflected an uneasiness about the black presence in Evansville. To the typical white observer, all blacks were alike—and alien to the orderly development of the city.[1]

As W. E. B. Du Bois observed in 1899, however, "wide variation in the antecedents, wealth, intelligence and general efficiency have already been differentiated within this group."[2] In some cities, like Boston and Charleston, a well-developed class structure had developed before the Civil War. In others, like Cleveland and many cities of the East and the Midwest,

> only an embryonic black class structure existed [before 1860]. The black community at that time was roughly divided into two broad groups: unskilled laborers on the one hand; skilled artisans, together with a few professionals and businessmen, on the other.[3]

In such cities as Evansville, steady population growth after the war "allowed social and economic differentiation within the black community to develop to a much greater extent."[4] The absence of even moderately wealthy blacks and the prevalence of illiteracy, crime, and poverty prevented most white observers from seeing the emergence of differences among social strata. In addition, the pace of industrialization and the smaller size of the black community, as compared with other cities to the north and east, helped to keep Evansville's black society from becoming as clearly divided into upper, middle, and lower classes as, for example, Cleveland and Detroit. Nonetheless, the patterns of family structure, church and club membership, residence, education, and occupation revealed that blacks in Evansville had to develop diverse life styles and to differentiate themselves from each other.[5]

The most important social institution among blacks in Evansville—as else-where—was the family. The traditional picture of the black family as an unstable social unit, the product of slavery and urban disorder, has been discredited by a series of studies of Afro-American familiy life in the North and the South, both before and after the Civil War. Despite the harshness of life, the typical family in Evansville was not disorganized or pathological. The continued existence of the black family in this rapidly industrializing community reflected the strength of traditional ideals and the ability to cope with the demands of urban life.[6]

TABLE 11:   Family Headship among Evansville and Vanderburgh County
Blacks, 1880 and 1900, by Percent

Section/ Year	Total Black Families:		Two-Parent Black Families	One-Parent Black Families	Female-Headed Families
	Number	Percent			
Rural					
1880	210	100.0	97.6	2.4	1.9
1900	83	100.0	84.3	15.7	6.1
Urban					
1880	574	100.0	78.0	22.0	21.4
Ward 1	190	100.0	74.2	25.8	25.8
Ward 2	113	100.0	69.9	30.1	30.1
Ward 3	64	100.0	75.0	25.0	23.4
Ward 4	49	100.0	98.0	2.0	2.0
Ward 5	33	100.0	84.8	15.2	15.2
Ward 6	125	100.0	83.2	16.8	7.2
1900	1370	100.0	71.5	28.5	22.4
Ward 1	145	100.0	74.5	25.5	22.1
Ward 2	204	100.0	64.2	35.8	29.4
Ward 3	130	100.0	60.8	39.2	30.8
Ward 4	174	100.0	80.5	19.5	11.5
Ward 5	90	100.0	74.4	25.6	20.0
Ward 6	79	100.0	79.7	20.3	15.2
Ward 7	548	100.0	71.5	28.5	23.2

Sources: Tenth Census, Population Schedules for Vanderburgh County, 1880; Twelfth Census, Population Schedules for Vanderburgh County, 1900. This table excludes single-member and public households. It is based on Darrel E. Bigham, "The Black Family in Evansville and Vanderburgh County, Indiana, in 1880," *Indiana Magazine of History*, LXXV (June, 1979), 124, Table I, and "The Black Family in Evansville and Vanderburgh County, Indiana: A 1900 Postscript," ibid., LXXVIII (June, 1982), 158, Table I.

The vast majority of black families in Evansville (Table 11) contained two parents, although the percentage varied from district to district. Two-parent families were lowest in the waterfront and downtown regions (Wards 2 and 3) and highest in the north and west portions (Wards 4 and 6). Given the common heritage of upper South roots among the Afro-Americans who settled in the urban and rural parts of Vanderburgh County, the table also suggests that the urban experience was an important factor in determining family structure. Urban stress—notably public health problems and low-paying, insecure employment, which encouraged the death and desertion of male heads—combined with the availability of employment for women to make for a higher incidence of female-headed families in the city of Evansville. As a result, black families were more likely to be headed by a woman than were white families, including those of German extraction. But the two-parent family remained the core of urban society.[7]

In general, female-headed families were on the lower end of the social ladder. In 1880 (Table 12) there were no female-headed families when the family head was a professional, a proprietor, or a skilled worker. By contrast, when service workers were family heads, slightly over 38 percent were females. When the family head listed no occupation, 83 percent of the families were headed by females, usually widows. In short, the lower the status of the family head, the more likely it was that families would have one parent, not two, and that single parent was most often a woman. That guaranteed not only a more difficult time coping with urban stress, given the absence of incomes from two parents, but also less respectability in a society which valued a couple-headed family. It is important to add, however, that in most cases female-headed families included relatives and/or boarders and lodgers who provided financial support and/or child care. Most of the working female heads, moreover, were washwomen. Although menial, such work allowed mothers the opportunity to care for their children while also securing a small family income.[8]

TABLE 12:   Black Family Headship by Occupation, Evansville, 1880

	Male		Female		
Occupation	Number	Percent	Number	Percent	TOTAL
Professional/					
Proprietor	16	100.0	0	0	16
Skilled	16	100.0	0	0	16
Semiskilled	51	100.0	0	0	0
Unskilled	252	99.6	1	0.4	253
Service	104	61.9	64	38.1	168
None	12	17.1	58	82.9	70
TOTAL	451		123		574

Sources: Same as Table 11. The occupational categories represent a simplified form of those used previously. The chief difference is that washwomen are counted here in a separate service category, not in that of unskilled laborer. The virtual absence of women from the ranks of common laborer accounts for the low percentage of female heads among the unskilled.

The addition of boarders and lodgers was a distinctive feature of Evansville black society. Unlike family headship, family composition did not reflect status. In 1880 and 1900, as disclosed on Table 13, about three in ten Evansville families were augmented. Despite Victorian notions that taking in boarders and lodgers was unrespectable, harsh conditions led black families to augmentation, and that helped to preserve the family. For blacks to have attempted to use only the nuclear, isolated family in the city would have been self-destructive. The inclusion of boarders and lodgers supplemented family income and also benefitted those who were added to the household by sheltering them from urban stress. The addition of relatives was also important. As Table 13 indicates, extended families were also more prevalent in the city than in its rural environs. Relatives could provide additional family income and child care. This also allowed the perpetuation of kin networks in the city, thus maintaining family ties and offering a haven for relatives, many of whom were young. That helps to explain why family extension was not limited to the well-to-do, who could afford to house relatives. The typical extended family in Evansville was two-generational and included a brother, sister, niece, or nephew of the head of the family or his spouse.[9]

TABLE 13:   Black Family Structure, Evansville and Vanderburgh County, 1880 and 1900

Type of Family and Year	Rural		Urban	
	Number	Percent	Number	Percent
Nuclear				
1880	155	73.8	293	51.0
1900	60	72.3	722	52.7
Extended				
1880	26	12.4	94	16.4
1900	14	16.9	254	18.5
Augmented				
1880	29	13.8	187	32.5
1900	9	10.8	394	28.8
TOTAL				
1880	210	100.0	574	100.0
1900	83	100.0	1370	100.0

Sources: Same as Table 11.

Probably a clearer indication of the development of social strata in the city was the black church.

Church membership was perhaps the most important indicator of status in the black community because, as one scholar observed in 1913, it was often "the only institution which the Negro may call his own . . . . A new church may be built, a new pastor installed, new members received and all the machinery of the church set in motion without even consulting a white person. In a word, the church is the Negro's own institution, developing according to his own standards and more nearly than anything else represents the real life of the race."[10]

Segregated churches had been a fact of life for Evansville blacks since the winter of 1842-1843. Blacks were as a rule excluded from the city's white churches, although by the turn of the century some attended Roman Catholic services. A regional German Evangelical Lutheran conference met in Evansville in 1896, and delegates discussed a report from a "committee on colored missions" and agreed that "more money should be appropriated to provide each mission with a suitable church, as many of them are too poor to pay for them . . . [and] the committee was instructed to collect money for that purpose."[11] Extant records, however, provide no documentation of a Lutheran congregation for Evansville blacks until 1938.

Between 1865 and 1900, however, Afro-Americans organized a score of churches on their own. The precise relationship between the prewar and the postwar AME church is somewhat clouded, since it was listed irregularly in city directories between 1858 and 1865, when an AME church was reported on Leet Street, but by the mid-1860s it appears that the congregation had moved to a site on Walnut, near Fifth. Pastors of the AME churches were rotated every two years, but the service of J. H. Alexander between 1874 and 1876 must have been outstanding, for by 1876 the church was known as Alexander Chapel. The congregation built a new structure on the same site, which was one block to the southeast of Evans Hall. Alexander had 325 members in 1889.[12]

The oldest church in continuity of record-keeping was Liberty Baptist, which rapidly became the largest Afro-American church in the city. The first pastor, according to tradition, was a white man named Woods, who served briefly until the election of Green McFarland in 1866. Another founder of the congregation was A. L. Robinson, the antislavery attorney and judge, who was appointed clerk at the organizational meeting. One of the first newspaper accounts of Liberty was the baptism of six or seven new members in the Ohio on July 8, 1866, an event witnessed by a large crowd of blacks and whites. Under the leadership of McFarland and J. D. Rouse, the congregation grew to a membership of nearly 800 in 1889. McFarland's death and the hiring of Rouse, an ex-slave who had come to the city with his parents in 1865, led to a highly publicized schism in the church in September 1882, and a month later the dissidents formed their own congregation, which they named McFarland Chapel. The group erected a building in 1884 at Cherry and Church streets and dedicated another structure three years later. The first pastor was W. H. Anderson, a native of the Lost Creek Settlement in Vigo County and a veteran of the Union army, who served until his death in 1919. In 1889 McFarland claimed 300 members.[13]

In addition to these churches—the largest and the most influential in the black community well into the twentieth century—a number of others were

7. Alexander Chapel AME Church, near Fifth and Walnut streets. The building, completed in 1889, was razed during urban renewal in the 1960s. John Payne.

8. Liberty Baptist Church, Seventh and Oak streets. This edifice was completed seven months after a cyclone destroyed its predecessor in the spring of 1886. *Indiana Magazine of History*, December 1980.

9. J. D. Rouse, pastor of Liberty Baptist Church, 1882–1929. Willard Library.

established. A Baptist church was organized in Independence, near Sunnyside Mine, in 1870, and a building was erected at the northwest corner of Twelfth Avenue and West Virginia Street. A new edifice was completed in 1883, and by 1889, the new congregation—called Independence Missionary Baptist Church—claimed 125 members. A second Methodist church, Zion, was founded in the mid-1870s, and by the 1890s the congregation, at the corner of Fulton Avenue and Nevada Street, was known as Hood's Chapel AME Zion. Another congregation formed in the 1880s was Fifth M. E. Church, which rented space at the northeast corner of Garfield and Illinois on the near northside. Like St. John's M. E. Church, organized in the early 1890s and situated at 33 Bland Avenue in Baptisttown, it was affiliated with neither the AME nor the AME Zion churches, but rather with the Central Conference of the white Methodist Episcopal Church, North. Two other Baptist congregations were formed on the northside in the mid-1890s: Mt. Zion, on Louisiana between Heidelbach and Governor; and Free Will, located near Nevada and Fulton. A "Colored Christian Church" was also established on Canal Street in the late 1890s.[14]

These churches, all but four of which were Baptist, marked not only the center and the enclaves of black Evansville but also the levels of black society. Liberty was the most influential and affluent. After a cyclone devastated the newly finished church in 1886, the congregation rebuilt the edifice at a cost of $7,000. None of the Evansville black churches, however, were elite institutions like Mt. Zion Congregational and St. Andrew's Episcopal churches in Cleveland. Members of all classes attended the leading churches each Sunday. Accordingly, "these congregations (especially those of the Baptist denomination) generally reflected the religious aspirations of the typical urban black."[15]

As W. E. B. Du Bois explained, the Baptist minister was "the elected chairman of a pure democracy, who, if he can command a large enough following, becomes a virtual dictator; he thus has the chance to be a wise leader or a demagogue, or, as in many cases, a little of both."[16] He provided a message which was basically conservative in theology and social theory. Rouse's Sunday School superintendent, J. D. Cox, admonished parents in a highly publicized statement in April 1899 to "help solve the race problem . . . by having good principles instilled in your boys and girls."[17] But it was the form, not the content, of Baptist services that offended some upper-class blacks. The typical black man or woman "enjoyed the singing, chanting, and enthusiasm that accompanied the Baptist rituals, and expected the sermon to be the emotional climax to [the preacher's] service."[18]

The frequent revival meetings at these churches were originally incomprehensible and amusing to white observers. In December 1875, protracted meetings at Liberty and Alexander led to "a painful state of excitement in consequence. . . ." Conversions followed the singing of "unchurchlike songs, the groans of mourners at the anxious seat . . . the entreaties and menaces of friends and relatives . . . [and] the shouting and screaming of men and women in a ferment of real or assumed enthusiasm." The Republican newspaper noted derisively that after Sunday evening services the black enthusiasts took to the streets and behaved in uncivilized fashion. The converts reported "visions which are absurd and laughable. The Lord appears to them in every imaginable shape and form."[19]

Because they appealed to the masses, the churches were involved in many aspects of the life of the black community. The AME church had a Sunday School as early as 1858, for instance, and assisted actively in the development of the early black schools. Sunday services, which provided social as well as spiritual relief, encompassed an entire day. Each of the churches had organizations for men, women, and young people—as in Liberty's Ladies' Home and Foreign Mission Society. The churches also touched the lives of black Evansvillians in other ways. A Union Aid Society was reorganized in the fall of 1879 at Liberty Baptist Church. Chaired by Adam Rouse, father of Dennis, the society aimed at providing benevolent aid to the black community. Black churches were also used for meetings of political organizations, fraternal societies, and Emancipation Day planning groups.[20]

Given the absence of membership lists, it is difficult to reconstruct a precise profile of each congregation, but extant records of church incorporation and the election of trustees offer clues. Although its members came from all classes, Liberty's trustees consistently represented middle- and upper-class blacks. In the early 1890s, for example, the trustees included Willis Green; Julius Coleman, a laborer who was active in Republican politics; Grandville Waddell, owner of a barbershop on Water Street; Robert Babb, a houseman; George Hines, a hod carrier (among the elite of black workers); and Henry Dillard, identified in the 1891 directory of Evansville by "moving car." The same could be noted of the trustees of Alexander Chapel. In 1890 they constituted Charles Asbury, a foreman at Igleheart Brothers Mill; David Allen, a grocer at 1411 Canal; Nathaniel Allen, owner of a barbershop on Upper First Street; Henry Porter, a hod carrier; and Simon Walker, a paperhanger. The church clerk was W. A. Rucker, owner of a barbershop on Upper First Street.[21]

Records of church leadership indicate that only these two churches initially included black Evansville's higher classes. The trustees of McFarland Chapel in the 1890s were laborers and teamsters, as were those of Independence Missionary Baptist Church. The AME Zion church on Fulton Avenue adopted articles of incorporation in October 1886. Of the thirty-two men and women who attested to the formation of the new church, twenty-three were unable to read and write, as indicated by the "x" after their names. All resided nearby, and of those identifiable in the city directory all were laborers or miners.[22]

Although the people who attended Liberty and Alexander were relatively better off than other black Protestants, their pastors and their members engaged in a high degree of cooperative activity with other black Protestants, which bespoke the emergence of a strong sense of racial cohesion. One form was the interchange of pastors with other congregations, both in Evansville and in the Kentucky towns of Henderson and Owensboro—and even the faraway metropolis of Indianapolis. It was a matter of great local pride when J. D.

Rouse gave the guest sermon at the reopening of the largest black Baptist church in Indiana, Second Baptist of Indianapolis, in August 1894. Similarly, jointly sponsored evangelistic services unified the city's blacks, as did the yearly celebration marking the continued tenure of a black minister. Given the length of his service and the influence of his church, the anniversary of J. D. Rouse was one of the most important social as well as religious events of the year. Black clergymen also cooperated in the planning and observance of Emancipation Day and were prominent figures, as noted in chapter 3, in annual high school graduation activities.[23]

Intraracial cooperation was especially evident in 1894. On June 8 Rouse presided at the local jubilee for the rejection by the Kentucky Supreme Court of a law allowing for the creation of racially separate railroad cars. The celebration took place at Alexander Chapel and attracted spokesmen from most of Evansville's black churches. Only a week earlier, the city's seven black pastors had organized the Colored Ministerial Alliance. (An alliance of white ministers had existed since the late 1860s). The CMA invited any pastor to join and was designed to provide weekly discussions of matters of interest. The alliance usually dealt with theological and pastoral matters, but also became a means whereby blacks could collectively exercise their influence in matters affecting the race.[24]

Fraternal and benevolent societies offered another important focal point for group activity. The earliest organizations appeared during and immediately after the Civil War. On Emancipation Day in 1869, for instance, a large crowd proceeded to Blackford's Grove for a picnic and speeches. The procession was led by an Afro-American brass band which was followed by the members of the Mutual Aid Society. By 1900 there were at least twenty-two such organizations of varied size and function. In this period of United States history, whites as well as blacks joined lodges and mutual aid organizations in unprecedented numbers, and these organizations "became an important social phenomenon." As mutual benefit societies, like churches, they often paid "a small weekly stipend to members who became ill and help[ed] to pay funeral costs and support the widows of those who died." In addition, "the imposing rituals and colorful regalia of the lodges, combined with the opportunity for social intercourse that they provided, helped restore a sense of community participation to what was becoming an increasingly atomized society."[25]

By 1900 the most important associations for black men and women were the United Brothers of Friendship, the Masons, and the Odd Fellows. The United Brothers of Friendship claimed three lodges (for men) and eight temples (for women); the Masons had four lodges and a chapter of the Order of the Eastern Star for women; and the Odd Fellows had two lodges and two chapters of the Household of Ruth for women. Blacks also organized a variety of other groups—for example, the Evening Star Brass Band, formed by Richard Amos in June 1868, which lasted until about 1892; Carter's Quadrille Band, created by Augustus Carter in 1878 and active until the mid-1890s; and the

Colonel John F. Grill Post No. 541 of the Grand Army of the Republic in December, 1888.[26]

Probably the most important of these groups was the United Brothers of Friendship, founded in Louisville in 1861. Its purpose was to "visit the sick, relieve the distressed, watch over and bury the dead, comfort the widow, and guard the orphans."[27] The first Evansville lodge, Asbury No. 1, was established shortly after the end of the war by Charles Asbury, who like many other men and women involved in fraternal societies was also prominent in church affairs. The first published reference to the chapter was its sponsorship of an "Ethiopian Festival" at the Masonic Hall in May 1867. "The Ethiopian damsels were arrayed in the most gorgeous attire," sniffed the *Journal*, "and we presume to their sooty beaux looked extremely fascinating. Out of curiosity we looked in for a moment, and must confess that the order prevailing would have done credit to any assembly."[28]

The organization was inactive for about four years and revived in late 1871 or early 1872. In August of 1872, in celebration of its reorganization, it sponsored a parade and a gala picnic. Prominent in the event were Rev. Green McFarland, J. H. Gray (a saloonkeeper), Alfred Carter (a confectioner), Charles Sheldon, and J. H. Townsend (the teacher). Members traveled to Henderson, Kentucky, in October 1873 to celebrate the creation of a lodge there. Like other fraternal organizations, the UBF also sponsored annual Emancipation Day observances. The most important event of the group's year—as it was for other societies—was the "Annual Sermon," a celebration usually held in the spring. The event included a parade through the downtown to a church, where members took part in organizational rituals and heard from one of the city's leading pastors.[29]

The Evansville UBF, which produced a national grand master (F. D. Morton) and a state grand master (Asbury), attracted members of the higher levels of Evansville black society. The roster of the first official list of the officers and the trustees of the Asbury lodge in 1872 included, in addition to Charles Asbury, two barbers, a driver, and four laborers. (Asbury and the two barbers were also trustees of Alexander Chapel.) The founders of Lodge No. 9, formed in 1895, included two drivers, two engineers, a barber, a joiner at Blount Plow Company, and a laborer. The first "worthy princess" of Mt. Carmel Temple, established probably in 1868, was the wife of James M. Townsend. In 1889, 300 men and women belonged to the UBF lodges and temples.[30]

Also prominent were the lodges of the Masons, the first of which, Olive Branch No. 23, was organized in 1870. On July 4 of that year the black Masons and their ladies' auxiliary sponsored an Independence Day celebration at Masonic Hall for the Afro-American community. An examination of the early leadership of McFarland Lodge, a reorganized group which included Olive Branch and which was named after the Rev. Green McFarland, reveals that the Masons were also prominent in church and social affairs. The founders included Adam Rouse, a janitor, and John Banks, foreman at a tobacco factory and a trustee of Alexander Chapel. Worshipful masters of this lodge, formed in the mid-1870s, were J. D. Rouse and Lewis Anderson, for many years a trustee of Independence Church. Pythagoras Lodge, formed in 1887, included in its leadership two trustees of Alexander Chapel. The two lodges claimed about ninety members in 1889.[31]

A third important fraternal organization was the United Order of Odd Fellows. The first lodge, Vanderburgh, was chartered on January 7, 1876, and by 1880 there was a second lodge, Pride of Hope. Like the United Brothers of Friendship, the Odd Fellows celebrated their annual thanksgiving with an "Annual Sermon." On Sunday afternoon, March 5, 1893, for example, Evans Hall was filled with black citizens, who heard Rev. David Irwin of the AME Zion church deliver the message. The two Evansville lodges were joined by the Henderson lodge in the ceremony presided over by J. R. Blackburn, the most prominent black educator of the era. The Odd Fellows were also in charge, from time to time, of Emancipation Day observances. Progress was so marked that local Odd Fellows hosted the convention of the thirty Indiana lodges in August 1893. According to a story in an Indianapolis black newspaper, "the good people of Evansville are vieing [sic] with each other in making it pleasant for their visitors, which combined with the other attractions that charming Evansville is noted for, the occasion cannot help being an enjoyable, profitable success." The observer stated that the event eloquently testified to the importance of the secret society "as a rock in a weary land ... [and] shelter in a mighty storm."[32]

The Odd Fellows also attracted the black community's elite. Trustees of the Pride of Hope Lodge in 1886 included a barber and an expressman. In 1888 they comprised an expressman, a janitor, and a barber, and in 1893 a barber, an expressman, and a laborer. One of the most prominent was William Glover, the barber. In 1889 there were seventy-five members of the Odd Fellows in Evansville.[33]

Although membership lists of the fraternal orders have not generally survived, the extant records of the elections of trustees suggest that the dominance of the older elite of Afro-Americans in the United Brothers of Friendship, the Masons, and the Odd Fellows reflected the fact that prior to the 1890s these lodges were the only ones in Evansville. By the late 1890s the Knights of Tabor had founded an Evansville chapter, and it appears that its membership was drawn from the same social strata as the older lodges and clubs. Growing rapidly, the Taborites hosted the state convention in 1899. Prominent in local arrangements were Hugh Rouse, son of the Baptist pastor; Patsy Woods, the first "worthy princess" of a temple of the United Brothers of Friendship; and Georgia Coffee, wife of the prominent civic leader, John.[34]

Family life, churches, and fraternal societies revealed, in a word, patterns of social organization among Evansville's blacks which were emerging in the decades after the end of the Civil War. Such activities were part of "a broad nexus of socioeconomic relationships and cultural values" which separated the black upper- and middle-classes from the bulk of the black community.[35]

In this era a small upper class dominated Evansville's black community. Composed of a handful of small entrepreneurs, craftsmen, barbers who owned their own shops, physicians, attorneys, and educators, it established standards by which many governed their lives. The older Afro-American upper class had roots in prewar Evansville or Vanderburgh County. The most notable were Lena [sp?] McDaniel and Mary Morton, who had property valued at several thousand dollars each in the 1860 and 1870 censuses, and the James Carter family. Carter died in the 1860s, and his widow took over his business. A son, Alfred, founded a small confectionery in the decade, during which time another relative, Augustus ("Gus")—possibly a nephew—established a barbershop. Both were prominent in civic affairs in the postwar period. Alfred Carter, born in the 1840s, was foreman of the first black jury in the county's history in October 1870. Four years later, he served as a witness for several black women who claimed they had been wrongfully arrested on Fourth Street. Carter testified that the three were not prostitutes; the three were released. "The affair caused considerable stir in colored circles," wrote the Republican paper, "where the action of the officers is looked upon as not less than an outrage."[36] One of the first recorded black protests against white injustice in the city's history, the event illustrated Alfred Carter's standing among whites as well as blacks.

Joining the older black elite shortly after 1865 were others whose influence was also substantial. Born in Knight Township, sons of a relatively well-to-do black farmer, James and Richard Amos rose to prominence in this era—James as a barber and Richard as a musician, and both as prominent Republicans. Adam Rouse, born in Kentucky, was by 1870 a foreman in a tobacco factory and the owner of a comparatively large amount of property. By 1880 he had secured the post of courthouse janitor. Both he and Charles Asbury were prominent in church and club activities. Also of note was Willis Green. When he died in 1908 at the age of sixty-six, he owned a number of lots and houses in Baptisttown and "Greenville," a section on Green River Road.[37]

Although these men and women had good rapport with white leaders, unlike the Afro-American elite in some other cities in the North this group resided in or near the incipient ghetto, not in integrated areas removed from the black masses. Their clientele was—with the exception of the barbers—exclusively black. Having little or no formal education, they provided much of the leadership and financial resources—an "interlocking directorate"—for the development of black churches, clubs, and schools. All of them but the Amoses were defined by census enumerators as mulattoes, and it is obvious that that, as well as their desire to emulate the lifestyles of affluent whites, meant that the older black elite was much shaped by the attitudes and values of white leaders. This elite sought to separate its way of life from the black masses, which white leaders deemed shiftless and irresponsible. Despite these aspirations, however, no black leader achieved equal status in the white community. For example, in the 1903 Christmas Art Supplement of the *Evansville Journal-News*—a "Who's Who" of the city—white leaders were prominently featured in the first section, which was followed by features on local businesses. At the back were biographical sketches of the two men whom the newspaper identified as Evansville's black leaders— S. S. Dupee and J. D. Rouse—and both were praised for their support of Booker T. Washington's ideals.[38]

At the turn of the century Evansville's black elite was undergoing a transition, but not nearly as substantive as that in Chicago, Cleveland, or Philadelphia. Joining the ranks of the Evansville upper class were several barbers who owned their own shops, like Grandville Waddell, William Glover, and William Jones; three physicians, S. S. Dupee, George Washington Buckner, and Jeremiah Jackson; a real estate agent, Logan H. Stewart; an educator, J. R. Blackburn, principal of Clark High School, who earned about $1,300 in 1899, when the typical black workers earned $100 or $200 a year; and an undertaker, W. A. Gaines. The demise of the black skilled artisan and the black barbershops which catered to white men meant that the newer elite emerged primarily on the basis of providing services to blacks. Given the lack of an integrationist tradition in Evansville, it is worth noting that the older and the newer elites differed primarily in the manner in which they appealed for influence and prestige among whites. Like their predecessors, they tended to be light-skinned, but unlike them they had come of age in an era which was more blatantly racist, and hence they were more favorably disposed to Booker T. Washington's dicta about accepting second-class citizenship and proving merit by hard work and virtuous behavior. The newer elite also stressed the need to develop and sustain black-owned businesses.[39]

The upper-class element was a minute segment of Afro-American society. Although there was no appreciable difference in the birthplaces—Kentucky—of the older and newer elites, the rise in the number of professionals meant that the educational level of the members of the newer elite was somewhat higher. One example was George Washington Buckner, who migrated to Indiana from his native Kentucky and received much of his public school education in Indianapolis. He attended the state normal school at Terre Haute before taking a medical course at the Eclectic Medical College in the capital city, from which he graduated in 1890. He began practicing medicine in Evansville shortly thereafter and also for a time was a teacher and principal. Another was S. S. Dupee, who entered Howard University's medical course after his graduation from Fisk University in 1894. Dupee graduated from the Freedmen's Hospital in 1898 and practiced medicine in New York City for six months. In late 1898 he arrived in the Crescent City, where he set up a practice and also entered actively into civic affairs: he revived a local chapter of the Knights of Tabor, and was prominent in Republican politics. He was recognized as an able physician by white peers, one of whom declared: "It is a pity Dupee is a colored man. The colored people almost worship him, and because of his many miraculous cures have nicknamed him 'Black Jesus.' "[40]

The ascendant elite formed a tenuous union with others of their race. They were founders and leaders of fraternal societies, churches, literary groups, and political organizations—usually for the party of Lincoln. They resided in or near Baptisttown. The message they delivered was also conservative. As Dupee

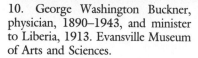

10. George Washington Buckner, physician, 1890–1943, and minister to Liberia, 1913. Evansville Museum of Arts and Sciences.

11. S. S. Dupee, Evansville physician, 1899–1913. Willard Library.

observed, the "race problem" would be solved by teaching children how to develop good habits and by maintaining loyalty to the Republican party. Toward that end he urged school teachers to be aware of their duty to instill spiritual values and school administrators to hire teachers who would care for the welfare of their students, not money. He implored parents to be more observant about their children and ministers to become more aware of literature which would promote proper virtues. He also asked whites to reward only those blacks who followed these recommendations.[41]

Standing slightly below these persons in income and social status was the black middle class. If occupation is used as the chief measurement, teachers, clergymen, most artisans, clerical workers, and small businessmen constituted the backbone of the group, which in 1900 represented no more than 8 percent of the black population, as compared with an estimated 18 percent in Boston in 1914 and 20 percent in Cleveland. It was nonetheless larger than the upper elite, which in 1900 claimed at most 1 or 2 percent of the population. Some factory workers and service workers, especially janitors, may have belonged to the black middle class, particularly if their spouses worked. Income levels for this stratum are somewhat difficult to identify, but one clue is the pay of teachers: in the 1899-1900 term, between $450 and $550 per year. By standards of the black community, these persons lived comfortably.[42]

With exceptions such as city hall or courthouse janitors, Evansville blacks in this class had few if any contacts with whites. Like the black elite, they also developed lifestyles which distinguished them from the black masses. One of the primary means of achieving this was club life. In addition to fraternal and secret societies, middle class blacks formed a plethora of literary, social, and recreational organizations. Many of these activities were developed through the churches. An organ of middle class values, the "Colored Folk" column carried descriptions of numerous social gatherings sponsored by such groups. A typical column announced that the I. H. N. Club "would give a free entertainment" at the Mt. Zion Baptist Church consisting of recitations, duets, solos, and readings. It also noted that Miss Georgia Williams, a teacher at Clark High School, was visiting the Pan-American Exposition in Buffalo. "She is quite a cultured and refined young lady and is well thought of by her acquaintances."[43]

An extremely important element in middle class society was the excursion, initially associated with the annual Emancipation Day celebrations and the establishment or anniversary of fraternal orders. At first this included only Henderson or Owensboro because these Kentucky cities were accessible by steamboat. By the 1890s, however, the expansion of railroad service brought more frequent excursions at special rates, usually on Sunday, to more distant places. Trainloads of blacks from other cities also visited Evansville regularly. The local agent of one line placed this advertisement in the July 26, 1887, newspaper:

Grand Excursion August 4

The colored people of Evansville who wish to visit Corydon, Waverly, Morganfield, Uniontown, Marion, and all points on the Ohio Valley Railway, can secure low round trip rates by boat and rail via Henderson and the Ohio Valley Road.[44]

Although such men as Robert Nicholas and Jeff Coleman—city policeman and fireman, respectively—were prominent, the quintessence of middle class aspirations was Lucy Wilson McFarland. Born in Vanderburgh County, she was hired as a teacher in 1870 in the new public school for blacks, and in 1876—at the age of twenty-six—she became principal of Clark Street School, a position she held until 1897. She married W. Riley McFarland, a stock keeper, and the two resided on East Franklin Street in Jimtown. By the time of her death in June, 1900, she had acquired property reputedly worth $7,000.[45]

Praised at her death as "one of the most publicly spirited and highly useful women of which the state of Indiana can boast," Mrs. McFarland was described as an educator, clubwoman, and "substantial taxpayer" whose object was "the betterment of the condition and elevation of her race and the good of the community at large. . . ." At her death she belonged to the auxiliaries of five fraternal orders and was state grand matron of the Order of the Eastern Star and charter member of the Zella chapter of Evansville. Her funeral, conducted at Liberty by prominent Baptist and Methodist clergymen, was said to have been "the most elaborate ever witnessed in this city among colored people."

Thousands paid respects to one "whose life, character and services they deemed worthy of earnest emulation and whose death they deeply mourned."[46]

Such affluent persons epitomized the "strive and succeed" ethic which animated her peers. Motivated by the aversion to African traditions and black skin, members of the elite tried to show—as one Cleveland editor observed in 1915—that "we have been thinking black for a long while. Let us try the alternative and in conjunction with our change of thought be prepared to play the game EFFICIENTLY AND WELL."[47] Those who purchased *The Freeman* were treated to a barrage of advertisements for products designed to make blacks look white. Madame M. C. Turner's "Great French System," for instance, was promoted in 1897 as a guarantee of "Soft, Straight, and Glossy Hair"; it also included "Mystic Face Bleach" which in "eight or ten days" would leave the skin "about two shades lighter" and give "the complexion of a soft and youthful tenderness."[48] Not surprisingly, Mt. Zion Baptist Church, like others, praised the extension of Anglo-Saxon culture into Africa, holding a missionary service in April 1899, in which one orator spoke of "Livingstone, Africa's Friend."[49]

This idealization of white culture sometimes took curious twists. A poignant illustration of that occurred in December 1901, when thirty-five of the leading ladies of the city—among them Mrs. Annie Morgan Viele, Mrs. Mose Strouse, Miss Louise Dunkerson, and Miss Bessie Heilman—put on an amateur minstrel show for the benefit of the Free Kindergarten Association. Headlined as "sweet ladies in black face," the event was received enthusiastically by a large white audience. The society women reportedly charmed the crowd with their "ludicrous" costumes and jokes.[50]

As if to underscore this dubious form of respect for black culture, the editor of the "Colored Folk" column wrote that

> [a] fact that our people are ever on the alert to emulate the example set by the white race is demonstrated in the announcement of "The Ladies' Minstrel," which is to come off during the latter part of the month. Not long ago the best young white ladies of our city gave a "Minstrel Show" and it was not only a success financially but met the commendations of all the leading citizens. The members of the organization of the club are some of our best young ladies, and we assure you that the performance will not only be amusing but will be praised by the old and young alike. . . . If there ever was a time when our people should work for the upbuilding of those institutions, which have for their motto the taking care of the sick and burying the dead, it is now. Young ladies, if you hear any knockers on your entertainment, heed them not.[51]

Such perspectives must also have "led to consternation and a good deal of frustration" among lower class blacks, who looked to middle- and upper-class blacks "for guidance and standards and sought to emulate, to some degree, the bourgeoisie life-style."[52] A vast majority worked as day laborers or domestics, and wages were not only low but uncertain. A good job—for example, being a porter—paid at most $6.00 a week. These positions offered little chance for advancement. The low level of residential persistence underscored that fact. Of the proportionately few blacks at the turn of the century who owned their homes, only sixty-five of them were from the lower class. Consequently, in many families women as well as men worked, and "the long hours, low pay, and servile demeanor that the job required [added] the badge of social inferiority" to black women in addition to placing greater stress on the integrity of the black family.[53]

Although the paucity of historical records makes the reconstruction of the life-style of lower class blacks difficult, one can conclude that most households included two parents as well as relatives and/or boarders. The daily lives of ordinary blacks were devoid of frills, including clubs and recreational activities. Housing selections were limited to cheap boarding and lodging houses or rental housing in or near the old canal or near the mouth of Pigeon Creek. Prior to 1900 there were few options for recreation other than an occasional steamboat or railroad excursion, a picnic on Emancipation Day or the Fourth of July, or—probably more common—an evening in a local saloon or "dive." There were no black nightclubs or vaudeville houses. For most the only focus outside the family was the church. Although statistics of church membership and attendance are extremely limited, the proliferation of laborer-dominated churches in the 1890s attests to the centrality of religious affiliation for social and recreational as well as spiritual needs.[54]

It is little wonder, however, that there was also "a deviant subculture involving gambling, drinking, and sexual promiscuity . . . among a portion of the black lower class."[55] This element had always been present in Afro-American culture in Evansville, and by 1900 was a permanent part of life in three portions of the city—Baptisttown, the Midway, and the "Tenderloin," or High Street. For example, in census district 96, which comprised a section of the "lower" part of the city, one-fourth of the 638 residents were black. Over a third of the work force had been unemployed during part or all of the previous year. The average length of unemployment was four months. Sixty-seven of the adults were illiterate. Census District 126 in Baptisttown had a population of 847, 678 of whom were Afro-American. Of those old enough to work, 52 percent had been unemployed for part or all of the previous year, and the average length of unemployment was 3.5 months. Illiteracy was also rampant here. These two districts were notoriously vice-ridden, and the stereotypical black male was a garishly dressed youth with a bowler and a Havana cigar. Although the typical lower class black was not an irresponsible dandy and was concerned with the survival of his family in the face of difficult odds, he was increasingly beset by a culture of poverty in which such a role model had great appeal.[56]

Although class differences in the black community were important, racial discrimination transcended those distinctions. Where the welfare of the race was concerned, Evansville's affluent blacks—like those in Milwaukee, Nashville, or Raleigh—maintained a tenuous unity with the masses.[57] Nowhere would that fragile relationship be illustrated more clearly than in the political arena. What to do with the vote, and how, more generally, to deal with the vagaries of an increasingly segregated city constituted the major issue facing leaders and ordinary people alike from the Civil War onward.

We Ask Only a Fair Trial: Political Allegiance and Racial Strategies, 1865–1900

 On May 24, 1899, the Order of the Chosen Friends held its twentieth anniversary celebration—a "colored cake walk"—which featured "Jubilee singing [and] wing and buck dancing by the best talent."[1] Staged by the city's black elite for the entertainment of whites at Evans Hall, the event encapsulated the perceived ideal relationship between the races. Whites expected blacks to behave stereotypically, exhibiting childlike and sensual tendencies, and in return blacks assumed that they would receive respect from the white community.

Coping with second-class status was an extraordinary task, and that challenge extended to the political arena, where in theory blacks and whites had equal chances to secure benefits for themselves. In reality, political opportunity was conditional, and the black vote was treated as an object of manipulation. White leaders selected black leaders and presumed that blacks would not use their political power to attack the inferior status to which they had been assigned.[2]

As elsewhere, Evansville blacks were a virtual appendage of the Republican party. The leadership of the black community, which comprised teachers and ministers, many of whom were ex-slaves and/or Union army veterans, viewed the Republican party as the source of emancipation, civil equality, and the suffrage. Not surprisingly, the lines between religion and politics were blurred. The Emancipation Day observance of 1868, like every other one for decades to come, included speeches by black teachers and preachers, each of whom stressed the dependence of Afro-American progress upon loyalty to the Grand Old Party. The most prominent figure of the immediate postwar period was teacher-clergyman James M. Townsend, Oberlin alumnus and veteran of the 54th Massachusetts. The founders of the Colored Grant and Wilson Club, the first black political organization (1872), were lay leaders and clergymen of the black churches. The mixture of politics and religion was also evident on August 15, 1870, when black Senator Hiram Revels of Mississippi lectured at the Opera House to a large and apparently racially mixed audience. Proceeds from the affair benefitted the AME church. "The colored people evidently felt proud of their Senator," noted the *Evansville Journal*, "and indeed he seems to be fully up to the average of Congressmen. . . ."[3]

The most articulate (and persistent) spokesman for this position was Robert Nicholas, a Union army veteran. In the "tenth annual address to the emancipated race and to the American public" in 1875, Nicholas observed that emancipation had "imposed upon us a debt, which it will take generations yet to come to pay. It has been often repeated that we are incapable of comprehending the responsibilities upon us as citizens." He added, "Be this true or not, we ask only a fair trial, and we are willing to abide the consequences, and we will in a few years demonstrate to the world that we are intelligent as well as free." Nicholas noted with pride that he was the first black policeman in Evansville, "if not in the whole state." Expressing his gratitude to the City Council for the confidence it had shown in him, he stated—like so many "first blacks" after him—that he hoped he would "not be a 'stumbling block' to those who come after me . . . [as] any incompetency or neglect of duty on my part would be speedily furnished to the authorities." Recalling that the use of black soldiers had also brought expressions of doubt and ridicule, he asserted that his appointment demonstrated "that you have only struck the channel of other true men and hurled to the breeze those principles which we will be delighted to honor."[4]

The duties of the black community, he concluded, were

> to educate our children and ourselves in all the useful branches, and to strain every nerve, and leave nothing undone which shall tend to fit us for the duties and responsibilities of the undeveloped future. Cultivate and raise the standard of morals among our people, and educate, because just as the precepts of faith . . . raise our souls above the interest of this world, so will the pursuit of education inspire us with a love of the beautiful and the just and a hatred of what is wrong, and will teach us these beautiful truths first proclaimed by the Savior of mankind.[5]

Unlike blacks in cities like Boston and Cleveland which had integrationist traditions, Nicholas and his peers resided in an exclusionist community. The passage of the Civil Rights Act of 1875, which promised equal access to public places, had no apparent effect on Evansville. Black leaders like Alfred Carter advised prudence and courtesy on the part of blacks—that is, going only where they would be welcome. Especially after the ratification of the Fifteenth Amendment in 1870, Democratic leaders like Charles Denby raised the spectre of social equality in campaign debates with Republicans, and in a city in which voter loyalties were nearly evenly divided, Negro-baiting was an important electoral tool. Judge W. E. Niblack, Democratic Congressman from the First District, successfully campaigned for re-election in 1870 by claiming, among other things, that "we're not free because we cannot prevent whom we please from voting."[6] Even Republican leaders were quick to qualify their support of the freedmen. Declared the editor of the *Journal*, support for Reconstruction amendments to the Constitution were guarantees that blacks would remain in the South where they belonged: "[S]how your disapproval . . . and you may have them leave the South in a body."[7]

Despite this type of rhetoric, loyalty to the party of Abraham Lincoln remained strong among Afro-Americans. Nominated as temporary chairman of the Colored Grant and Wilson Club's first convention, James H. Gray, a janitor, noted that

> two years had elapsed since he had become a citizen, and to be called upon to preside over a meeting of citizens, who, like himself, had but recently become such, to discuss and decide upon their action in regard to the questions agitating the parties of the country, was an unaccustomed honor.[8]

A committee on permanent organization proceeded to nominate a slate of officers, and Alfred Carter, the confectioner, was elected president. As George H. Jackson, another speaker, declared, it was time that "colored men consider who were the true men and who were the traitors. . . . [N]umerous men who have never had time to notice a colored man before were now very attentive to them. . . ."[9] The convention then selected James M. Townsend as their representative on the Republican County Executive Committee. The practice of allowing a single black to take part in GOP affairs at that level continued into the 1890s.[10]

Such an organization attested to the emergence of a black subculture in Evansville, and it assumed blacks could count on the Republican party to provide for their welfare, in return for which the party of Lincoln could count on the black vote. After black men began to vote in the fall elections of 1870, the political climate of the city was significantly altered, for Democrats—despite their antipathy to the Fifteenth Amendment—had to accept the reality of the black vote. The *Journal* ridiculed the Democrats' response: "Before the war the d——d nigger was a slave; after the war the ignorant negro was free; at the present time our intelligent colored fellow-citizen is a voter."[11]

Accordingly, Republicans complained that Democrats harrassed and even prevented blacks from voting. Democrats responded that Republicans exploited ignorant blacks, especially by "importing" them from Kentucky at election time and creating the "floating vote."[12] In the October 1870 election, for instance, Republicans claimed that Democrats, who controlled city administration, had offered one black voter the alternatives of voting Democratic or going to jail. (The black man chose jail, boasted the Republican editor, rather than ignore his conscience.) Democrats responded that black voters were being bribed to come from Kentucky to Evansville and support the Republican party. A Republican leader replied, "Every intelligent man . . . has known that there were over five hundred colored men in the county entitled to vote, and no more than this number voted."[13] The Republicans swept the county elections, he added, because the Democratic campaign was ineffective, not because of the number of black voters. In city elections the following spring, Democratic complaints about voting irregularities led him to declare that the real issue was "hostility to the enterprise" of Negro suffrage.[14]

Similar rhetoric accompanied every election for twenty years. The fall election of 1876 was especially vicious. Republicans ridiculed Democrats for bringing the former body servant of James K. Polk as an election-eve speaker. The servant had claimed he would rather live in a slave state than in the North, "where the people treat the colored folks 'wusser than a dog.' " In response to his query as to what the civil rights bill had done for blacks, Robert Nicholas reportedly shouted from the audience, "It put you in the St. George Hotel [the city's finest hotel] today."[15] During the same week the Republicans brought Frederick Douglass to town. His address to a large, racially mixed crowd was well received. The nation's most famous black labeled Democrats as "the sectional party and the party of the South. It is something like a snake which you catch by the head with a crooked stick. The tail slashes all around, but the head, the brains, are always in the same place."[16]

Numerous allegations of fraud and intimidation surfaced in that campaign. in response to Democratic claims regarding imported voters, the Republican newspaper ridiculed two enthusiastic young Democrats who had sought "importations being colonized in Union Township." Spying "an old darkey trudging along the road," they inquired of his origins, and after learning that he was from Kentucky, were chagrined to discover that he planned to vote for Rutherford B. Hayes.

> "How long have you been over here?" asked his catechiser. There was a long pause, during which they felt their hearts beat and their eagerness became almost apparent. The old man paused because he was looking down the road to where a half dozen small editions of himself were tumbling over the fence to meet him. "Well," he said, "I's lived here for *nigh onto thirteen years!*" The young men drove on hastily and came back last night, a little disgusted. Imported voters don't hang around on trees, waiting to be knocked off.[17]

The 1876 campaign was one of the nastiest in local history. Violence against blacks was commonplace on the day of the presidential election, November 7. White ruffians (and some black ones as well)—special election officers appointed by Democratic-controlled county government—were out in force, and, according to Republicans,

> filled out with a little brief authority [and they] strutted through their momentary life acting as they pleased. The poor colored man seemed to be the special object of their wrath, and on him they wreaked all their spite. If a skull was to be broken it was a colored skull; if a man was to be arrested without cause and sent to the filthy lock-up in order to give the public a wholesome idea of the power of

the special idiots, it was a colored man; if anybody wanted to pitch on to a peaceable citizen and abuse him with the full consent of the special lunatics that citizen was sure to be colored.[18]

City and county elections thereafter were filled with reports of drunkenness, fisticuffs, and voting irregularities. A corollary was the ritualistic plea of white and black Republicans to black voters to remain true to the party of Lincoln. A prominent black, for example, would write an appeal to black voters in the *Journal* attesting to the integrity of the white GOP candidates and warning of the perils which would follow the election of Democrats. Similar alarms were raised at election-eve rallies of black Republican clubs. By contrast, Democrats would warn party faithful to be on the lookout for black "repeaters" from Kentucky. "Lest some of the rascals may escape, let the vote of every stranger be challenged, whether he be white or black," wrote the Democratic editor in 1884.[19]

All this helped to create an infrastructure which enabled black Evansvillians to gain a degree of autonomy. Black political organizations emerged on the precinct, ward, and county levels. A few Democratic clubs were present as early as 1872, but there is no evidence of a black's being named to Democratic central committees or county and state conventions. In return for political loyalty, limited rewards were available. In April 1880 the Republican mayor added three blacks to the police force and one each to hose houses 5 and 9. Frederick Douglass Morton was appointed clerk of police court, one of the highest political positions attained between 1865 and 1915. After 1890 rewards were limited to service on newly created all-black Hose House No. 9, janitorships at public buildings, and the post of township physician. One black was named annually to the Republican party central committee, which limited black Evansville to a single spokesman recognized by the white community. Such modest political power depended on the good graces of white leaders, and even that was pared by 1900.[20]

Given these sparse rewards, the animosity of Democrats, and the poverty and illiteracy of most Evansville blacks, how did the black community influence Evansville elections? Although blacks resided in most precincts in 1870, most lived in precinct 1, which comprised a large part of what would later be known as Baptisttown. Many were in contiguous precincts nearby (2, 4, and 11). Numbers 2 and 4 included the area bounded by Fourth, Walnut, Fifth, and Chestnut streets. Precinct 11 was the region north and east of Eighth and Canal streets. Precinct 6 also included a number of blacks who lived on Lower Water, Clark, and High streets. Precincts 1, 2, and 11 voted Republican in the 1870s. Precinct 4 was usually Republican, but narrowly so, and the riverfront precinct 6, which had the lowest percentage of black residents among these five, voted consistently Democratic, but by a narrow margin. Such election returns suggest that blacks in the immediate postwar era were loyal Republicans, but records documenting voter participation and directly connecting blacks to Republican candidates have not survived. Thus these election statistics must be used cautiously.[21]

The entrance of blacks into Evansville elections evoked Democratic fears that a Republican machine was being created which depended on the votes of the former slaves. There appeared to be justification for that concern. In the eleven campaigns between 1870 and 1890 for city, county, and state offices, Republicans lost the city only once (1882) and the entire county only twice (1882 and 1884). All these elections, however, were decided by close margins. The largest Republican share of the vote was 54 percent, and as a rule the party of Lincoln won by less than 500 votes. It should also be noted that the number of voters increased significantly in the period, not simply because of the influx of Southern blacks, and Democrats benefited enormously from the large numbers of Bavarian and Alsatian Catholics who settled in the city. Nevertheless, without the black vote the Republican party would have been at a disadvantage vis-a-vis the Democracy in the Gilded Age.[22]

Through the 1880s it was essential for Republicans to keep their black troops in line and for Democrats to try to breach that by whatever means they could. During the massive torchlight parades common to the era was the inclusion of the various "colored Republican" clubs, each resplendent in uniforms and usually accompanied by a band, marched on election eve. These units were always located, however, at the end. On October 22, 1884, for example, the massive GOP parade to welcome presidential candidate James G. Blaine to Evansville had five divisions, the last of which comprised eight black units headed by Frederick Douglass Morton. A band led the black marchers, which included 100 in Company E dressed in blue capes and white caps; Company D, with sixty outfitted in red uniforms; a "broom brigade" of fifteen men wearing silk hats and carrying brooms to signify a Republican sweep; and a glee club of twenty-four men and women wearing white suits and dresses trimmed with gold stars. The Republican daily also reminded black voters of their indebtedness to the Republican cause and urged them to avoid saloons, not to take offense at insults, to ignore rumors, and to go to the polls quietly and firmly. If challenged, they were to insist on their rights and state that they were complying with the law.[23]

Throughout the 1880s black leaders remained intensely loyal to Republicanism. In the 1888 campaign Rev. J. D. Rouse, for instance, took an especially active role in attacking Democratic efforts to secure black support. He argued, as did most blacks in the era, that the Democrats had opposed emancipation, civil rights, and suffrage for blacks and beneath the surface still thought of Afro-Americans as "niggers, mokes, or coons." As in the past, the "old soldiers" like Robert Nicholas presented themselves as the conscience of the black community. At a rally at Evans Hall at which Rouse and Morton spoke, Nicholas inquired if blacks could be served a glass of soda or a saucer of ice cream in a business owned by a Democrat. If elected, Democrats would, he asserted, seek to return blacks to their prewar status. Voters appeared to agree. Precinct 3, bounded by Oak, Eighth, Canal, Lincoln, Line, Powell, and Fourth streets, had the highest percentage of black voters in the decade. In each election between 1882 and 1890, this precinct was solidly Republican.[24]

By the early 1890s, however, some important changes began to emerge. The river city was not unique in this respect, as the number of blacks affiliating with the Democratic party throughout Indiana began to increase as the Democracy turned to courting the black vote. In an age in which voting occurred in public view, in private residences and saloons, various forms of political persuasion came to be used by both parties. Particularly common was the $2 payoff. Although most rank-and-file Democrats remained hostile to blacks, some of their leaders asserted that blacks had paid their debts to the Republican party and that the low level at which Republicans repaid their black supporters added insult to injury. A national convention of black independents meeting in Indianapolis in 1888 reflected that opinion. Charles H. Sheldon of Evansville, a saloonkeeper who had shown maverick tendencies since the 1872 convention of black Republicans, was elected temporary chairman of the convention, which endorsed Grover Cleveland for the presidency.[25]

The restiveness of black voters was also symptomatic of shifts in white Republican loyalties. As Jim Crow practices flourished, Republican leaders who had once portrayed black voters as educable children now seemed to join in the chorus of those who treated blacks scornfully. In the spring of 1890 the editor of the *Journal* declared,

> Not one colored man out of a hundred is fit to hold office. They are ignorant through no fault of their own. ... No matter how kindly Republicans feel toward colored people, they cannot hand the destinies of a community over to ignorant rulers.[26]

Paltry political rewards also stimulated black restlessness. Street and alley improvements and sanitation projects, for example, which dominated City Council deliberations in this period, did not extend to black enclaves, and black sections continued to be associated with crime and vice. And the number as well as the level of political appointments were steadily declining.[27] A reflection of this was the formation in 1894 of the Bruce Club (named after the Republican governor). Led by the newly arrived attorney, J. H. Lott, teacher George A. Williams, veteran Republican loyalist Richard Amos, and four others, the club boasted of its part in electing the Republican slate. After the election, the leaders met with white Republican officials to discuss

> the patronage that the colored people believe themselves entitled to by reason of their fight for the success of the Grand Old Party. ... [A]ll of the janitorships at the court house should be given to colored men since they can secure no clerkships or other positions higher than janitor.[28]

The appeal fell on deaf ears, as the white officials listening to the request merely thanked the petitioners for their help in the previous election and subsequently appointed only one black janitor and one fireman. Yet the emergence of the Bruce Club, which had a brief life-span, signified the sense of unease which was growing in the black community in the 1890s. It was the first of several well-publicized efforts to remind white political leaders not to take black Evansville for granted.[29]

The emergence of articulate spokesmen for the Democrats may also have contributed to the restlessness of black Evansvillians. The coming to the city of George Washington Buckner in 1890 was especially important in this regard. Precisely why the thirty-five year-old physician was a staunch Democrat is unclear. He soon became an ally of John W. Boehne, Sr., a staunch Lutheran layman who as Democratic city councilman was an outspoken opponent of vice. Because of the connections of Buckner's wife with other Fisk University graduates and due to his professional standing, Buckner became a member of the black upper class, and his home was a cultural center for black Evansville and a waystation for prominent blacks traveling through the region. His carefully cultivated relationship with local Democrats, however, was fraught with peril. Undoubtedly due to partisan politics, Buckner, who also taught school, was charged anonymously in the Republican newspaper for various infractions of school rules. In 1895 the paper also reported that he had been censured by the local health department for failing to report a case of diphtheria properly. In reply, Buckner complained "that harsh treatment had been given him on account of his color. . . ."[30]

Buckner was able, nonetheless, to enlist hundreds of blacks in the Colored Akin Club, organized for the municipal election of 1897. He also edited sporadically the newly formed "Colored Folks" column in the Democratic daily. When William Akin and his slate were elected, the *Courier* attributed the feat in part to the awareness of the "better class" of Afro-Americans that it was their vote which kept the Republican bosses in power and which determined which party won. Buckner, who helped Akin win reelection in 1899, wrote that the old methods of herding transient blacks into pens and treating them like cattle at election time were no longer acceptable. In rhetoric reminiscent of earlier Democrats, Republicans seemed to acknowledge that Buckner bespoke a shift in black loyalties, because they charged in 1899 that it was only black votes which kept Mayor Akin in power.[31]

Growing residential segregation also abetted the clout of black voters. *The Freeman* was aware of this shortly after the Republican city council created the Seventh Ward in 1892 and placed all of the heavily black precincts of adjoining Wards 1 and 6 in it. That year black Republican leaders considered running a candidate for the city council, but decided against it when white leaders objected. (Independent candidates ran in 1893 and 1895, losing by wide margins.) Seventh Ward blacks amassed enough votes at the ward convention in March 1897, however, to nominate Robert Nicholas for city council—the first black Republican candidate in the city's history. The entire Republican slate, however, lost in the Akin sweep of that election. Seventh Ward Republicans also elected six blacks to the county convention of May 1894, and also a delegate to the congressional, senatorial, and state conventions of 1898.[32]

By the late 1890s Democratic and Republican leaders alike openly recognized the fact that the black vote was the key to their success. In November 1901 the *Courier* offered graphic evidence: about 3,100 black voters resided in the First Congressional District, and 1,800 of them were in Vanderburgh County. Of these, 1,611 were residents of Pigeon Township, and most of them lived in the Seventh Ward.[33]

As in Louisville, black leaders as a rule did not remain aloof from politics, as Booker T. Washington had advised, but they disagreed over the means of using their clout. Buckner argued that the political rewards were more substantial in the party of Jackson, which did not take blacks for granted. An unidentified few entertained the idea of forming a separate party, asserting that only in uniting along racial lines could blacks progress, as neither party could be trusted. The *Journal* selected the blacks it considered most influential—Reverends Anderson and Rouse, principal John R. Blackburn, and Mrs. Lucy McFarland—for their comments on this proposal. All said the same thing: that because blacks were poor, illiterate, and unorganized, such an effort would encourage political charlatans, and that blacks were better off working with whites for racial improvement. Interestingly enough, none of those interviewed endorsed either political party. Anderson advised, for example, "the negro voter who can not accept the policy of the republican [sic] party to vote and affiliate with the party whose doctrine is in accord with his political convictions."[34]

Most leaders, however, reflected the views of the young physician, Dupee, who urged blacks to remain Republican. They also encouraged the masses to cease the practice of accepting payment for their votes. By so doing, blacks would end the reign of political bosses and secure greater influence within the GOP.[35]

Whites, unfortunately, were not sensitive to this debate, and neither were some black politicos, who—being closer to the masses—understood the appeal of a few dollars or a pint of whiskey at election time. The poverty, disorganization, and illiteracy of the black community, combined with the loose voting practices of the day, meant that at election time both parties treated black voters as purchasable commodities. "Boodle" and vote-tampering were the keys to winning elections. Whistling in the dark, the *Journal* observed in 1891 that "the colored voter must not figure so largely. . . . He is as good . . as the white voter, but not better. When he sulks and stays away from the polls because he is not supplied with boodle," the editor added, "let him sulk and stay away. . . . If he wants to sacrifice his freedom and citizenship, he can do so. He will suffer worse than the white. . . "[36]

Reality, nevertheless, dictated that both parties seek the black vote in ways which were often unsavory. In the 1899 city elections, Republicans accused Democrats of offering free food and drink to induce black Republicans to enter certain saloons on "the Midway," and once inside they were prevented from leaving because city officials imposed a smallpox quarantine on the saloons. Democrats reportedly had to get 400 black votes or else suffer defeat. After the 1900 election Democratic workers boasted, "we are breaking even with you on the nigger today. . . ." It was time "leaders of the race, so-called, were giving attention to this matter, in the interest of their people," asserted one Republican official.[37]

All this notwithstanding, black voters generally remained loyal to the Republican party. Political independence, moreover, usually applied to local tickets, not to state or national ones. As elsewhere, the memory of historic ties to the party was powerful, and Democratic leaders did not sustain the black support they received with ample patronage and elective positions. Some were rewarded the traditional black posts when Mayor Akin took office, but Democrats did not elect any black precinct workers or convention delegates. Attitudes toward blacks among local Democrats, whose origins were in the upper South and southern Germany, moreover, ranged from custodial to hostile. The *Courier*, for example, referred to Nicholas's candidacy in 1897 as "A Dark Spot on the Ticket."[38]

For the most part, precincts with large numbers of blacks voted Republican in the 1890s. Precincts 6, 7, 8, 37, and 38, all in Ward 7, voted solidly for Republicans in every election between the spring of 1892 and the spring of 1897, when Akin's ticket took all but one heavily black precinct. Thereafter Republicans did well in those precincts, except for the municipal elections of 1899. Black Republican organizations remained strong, and election-eve rallies continued to feature ex-slaves and Union veterans. A majority of black leaders, including Dr. Willis Green and Frederick Douglass Morton among older blacks and William Glover and George A. Williams among younger men, were in the GOP camp.[39]

By the turn of the century, three decades of the suffrage had produced a sad cycle. The vote, for many, seemed purchasable, and neither party was interested in returning justice for the vote. Realistic enough to acknowledge that the black vote would not disappear through threats of violence, Democrats resorted to the same election tactics as their opponents. Republicans sought to hold onto power by appeals to traditional ties and by payoffs to loyal supporters. Cleaning up voting practices in black sections was thus a dream which few white leaders wished to pursue.

Ironically, the increasingly segregated society contributed to the making of a black leadership structure. As in the case of churches, clubs, and fraternal societies, racial discrimination had the unintended effect of producing a semiautonomous group of political leaders whose power depended upon their ability to deliver the black vote. The earliest of these were clergymen and teachers, but by the 1890s they were being replaced by businessmen and other professionals whose clientele was Afro-American. Politics, in addition, offered a chance at upward mobility to enterprising young men. The most notable of these was Ernest G. Tidrington, a mulatto born in Tennessee in 1882, who arrived in the city with his mother shortly after birth. By his teens he had earned a reputation for energetic and resourceful work on behalf of the Republican party. His mentor was the saloonkeeper, Charles Ossenberg.[40]

The emergence of a black infrastructure, replete with leadership and a myriad of social organizations, was not only a product of racial discrimination but also a means whereby black Evansvillians learned to cope with second-class status. In general, their leaders acquiesced in the decisions made regarding their place in the city. A notable exception was the outcry over the separate coach law, the only recorded evidence of local protest against de jure segregation between 1865 and 1900. In the fall of 1893, some Evansville blacks planned a national convention "on the race question" in the city. The proposed convention, wrote chairman W. H. Beecher, an Evansville teacher, to *The Freeman* in early November, was cancelled in order that Bishop Henry M. Turner's national convention on the race question, scheduled for Cincinnati in late November, might succeed. Both meetings sought to deal with de jure racial discrimination and lynching. At the Cincinnati gathering, Booker T. Washington's supporters argued that the remedy was economic—to have twenty men worth $1,000 in each town in America. By contrast, Turner, a Union army chaplain and Reconstruction leader, advocated a return to Africa. This unique gathering ultimately rejected Turner's solution, but after it a National Equal Rights Council was formed, and two Evansville men—Rev. W. H. Anderson and George A. Williams—were selected as Indiana's two representatives. Williams was also chosen secretary of the organization.[41]

The aims of the organization, wrote Anderson and Williams in the May 5, 1894 issue of *The Freeman*, were to

> prove ourselves worthy of better treatment in this country than we are now receiving as a race. . . . [O]ur moral, religious, intellectual, and financial forces [should be concentrated] so as to be felt in the assertion of our rights. . . . [We need t]o organize National Equal Rights Councils to raise money to employ detectives and lawyers, colored and white, to bring justice to these mobs and defend our equal rights in the courts. . . . The great christian [sic] heart of this country is opposed to mob violence, but it is not organized against it. . . .[42]

Toward that end Anderson and Williams urged greater involvement in Republican party affairs. In conjunction with some Kentucky blacks, they also challenged a recently passed Kentucky law which provided that white and black passengers be provided separate compartments while traveling in the state. Passenger trains departing Evansville for Southern destinations were outfitted with "Jim Crow" cars, even though those trains had to traverse several miles of Indiana soil before crossing into Kentucky.

To test the law, Anderson, his wife, and some parishioners boarded an L & N train at Evansville and sat in the "whites only" section after the train crossed into Kentucky. They were put off the train at Owensboro for violating Kentucky law. Anderson and the others retained attorney J. H. Lott, in addition to three white attorneys, to sue the state of Kentucky. In early June a United States Circuit Court judge ruled in their behalf. The law was deemed unconstitutional because it sought to regulate interstate commerce. Most of

Evansville's black leaders addressed a large and joyous crowd at Alexander Chapel on June 7, 1894, to "jollify over the victory of the colored people. . . ." Resolutions were passed praising Anderson and Lott because "[t]his decision affects not only the colored people of Kentucky but of the entire nation." Funds were solicited for the plaintiffs, "there being a general belief that the case will be appealed to the Supreme Court of the United States."[43]

The appeal was made, but the challenge—like the Equal Rights Council— was a victim of the rising "separate but equal" thinking of the courts. In addition, Lott left Evansville for the greener pastures of Indianapolis, where he established a successful law practice. The effort was, however ephemeral, an important sign of black opposition to the spread of Jim Crow. The first effort of its kind in the city's history—and the last for over ten years—it illustrated that a sense of race solidarity transcended religious and class interests. (The event may have also stimulated the formation of the Bruce Club and of the Colored Ministerial Association, both formed in the same year.)[44] One suspects that this protest occurred because of a fortuitous mix of circumstances: the appearance of the Equal Rights Council, two leaders of which were Evansvillians; the arrival of the talented attorney, Lott, who, like the younger members of the middle class, had a higher level of education; and the fact that many blacks used passenger trains to visit their Kentucky relatives.[45]

The hegemony of Jim Crow after the mid-nineties, coupled with the strength of the tradition of discrimination in Evansville and the relatively small size of the black community, strengthened the accommodationist approach advocated by Booker T. Washington, the "Wizard of Tuskegee." Visiting Evansville in late June 1897, he asserted that

> there was but one thing before which all distinctions, all differences, all likes and dislikes faded away, and that was the "almighty dollar." Hence to put the negro on the plane of equality with his fellow men, to give him power, and cause him to be respected, he must be enabled to earn this dollar—this leveler of all class distinctions and prejudice. To earn this dollar . . . the negro must compete with the white man. . . . [T]he negro, in his present state, is not capable of successfully competing. . . . [It was necessary] not only to educate him, for this was a comparatively easy task, but to teach him what to do with his education when once acquired. . . .[46]

Predictably praised by the local press, Washington offered a racial strategy which took into account the growing hostility of whites toward blacks and the growing importance of businesses and professions which served an Afro-American clientele. That approach was increasingly evident among Evansville's black leaders.[47]

Reflecting this position, Reverend Anderson—who had earlier advocated litigation—argued at the graduation of Clark High School in 1901 that although the constitution stated that all men were equal, in practice blacks had to earn their status. Schools provided only the foundation of knowledge, he asserted, as hard work and sound moral character were also necessary. An even more cautious approach was urged by S. S. Dupee, who contended that civic equality and social equality were not synonymous. The solution to the "negro problem" lay in teaching black children the virtues of self-reliance, thrift, and charity. He warned Evansville blacks not to follow the advice of those who insisted on a direct attack on racial questions. Such acts would surely lead to the blacks' losing favor with whites. Toward that end, he also insisted on loyalty to the party of Lincoln.[48]

Unlike most of his peers, Anderson did not think it ill-advised to protest while emphasizing economic security. In the litigation against the state of Kentucky in 1894, he insisted that one of the attorneys be black. He perceived that as one means of encouraging self-reliance. Later he would argue that if a black business existed—for example, a funeral parlor—blacks should patronize it and not its white competitor.[49]

By the late 1890s, however, few Evansville blacks openly challenged segregation or disagreed with the strategy urged by Washington. The absence of protest, as Rabinowitz has noted about the urban South, emanated not only from fear of white disapproval, but also the lack of white support in the courts and the economic reality that white proprietors and professionals would not risk alienating their white customers to please a handful of poor black clients. Some problems resulted, however, from the means of attaining the goals that the Tuskegee educator had set forth. Even though younger, more educated men like Dupee had only black clients, they emphasized self-help and exhibited a tendency to overlook discrimination with an almost obsessive concern with white perception of their acts. Possibly this was because whites determined such important matters as which blacks received the top positions—school principals, township physicians, and the other meager rewards over which blacks were forced to fight. By the turn of the century a rift appeared to be emerging between some professionals and businessmen like Dupee and clergymen like Anderson, both of whom claimed to speak for the black community. Dupee thought most ministers too concerned with the life hereafter, instead of solid citizenship on earth. He was especially critical of Anderson for his insistence on the patronage of black businessmen and professionals, which he said made blacks appear ridiculous to whites. Anderson vigorously disagreed.[50]

As in other Northern black communities, the growth of the black population led to changes in leadership and to the development of all-black institutions. Unlike cities like Chicago with larger numbers of blacks, fewer separate institutions were proposed in Evansville because the community was too small to support them. Combined with the absence of an integrationist tradition common to cities and towns of the northern Midwest, this meant that few leaders rejected the conservative view of social change—"strive and succeed." That was reinforced by the racial values of the time and by the fact that middle- and upper-class blacks had risen from poverty to a modicum of respectability.[51]

Like Cleveland, Detroit, and Newark, which prior to 1915 had small black communities, black Evansville was more dependent upon white organizations and resources than those in cities with black communities large enough to support black-run hospitals, banks, insurance companies, or orphan asylums. The tradition of black dependency, spawned by the legacy of slavery and the virulent form of racism found in the Ohio River Valley, was thus strengthened, and white paternalism and control remained a central fact of life to black Evansvillians. Patron-client relationships were especially notable in the political arena, where the black vote—like black labor—was perceived as a tool of white leadership.[52]

It is undeniable, however, that by the 1890s there was a greater degree of independence. The appearance of black political candidates, the decline of the absolute bond between white Republicans and Afro-Americans, and the formation of such groups as the Colored Ministerial Association attested to the emergence of a modest amount of community autonomy. Booker T. Washington's self-help strategy also encouraged the development of black businesses and professions. All changes have to be seen, however, within the context of a city described by one Indianapolis journalist in 1899 as the most "wide open" in Indiana. A key to his comment was the manipulation of the black vote, a symptom of the maladies resulting from deeply engrained racial prejudice in the river city.[53]

PART III

The Consolidation of a Ghetto, 1900–1930

SEVEN

Population and Housing, 1900–1930

 At the turn of the century there were 7,518 blacks in Evansville, a third more than in 1890 and over four times the number in 1870. Afro-Americans accounted for nearly 13 percent of the city's residents. By number and proportion, Evansville's black population ranked high among cities in the North. Combined with the proliferation of social organizations and the emergence of a small business-professional community, black Evansville seemed to promise even greater growth and development. After a visit to the city, George Stewart, editor of the *Indianapolis Recorder*, wrote in June 1903 that there were two striking facts about Evansville: the absence of racial prejudice and the evidences of material progress among its black citizens. "[Y]oung men are in charge of most everything," he declared, "and with older mens [*sic*] counsel they are moving everything that is not securly [*sic*] nailed down."[1]

The editor's praise of Evansville was effusive. As in Indianapolis, he argued, members of churches and lodges were united with professional men. Baptists even worked with Methodists—a "really strange" phenomenon. He also offered statistical evidence. There were 2,270 black voters and, to Stewart, their clout was shown by the presence of four janitors in public buildings, two "assistant city physicians," a black-staffed fire house, and a black deputy sheriff, Ernest Tidrington, who at age twenty-four was "a hustler," the leading black Republican and principal spokesman for his race. There were five physicians, a druggist, an attorney, two grocers, plenty of barbers, seven saloonkeepers, and a hotelkeeper, W. H. Bell, who also owned ten teams of horses and worked as a street contractor. Willis Green, the physician, was reportedly worth $100,000, and was a land developer in "Greenville" and Oakdale, small black enclaves on the southside. Stewart also counted five black schools, thirty teachers, and a new newspaper, to be launched July 4, as proof of the cultural advancement of the black community. There were also several prominent social clubs, especially the "Dukes" and the "Duchesses," and the high school had recently graduated its twenty-third class.[2]

That this analysis was not only superficial but sanguine was made rudely apparent within a week. Beginning on July 3 the city experienced the worst racial disturbance in its history. By 1910 the population of black Evansville had declined by 1,300. While many Northern cities were experiencing significant gains in the number of blacks, especially after 1915, Evansville underwent a period of stagnation which lasted until the Second World War. (See Table 14.)[3]

That a major outbreak of racial strife was likely should have been apparent to city fathers. Several nasty interracial clashes between small groups of whites and blacks occurred in February, 1903, all related to claims by whites that blacks were infringing upon their territory. In late May a *Courier* headline blared that a drunken black had tried to kill a police officer. Both dailies carried numerous stories on the "Negro problem" in the nation as well as in the city, and racist cartoons, especially in the *Courier*, portrayed blacks unflatteringly. On the morning of July 3, the *Journal-News* reported an attempted assault on a white woman by a black man the previous night.[4]

A city with 300 saloons and countless unlicensed "dives," Evansville awoke on the morning of Independence Day to learn that late on the afternoon of July 3 a black man had seriously wounded a white policeman, Louis Massey. The alleged assailant had gotten into an argument with the porter at Ossenberg's Saloon on Tenth between Oak and Canal and had left the saloon with the promise to return to settle the score. Apprised of the threat, Massey—according to accounts provided newspaper reporters and the coroner—located the man at Ninth and Oak. Two eyewitnesses said that as Massey approached him from the rear, he turned and fired three times. Massey replied with four shots before collapsing. He was rushed to Deaconess Hospital, and his assailant, who was also wounded, was apprehended and placed in the County Jail.[5]

Twenty-four hours later, Massey died, the first policeman killed by an arrested man in the city's history. Given the presence of 30,000 visitors in the city for the Fourth of July, the availability of alcoholic beverages, the racial climate of the times, and the absence of an ordinance prohibiting the discharge of firearms within city limits, it is hardly surprising that several hundred hostile whites gathered outside the jail on the evening of the Fourth to seek justice for the fallen officer. The suspect, identified as Robert Lee, reportedly had confessed to shooting Massey. Although the crowd was dispersed, on the next night, Sunday, approximately 1,000 gathered at the jail and a number of men tried to enter the premises. Claiming that black gangs had threatened them, groups of whites also began to terrorize black neighborhoods. Mayor Charles Covert, a Republican, closed all saloons and ordered citizens to stay in their homes. Democrats criticized the mayor for overreacting to Fourth of July festivities. Governor Winfield Durbin, also a Republican, and the *Journal* disagreed. On the morning of the sixth the governor responded to the sheriff's plea for help by ordering the local militia to arms to protect Lee and the jail and to restore order.

That evening a large gathering confronted the 100 troopers at the courthouse. One of the onlookers apparently fired a shot, and the troops responded by firing into the crowd. Twelve were killed and thirty wounded. Most of those who were shot were laborers, although one of the fatalities was a young girl who had been observing the fracas. To return the rule of law to the beleaguered city, the governor ordered 300 militiamen to Evansville. He also prevented Evansville authorities from bringing Lee back to the city from Vincennes, where he had been removed for safekeeping. Barely alive, Lee was instead taken to Jeffersonville prison. By the morning of the tenth, order had been restored, and the troops departed, although saloons remained closed for several days thereafter. Portrayed as a murderer by both dailies, Lee died on July 31 without having gone to trial.[6]

The black community lived in a state of terror from July 4 through July 10. No one was safe outdoors, and scores of homes and shops were riddled with bullets. Fearing violence, the members of Hose House No. 9 resigned on the sixth, and consequently the fear of fire was intensified. Blacks reportedly could be found walking on the railroad tracks leading in every direction from the city, and 500 went to Henderson, Kentucky, for refuge. Charles Hunter, an AME pastor, observed that had blacks stayed off the streets from the beginning of the crisis, they might not have suffered reprisals. He acknowledged, however, that there was no telling what might have happened without the presence of the militia.[7]

Even before the troops left, white Evansville began to search for an explanation for the tragedy. The *Courier* ran an editorial on July 7 and an unflattering cartoon which attributed the riot to the importation of "worthless blacks" as voters. The crowd which railed against the alleged murderer, according to the editor, did not consist of a few rowdies but was representative of all classes in the city. By contrast, the *Journal-News* deplored the outbreak of mob rule and—listing the lynchings in the United States in 1903—insisted that criticisms that Evansville was a wide-open town were unwarranted. Reprinting editorials from newspapers in Pittsburgh, New York, and other cities, the editor associated the riot with an upsurge of the mob spirit across the nation. The chief issue for him was the blight that the episode had brought to the city's image, for the perpetrators were a handful of poor blacks and poor whites who had sparked the latent spirit of mob rule. The Evansville Businessmen's Association agreed, saying the Republican city and county administration had done its best to curb lawlessness.[8]

About a week after the troops departed, a county grand jury lent some support to that view. It criticized those who had blamed the militia for the killings and attacked the spirit of lawlessness aroused in the crisis. It further declared that the major source of trouble was lax enforcement of the law, especially regarding liquor. On July 20 two Democratic members of the City Council took a different approach. Tracing the events of July 5 and 6 to "the vicious, shiftless, lawless element which finds its home in the low down negro dives [sic] of the city," they proposed that any saloonkeeper lose his license if he "allows any negro to sit or lie down at any hour day or night either in the saloon or anywhere about the premises. . . ." A month later, the Republican-controlled council adopted an ordinance requiring a liquor license for all liquor

12. A Democratic cartoonist's explanation of the 1903 riot. *Evansville Courier*, July 7, 1903.

sales within city limits, raising the cost of the license from $75 to $250 a year, and abolishing the granting of licenses of less than six months' duration. On September 21 the council granted 276 licenses under the new ordinance.[9]

The violence had profound influence on black Evansville. Aside from property damage and threats to the personal safety of hundreds of blacks, it blunted the development of the business and professional community. The proposed newspaper did not get off the ground. Within a year three prominent professionals had left town. It is impossible to determine how many others decided not to settle in Evansville because of its reputation. It is unclear how many of those ordinary people who fled for their lives failed to return. During the summer of 1903, moreover, there were numerous instances of rowdyism in which white youths attacked black citizens or vandalized their property without provocation.[10]

The disturbances also reaffirmed the prevailing view among black leaders that the best racial strategy was that advocated by Booker T. Washington. Two different but related arguments within that framework were offered. On July 17 leading members of the Colored Ministerial Alliance, including Rouse, Anderson, and W. W. Townsend, met to discuss recent events and concluded that the chief cause had been the prevalence of the lynch-mob spirit in the nation. The eight clergymen also wrote the newspapers that, although most blacks were law-abiding, a few had abetted that spirit through their irresponsible behavior. They called on city authorities to close all illegal vice dens and to raise the cost of a liquor license. They also requested the proprietor of a dance hall in Baptisttown to cease offering nightly dances, which the pastors claimed were injurious to the morals of black youth.[11]

Dr. Dupee took a somewhat different tack. In a lengthy letter to the editor of the Republican daily on July 18, he attributed the outbreak of violence almost exclusively to the black community. Accusing race leaders of poor direction, he described the black masses as spoiled and lazy, a logical result of the exploitation of poorly educated people. "It would not hurt," he added, "for us to humiliate ourselves a little. . . . We must . . . show to the white people that we are bent upon ameliorating conditions." The young physician went on to insist that only when blacks were "earning their bread by the sweat of their own brow" could they gain self-respect and esteem.[12] In his first reference to the riot in the "Colored Folk" column, he called on black pastors and teachers to do a better job of instilling moral precepts among the youth. In a subsequent column he argued that the use of "Equality Buttons" showing President Theodore Roosevelt and Booker T. Washington dining together at the White House was foolish, as it would "create public sentiment against the black man."[13]

The approach urged by Dupee seemed appropriate to most whites, as the separation between the races and stricter controls on blacks intensified after 1903. The immediate response of the City Council to the riot was, in addition to the new liquor ordinance, a ban on the discharge of firearms in city limits.[14] Between 1903 and 1916, as noted in chapter 8, the pace of de jure as well as de facto segregation quickened.

TABLE 14:   The Black Population of Evansville, 1900-1950

Year	Total	Black	Percent Black	Percent Increase
1900	59,007	7,518	12.7	35.9
1910	69,647	6,266	9.0	(16.7)
1920	85,264	6,394	7.4	2.0
1930	102,249	6,514	6.3	1.8
1940	97,062	6,862	7.1	5.3
1950	128,636	8,483	6.6	19.1

Sources: Bureau of the Census, Department of Commerce, *Twelfth Census of the United States, Taken in the Year 1900,* volume I, *Population,* part 1 (Washington, D.C., 1901), 615; *Negro Population, 1790–1915* (Washington, D.C., 1918), 106; *Fourteenth Census of the United States Taken in the Year 1920,* volume III: *Population 1920* (Washington, D.C., 1922), 296; *Fifteenth Census of the United States, 1930,* volume III, part 1, *Population* (Washington, D.C., 1932), 700; *Sixteenth Census of the United States: 1940, Population,* volume II: *Characteristics of the Population,* part 2: *Florida-Iowa* (Washington, D.C., 1943), 705, 784; *Census of Population: 1950,* volume II: *Characteristics of the Population,* part 14: *Indiana* (Washington, D.C., 1952), 31.

As indelibly as the violent events of July 1903 marked the character of the city, however, economic and transportation factors were more important in determining population and housing patterns. On the one hand, limited occupational opportunities combined with increased racial discrimination to make for a stifling climate for those who sought upward mobility. The race riot was a symptom of that. On the other hand, improved rail connections between South and North and the opening of employment in factories in more northerly cities, especially Chicago, made Evansville a less logical terminus for Southern blacks seeking to make a new start. Until the Second World War brought an increase in the quality and quantity of jobs for blacks in Evansville, the demographic changes which greatly altered the composition of Northern cities barely touched black Evansville.[15]

Black population in the entire lower Ohio Valley, in fact, experienced a decline between 1900 and 1910 and either stabilized or declined further thereafter. In areas of Kentucky adjoining the Ohio River, the major source of Evansville's black community, the black population of Henderson County decreased from 8,804 in 1900 to 6,818 in 1910, and that of Daviess and Union counties from 5,554 and 3,113, respectively, to 5,195 and 2,414. In southwest Indiana it also declined in Gibson County (1,481 to 1,445) and Posey County (1,226 to 963). Similar declines occurred in neighboring Warrick, Knox, and Perry counties. In the same decade, the population of black Indianapolis increased from 15,931 to 21,816. Black Chicago grew from 30,150 to 44,103, and black Cincinnati from 14,482 to 19,639. The total increase in the black population of Indiana in the decade was from 57,505 to 60,320, and no southern Indiana county experienced any increase. Only ten of the state's ninety-two counties, in fact, did.[16]

An examination of the 1910 federal population schedules of Evansville and rural Vanderburgh County reveals that of the 6,266 Afro-Americans residing in the city, only one in three was a native of Indiana (as compared with three of four whites). Of those born elsewhere, 70 percent were natives of Kentucky; 20 percent had been born in other states in the South. (In 1880, 27 percent, and in 1900, 37 percent were natives of Indiana.) The high transiency rate is also suggested by the fact that, in 1910, 59 percent of the black population was male, of whom only a third were married and living with their spouses. During the first decade of the twentieth century, in short, the proportion of youthful, childless males in their twenties and thirties increased. That there were more blacks in the 21–40 age bracket (41.5 percent, as compared with 34.9 in 1900) and less in the 20 or below category (28.7 percent, as compared with 37.9) suggests that in the previous decade family formation had been disrupted. Perhaps one victim of the racial disturbance of 1903 was the black family, which in 1880 and 1900 had accounted for a larger share of the black population.[17]

TABLE 15:   Distribution of Population by Ward, 1910

Ward	Total Population	Number Black	Percent Black
1	9,825	565	5.8
2	4,316	717	16.6
3	5,600	582	10.4
4	15,229	906	5.9
5	10,590	403	3.8
6	13,591	460	3.4
7	10,496	2,633	25.1
Total	69,647	6,266	9.0

Source: *Negro Population, 1790–1915,* p. 106; Bureau of the Census, Department of Commerce and Labor, *Thirteenth Census of the United States Taken in the Year 1910: Abstract of the Census with Supplement for Indiana* (Washington, D.C., 1913), 623.

During the decade blacks had also become more residentially clustered. As shown on Table 15, Ward 7 on the near eastside was one-quarter black, and its black population represented over 42 percent of the total in Evansville. Ward 2, which adjoined this ward and included enclaves on Fourth and Fifth streets, was one-sixth black. Slightly over 900 resided in the lower waterfront section, Ward 4. Over 4,250 of the 6,266 blacks in Evansville, in short, resided in three wards.[18]

The centripetal tendency of the population becomes clearer through examination of the enumeration districts in the 1910 census. Of the seventy districts within the city limits, twenty-five had no black residents. By contrast, thirteen accounted for three-quarters of the black population. Most adjoined each other in Wards 2, 4, and 7. Districts 141 to 145 in the Seventh Ward constituted 41.5 percent of the city's blacks. In nine of these districts the population was at least 20 percent black. In two, 144 and 145, two-thirds were.[19]

When examined street by street, the population schedules reveal clustering even more clearly. Of the approximately 225 streets in the city, two-thirds had no blacks residing on them. Blacks dwelling on portions of Canal, Cherry, Upper Fifth and Fourth, Gordon, South Governor, Lincoln, and Oak represented one-fourth of the total in the city. If one adds two or three-block portions of seventeen other streets—for example, Church, McCormick, Douglas, and Elliott—one can determine that half of the city's blacks lived on about 10 percent of the city's streets. Another 22 percent had addresses on fourteen other streets. All told, about three of every four blacks resided on less than one-fifth of the streets in the city.[20]

Using the census district as the basic unit of examination, one discovers that the index of dissimilarity rose from 45 to 49 between 1900 and 1910, a slight increase and an indication that residential segregation was partially complete. It must also be noted that such segregation was not exclusively racial, moreover, as about 80 percent of the German-born resided in clusters on the north- and westsides, and for them the index of segregation in 1910 was 40. One must add, however, that in all wards except the Seventh the proportion of second-generation German-Americans was at least 25 percent, an indication that residential mobility existed among the children of these newcomers.[21]

Although the racial dissimilarity index and the survival of smaller enclaves outside Baptisttown suggest that a racial ghetto had not formed by 1910, one must also observe that an ever-increasing share of the city's blacks—60 percent in 1910—dwelled within a four-block radius of the center of Baptisttown. On the short streets and alleys, as well as segments of larger streets in the area, the percentage of blacks was high—50 to 100. The smaller enclaves, like Oakdale, accounted for about a fifth of the total black population, and in them, like Baptisttown, most of the streets were largely black. (The remaining 20 percent were enumerated in white-owned homes, hotels, and steamboats.)[22]

Blacks also resided in crowded and inferior settings. About one in ten resided in dwellings in which there were two or more households, as compared with less than one in twenty whites. Approximately 56 percent of the community's blacks could be found in households of three to six persons, as compared with about 62 percent of Evansville's whites. By contrast, black households containing nine to twenty persons accounted for 16 percent of the black population, as compared with white households of similar size which included 9 percent of the total. One-third of black Evansvillians lived in households augmented with boarders and/or lodgers, moreover, as contrasted with 15 percent of white Evansvillians. And about nine-tenths of black household heads rented their homes, as compared with slightly more than four in ten whites. The percentage of blacks who owned their own homes, it should be added, was about twice that of blacks in Chicago, Cincinnati, and Louisville, slightly less than those in Indianapolis, and less than half of those in Terre Haute.[23]

The quality of black housing was deplorable. Homes on Church Street, for instance, were of such poor quality that the fire chief condemned most of them in early 1904. Blacks who lived there refused to pay rent because of the condition of their homes, but they also refused to vacate because they did not know where else they could live. Several years later, during the administration of Mayor John W. Boehne, the city engineer completed the first citywide study of housing conditions and recommended that homes on Douglas, Reilly, Mitchell, and Gordon be vacated, and that Brower, Ballard, Elliott, and Garvin streets be extended through that region in order to eliminate blighted homes located on tiny lots and improve traffic flow on the eastside. At the urging of housing reformer Albion Fellows Bacon, the City Council also adopted the city's first housing law, by which a city housing inspector was appointed. Despite remonstrances from blacks and cries of foul from Republicans who claimed the Democrats were seeking to eliminate the black vote, the board of public works voted to implement the plan, but implementation was stalled and then dropped because of the election of a Republican city administration in 1910.[24]

Housing reform was resurrected in 1914, the first year of the administration of Democrat Benjamin Bosse. The city building commissioner condemned rental dwellings housing 180 blacks on Fourth Street between Walnut and Locust as breeding places for contagious disease and crime. Resistance from whites who owned the buildings slowed his efforts. Later in the year the commissioner was authorized by a committee comprising Mrs. Bacon, leader of the effort to enact the state's first housing law (1913), and representatives of the forerunner of the Chamber of Commerce, to survey housing conditions.

The group learned that at least thirty houses on High Street and in Baptisttown needed to be razed. Emil Weil, chairman of the joint housing committee, proposed eliminating blighted housing for blacks in the area near Fourth and Chandler, an attractive middle-class white neighborhood, and moving the blacks to Oakdale. Few on the committee seemed to be interested in the fate of the people living in these dwellings. Mrs. Bacon and industrialist Richard Rosencranz, son of philanthropist A. C. Rosencranz, stood alone in urging gradual change because of the dearth of low-income housing in the city. Most committee members were, however, impatient. Several members of the committee complained that change would not occur because of the value of Baptisttown to local politicians, and one—physician William E. French—suggested that the entire area should be razed and turned into a park for whites. Another member, Rev. William Brightmire, a member of the city's "Morals Committee," assured everyone that after Billy Sunday's revival meeting in the city later that summer the problem would take care of itself because there would be no more unclean souls.[25]

Whatever their solutions (and disagreement led the committee to adjourn and not set another meeting date), it was clear that committee members—as

Howard Rabinowitz has observed about housing reformers in the urban South—had "discovered" black slums only because they were forced to. The opening of new subdivisions on the eastside and the use of Fourth Street for commuting, for example, created the kinds of concerns expressed by men like Weil. Mrs. Bacon revealed as much about her perspectives on race relations as her knowledge of housing conditions when she declared that because blacks kept to themselves and cared for their own, she had not realized, until visiting Baptisttown, "how uniformly miserable and unsanitary were their dwellings."[26] When introduced to the existence of such conditions, she seemed less interested in the social forces creating them than in their aesthetic quality.

In early 1915 the works board approved the opening of Elliott from Lincoln to Canal, a plan which would eliminate what the *Journal-News* called "the unspeakable Green's Alley." This was to be accomplished by charging property owners abutting the street improvement half of the cost and paying for the remainder via the city's general fund, as the project was deemed to have communitywide benefit. Property owners, however, blocked full implementation of the plan. The commissioner announced in September 1915 that his deparment had been able over the previous two years to force improvements in 215 homes, raze 63, and plan for the razing of 40 more. Much of this work involved housing for blacks. Building violations were the worst, he added, in Oakdale.[27]

In mid-1915, Mrs. Bacon wrote a newspaper column on "Better Homes for a Better Evansville." Recalling the joint committee's work in the previous year, which was patterned after studies in other cities, she implored the community to reconsider the merits of the "Model Block" plan which had given rise to the committee. During the following week members of a new committee toured blighted areas in Upper Fourth and Upper Third, High Street, and Baptisttown. Rosencranz was especially active in this effort, designed to raise $100,000 via selling stock in a model homes building committee. As in previous efforts, progress was stalled.

In May 1916, Mayor Bosse, Rosencranz (head of what was now called the Baptisttown Committee), and others from the Chamber of Commerce adopted a ten-year plan to "redeem Baptisttown." The plan focused on the most notorious regions—for example, Green's Alley, Short Eleventh Street, Day's Row, and Douglas and Reilly streets—and proposed the building of several thoroughfares by extending Elliott, Cherry, Ballard, Garvin, and Oak streets through Baptisttown. The mayor proposed that as a start Green's Alley be replaced by a park and that seventy-five good building sites be bought and homes built for the families which would be displaced. In its report to the Chamber of Commerce in July, the committee also noted that few homes in Baptisttown were connected to city sewers, and that most used cisterns for their water supply. The committee also attempted to persuade Canal Street property owners to accept the widening of the street to provide for a twenty-four foot wide park in the center, through which the traction line would run from Eighth and Grant streets to the city limits.[28]

The passage of a second state housing law in 1917, empowering state health officers to order corrective action when a dwelling was deemed unfit for human habitation, may have helped city officials remove Green's Alley via the extension of Elliott Street, but the seventy-five homes were not built. Canal Street improvements were also not implemented. There were many reasons for the lack of success. Some blacks complained they had not been involved in the planning process, and others feared the loss of what little they had, knowing that replacement housing was scarce and expensive. Republicans continually charged that the real motive for the reform was the Democrats' desire to pare the number of black voters. Slum landlords raised obstacles. Some progressives, moreover, charged the mayor with duplicity—using rhetoric designed to please reformers, while not actively pushing for change, as his election depended on black votes delivered by Seventh Ward leaders who delivered the vote in return for city government's giving them a free hand to exploit the region. The coming of World War I was also a factor, for the State Defense Council urged suspension of local capital improvement projects during the war. Whatever the reason, Baptisttown remained generally untouched until the late 1930s.

Growing up in the region in the 1910s and 1920s, Douglas Lander recalled the center of Baptisttown as a myriad of small "eat shops," saloons, and ramshackle homes. At Tenth and Canal was the symbol of the region's status— the largest junkyard in the city. Bad housing was not, as a rule, eliminated by the passage of legislation and the efforts of a few diligent reformers.[29]

The tendency toward greater concentration of blacks in the area was not only aided by such early forms of slum removal but also sparked by outbursts of hostility to those few blacks who dared to consider moving into regions tacitly understood as for whites only. The most notable instance occurred in the summer of 1907, when Moses and Beulah Davis, schoolteachers, attempted to purchase a home in the Tuxedo Place subdivision on Linwood Avenue. Neighbors strenuously objected, and even asked the school board to exert pressure to prevent the couple from moving in. The board's president, A. C. Rosencranz, resisted, arguing that "the colored people have a perfect right to live in property they purchase." Neighborhood opposition persisted, however: nearby grocers were persuaded, for example, to agree not to sell to the Davises. Bowing to pressure, the couple decided to purchase another home, this time in a white area between Tenth and Chestnut. The Republican paper chastised the two for "forcing themselves into this pretty neighborhood," and said "[e]veryone interested in the deal that has settled the negroes on Chestnut Street is being execrated. . . . Why don't they go among negroes and buy property if they want to own a home? . . ." The Davises moved in, nevertheless, despite fears expressed in the *Journal-News* that "the importation of negroes anxious to 'settle down among white folks' . . . [would] become a habit. . . ." Rosencranz replied caustically that there would have been no opposition had Moses Davis "been a white gambler or pimp. . . . The spirit displayed in the prosecution of these people is contemptible and unworthy of this age." Replied the Republican editor, Evansville was a Southern city with distinctive districts for blacks, and

[even] the colored ministers, who are educated men, have found it advantageous to live among their own people. This fact may not have dawned upon Mr. and Mrs. Davis, but a little inquiry will acquaint them with the truth of the statement.[30]

Although the Davises moved to 1101 Chestnut and remained there until Moses left town in 1917 for the war in France, they were the only blacks on the block, and after they departed the area was all white for several decades. (The Memphis *Commercial-Appeal* found the case amusing, for it illustrated to its editors the hypocrisy of the North on racial matters.) Associating the coming of blacks with the probable decline in property value and the likelihood of race-mixing, some white leaders even suggested that the case reinforced the need for the community to segregate blacks by ordinance.[31]

Such a formal device, however, was not passed because it was not needed. Custom, the threat of retaliation, and the restrictive covenant were sufficient. The most effective means was word of mouth, recalled Alfred E. Porter, and that meant that most blacks never considered living anywhere else but where most blacks had always lived. In addition, newspaper advertisements listed rental property and homes for sale according to racial preferences. Also power-ful was the provision—introduced into deed records about 1909—that prop-erty could not be sold, rented, or leased to blacks.[32]

A profile of the post-1910 black population indicated that stabilization was occurring not only in numbers but also in sex ratio, marital status, and age distribution. That is, the sharp increase in the proportion of single, Kentucky-born males in their twenties and thirties revealed in the 1910 census was not present in the censuses of 1920 and 1930. In the former there were ninety-nine males per 100 females in Evansville, and in the latter the ratio was ninety-seven to 100. (For native whites it was ninety-four to 100.) The sex ratio among Evansville blacks in 1930 was virtually the same as the rate in Cairo, Illinois, Des Moines, Iowa, Terre Haute, and Springfield, Illinois. By contrast, in the more northerly industrial cities like Chicago, Flint, Pontiac, Milwaukee, and Warren, Ohio, the number of males to females was considerably higher. To the south the number was much lower—about eighty to 100.[33]

Marital condition and age distribution indicated other changes. In 1930 the proportion of single black males aged fifteen and over had dropped to 36.6 percent, over three percentage points lower than twenty years before. The per-centage of single women in that bracket, 25.8, was essentially unchanged. The number of black families, 1,720, was almost exactly what it had been in 1920 and higher than the total in 1910. By age, the distribution of population among black men and women in each age bracket revealed that there was little difference. That there were proportionally more women than men in their twenties perhaps reflected the number of young men who had left the city to seek their fortune elsewhere. When blacks and whites are compared, there were more blacks than whites aged twenty to forty-four and slightly more whites under age ten and over age sixty-five. Higher infant mortality rates and lower life expectancy continued to plague the black community.[34]

Perhaps even more striking was the steady increase of residential segregation. As revealed in Table 16, in 1920 the percentage of blacks equalled or exceeded the citywide proportion in only three of the eight wards: 2, 3, and 7. (Ward lines were redrawn in the Bosse administration. Precinct 4 in Ward 1, precincts 6 and 7 in Ward 2, and precinct 2 in Ward 3 adjoined Ward 7, the boundaries of which remained virtually unchanged.) Blacks in these three wards accounted for 68 percent of the city's total, and one-third of the total dwelled in the Seventh Ward. During the following decade, the number of blacks dropped in six of the eight wards. Especially significant was the decline in the Fifth Ward on the westside. Ward 7's share of the total black population increased to about 40 percent. (In 1910 it had been 25 percent.) The Second Ward, which included the downtown hotels and restaurants and the residences of many of the city's affluent, claimed slightly fewer blacks in 1930, but the total, 1,356, was about one-fifth of the entire black community.[35]

TABLE 16:   Black Population by Ward, 1920 and 1930

Ward	Total		Black		Percent Black	
	1920	1930	1920	1930	1920	1930
1	9,816	15,526	520	587	5.3	3.8
2	10,039	10,222	1,402	1,356	14.0	13.3
3	10,892	9,942	811	773	7.4	7.8
4	8,774	8,864	555	485	6.3	5.5
5	12,035	10,166	178	12	1.5	0.1
6	11,163	15,488	293	249	2.6	1.6
7	9,783	12,952	2,140	2,502	21.9	19.3
8	12,762	10,782	405	292	3.2	2.7
Unwarded	0	8,307	0	258	0	3.1
Total	85,264	102,249	6,394	6,514	7.5	6.4

Sources: Fourteenth Census, 1920, *Population*, III:305; Fifteenth Census, 1930, *Population*, III:1, 744.

When examined by region and street of residence, the advancing centripetal pattern clearly emerges. In 1914 about 62 percent of the city's blacks lived in the near downtown region to the north and east of Canal and Eighth. By the time the 1929 city directory was published, that had risen to 69.8 percent. Examined by street, city directories disclose a higher degree of residential separation. No blacks resided on 82.5 percent of the city's streets in 1914, but 76.4 percent of the heads of household dwelled on streets in and near Baptisttown. In 1919, 44 percent of the black community lived on twelve streets—Bellemeade, Canal, Elliott, North Evans, South Fifth, North Fulton, Gordon,

West Iowa, Lincoln, Oak, South Seventh, and West Virginia. In 1924 and 1929, blacks were residents on only 16.9 percent of the city's streets, few of which were outside Baptisttown. Put another way, close to nine of every ten thoroughfares were all white. (By contrast, persons with German surnames could be found on at least half the streets of the city.)[36]

Certain portions of the city remained as closed to blacks as they had been since 1865. Probably the most exclusive was Howell, a westside community of upper-South whites organized around the L&N railroad yards in the 1880s and annexed in 1916. No blacks were ever enumerated there, and the members of the black community were aware of the unwritten rule that blacks did not spend the night in that community. In addition, the regions with the highest share of German Americans were also unlikely to have black residents. Streets on which at least 50 percent of its residents were of German extraction consti-tuted 29 percent of the total in 1929, and on those blacks lived on only three. On the twenty streets with at least a 50 percent black population, however, only two had German Americans on them.)[37]

By the fall of 1925, when a site for the new high school was being debated before the school board, "the principal negro district" was described as beginning

> at Fourth and Walnut, along Fourth to Mulberry, Mulberry to Eighth, Eighth to Bellemeade, Bellemeade to Line, Line to Chandler, Chandler to Elliott, Elliott to Gum, Gum to Garvin, Garvin to Mulberry, Mulberry to McCormick, McCor-mick to Lincoln, Lincoln to Evans, Evans to Canal, Canal to Denby, Denby to John, John to Main, Main to William, William to Heidelbach, Heidelbach to Walnut, Walnut to Tenth, Tenth to Oak, Oak to Fifth, Fifth to Walnut, and then to the point of beginning.[38]

That the proportion of blacks living in predominantly black neighbor-hoods in the Baptisttown region was on the rise was especially evident in the city directory published on the eve of the school relocation controversy. According to the city directory of 1924, 952, or 73 percent of the total listed (1,212), were residents of the region defined by opponents of the school board's plans as "the Negro district." (See Map 5.) Most blacks lived, more-over, with other blacks. Within Baptisttown, for example, 58 percent resided on streets on which at least 75 percent of their neighbors were black. Of the remainder, all but a few dwelled on streets which were at least 50 percent black. In enclaves outside Baptisttown, 46 percent resided on streets which were three-quarters or more black, and another 23 percent lived on streets which were from 50 to 75 percent Afro-American.[39]

The traditional center of black Evansville showed even greater signs of that trend five years later. Almost 76 percent of black Evansville lived there, and 59 percent of those were residents of city blocks which were at least three-quarters black. Another 31 percent were in neighborhoods which were 50 to 74 percent black. Similar evidences of increased concentration and racial separation were present.[40]

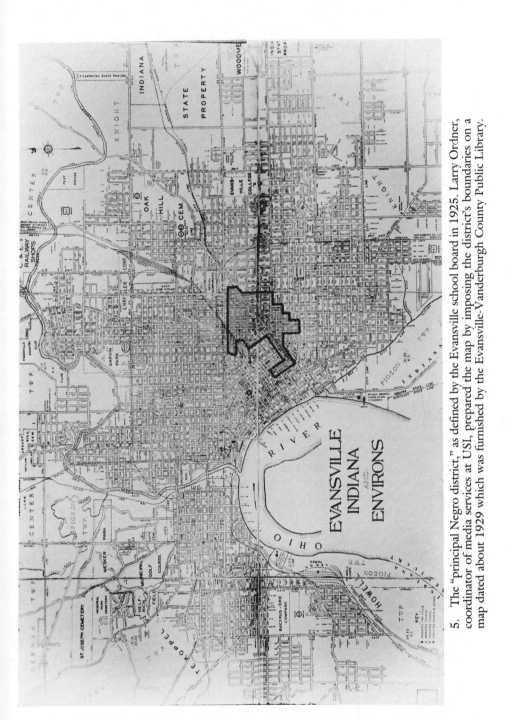

5. The "principal Negro district," as defined by the Evansville school board in 1925. Larry Ordner, coordinator of media services at USI, prepared the map by imposing the district's boundaries on a map dated about 1929 which was furnished by the Evansville-Vanderburgh County Public Library.

The growing number of blacks in Baptisttown predictably exerted pressure against the white neighborhoods to the northeast, east, and southeast. Slowly but surely the ghetto spread toward Kentucky Avenue. Charlotte Glover Moody recalled, for example, that when she was a child living on the 900 block of Cherry Street her block was racially mixed and the next block to the east was all white. By the time she was a young adult in the early 1930s blacks had moved into that block. Another reality was that housing remained crowded and inferior. Periodic housing surveys of Baptisttown through the early 1930s reported that most of the black-occupied housing was undesirable or uninhabitable.[41]

The decision of the school board in the mid-1920s to relocate the black high school and to consolidate black elementary schools (see chapter 9) on Lincoln Avenue near Governor was one of several factors accelerating the centripetal process prior to the Great Depression. Another was the changing economy of the community. The decline of river traffic, for instance, lowered the number of blacks in the Lower Water Street enclave. Also important was the removal of blighted housing on or near Fourth Street and the assault, however uneven, on vice-ridden regions in which blacks lived. The resistance of white suburbanites and the prohibitive cost of suburban housing, factors in other Northern cities, were not significant factors in Evansville, however, given the poverty of the black community and the strength of the written and unwritten rules about where blacks should live. The staunch resistance of artisans and laborers to black residential mobility was a powerful force. As Kenneth Kusmer has noted of Cleveland, workers and small entrepreneurs

> [were] highly prone to what social scientists have called "status anxieties." Having raised themselves above poverty, acquired a small home (with perhaps a large mortgage as well), and attained a modest level of income, they were fearful of association with any group bearing the stigma of low status. They naturally resented the encroachment of a racial group that American society had designated as inferior.[42]

Such socioeconomic sources of residential exclusiveness do not, however, tell the whole story. Hostility to blacks in predominantly German and upland Southern neighborhoods had been present from the middle of the nineteenth century onward. Throughout southwestern Indiana the regions with high concentrations of Germans—notably DuBois County—had from their inception contained the fewest numbers of blacks. Hoosiers in the lower Ohio Valley, moreover, also displayed the values and attitudes of the adjoining South. Hence the culture of the region must be seen as the most essential factor in making for residential patterns in the city of Evansville. As in Chicago, white hostility was the chief cause of the formation of the black ghetto, which was reinforced by the poverty of black Evansvillians.[43]

Evansville's black ghetto, in short, was not necessarily the product, as in Cleveland, of a series of unthinking choices.[44] At the turn of the century the city

had an incipient ghetto and several smaller enclaves, in each of which the proportion of black residents was steadily increasing. Although the number of
blacks declined, the largest black section and the physical separation of the races
grew. Increasing residential segregation in Evansville was an important proof
that migration alone was not the cause of ghetto development. The desire for
social control had much deeper roots than that. This was an ironic twist to
what George Stewart had reported in June 1903. The physical separation of the
races vividly illustrated a process which had been evolving over a lengthy period
of time and which matured in the 1920s.

EIGHT

Race Relations in the Progressive Era
1900–1916

 In *Growing Up*, Russell Baker remembered that in the 1930s the rules of his Baltimore neighborhood on race relations were absolute. Blacks were "unworthy and inconsequential": They had a place and stayed in it.[1] Similar rules, mostly unwritten, had also evolved in Evansville since the middle of the nineteenth century. The physical ghetto was stark testimony to that. Between the turn of the century and the Great Depression those proscriptions were considerably enlarged.[2]

The growing racial discrimination of the period reflected in part the spirit of the times. During the progressive era animosity toward Afro-Americans escalated in the United States, and some of its most virulent forms—the city's 1903 riot and lynchings in Henderson and Paducah in 1915 and 1916—were close to home. The muckraker Ray Stannard Baker attributed the outbreak of violence against blacks to the distrust that Southern white men had of their own judicial processes and "counseled that time, patience, and education were the only solutions to the negro problem."[3] White Evansville leaders were prone to blame "the Negro problem" on the presence of "worthless" blacks in the city, and some black leaders agreed. Rev. Charles Hunter of Alexander Chapel AME declared in September 1901, that the hostility of whites toward blacks was the result of the behavior of "idle, worthless, [and] vicious young negroes," a statement which received prominent treatment in the Republican newspaper (unlike comments in the same month by Rev. W. H. Anderson, associating the assassination of William McKinley and the proliferation of lynch mobs with the growing spirit of anarchy in the nation).[4]

Abetted by Republican abandonment of the freedmen, the adverse racial climate on the national level had powerful influence on black Evansvillians. During January 1906, the stage version of Thomas Dixon, Jr.'s *The Clansman* was performed at the Grand Theatre. The *Journal-News* "Colored Folk" column echoed the sentiments of the *Indianapolis Recorder* by describing the play as an attempt to stir up race prejudice. The white editor, however, insisted the play attacked only criminal behavior among blacks. White reception of Dixon's work was enthusiastic, and the play returned to the city for a second run in February 1909. The *Journal-News* portrayed it as a sequel to *Uncle Tom's Cabin* and a true story of Reconstruction. (In the final scene, a member of the Ku Klux Klan rescued the daughter of a white abolitionist from the clutches of a lecherous mulatto.)[5]

The black community was also influenced by other external expressions of racial animosity. In late 1906, for instance, President Theodore Roosevelt "summarily discharged three companies of the black 25th Regiment on unproven charges of rioting in Brownsville, Texas. No actions hurt and angered Negroes more than this one."[6] Hundreds of Hoosier blacks protested. On the evening of November 27, Evansville's black leadership convened a mass meeting at McFarland Chapel, which adopted a statement expressing regret that the conduct of a few in Texas has "brought disgrace and shame upon that brave and ilustrious regiment," urging a fair and speedy trial of the guilty parties, suggesting that the attacks on the president's motives were "unwarranted, unpatriotic, and senseless," and calling upon blacks not to listen to those who urged them not to enlist in the army. The statement concluded that the best means of presenting their case "to the proper authorities" was to send a copy of their resolutions to the Afro-American Council, which at the time was under the control of Booker T. Washington.[7]

Even this must have seemed effrontery to whites. Antiblack sentiment was strong, especially in the summer of 1910, when Jack Johnson fought Jim Jeffries for the heavyweight championship in Reno, Nevada. Local white leaders generally opposed the interracial match. When the black boxer won—a turn of events they had considered impossible—the newspapers reported disorders across the nation, as whites were disappointed and blacks jubilant. On the morning of July 5, six Evansville black men were hauled into court for having "celebrated the victory of the[ir] brother in much whiskey and boisterous manner. ..." Said one allegedly to a newspaper reporter, "It was sho' worth it." Another stated the judge "asked me could a nigger whip a white man. I didn't say nuthin' but knowed one niggah that could. ..." Particularly repulsive to one newspaper was Sam Watson,

> well-known negro character, [who] celebrated Johnson's victory by parading up and down Main street by waving a flag and telling what he knew about "de bestest man on deck." He was raked in by Bicycleman Friedie. He was ordered to leave the city and stay away until the first of the year.[8]

The state of race relations was also evident in the debate over the showing of two movies in 1915: *The Nigger*, which appeared in August, and *The Birth of a Nation*, the film version of *The Clansman*, which was shown in December. These films so offended some black leaders that they—led by Rev. Hugh Shannon, pastor of Alexander Chapel—called on Mayor Bosse to prohibit their being shown. The mayor viewed *The Nigger* with his chief of police and controller and decided to ban its showing. The film, starring William Farnum, portrayed an attack on a small white girl by a black man, the burning of the man at the stake, and the burning of "a whole flock of negroes in another part. The plot deal[t] with a man who becomes governor of his state and it is later found out that he has negro blood."[9] The theatre owner, however, protested that he had been unable to find a substitute film, and that combined with pressure from white citizens prompted the mayor to permit the showing of the movie on the evening of August 14. Afterwards 500 "representative business men and women . . . stated that there was nothing in the picture to cause race prejudice on the part of white people against negroes."[10]

Shannon's small group was, however, totally unsuccessful in the case of D. W. Griffith's work. The response to his earlier decision prompted the mayor to create a "board of censorship" to preview the film "and all future films on which complaints are made." This solution allowed him to appear to be fair to those on whose vote he depended and also to guarantee a decision pleasing to white bigotry. The board, all white, included such Bosse loyalists as Richard Rosencranz and Mrs. George Clifford. It listened to Shannon's committee, by now identified as the local chapter of the National Association for the Advancement of Colored People, which like chapters in many other cities was organized to oppose the showing of the Griffith movie. Its members then watched the film. Despite Shannon's "eloquent plea for the condemnation of the film on the ground that Thomas Dixon . . . had as his purpose the elimination of the colored people" and that the recent lynching in Henderson had underscored the need to restrain the lynch mob spirit, the committee decided to permit the showing of the movie. Members were "impressed with the fact that the picture depicts a very unhappy and unfortunate condition, but it reflects credit and not discredit on the present-day negro." They asserted that it portrayed "the vicious characteristics of the negro as the result of slavery and one is impressed with the wonderful development of the colored race since those unhappy days."[11]

As elsewhere, Griffith's picture was well received in Evansville. Aside from the objections of some black leaders, the only public criticism came from the progressive *Evansville Press*, a Scripps newspaper founded in July 1906. The paper reported that the film, shown on a nine by ten-foot screen, was accompanied by a thirty-piece orchestra and realistic sound effects. It was admittedly stirring and thrilling, but nevertheless one-sided in its treatment of Reconstruction. Observed the reporter,

> The hero refuses to shake the hand of a colored man to whom he has been introduced, though the colored man has at that time done him no harm. The audience applauds. You see a white man, single-handed, clean up on a dozen negro men. Negro men are shown pursuing white girls, raiding white homes, rioting in the streets. There is no "back-flash" showing what the negroes had endured under slavery to explain the outrages some of them committed at the first moment of freedom.[12]

Given that sort of climate and the small size of Evansville's middle and upper classes, the first NAACP chapter was ephemeral. The group had a handful of members and met intermittently. Its officers, however, were the younger, more well-educated members of the black elite. Sallie Stewart was secretary in 1915, and in 1917 W. E. Best was elected president and Logan Stewart secretary. The chapter disintegrated after the war. The protest against the showing of the Griffith movie was the only public reference to the existence of a chapter until its reorganization in early 1931. (Not surprisingly, it might be added, Bosse's review board ceased to exist after acting on this single instance of public controversy.)[13]

Nor is it surprising that local expressions of racial bigotry grew more blatant in these years. In the fall of 1907, for example, the local chapter of the Christian Endeavor Society invited Senator Benjamin Tillman of South Carolina to speak at Evans Hall. Hosted as well by some local Democrats, the well-known Negrophobe addressed an enthusiastic overflow crowd of 2,000, and in the course of his three-hour speech denounced the Fourteenth and Fifteenth amendments and defended lynching as a solution to what he termed "the nigger question." The Democratic daily reported that there was "little in his address that intelligent people of Evansville would not agree to, though few would have the hardihood to express themselves at the meeting."[14] Some whites disagreed. The mayor, Democrat John W. Boehne, and some members of Christian Endeavor expressed disgust at what they termed incendiary as well as inappropriate comments at a CE meeting. The Democratic newspaper replied by comparing Tillman's remarks to Daniel Webster's Seventh of March speech. Three years later, local historian Frank Gilbert decried the "hordes" of "ignorant, shiftless niggers" in Evansville. The root of the problem, he wrote, was education, which spoiled rather than helped blacks, all but a few of whom thought themselves equal if not superior to whites and too good to work. The solution was returning blacks to the rural South, where they were better suited.[15]

Whatever their origins, the evidences of racial separation grew more marked between 1900 and the First World War. Those few blacks who attempted to enter white neighborhoods—as the Davises learned in 1907— were subject to verbal and physical abuse. In 1914 white residents in the neighborhood of Second and Jefferson streets learned that the AME Zion congregation planned to purchase the former Jefferson Avenue Presbyterian Church edifice, which some white businessmen had earlier desired as a movie theatre. Neighborhood protest had blocked the efforts of the businessmen, but Zion's announcement so outraged whites that they dropped their objection to the theatre. The black congregation decided to locate their church in Oakdale.[16]

The high degree of existing separation of the races meant, however, that formal rules were less needed than in cities to the south. Hence, segregation by custom and by law coexisted. It was understood, for instance, that the city's YMCA was off limits to blacks, as was the YWCA, established in 1911. By contrast, a year after the gift to build two buildings from Andrew Carnegie led to the establishment of the Evansville Public Library in 1912, the library board opened a "colored Branch" at Cherry and Church streets, near McFarland Chapel.[17]

The record was also mixed in transportation and movie theatres. As Evansville was the last stop before Dixie, passenger trains departing the city southward had white and colored sections, as required by Kentucky law, even though a section of the trip was in southern Vanderburgh County. The state of Kentucky brought suit in Evansville in 1909, in fact, after whites complained that they were forced to mingle with blacks on a run from Evansville to Louisville. The problem appeared to stem from the fact that one railroad line provided a combination baggage and passenger car for blacks immediately behind the engine and could not turn the car around at its Evansville station, thus forcing whites in the next car to be close to blacks during part of the journey. On Evansville streetcars, by contrast, custom rather than law continued to dictate that blacks sit in the rear of the car. That was undoubtedly due to the infrequency with which blacks used the trolley. In the case of the new movie theatres, however, those owners who did admit blacks established Jim Crow sections in the balcony. At least one theatre—the Majestic—also had a separate entrance for blacks.[18]

The desire to formalize racial separation seemed to grow with the passing of time. The school board ruled in November 1909 that in teachers' meetings blacks and whites had to sit in separate sections. Probably because white and black parents and students had few public contacts, other rules were not needed until April 1918, when a group of black students refused to sing at a convention of music educators at the auditorium of Evansville High School. The students had learned that their parents, who had been invited to the concert, would be required to sit in a special section. Speaking for them in a closed door meeting prior to the concert was M. C. Bryant, principal of Third Avenue School, who explained to board member Abe Strouse and principal John Chewning that the Evansville children had been deeply hurt by the display of racial discrimination and that they felt they were singing "not for the music but for the entertainment of others." Said Mrs. Moses Davis (whose husband, ironically, was in the American army in France) "white people will go anywhere . . . sitting next to their colored chauffeurs. Yet they object [to] sitting next to a colored person in a theatre. It is not consistent and it wounds us to have the distinction made."[19]

Strouse and Chewning replied that the seating had been segregated because the clerk of the board had assumed that the practice of the movie theatres ought to be extended to school concerts. After a twenty-minute delay they decided to allow the black parents to sit where they wished. A day later, however, board member Howard Roosa, editor of the *Courier*, objected to the fact that black parents "were allowed to be seated promiscuously *[sic]* in the auditorium." Terming this a violation of board regulations segregating the races, "which works for the best interests of both," he declared that Bryant should be fired for advocating "race promiscuity." A week later, the board voted to severely reprimand Bryant and to segregate all future concerts. Roosa insisted lamely that "it is no more segregating against the colored people than it is against the white people. It has been proven that the two races can not mix."[20]

That argument was used with increasing frequency. The new facility for the treatment of tuberculosis, Boehne Camp Hospital, opened a "special ward" for blacks, and the city's three hospitals continued treating blacks in Jim Crow quarters, where conditions were crowded and often unsanitary. Patients were bedded next to each other without regard to the nature of their illnesses. As early as 1902, moreover, public meeting halls previously available to blacks for meetings, including the Masons' building, were closed to them, and as a result black fraternal orders had to rent or build their own structures. By 1904 the only public meeting hall that blacks could use was Evans Hall, but as S. S. Dupee observed, access could be obtained only by "influential members of the race."[21] Sometime between 1904 and 1910 blacks were also "barred from all the parks where refreshments are served. . . ."[22] Public celebrations, therefore, were even more segregated. Memorial services for the assassinated president in 1901 were held in different locations—the whites at Evans Hall, and the blacks at McFarland Chapel. Separate Decoration Day observances were held, and Fourth of July and Labor Day parades no longer had the obligatory black contingent at the end.[23]

Race consciousness was especially acute in the public schools. Symptomatic of that was the case of a hapless young girl, who was suspended for a week when parents at Blankenburg School complained to the school board that she was black. After an investigation by the health department "proved" that she was white, the board re-admitted her.[24] In this regard, the minutes of the school board reflect the continuation of a custodial approach to black educators, whose personal lives were of great interest to school board members. They were also filled with reminders of the largesse of whites toward black Evansville.[25]

During 1902, the Evansville school board, led by A. C. Rosencranz, commenced a revision of the school curriculum for blacks. Graduation requirements at the high school were cut from four to three years, the number of Latin and "higher mathematics" courses was lowered, Latin was made an optional course of study, and a number of commercial courses were added. The board sought "to take out of the curriculum the things that are of no practical benefit to the pupils and to substitute matters that are very essential . . . [for] the pupils of the school when they come to enter their life work."[26]

The commitment to vocational education was subsequently expanded. Such a course of study, to be sure, was also developed at the white schools, but in the black schools it became the core of the curriculum. The board contacted Wilberforce College in the fall of 1904 to locate a instructor to oversee domestic science, and through that effort hired Beulah Davis, a Hampton Institute graduate and a former Tuskegee Institute instructor, and her husband, Moses, who became head of the manual training program. These classes were offered, however, only at Clark.[27]

The Clark graduates who attended college usually went to Wilberforce and Fisk, but some went to the heavily white Indiana State Teachers College, Indiana University, and even the University of Chicago. Helen Best and Pauline Thompson, members of the class of 1915, recalled that of their class of nine, four became educators. After attending the teachers' college in Terre Haute, they returned to Evansville to teach. Increasingly, however, young men and women attempted to find work after graduation and not to continue their formal education.[28]

The spokesmen for vocational education in the black community were numerous. From the turn of the century to his death in 1913, S. S. Dupee was the most articulate defender of this strategy. In the spring of 1916, the secretary of the Colored YMCA and the two persons recently associated with the establishment of the local chapter of the NAACP, Hugh Shannon and Sallie Stewart, called on the secretary of the Evansville Chamber of Commerce to urge his assistance in the expansion of vocational education. Stewart reported that high school graduates with scientific and foreign language training were being hired as porters and trash haulers. Responding to unnamed black critics, they insisted that youth should be trained for the vocations which are in demand in order to guarantee "the immediate uplift of the race." Evansville needed beautiful lawns, they argued, not more black doctors or lawyers.[29]

In June 1916 a subcommittee on education—part of the larger Baptisttown concerns of the Chamber—met with "representative colored citizens" in the Chamber office to "ascertain the most striking needs of vocational education for the colored people of the city."[30] The group, which included principals Best, Cox, and Miller, Mr. and Mrs. Davis, testified to the need for more courses and better facilities for training carpenters, home decorators, gardeners, domestics, laundry and cigar workers, and custodians. The embryonic NAACP chapter supported this, but the strongest support was clearly among white leaders. The Chamber committee on Baptisttown seemed particularly interested in resolving the 40 percent truancy rate among black youth, for example, and vocational education was their solution, even though the truancy problem was symptomatic of deeper causes. The blacks who met with Chamber officials had no difficulty accepting an educational system which mired blacks in domestic and public service positions.[31]

This inquiry occurred as local schools engaged in a more comprehensive examination of the curriculum, due to new federal and state legislation on vocational training. A substantial expansion of vocational education in all schools followed. Toward that end, in the fall of 1917, the board authorized the expansion of Clark, but allocated money only for the purchase of 10,000 bricks and the payment of black students at fifteen cents an hour in the summer to build the addition. To be directed by Moses Davis, boys at Clark would thus receive what the board thought would be valuable practical training. (No white school, however, was built in this manner.) The project was not completed until 1920, in part because of Davis's enlistment in the AEF. (A. M. Meeks took Davis's place when the latter left. Davis did not return to Evansville when his term of service expired.) Using the same approach, in 1920 the board also opened a cafeteria at Clark, to be staffed and supplied by female students in cooking and domestic science classes.[32]

Such strategies revealed the continued refusal of the board to offer equal as well as separate education. Black students could obtain eighth grade and high school training only at Clark. The relative decline of river traffic and the rapid growth of Baptisttown meant that those students who wished more than a grade school education had to walk a considerable distance to obtain it. Blacks had no kindergarten facilities until January 1916, when A. C. Rosencranz donated a property at Gum and Elliott streets for that purpose. Five years earlier, he had also given property in Oakdale so that parents would not have to send their children all the way to Governor Street School. Students in grades one through six in that neighborhood, those in rural environs of the city, as well as others outside Baptisttown, Blankenburg, and Oakdale, thus faced a considerable trek to school. Especially difficult was the situation facing black orphans living at the asylum on West Indiana Street, who had to walk fifteen blocks to attend Third Avenue School.[33]

In the fall of 1919 Governor had 585 students, Clark 154, Third Avenue 231, and Oakdale twenty-six. None of the schools had an auditorium, and hence the black community was forced to use Evans Hall—razed in the early 1930s—for school programs. Playground equipment was not provided at Governor until May 1913, but the board never got around to building a swimming pool, as it had for whites. The physical condition of these schools was revealed by the board's capital needs inventory of June 1919: Third Avenue had no indoor toilets (only Howell, among white schools, shared that distinction); Governor needed electric lighting throughout the building; and Clark's laboratories were unheated.[34]

Salaries also continued to lag behind those of white educators. The board adopted its first salary schedule in 1914, which strengthened the discriminatory compensation practices of the past. Dominated by appointees of Mayor Bosse, the board set the maximum salary for the teachers and the principal of Clark High School at $900 and $1,250, respectively, while placing limits of $1,600 and $3,150, respectively, on their white counterparts. In the summer of 1918 the board replaced this de facto form of discrimination with an explicitly Jim Crow form: In the future black teachers were to be paid according to the white salary schedule of the previous year. This practice continued for several decades. Hence in March 1920 the board agreed to pay black elementary teachers $1,350, on the average, for the coming year, as compared with $1,500 among whites, and Principal Best was to receive $2,000. (The lowest salary for any white principal was $700 higher.)[35]

Despite these obstacles, Evansville's black community continued to support its schools. The addition to Clark was greeted enthusiastically, and shortly after the project was completed, the board agreed to a request from students and teachers that the school be renamed Frederick Douglass. Parents and teachers held fund-raising affairs—often concerts at Evans Hall—to purchase books

13.   A class at Governor Street School, about 1910. P. T. Miller, the principal, is standing in the center of the last row. Special Collections, University of Southern Indiana.

and equipment. Graduation ceremonies at the high school remained extremely important, and close ties between religious and educational leaders were evident at those well-attended gatherings. The thirst for evening school also remained great. In November 1907, for instance, fourteen classes were offered, six in the black schools. As an economy move, the board of the Bosse era pared the number of night classes, but demand in the black community remained high.[36]

The small cadre of black educators—thirty-three in 1920—wielded enormous influence in the black community, partially due to the length of their service. Especially notable were P. T. Miller, the principal of Governor Street School from 1906 until its closing in 1928, after which he served as assistant principal of Lincoln before his retirement in 1931; and J. D. Cox, principal of Third Avenue in 1907, a post which he held for several decades. Undoubtedly the most influential was William E. Best (1884–1959), a West Indian who received some undergraduate training in New York and graduated from Indiana State Teachers' College. He also attained a master's degree from Indiana University. Best was hired as principal of Clark in 1913, after having held a similar position in Mt. Vernon, Indiana. Recalled as a gracious, diplomatic, and highly intelligent person, he became the most highly respected spokesman for black Evansville in his thirty-eight years as the high school principal. He was also a devout lay member of Alexander Chapel, and was eventually ordained to the ministry.[37]

Black educators remained the backbone of the black middle and upper classes and the role models for hundreds of black Evansvillians. Among the most affluent and highly educated citizens of the community, they were involved in many civic activities outside the classroom. As demonstrated by the example of Best, the connection between teachers and the churches was especially strong. One event in March 1909 was typical. Two teachers, Georgia Williams and Ida Clark, arranged a program to help Alexander Chapel pay off its debt. Over 250 attended the elaborate affair, in which eighth grade pupils exhibited the "wand drill," W. F. Cooper sang a solo, three students performed scenes from *Julius Caesar*, and Moses Davis recited Mark Antony's funeral oration.[38]

Regardless of the loyalty of the black community to its schools, the devotion of its educators, and the linkages between the schools and the churches, the fact remained that the Evansville's racial climate was increasingly inhospitable. Despite the growing vocationalism of the schools, blacks trained in the skilled trades found little opportunity in the river city, and thus publicly supported vocational education either mired those who remained in the city in service positions or drove those with unwanted skills to other cities, where employment could be secured.

That ought not to have been unexpected, for in the first two decades of the twentieth century, black Evansvillians were subjected to an enormous amount of adverse reporting among those most influential in shaping public images of Afro-Americans. To be sure, some opinionmakers, like the leading local historian, John E. Iglehart, simply ignored blacks, but the black community was attacked by unflattering images, especially in newspaper editorials, cartoons, news articles, and headlines. Death notices continued to be segregated, and classified advertisements carried racial preferences in most housing and job listings. Based on two strains of Southern racism, the fundamental images of Afro-Americans in this era were the docile, child-like creature whose comic behavior was to be treated condescendingly, and the brutal, savage beast whose criminality was to be scorned and severely punished, often extralegally. Each of these had prominent advocates. The latter was more persuasive in periods of social stress, such as the summer of 1903. Sometimes both images, however, were intermingled.[39]

Democratic and Republican newspaper cartoons regularly reflected both positions. Blacks were ridiculed for their appetite for possum, sweet potatoes, and watermelon. Black men were frequently reported having extramarital sexual relations, only to be caught by their large, boisterous wives wielding rolling pins or washboards. They were also allegedly so fond of sweets and fried chicken that petty theft was a way of life among them.[40]

These stereotypes were, unfortunately, reinforced by those blacks who played the roles assigned to them, and sometimes black leaders themselves provided support for those who thought blacks subhuman. Probably most damn-

14.   Black roustabouts on the Evansville wharf, about 1910. The photograph
seems to have been staged, probably to reinforce stereotypes of black workers.
Photograph files, *Evansville Courier*.

ing were the observations of Dr. Dupee, who portrayed the black middle and
upper classes as threatened by the shiftless masses. Seeking the recognition of
white leadership, he provided ample fuel for those who believed that blacks
deserved second-class status.[41]

Although the image of the childlike, carefree, music-loving, and ignorant
black was attractive, as shown by the popularity of black and white minstrel
shows prior to the First World War, the more prevalent image was that of the
worthless, brutal creature who threatened the community's well-being, and
especially its white women.[42] If newspapers of this period are to be believed,
fighting, gambling, theft, prostitution, and lasciviousness were synonymous
with black Evansville. Adjectives such as bestial and savage were often
appended, like the word brutal, to "colored," even when reports of the lynchings of innocent black men in the South were printed. Initially a common feature of *Courier* articles during election campaigns, by the turn of the century
both newspapers exhibited little difference in this respect.[43]

This approach seems to have been most popular in the Progressive era
between 1899 and 1916. Typical was the newspaper report of the trial of several blacks following a "rough house" in Baptisttown. One defendant, Alex

Johnson, was described as "very black, big-eyed, with a pie demolishing mouth and an exceedingly dense look on his face."[44] Also commonplace were stories of wanton assaults on whites by blacks. A variation of this theme was the alleged proclivity of black men to make lewd comments to white women. Less frequent, but more serious, were stories of physical attacks on white women.[45] On July 23, 1907, for example, the *Journal-News* printed a story on page one of the arrest of a "bold negro" in a "sensational case" in which the man had allegedly "been annoying the [white] girl for the past week, meeting her on the street and jostling her about with his arm." The man purportedly "followed her about a great part of the time, too, until Monday afternoon, when he patted her on the shoulder." The paper rued the fact that the "big black man" would be tried only for assault and battery, despite his being, according to the paper, a "brazen offender."[46]

An especially lurid case was reported in early 1904, when a black man was arrested for sexual relations with a fourteen-year-old white girl. The man alleged that "he had been intimate and on the most familiar terms with the entire [white] family," which he said had sanctioned his living with the girl. His testimony "was overruled by the court." According to the Republican editor, the prosecutor made "an eloquent plea to the jury to rid Evansville of such brutal characters," and the jury of twelve white men found him guilty after deliberating ten minutes. He was then sentenced to twenty years at Michigan City prison.[47]

The case obviously evoked the fear, expressed by the Republican editor, that "race lines [were] eliminated and morality [was] low in Evansville." The revelation that the black man and the young white girl had been living together for several years, with the family's blessing, was especially shocking. "When the white has fallen so low as not to consider criminal relationship with the negro as unusual, the laws of the state should come to her rescue and raise her out of degradation."[48]

Enforcement of the state's antimiscegenation statute was a feature of local criminal justice—a practice which distinguished the city from many Northern communities. Usually the cases involved a black man and a white woman. As in the late nineteenth century white men were sometimes charged with soliciting black prostitutes, but in these cases—as in those not involving prostitutes—the punishment for the white man was light. The anti-miscegenation law and the tendency of judges to mete heavy sentences on black men may have blunted extralegal acts against black offenders.[49]

Reports of increased brutality strengthened the antiblack mood of the era, and that led to a series of police crackdowns on the black community.[50] Black clergymen like Rouse supported these, as they were scornful of the hundreds of idle young men in the city who were easy prey to the scores of low-life dens. Rouse gained front-page coverage in 1903 after becoming "spiritual advisor" to an unfortunate youth, George Jackson, who was convicted of murder and hanged at Michigan City. Before his execution, Jackson explained that his life should serve as a warning to wayward black youth.[51]

Unfortunately, the real problem was a discriminatory judicial system. Jackson's fate should have been a clue, as he had been arrested and convicted in less than a day. Despite defense motions for a new trial based on Jackson's ignorance of the seriousness of the charge against him and his drunken state at the time of his arrest, the youth was denied a review and promptly hanged.[52] The prevailing sentiment at the time was best expressed by the Evansville Businessmen's Association, forerunner of the Chamber of Commerce, which in October 1903 declared that "the greatest menace to peace and good order in the city is the number of worthless negroes (which bye the bye congregate in all river towns) who may be found in this city."[53]

Efforts toward that end, which tended to ignore the rights of black citizens, were expanded over the succeeding years. In August 1907, for instance, police began forcing "shiftless and loitering negroes without visible means of support, whose pastime [sic] is to get drunk and create trouble in fights . . . to go to work or leave the city." The safety board instituted what it termed "a weeding process such as it never has experienced [for] notorious Baptisttown." Its chairman, furniture manufacturer Benjamin Bosse, proposed abolition of the all-black hose house because he argued its crew was prone to drunkenness. The board also sought to clean up the waterfront, which would be "thoroughly scrubbed and washed of all offensive black humanity."[54]

Much discussion also surfaced regarding the use of cocaine by the city's blacks. Large quantities of the drug were apparently readily available from local pharmacists, some of whom sold it illegally to a largely black clientele. That "sniffing" and the injection of cocaine were commonplace prompted city authorities to arrest druggists who sold the drug without a prescription. That was followed by an effort to place the city's "immoral resorts" under supervision of the board of public health.[55] The mayor also proposed the creation of a city workhouse because many persons, mostly blacks, committed petty crimes in order to be jailed and "take life easy, fattening off the people's money."[56]

These efforts at social sanitation were uneven. During Boehne's term the sale of liquor in the city was curtailed, as were street-corner gatherings of blacks, socialists, and hucksters. Police increased their attention to vagrancy, cocaine use, prostitution, gambling, and drunkenness. Although a red light district was never formally created, it appears that city authorities and local madames worked out an informal understanding regarding the controlled practice of that vice within limited boundaries.[57]

Political considerations affected the implementation of other proposals. The city workhouse did not materialize because Boehne's advisors suggested the project was probably illegal. The elimination of the black fire crew was dropped because of the outrage the idea generated in the black community, which Boehne wished to bring into the Democratic fold. Most important, as newspaper and court records disclose, the vigorous prosecution of vice in the black community was not necessarily of political benefit. Payoffs from vice, in votes and political contributions, ultimately proved to be too attractive to Boehne's successors to be eliminated. Of all mayors prior to the 1940s, however, Boehne may have been the most earnest and thorough in efforts to clean up the city.[58]

Criminal records afford a unique insight into what all of this meant for black Evansvillians. During the administrations of three different mayors—Democrats Boehne in 1908 and Bosse in 1915, and Republican Charles Heilman in 1912—the arrest and conviction of blacks remained disproportionately high. In one six-month period in 1908, 38.4 percent of those arrested were black. Of these slightly over half were convicted, as compared with only a third of those whites who had been arrested. Blacks generally were charged, as in other cities, with petty larceny or drunk and disorderly conduct. Only 15 percent were indicted for crimes of violence, a quarter of which were homicides—a much lower rate than among whites.[59]

Similar patterns recurred in 1912 and 1915. In a six-month period in 1912 police arrested 323, 35.6 percent of whom were Afro-American. Of these, 47.8 percent were convicted, as compared with 16.8 percent of the whites. Petty larceny was the charge in 60 percent of the cases involving blacks, but violent crimes were charged in only thirteen cases. In 1915 city police arrested 301 in that six-month span, and of these 110, or 36.5 percent, were blacks, about two-thirds of whom were convicted. The conviction rate among whites, by contrast, was one-third. Petty theft was the leading cause of the arrest of blacks, accounting for 58.2 percent of the cases. Ten cases of violent crimes were recorded, half of which led to acquittals.[60]

The consistently high proportion of arrest and conviction suggested the continuation of post-Civil War patterns of capricious vigor encouraged by the prejudices and whims of judges, policemen, and all-white juries, and abetted by the low social status and economic clout of blacks. That is underscored in both a statistical overview of arrest and conviction patterns and an examination of specific cases. In what was an all-too-common occurrence, the *Journal-News* of January 23, 1905, carried a bold headline, "Negroes Assail 10-Year-Old-Girl" and the subheadlines, "Child Dragged through a Field" and "Approach of Market Wagon Causes Brutes to Throw Victim into Ditch—Bloodhounds on Trail." The Perry Township incident purportedly happened in the same neighborhood in which a girl had been allegedly raped and killed six years earlier, and "the negro who committed that crime was never caught." It was fortunate that this case occurred in the dead of winter and not under circumstances resembling those of July 1903, for on the following day the newspaper retracted the story—in much smaller type—acknowledging that the girl had lied.[61]

Stereotypes of black criminality helped create this unfortunate story, which doubtlessly reinforced an adverse climate in which assaults on innocent blacks were as commonplace as arrests and convictions. In the spring of 1901, for example, a black section hand was speedily convicted of manslaughter in the death of a white man, although he claimed to be defending himself against the racial taunts and physical abuse of the drunken white. In late December 1906 a railway foreman shot and killed a black man whom he claimed had threatened him. The county coroner promptly ruled self-defense, and the white was freed, despite pleas from Rouse and other members of the Colored Ministerial Association for a more thorough inquiry. By contrast, when blacks committed crimes against whites justice was swift and sure, as two cases in 1908 demonstrate: that of a man who reportedly killed a married white woman with whom he had been sexually intimate, and received a life sentence for second-degree manslaughter; and that of a drunken coal miner killed by a white policeman who had mistakenly broken into his dwelling looking for a fugitive and shot the miner instead, who the policeman said had threatened his life.[62]

The most striking instance occurred in February 1913, when the son of B. F. Von Behren, prominent furniture manufacturer and civic leader, shot and killed three black workers in cold blood at his father's factory. "This is what comes of your hiring those Negroes out there for me to boss," shouted the youth as he was taken to the police station, where he was arraigned on a charge of first-degree murder. The accused murderer told reporters there that he had been threatened by one of the blacks. Members of the Colored Ministerial Alliance expressed sympathy for the slain workers and called for a suspension of judgment until the law had taken its course. They also praised the expressions of sympathy which had been shown to the families of the alleged killer as well as those of his victims. White leaders were mute on the matter.[63]

The Von Behren family hired three prominent attorneys to defend their son, and in May—a day before his trial was to begin—the regular judge in the case surrendered his position to a special judge. In a private session the special judge permitted the youth to withdraw his plea of insanity and to enter a plea of guilty to the charge of manslaughter in the death of one of the three workers. Von Behren was subsequently sentenced to two to twenty-one years at Jeffersonville prison, whence he departed immediately. The judge claimed that under the circumstances the youth had been given the maximum penalty. He also asserted that otherwise the young man would have been acquitted by reason of insanity or there would have been a hung jury.[64]

The Democratic editor promptly supported the decision of this Democratic judge, but the Republican editor declared that ordinary people would think that favoritism had been shown. To him, the obvious problem was the politics and the social status of the Von Behren family. The *Press* ridiculed the decision by inquiring if all murderers henceforth would receive comfortable jail accommodations, secret hearings, and light sentences in order to spare them the embarrassment of a public trial.[65]

None of the newspapers had ever hinted that race was a central issue. That was especially noteworthy in light of the fact that less than two weeks after the Von Behren shooting, a black man had shot a white man, who happened to be a Republican candidate for county surveyor, in what he termed self-defense. The next day a jury found him guilty of murder and sentenced him to life imprisonment. Even if the black man had been well off, it is highly unlikely that he would have secured the same verdict as Von Behren. Had he been white, it is also likely that the course of justice would not have been so swift.[66]

However critical they were of the behavior of the black masses, black leaders were sensitive to these nuances, and—as in the shooting in 1906—spoke out when the interests of the race were at stake. In mid-May Rev. W. W. Townsend circulated a petition to remove the county prosecutor because he permitted a secret hearing and did not insist on a trial after the grand jury had indicted the white youth. Five hundred blacks signed the petition, which was turned over to the members of the Colored Ministerial Association, the "Colored Law and Order League," and the National Negro Business League chapter for action, but there is no record of its fate. One may safely assume it was ignored by white authorities. The only black attorney at the time, John H. Wilson, also filed a lawsuit against young Von Behren on behalf of the mother of one of the other two slain men and requested a special prosecutor in the two murder cases still pending. Both requests were dismissed.[67]

Given the absence of black jurors, the paucity of black attorneys, the poverty and illiteracy of most blacks, and the predilections of white authorities, the outcomes of the two cases of homicide in February 1913 were hardly surprising. They afford a vivid illustration of the state of race relations and of the rights and opportunities of black Evansvillians on the eve of America's entrance into World War I. These cases, rooted in many decades of racism, help to explain why the decade of the 1920s, in which the Red Scare and the Ku Klux Klan would predominate, represented the maturation of racial discrimination in Evansville, not—as in some other cities in the North—its birth.

Race Relations in the Era of the First World War and the Ku Klux Klan 1917–1930

Evansville's black community approached the First World War with hopes that their loyal and enthusiastic support would lead to an improvement in their living conditions.[1] A few days after America entered the war, Evansville's blacks demonstrated that they, too, wished to support the war effort wholeheartedly. The city's "Patriotic Day" at the newly built Coliseum on April 14, 1917, included a program of drills and music by black pupils. Leaders of the Colored YMCA volunteered their services by developing a Boy Scout troop, supporting Red Cross and Liberty Loan drives, and offering their grounds for the drilling of black enlistees and draftees. Ernest Tidrington, the lone black policeman and leader of the Pythians, unofficially attempted to raise a "Southern Indiana Colored Battalion" of the Indiana National Guard. Out of that came the guard's first black company.[2]

Such efforts occurred despite the fact that no blacks served on the draft registration drive committee or the draft board, or on the campaign steering committees of the Red Cross, Liberty Loan, Patriot Fund (a forerunner of the Community Chest), or the Evansville College fund drive. Nevertheless, a bold headline in the *Journal-News* on May 28, 1918, announced, "Colored People Are Patriotic." The paper noted that Logan Stewart was head of the "Colored Division" of the Patriot Fund (located at the bottom of the group's organizational chart). Black draftees were not inducted in large numbers until August 1918, when the call for white registrants fell off. Consequently the black community organized a gala send-off ceremony that month, which Tidrington chaired. A parade led by members of the fraternal lodges and the Boy Scouts preceded a rousing farewell at the Coliseum, where Tidrington delivered an oration on "The Negro Soldier" and funeral director W. A. Gaines urged the young men to do their best in the fight against the slavery and torture that their forefathers had suffered under and defeated. Subsequently Sallie Stewart organ-

15. Black schoolchildren in the parade sending off black troops in the late summer of 1918. Photograph files, *Evansville Courier*.

ized a committee which raised $450 to finance a day nursery for children whose fathers were in France and whose mothers had gone to work.[3]

The substantial effort of the black community did nothing, however, to weaken the grip of Jim Crow. The school board's actions following the April 1918 concert illustrated that vividly. While the war was being waged, the exploits of black soldiers from the city were unpublicized in the city's newspapers, even though one—Alfred T. Duncan, who served in a trench mortar battalion of the 92nd Division—received a distinguished service medal from the French government for his valor. Shortly after the armistice, black veterans organized a branch of the American Legion. Black pastors were invited to participate in planning for the first of the "welcome home" ceremonies in the city, but the parade on January 22, 1919, was a clue to the status that the veterans would have: black troops brought up the rear. Nine months later a massive parade led by General Leonard Wood again found black veterans at the end. The "Honor Roll," the so-called official war record of the city, overlooked blacks, as did John E. Iglehart's history of the city published a few years later.[4]

In the period immediately before and after the war, Evansville experienced no race riots, unlike such Northern cities as East St. Louis and Chicago. As compared with Cleveland, which also had no racial disturbances in this period, Evansville's industries were not diversified. In Chicago, which also had little diversification, the stockyards were the focal point of racial hostility. Evansville's blacks did, however, have access to menial jobs, especially in service, and thus did not threaten the territory of white workers in the city's foundries, furniture factories, and newly emerging refrigerator and truck manufacturing plants. Like Cleveland, the residential pattern of black settlement was also an important factor in mitigating racial disturbances. Black workers did not have to pass through hostile German and upper Southern neighborhoods on their way to work, and they had the modest opportunity to expand their residential sections into the poorer white neighborhoods to the east and northeast of Baptisttown which were being vacated for more affluent residential subdivisions. This "safety valve" reduced the possibility of contested neighborhoods and lessened racial tensions in a critical period of race relations.[5]

One must also add that although Evansville's "black belt" had been taking shape for many years and, as in Chicago, social interchange between whites and blacks was exceedingly rare, the population of black Evansville did not increase between 1910 and 1940. That may have been the most important factor lessening the possibility of interracial clashes. The conflicts in Northern cities after 1915 were thus perhaps similar to those of Evansville in 1865 and 1903.[6]

The "Southern way" in race relations, which was becoming the "American way" by the 1920s, had been part of the culture of Evansville for decades. Separation of the races was becoming well established, but unlike the South Evansville's blacks retained their right to vote, which was used to gain modest concessions from local government. The principle of Jim Crow was not, moreover, as rigidly or as dogmatically applied in social relations for other reasons: the antislavery traditions of the Old Northwest and the efforts of a handful of white leaders (like industrialist A. C. Rosencranz, his son, Richard, and the rabbis of the Reformed Jewish Temple) to obtain a modicum of racial tolerance. Also important was Northern urban life, where the growth of the ghetto was rapid, and blacks were rapidly becoming separated from the rest of the community. Because contacts between blacks and whites were infrequent, custom rather than statute continued to dominate interracial relations. As William E. Wilson recalled, lower-class whites were especially vocal in their hostility to blacks.[7]

Perhaps most of all because of the small size of the black community, and especially of its middle and upper classes, the rise of the local Ku Klux Klan after 1921 was essentially unrelated to racial matters, as it was in many other cities.[8] There is no doubt that some men joined the Klan as a means of controlling the black community, but for most the Hooded Order held other promises. (See chapter 12.) Klan-era rhetoric, moreover, did not appreciably differ from the language of earlier days. Headlines and news stories identified blacks by race and not by name, as in the case of the May 4, 1921, issue of the *Courier*, which carried a large headline, "NEGRO IS NAMED," over the story describing the fact that Logan Stewart had been selected as the Republican candidate for the Seventh Ward City Council seat. News about blacks tended to stress criminal behavior, as in these headlines in the relatively liberal *Press* in 1924 and 1926: "Wave of Holdups Hits City; Negroes Held to Trial When Captured After Daring Act"; and "Evansville Negro Is Held In Assault."[9] Like its competitors, the *Press* also perpetuated the image of blacks as buffoons. In October 1924 it spoofed the campaign by announcing the candidacy of "Wash Funk of Baptisttown," and in the dialect that newspapers of the day seemed to enjoy printing, said that a vote for him was "like pouring gravy oveh yo' sweet potatoes. Hoddog!"[10]

Policemen and court officials also enforced the law as they had for many years, and the coming of the Klan to political power did little to change that. Throughout the decade violations of the liquor law and drunkenness were the most common in the local courts: 218 cases of the former and 597 of the latter between September 1921 and December 1922; and 219 and 704 cases, respectively, between December 1922, and November 1923. Similar statistics appeared in 1926 and 1927. Blacks were involved in about one-quarter of these cases. In the last year of Democratic city administration, 1925, police arrested blacks in slightly over 21 percent of all cases in City Court, and in the first year of the Klan-dominated Males administration, 1926, the proportion was nearly the same—20.2 percent. In police department record books between 1927 and 1929, blacks constituted 25 percent of the listings, and their crimes were chiefly petty theft, vagrancy, and drunkenness. The primary change instituted in law enforcement in the black community during the Klan era of county and city rule, ironically, was the hiring of more black policemen. (See chapter 12 for more detail.) Arrest and conviction rates, however, did not change.[11]

There is little doubt that during the 1920s the lines separating the races were as sharp, if not sharper, than ever before. In addition to movie theatres, waiting rooms in the city's new bus terminals were segregated. The closing of Black's Hotel (see chapter 10) meant that blacks traveling through the city had to find shelter in rooming houses or with relatives. Parks were closed to blacks, except for Barnett's Grove, east of town, which was reached by the interurban.

Segregated health care facilities, moreover, were expanded at Boehne Camp Hospital and Welborn-Walker Hospital. In both, black leaders promoted the improvement of health care while leaving segregation untouched. Health campaigns had been sponsored by the Negro Businessmen's League since at least 1915 and were a response to a death rate which was 50 percent higher among blacks than whites, in large part due to consumption. By the fall of 1928 a colored auxiliary of the county tuberculosis association was organized, in cooperation with Boehne Hospital and the Public Health Nursing Association, and Sallie Wyatt Stewart was selected as chairperson. As a result of the vigorous "Health and Cleanup Campaign" in Baptisttown, a new facility for blacks was opened in April 1929 at Boehne. Formerly the custodian's cottage, the space could handle eight patients.[12]

About the same time a group of black leaders, including Drs. Buckner and Jackson, attempted to build a hospital for the black community. To be named Mercy, the project was to handle fifty patients, as the city's three hospitals had limited space for blacks. Commenced in the summer of 1928, this ambitious effort failed, but in 1929 the private Welborn-Walker Hospital opened a Jim Crow "annex" at Sycamore and Elliott streets, probably as a result of the requests of the same black leaders. Open for several decades, local blacks eventually nicknamed this twelve-bed center "the butcher shop."[13]

16.   Douglass High School in 1924. The manual training building in the rear was erected after the First World War by Douglass students under the supervision of A. M. Meeks. The Douglass yearbook, *The Dougite*, 1924, was lent to the author by the late Douglas Lander.

17.   Douglass High School orchestra, mid-1920s. Alfred Porter, music instructor, is standing. Special Collections, University of Southern Indiana.

18. Douglass High School graduating class, about 1920. Photograph files, *Evansville Courier*.

19. Domestic Science class, Douglass High School. *The Dougite*, 1924.

20.   Douglass High School band, early 1920s. Special Collections, University
of Southern Indiana.

Perhaps the most vivid illustration of the racial mores of the 1920s, however, was the consolidation of all but one of the city's black schools into a new
one. Unlike Indianapolis and Gary, which did not establish fully segregated
schools until, 1927, Evansville had always had such schools. Like these cities,
the building of a new school exclusively for blacks was not a direct result of the
Klan.

In April 1924 the *Evansville Courier* reported that the school board had
begun to consider moving Douglass High School, as "it was not situated near
the center of the colored population."[14] By the end of the year the board,
appointed by Democratic mayors Benjamin Bosse and William Elmendorf,
adopted a five-year capital plan which included purchasing a site on Lincoln for
about $60,000 during the 1925–1926 term and erecting a building on it at a
cost of $400,000 during 1928–1929. Within five months it announced that it
had purchased all the lots in the block bounded by Lincoln, Garvin, McCormick, and Bellemeade—immediately to the east of the heart of Baptisttown—
and that it had decided to fence the entire block off as a playground for black
children, since Douglass and Governor schools had "the poorest playground
facilities of any of the public schools." A new elementary and high school was
to be built there, as present school arrangements were "very bad": the Douglass
and Governor school buildings were "ill-arranged and unsightly," and "[the
colored boys and girls should be encouraged by surroundings in which they
may take more pride."[15]

The plan drew immediate fire from residents to the south and east of the proposed school, as well as some others who were linked to the Ku Klux Klan, who claimed that the new school would encourage blacks to settle in their neighborhoods and thus devalue their property. Remonstrators appeared at several board meetings in May and August, but they did not deter the board from hiring an architect to develop plans for a new building. In September, however, the opponents—calling themselves the East Side Voters and Taxpayers League—informed the board that they had completed a study of their own and insisted that the board examine it. Given the fact that their study was presented during the early phases of a heated city election, the board was forced to take it seriously.[16]

After describing what they labeled "the Negro District," the opponents asserted that

> we must look for the negro to move and the district to grow northward toward Division Street. . . . Then too, the property in that direction is the kind which can be, figuratively speaking, attacked by the negro without doing serious damage. If such is true, nothing should be done which will hinder or tend to change the natural direction of the growing negro settlement. . . . [W]ith these streets [Lincoln and Garvin] made more important [as thoroughfares by the City Planning Commission], they will create natural barriers. . . . There is no animosity between the two races in Evansville; but both races believe that it is not conducive to good feeling, harmony, and the proper development of the city that they should intermingle to a great extent and especially is it not good for the colored people to reside in a locality given over to first class dwellings. The negro cannot afford expensive property, [and] does not desire to live away from his associates; but one such occupant can do serious damage to a first class residential district.[17]

Critics proposed that the school board hire an expert to look for alternative sites. They suggested several, including one to the northwest, bounded by Lincoln, Gordon, Canal, and Governor, even though that one and the others were admittedly more expensive and failed to meet state requirements preventing the location of school buildings near factories or railroad tracks. The board took the report under advisement and asked the school business manager to complete a feasibility study.[18]

On January 4, 1926, the business manager reported that the alternative sites were large enough for a new school and relatively inexpensive. Members of the board then met with remonstrators and instructed them to "provide ways and means of taking [the] present site off the hands of the school city at the purchase price, and . . . [h]ave [the] Real Estate Board appraise said property with no expense involved to the Board of Education." The protestors were also asked to secure options to purchase the alternative sites. In May, they announced to the board that they had made little headway. The debate quieted sharply thereafter, as the board took the tactic of allowing the remonstrators more time to meet its requests, probably knowing that they would be unable to do so.[19]

In the meantime, newly elected Mayor Herbert Males, a Klansman, appointed two new members to the five-member board, one of whom was Rev. J. L. Rake, pastor of the First Baptist Church and an advocate of religious instruction in the schools. The president of the board was banker C. B. Enlow, an Elmendorf appointee who had supported Males's candidacy. The new board waited until October 1927—more than a year after the alternatives were presented to the remonstrators—to announce that it would proceed with the original plan to build a school on the site it had purchased. By then, Klan activity in the city had waned. In late December the board arranged for the vacating of Mulberry Street between McCormick and Garvin, the purchasing of houses on that block, and the hiring of architects to plan a building to be located on Lincoln, between Garvin and McCormick. Sod was broken for the new building on March 1, 1928, and work on the project proceeded rapidly. School leaders boasted that the building was completed five months ahead of schedule and at the cost of $275,000, or twenty-four cents a square foot, "the smallest . . . of any modern school building erected here."[20]

The new school, opened in September 1928, included classrooms for elementary and secondary instruction and a combined manual instruction-gymnasium facility which seated 1,800. Rake, board president in 1928, and superintendent John Chewning spoke at the dedication ceremonies October 6. A few months later, Mayor Males, in his annual address to the City Council, echoed the comments of the two when he declared that the new structure was an expression of "true Americanism," as it guaranteed "equal educational opportunities to all children of the city."[21]

The absence of black speakers at the dedication was a symptom of the fact that Males's comments were either naive or hypocritical. Black organizations were not involved in the planning for the school and had not been asked to respond to the remonstrators. Neither had they been asked if they wished three neighborhood grade schools—Clark, Governor, and Oakdale—replaced by a central school on the edge of Baptisttown, which would require a number of students to travel a considerable distance to school. Even the naming of the school was secured without black participation. When a committee of school patrons petitioned the board in March 1928 to perpetuate the name Frederick Douglass, the board announced it had already selected a name—Lincoln—and that a stone cast with the letter L had been ordered.[22]

Like the building of "the butcher shop," the school board's decision reinforced the trend toward the concentration of blacks in the Baptisttown region. The new school was, nevertheless, the object of considerable pride in the black community. The building of Lincoln did narrow the hiatus somewhat between educational offerings for whites and blacks, but the gap remained large. The number of teachers remained the same through the 1920s, despite enrollment increases. During 1929–1930 there were thirteen teachers at the high school, seventeen at Lincoln elementary, and three at Third Avenue—a ratio of nineteen students per teacher at the high school and forty-four to one on the elementary level. In both cases the ratio was higher than that of the white

21. Charles E. Rochelle (left) and William E. Best (right), principals of Lincoln High School between 1913 and 1962, with two students. Special Collections, University of Southern Indiana.

schools. Salaries for black teachers also continued to differ from those of white teachers. William E. Best, for example—a veteran of sixteen years in the Evansville schools—was paid $3,300 for 1929-1930; compensation for the white principals ranged from $4,600 to $4,800. White high school teachers averaged $450 more per year than their black counterparts, and white elementary teachers $200 more.[23]

Other qualitative and quantitative differences persisted. Kindergarten classes were available for blacks only at Lincoln, not at Third Avenue. School nurses were provided at white schools but not at black schools. Annual "Field Day" exercises for black elementary students were offered for the first time in 1921—many years after the event was provided for white students—but they were not only segregated but held on a different day. The first school athletic director was hired in the same year, and interscholastic athletic events began to be scheduled—but only with other black schools. In the fall of 1921, Douglass fielded its first football team (playing its initial game with Douglass High of Henderson). The 1924 team, coached by John Shelburne and aided by Charles Rochelle, athletic business manager, extended its schedule to teams from Paducah, Louisville, Owensboro, St. Louis, Terre Haute, and East Chicago—long treks for athletes and their fans. High school students also formed many clubs, but competition in such activities as debate was limited to other black schools. Improved educational offerings undoubtedly contributed to the lowering of the illiteracy rate from 14.6 to 8.7 percent between 1920 and 1930. But unequal education's effects remained strong, as the rate in 1930 was six times higher than the rate for native whites. It remained sixteenth highest among the largest cities of America and higher than any city in Indiana, Illinois, or Michigan.[24]

As in the past, such circumstances motivated parents, teachers, and students to seek funds and volunteer support in the black community. Since the school board did not fund the purchase of band uniforms or instruments for black students, in the fall of 1920 the Evansville Federation of Colored Women and a group of black teachers raised $600 to buy instruments for the new band at Governor School. The following spring the proceeds from the first Field Day event were used to purchase band instruments and baseball uniforms. Governor's new football team, organized in the fall of 1923, took the field with equipment and uniforms purchased by parents, students, and teachers, and their coaches were volunteers. When Principal Best requested school board funding for a school newspaper at the high school in 1923, the request was taken "under advisement." Eventually the paper, like the yearbook which followed, was financed by donations.[25]

Black Evansville was understandably and justifiably proud of its students and faculty, but the struggle to maintain dignity in the face of racism was monumental. On the one hand, the community could look with pride to the fact that 2,000 regularly packed the Lincoln field to watch football games, where the Lions regularly defeated most opponents by large margins. Lincoln sponsored, moreover, several renowned musical organizations—a chorus, a band and orchestra, a harmonica band, and an elementary choir. Each had at least thirty members. The choir director was W. F. Cooper; Alfred Porter directed the band and orchestra; and Rochelle was in charge of the harmonica band, a favorite among white civic organizations. Douglass and Lincoln students consistently received extremely high ratings in attendance contests with other public schools, and in September 1928, they won Superintendent Chewning's contest for the best student body in the city. Criteria in the contest included attendance, citizenship, and extracurricular activities. And despite the emphasis on vocational training, a number of the high school graduates went on to college. The Douglass class of 1924, for example, included four who attended Howard, four who enrolled at the teachers' college in Terre Haute, and four at other schools.[26]

On the other hand, black students and faculty were often reminded that theirs was a unique part of local public education. A rumor in the late twenties that Lincoln and Central high schools were about to play an exhibition football match for charity led to a curt announcement from Superintendent Chewning that blacks would never play whites in his schools. Chewning also insisted that the band and orchestra play only spirituals. (That was probably a clue to the popularity of the harmonica band.) The Lincoln band also marched at the end in local parades.[27]

22. Douglass High School football team. William Best (standing, left) was the manager, and John Shelburne (standing, right) was the coach. *The Dougite*, 1924.

In spite of that, there was no doubt about the dedication of and the ability of teachers in the black schools. Among those joining the Douglass staff in the 1920s were Rochelle and Porter, Indiana State Teachers College graduates, both of whom remained on the high school staff until its closing in 1962. Together with such loyalists as Best, Sallie Stewart (subsequently dean of girls at Lincoln), and Fannie Snow, they consistently rated well under the "success system" of evaluation. That teachers were gaining in self-confidence and leadership skills was evident in 1924, when they organized a federation for social and professional benefit which would cooperate with the federation of white teachers in matters of common interest. Their commitment to community progress was also evident in the financial support that black teachers had given the drive to bring a college to Evansville in 1918. P. T. Miller, for example, had donated $100, a substantial portion of his salary. Yet blacks were, ironically, denied admission to the school, forcing students who wished higher education to travel at least 100 miles to the nearest college which would admit them and denying teachers access to courses which would enrich their work.[28]

Such relatively well-paid and articulate persons, however, were not universally praised in the black community. The most notorious instance of this was the charge filed by Tidrington, the black Seventh Ward power, against Principal Best in early 1928. Alleging immoral activities were occurring at Douglass—reminiscent of similar incidents involving anonymous persons and unspecified charges extending back to the 1880s—Tidrington claimed he had proof that Best had engaged in illicit relations with several students. When pressed by the board of education for evidence, he produced none, and the board unanimously exonerated Best and his students. The tone of the accusa-

23. The "Indiana Five"—Cardwell Osburn, Riddles Woodard, Milton Parish, Reuben Reeves, and Pete Whitney—and their singer, Nannie Glover. The group performed jazz concerts in the late 1920s on Evansville's first radio station, WGBF; the photograph was taken in its studio. Special collections, University of Southern Indiana.

tion suggested that what was really at stake was Tidrington's resentment of Best's influence in the white and black communities. Such incidents were rare, and the teachers in the black community seemed to fit harmoniously into a variety of programs designed to produce racial progress. The staunch support which teachers gave the black clergymen, and vice versa, continued to be much in evidence.[29]

The racial climate of the Klan-dominated 1920s, best revealed in the educational sector, was symptomatic of deeply rooted discrimination extending far before the turn of the century. The Klan was, moreover, preoccupied with law and order and anti-Catholic themes. Hence there was little need for, or interest in, an exclusionary zoning ordinance or physical intimidation of the black populace, practices developed in other Northern cities.

Some signs of change in race relations, in fact, surfaced in the decade. Identification by race in the city directory—a practice going back to 1891—unacccountably ceased in 1926. Racial terminology in the newspapers of the twenties shifted from "colored" to "Negro," and the use of adjectives like "brutal" and "worthless" was less frequent. More important, newspapers began to include some stories about the achievements of blacks, instead of stressing crime and childish behavior. Beginning in 1921, they also published weekly reports from correspondents at the various city schools. These columns were generally of equal length and undifferentiated by race. News of the exploits of the black high school teams, moreover, began to appear on the sports pages, although the amount and quality of coverage differed from that provided white schools. These developments were symptomatic of the hiring of journalists who were relatively more educated and progressive than their predecessors.[30]

During the 1920s there were other improvements in the quality of interracial contacts. Some semiprofessional athletic competition by the late twenties cut across racial lines, for example, and the district meeting of the GAR in October 1929 was an integrated affair.[31] Most substantial, however, was the formation of the Inter-Racial Commission. Seven blacks and twelve whites— some of whom had been members of the Baptisttown Committee—were invited by Jewish merchant Mose Strouse to the initial meeting on October 25, 1927, and three weeks later the nineteen formally created the commission by adopting a constitution. The purpose of the organization was

> to promote a better understanding and a more helpful relationship between the various racial groups living in Evansville; to investigate the physical, intellectual and social conditions under which the colored people live; to develop a program of service through material support, counsel, and cooperation with the leaders of that racial group; to keep the public informed upon such problems as exist and suggest methods whereby these conditions may be met; [and] to secure as far as possible the necessary equipment to deal with such conditions as need attention.[32]

The commission's first president was A. E. Craig, who was also the president of Evansville College. Other officers were Percy Logsdon, a prominent white businessman, W. E. Best, Sallie Stewart, and Richard Rosencranz. Harper and Best chaired the first committee of the organization, established to survey the state of the black community, and on January 23, 1928 its members reported two matters were of special concern—the poor health of the average black resident, and the future of the Colored YMCA. The latter had been recently closed by the board of the white YMCA, which had governed it for its twenty financially strapped years, because the recent discontinuation of the Community Fund had eliminated the black branch's chief source of income. Within a month a committee consisting of Strouse, Rosencranz, and Anna Bosse, widow of the former mayor, recommended that the IRC assist in securing a lease and renovating the Colored YMCA for use as a community center. Leaders insisted "that the Commission would stand as a counsellor and helper in this matter and that the attitude of the Commission would be to do something with the people working on this project and not something for them."[33]

On April 23, 1928, the IRC approved the creation of the Community Association, an all-black committee which would administer the community center. Strouse, Rosencranz, and Bosse were named members of a permanent subcommittee to advise the Community Association, and over the following several months raised nearly $4,700 to renovate and equip the former YMCA building. The Community Center was opened on October 29. In the same month the IRC announced that its membership had been expanded to twenty-six, twelve of whom were black. In addition to those mentioned earlier, Afro-American members included such prominent citizens as Rev. L. S. Smith of Liberty Baptist Church—Rouse's successor—and T. B. Neely, former secretary of the Cherry Street YMCA and now secretary of the Community Center. White members—aside from those listed before—included Albion Fellows Bacon, Protestant pastors Henry Marcotte and Ewald Kochritz, and Rabbi Jack Skirball. Most had been associated with progressive causes in the decade, notably campaigns for city manager government, housing improvement, and election reform. Skirball had been one of the most vocal critics of the Ku Klux Klan.[34]

The IRC also helped to organize the Colored Auxiliary of the Vanderburgh County Tuberculosis Association, which in June 1928 conducted an investigation of housing and health in Baptisttown. The group, chaired by Mrs. Stewart, discovered virtually the same wretched living conditions that a Chamber of Commerce committee had reported in 1916. It subsequently sought to inform residents of means of ameliorating those conditions and was able, as noted earlier, to have the services of Boehne Camp Hospital expanded for black residents. It may also have been behind the drive to establish a black hospital. Mrs. Stewart's committee sought as well to have the city build a park for blacks and to improve the condition of the Booker T. Washington pool, the only public swimming pool for blacks, which had been opened in the early twenties. It subsequently campaigned for a playground and public housing.[35]

Although the IRC was the only organization in which blacks and whites met regularly and the only biracial group dedicated to improving the lot of black Evansville, its focus remained the "Negro problem." White-dominated from the outset, it was never chaired by a black, and the Community Association which it created had to report to the IRC via a subcommittee of whites. Ownership of the Community Center facility remained in the hands of white YMCA directors, to whom the Community Association also had to report annually. Most important, the IRC never attacked segregation, choosing instead to ameliorate the living conditions of blacks in their separate world. It was, in short, a paternalistic organization which, like similar organizations formed in Louisville in the 1920s, believed blacks "had their place."[36]

By the onset of the Great Depression, Evansville remained a highly segregated community. Probably because of the city's rapid growth in the decade, when the population increased nearly 20 percent and exceeded 100,000 by 1930, lines between the races did not need to be as formally defined as in Southern cities. White mobility, encouraged by the streetcar, the bus, and the automobile, combined with a stable black populace to produce an environment in which interracial contacts were infrequent and racial divisions were probably more customary than legalized. That white Evansville prospered while black

Evansville remained stagnant indicated that many blacks either remained only briefly in the city or bypassed it altogether on their trek northward. Racial discrimination was the root of this, and its chief evidence was found in the continued lack of economic opportunity for blacks.

TEN

Economic Stagnation in an Age of Industrial Vitality, 1900–1929

 From the turn of the century until the Great Depression many Northern cities attracted thousands of Southern blacks, who in turn helped to transform the face of the urban North. The chief reason for this was economic opportunity, chiefly after 1915, when European sources of factory labor began to dry up and the boll weevil and disastrous floods made life miserable for Southern tenant farmers.[1]

During this time the city of Evansville witnessed substantial economic change, broadening its base to include the manufacture of consumer durables. An impressive number of white-collar positions were also created. Between 1899 and 1930 the number of wage earners increased more than eightfold, to 43,000. Another 6,000 workers came to be employed in commerce and trade. The competition of railroads, automobiles, trucks, and buses, by contrast, caused river-related employment to experience a relative decline. Evansville became the economic, cultural, and political hub of a three-state region integrated into a national market. Older industries, like Igleheart Brothers Mill, which manufactured "Swans Down" Cake Flour, were joined by Mead Johnson and Company, noted for nutritional products for infants; Servel, a manufacturer of gas-powered refrigerators; Bucyrus-Erie, producer of heavy construction equipment; and Graham Brothers, a maker of trucks. Symptomatic of city development was the establishment of a Chamber of Commerce, a philharmonic orchestra, a public museum, and a college. City government also began to exhibit signs of modernization with the formation of a city planning commission, a parks department, and the erection of such public facilities as the first city-owned baseball park in the nation and a veterans' coliseum. With the completion of the first skyscraper, the Citizens Bank building (1914), the urban landscape came to be dominated by the physical evidences of material progress.[2]

Black Evansville, however, played only a peripheral part in this process. In general, pre-1900 patterns of employment and economic opportunity persisted, a symptom of the pervasive racial discrimination of the age. That may have been the chief reason for the decline and subsequent stabilization of the black population in Evansville between 1900 and the early 1940s.

TABLE 17: Occupation by Race and Ethnicity, 1910 (by Percent)

	White		German-Born		Black	
Occupation	1910	1930	1910	1930	1910	1930
High White Collar						
Professional	3.4	3.2	6.4	3.9	1.8	2.6
Major Proprietor,						
Manager, Official	3.0	2.5	2.1	7.1	0	0.1
Low White Collar						
Semiprofessional	1.9	3.0	2.1	2.0	0	1.3
Clerical/Sales	13.5	21.3	2.1	13.0	0	1.9
Minor Proprietor,						
Manager, Official	8.5	7.1	21.3	13.7	3.6	1.0
Blue Collar						
Skilled	17.9	16.9	21.3	20.0	2.7	2.5
Semiskilled/						
Service	32.9	37.6	31.9	27.9	60.4	62.7
Unskilled	17.9	6.9	12.8	5.3	31.5	26.5
Miscellaneous/						
Unclear	0.9	1.5	0	7.1	0	1.5
Total	100.0	100.0	100.0	100.0	100.0	100.0

Sources: Thirteenth Census, Population Schedules for Vanderburgh County, 1910; Fifteenth Census, 1930, volume IV: *Occupations* (Washington, D.C. 1933), 495–98.

The occupational level of black workers in 1910 (Table 17) remained poor. Over nine of every ten workers were employed at the same sort of work as they had been for decades. Fewer, in fact, held skilled employment than ten years earlier, but a slightly larger percentage were petty proprietors, managers, and officials. The proportion of professionals, most of whom were educators and clergymen, continued to be slight. Among whites, by contrast, one-fifth of the workers were skilled and another quarter classified as low white collar. Particularly significant was the fact that about one in seven were in clerical or sales positions, and the proportion in semiskilled and unskilled labor was about half that among blacks. Twenty years later, in the early months of the Great Depression, black Evansvillians were mired at the same occupational levels. There were, however, minor increases in the percentages of semiprofessionals, clerks and salespersons, professionals, and major proprietors, managers, and officials.[3]

Among whites perhaps the most marked shifts had occurred in lower white collar, semiskilled, and unskilled employment. The increase in the first two reflected the expansion of clerical and sales positions and the introduction of automotive and refrigerator manufacturing. The decline of the third category was symptomatic of the rise of assembly-line and clerical labor and the decrease in such unskilled employment as steamboat laborer, and the greater specificity with which census enumerators recorded employment data.[4]

As Table 17 reveals, blacks made at best small gains in the first thirty years of the twentieth century, but those advancements were much less impressive than those attained by white newcomers, many of whom were German. As shown on Tables 8, 9, and 17, for example, the German-born secured an increased share of higher status white collar positions, especially clerical and sales, while the proportion of those in skilled employment decreased, largely due to the rise of mass production work. In 1900 about three in four held blue-collar positions, but in 1930 about one in two did.

Census data regarding occupational level by birthplace and data from city directories reinforce the conclusion that the children and grandchildren of German newcomers enjoyed a much faster rate of advancement in status than that of Afro-Americans. In 1900, for instance (Tables 8–9), about 70 percent of native whites whose parents were foreign-born held blue-collar positions, but thirty years later (Table 20), the proportion of native-born blue collar workers had dropped to about 62 percent, while the share of clerical and sales workers increased markedly.[5] The city directory of 1924 discloses similar patterns. Those with German surnames held approximately the same share of white collar and skilled blue collar positions as the entire white population, and in each case the percentage was much higher than that among blacks. The opposite was the case with semiskilled, service, and unskilled positions. The occupational expectations of black and white newcomers were about as disparate in 1930 as they had been sixty years earlier. The case of the black porter at National City Bank, praised by an Evansville newspaper in 1922 for years of faithful and considerate service, is illustrative. The position was the highest level to which any black could aspire in downtown Evansville until the Second World War.[6]

There was also little change in the sector of the Evansville economy in which blacks were located. For the most part, Afro-Americans were excluded from the rapidly growing manufacturing and commercial sectors, although they did enjoy some slight advances between 1900 and 1930. The percentage of blacks engaged in manufacturing and commerce rose slightly by 1910 (Table 18). Nevertheless, about five of every ten workers were employed in public or domestic service, and one in ten had a job in transportation. About the same number were employed in education or government. Virtually none worked in construction or utilities.[7] According to the federal census of 1930 (Table 20), service remained the most significant activity of the black community, although the proportion of those engaged in manufacturing had risen to nearly 19 percent. Transportation—chiefly the railroads—continued to be a major employer and the proportion of blacks in coal mining was greater than in 1910. About the same proportion were in commerce as twenty years earlier.[8]

The modest progress evident in the 1930 census, however, is misleading. First, employment data was more specifically labeled. Workers who in 1910

TABLE 18: Occupations by Race, Ethnicity, and Sex, 1930

Occupation/Sex	Total	Native White	Foreign-born White	Black
1. High White Collar:				
a. Professional				
Male				
Number	811	731	29	51
Percent	2.7	2.6	3.6	2.3
Female				
Number	531	492	6	33
Percent	4.8	4.9	6.2	3.1
b. Major Proprietor, Manager, Official				
Male				
Number	966	899	63	4
Percent	3.1	3.2	7.8	0.2
Female				
Number	33	32	1	0
Percent	0.3	0.3	1.0	0
2. Low White Collar:				
a. Semiprofessional				
Male				
Number	512	469	11	32
Percent	1.6	1.6	1.4	1.4
Female				
Number	727	710	7	10
Percent	6.5	7.1	7.2	0.9
b. Clerical/Sales				
Male				
Number	5,178	5,062	94	22
Percent	16.4	17.7	11.7	1.0
Female				
Number	3,288	3,253	23	12
Percent	29.4	32.5	23.7	1.1
c. Minor Proprietor, Manager, Official				
Male				
Number	2,485	2,327	114	44
Percent	7.9	8.2	14.2	2.0
Female				
Number	357	329	9	19
Percent	3.2	3.3	9.3	1.8
3. Blue Collar:				
a. Skilled				
Male				
Number	6,694	6,432	180	82
Percent	21.2	22.5	22.4	3.7

Female				
Number	44	44	0	0
Percent	0.4	0.4	0	0
b. Semiskilled/ Service				
Male				
Number	11,018	9,667	201	1,150
Percent	34.9	33.9	25.0	51.6
Female				
Number	5,840	4,875	50	915
Percent	52.3	48.7	51.5	85.8
c. Unskilled				
Male				
Number	2,950	2,107	48	795
Percent	9.3	7.4	6.0	35.7
Female				
Number	253	176	0	77
Percent	2.3	1.8	0	7.2
4. Miscellaneous/ Unknown:				
Male				
Number	949	838	63	48
Percent	3.0	2.9	7.8	2.2
Female				
Number	98	97	1	0
Percent	0.9	1.0	1.0	0
5. Total				
Male				
Number	31,563	28,532	803	2,228
Percent	100.0	100.0	100.0	100.0
Female				
Number	11,171	10,008	97	1,066
Percent	100.0	100.0	100.0	100.0

Source: Fifteenth Census, 1930, volume IV: *Occupations*, pp. 495–98. The table was derived from data provided on those pages. The author has excluded five males and one female of "other races" from his calculations. Some occupational listings for white collar workers were vague—for example, "retail dealers." The author somewhat arbitrarily assigned one third of them to the category of major proprietor and two-thirds to minor proprietor. The census data did not include the category of native white with foreign-born parent(s).

might have been listed as laborers, with no reference to the nature of their employment, were assigned to manufacturing or commerce in 1930. Second, of the 374 black men listed in manufacturing, 252 were at the lowest level—that is, neither skilled workers nor operatives, but "laborers not otherwise specified." Among the 243 black women in manufacturing, 117 were employed as menial workers at H. Fendrich Cigar Factory and seventy-seven were "laborers not otherwise specified." None worked in the city's newer industries—automotive and refrigeration. In addition, among the "newer" occupations, such as electrician, plumber, gas and steam fitter, tool and die maker, machinist, and sheet metal worker—jobs which employed 1,555 white men—there were only one black plumber or gas and steam fitter, four machinists, and one tool and die maker. Of the 172 construction workers, 145 were common laborers or helpers. All but a handful of those in transportation were chauffeurs, drivers, and steam railroad laborers.[9]

Third, as in the status of employment, the type of work available to blacks and whites also demonstrated the unevenness of the rates of progress. As revealed on Tables 19 and 20, most white workers, native and foreign-born, claimed an ever-increasing share of manufacturing and commerce positions, but the remainder were significantly represented in most of the other sectors of the economy. By contrast, proportionately few of them were found in service, and a decreasing share worked in transportation. As shown by Table 20, in 1930 about the same percentage of the white work force was employed in Evansville's factories as that of the black workers in public and domestic service.[10]

TABLE 19:   Sector of Employment, by Race and Ethnicity, 1910
(by percent)

Sector	White	Black	German-Born	Native White/Foreign Born Parents
Primary				
Agriculture	9.7	0	12.8	14.3
Mining	1.6	2.6	2.1	0.8
Secondary				
Manufacturing	35.5	11.7	29.8	32.2
Construction/				
Utilities	2.5	1.8	4.3	2.0
Labor	0.9	1.8	0	0.8
Tertiary				
Commerce	23.3	6.3	29.8	22.9
Transportation	8.8	9.9	2.1	7.8
Public Service	3.9	22.5	2.1	4.1
Domestic Service	6.4	25.2	4.3	8.2
Professions	1.6	0.9	2.1	1.2
Education/Government	3.2	7.2	6.4	3.7
Unclear	2.6	9.9	4.3	2.0
Total	100.0	100.0	100.0	100.0
Number	771	111	47	245

Source: Thirteenth Census, Population Schedules for Vanderburgh County, 1910. The same sample was utilized as in Table 17.

TABLE 20:   Sector of Employment, by Race and Ethnicity, 1930
(by percent)

Sector	White	Black	Foreign-Born	Blacks in this Sector
Primary				
Agriculture	1.4	1.0	2.9	5.5
Mining	1.0	5.0	1.9	29.2
Secondary				
Manufacturing	36.7	18.8	25.9	4.4
Construction/				
Utilities	5.7	5.2	6.8	7.0
Labor	2.8	9.1	10.9	20.5
Tertiary				
Commerce	26.4	5.9	28.3	1.8
Transportation	9.2	10.1	5.3	8.4
Public Service	6.3	19.0	7.1	20.0
Domestic Service	2.8	20.9	3.1	38.6
Professions	4.6	2.5	4.9	4.3
Education/Government	3.1	2.5	2.9	6.3
Unclear	0	0	0	0
Total	100.0	100.0	100.0	
Number	38,540	3,294	900	

Source: Fifteenth Census, 1930, volume IV: *Population*, 495–98. Data for native whites with one or both parents foreign-born was not provided in the printed census.

Examination of the twenty most common jobs in black Evansville (Tables 21 and 22) affords added evidence of the continuity of the city's economic climate for the descendants of former slaves. To be sure, some change took place, but only four of the jobs cited in 1900—barber, cook, hostler, and steamboat laborer—did not appear on the 1930 list. (Hod carriers appeared in 1930 as helpers in construction.) The decline in the rank of the latter three was due to the demise of horse-drawn vehicles and steamboat traffic. The relative decline in the importance of barbers resulted from the stabilization of the number of barbers (twenty) through the 1920s and the slight increase in the number of white barbers, a symptom of the increasing racial separation of the times. It is also important to note the slight increase in the position of retail dealers, all small in scale of operations. That was symptomatic of the centripetal patterns of black residences and the business opportunities which followed.

Miners, janitors, and sextons also increased in relative rank. The number of miners increased from 1900 to 1920 and then dropped considerably in the 1920s from 830 to 383 because of an overall decline in the bituminous coal industry brought about by overdevelopment and the increased use of fuel oil. The number of black coal miners did not, however, drop as sharply, evidence perhaps of the willingness of blacks to work for low pay and under hazardous and uncertain circumstances. The increased use of black janitors and sextons underscored the growth of white businesses in the maturing years of the industrial city and the demand for black custodial help.[11]

TABLE 21: Twenty Leading Occupations Listed by
Evansville Blacks, 1900

Occupation	Number	Rank	Percent of Black Workers
Barber	37	18	1.0
Coachman	56	16	1.6
Coal Miner	88	11	2.4
Cook	312	3	8.7
Hod Carrier	34	19	0.9
Hostler	147	7	4.1
Housekeeper	65	15	1.8
Janitor	34	19	0.9
Laborer	250	5	6.9
Laborer, Day	607	1	16.8
Laborer, Rail	66	14	1.8
Laborer, Steamboat	265	4	7.3
Laborer, Other	126	9	3.5
Laundress	121	10	3.4
Porter	136	8	3.8
Schoolteacher	39	17	1.1
Servant	378	2	10.5
Teamster	75	13	2.1
Waiter	78	12	2.2
Washwoman	206	6	5.7
Total	3,120		86.5

Total Number of Black Workers: 3,606

Source: Thirteenth Census, Population Schedules for Vanderburgh County, 1900.

Despite increases in the variety and the number of jobs listed in 1930, the most prevalent occupations remained common labor and service (Table 22). The number and proportion of servants, in fact, grew, but certain domestic jobs—coachman, housekeeper, and laundress/washwoman—declined in number and rank. That was the result of several factors: the cost of maintaining large homes because of the graduated income tax and the onset of the Depression; the development of the automobile and of such labor-saving appliances as the electric washing machine and the electric iron; and the expansion of commercial laundries.[12]

TABLE 22:   Twenty Leading Occupations Listed by Blacks, 1930

Occupation	Number	Rank	Percent of Black Workers	Percent of All Workers
Chauffeurs and Drivers	89	10	2.7	9.0
Coal Miners	165	4	6.7	43.0
Draymen and Teamsters	31	18	0.9	16.0
Housekeepers and Stewardesses	31	18	0.9	10.5
Janitors and Sextons	181	3	5.5	49.9
Laborers, Clay and Stone	34	17	1.0	19.4
Laborers, Helpers in Construction	145	5	4.4	30.8
Laborers, Iron and Steel (excl. auto)	57	13	1.7	12.0
Laborers, Porters, Helpers in Stores	83	12	2.5	30.7
Laborers, Road and Street	39	15	1.2	34.2
Laborers, Steam Railroad	88	11	2.7	27.1
Laborers, Other Industries	91	9	2.8	15.7
Laborers, Unspecified	299	2	9.1	41.9
Laundresses	92	8	2.8	61.3
Operatives, Tobacco (F)	117	6	3.6	7.2
Porters (except stores)	107	7	3.3	91.5
Retail Dealers	31	18	0.9	2.3
Servants (M & F)	689	1	20.9	38.5
Teachers, School	45	14	1.4	6.6
Waiters and Waitresses	35	16	1.1	12.0
Total	2,459		74.1	

Total Number of Black Workers: 3,294

Source: Fifteenth Census, 1930, volume IV: *Population*, 495-98.

About 6 percent of the population in 1930, blacks were heavily over-represented in certain occupations (Table 22.) Virtually all of the porters in hotels, railroad and bus stations, factories, and other nonretail facilities were black, as were six in ten laundresses, half of the janitors and sextons, about four in ten miners, unspecified laborers, and domestics, one in three road and street laborers, porters and helpers in stores, laborers and helpers in construction, and one-quarter of the steam railroad workers. Blacks were also overrepresented in all but one of the other leading occupations except retail dealers. Only the percentage of teachers and tobacco operatives was approximately that of the black population as a whole.

TABLE 23:   Occupational Index by Sex, Race, and Ethnicity, 1900-1930

	1900	1910	1930
Males			
Blacks	626		617
Native Whites	n/a		483
Native Parents	490		n/a
Foreign Parent(s)	473		n/a
Foreign-Born Whites	463		437
All Workers	500		490
Females			
Blacks	608		579
Native Whites	n/a		475
Native Parents	496		n/a
Foreign Parent(s)	495		n/a
Foreign-Born Whites	504		457
All Workers	520		485
All White Workers		503	487
All Black Workers		605	599

Sources: Twelfth Census, 1900, *Occupations* (Washington, D.C. 1904), 556–59; Thirteenth Census, Population Schedules for Vanderburgh County, 1910; Fifteenth Census, 1930, volume IV: *Occupations*, 495–98. The format of this table is derived from Kusmer, *A Ghetto Takes Shape*, pp. 202, 279–80.

Occupational indexes for 1900 and 1930 also disclose the unevenness of progress (Table 23) The overall occupational index for black men moved up slightly, as it did for native and foreign-born whites. (In Cleveland black men advanced from 568 to 546.) Despite the increased number of black males in semiskilled and white collar positions, the occupational decline that they had experienced prior to 1900 was only slightly reversed. In an absolute and a relative sense—unlike blacks in many cities to the north—they made virtually no gains.[13]

The trend for black females on the occupational index was superficially more encouraging. As a group, black women encountered relatively greater improvement on the occupational index, climbing about 5 percent. That was due largely to the decline in the number of laundresses and washwomen, counted in calculation of the index as unskilled workers, and the increase in the number of cigar factory operatives and domestic servants, both counted as semiskilled workers. Although the occupational decline of 1865-1900 was somewhat halted, compared with white women, black women, like black men, experienced neither an absolute nor a relative improvement. The gap between black and white women, in fact, widened (Table 23). At the turn of the century, for example, young German women were more likely than in 1930 to be found in low-paying domestic work, for by the 1920s they had begun to enter clerical and sales positions.[14]

When the progress of all workers is considered, the overall occupational index of blacks advanced only about 1 percent, to 599 in 1930. The improvement was neither absolute nor relative, as the rise among whites was three times greater, and the level in 1930 was 487. In general, as William Harris has observed, however hard blacks ran to attain the American dream, the effort did not as a rule produce substantial reward.[15]

The continued presence of large numbers of black women in the work force underscored that. To be sure, the employment of women was increasingly common in twentieth-century American society. Awareness of that change, in a community in which most women were raised to consider work as not respectable, became especially pronounced during the early months of World War I, when the *Journal-News* reported that 9,000 women were at work in the city. The largest number, 2,400, were employed in the cigar factories, and the second largest, 1,688, were domestics. Perhaps most revealing was the fact that 579 professionals, 562 stenographers, bookkeepers, and typists, 580 clerks in retail stores, and 100 telephone operators were women. By 1930, the total number of employed women was 11,000—about one-quarter of all Evansville women.[16]

That women would seek employment was, of course, not unusual in the black community. One of every three black workers in 1930 was female, and slightly over two-fifths of all black women aged ten and above were employed. (That proportion placed Evansville near the national average and slightly below Chicago, Cincinnati, and Indianapolis.) Working remained an economic necessity. It was especially important to unmarried household heads, as proportionately more black women headed households. Nearly six of every ten widowed or divorced black women—about the same share as in other cities of 100,000 or more—were employed, four times the rate among whites in the same status.[17]

Although the gap narrowed somewhat, the percentage of married black women who worked remained substantially higher than that among married white women, especially those of German extraction. Because of low family income, in 1930 slightly over 28 percent of all married black women worked, over twice the level for all the married women in Evansville. Regardless of marital status, almost 36 percent of black homemakers were employed, as compared with 14.1 percent of those who were native white with native parents, 9.3 percent among those who were natives and had one or both parents born outside the United States, and 7.9 percent among those who were foreign-born.[18]

Black Evansville probably received with mixed emotions the news that many women were entering white collar positions, for that phase of social progress bypassed the Afro-American community. In 1930, 329 of the 545 black homemakers who had a job were in service, fifty-nine worked at home as laundresses or seamstresses, and 132 held positions in local factories, primarily those making cigars. Eighteen were professionals (mostly teachers). Just twelve employed black women were clerks or salespersons. Among native white home-makers who worked, 43.4 percent were in factories and 22.6 percent were cleri-cal or salespersons.[19]

Economic necessity also explained another feature of black employment: a disproportionately high number of youth and older persons in the work force. Although state statutes between 1897 and the late 1920s mandated school attendance and severely restricted the number of youth at work below age six-teen, the percentage of black youth aged ten to fifteen who had a job in 1930 (2.9) was one of the highest among Northern cities of 100,000 or more resi-dents, and black youth accounted for a disproportionately higher share of the employed young persons in the city. This was undoubtedly due to opportuni-ties in domestic service, particularly for young women. A typical case was that of Douglass student Lillian Lander, who like most of her friends worked in white homes before and after school. That meant leaving home before daybreak and returning after dark to prepare for classes and to rest. Proportionately more older persons were also employed—in 1910, for example, 9 percent of those over age sixty, as compared with 5 percent of whites. Work, in short, was important to black Evansville. About 32 percent of households in 1930 had at least two wage earners, and slightly over 37 percent of persons aged ten and above worked.[20]

Despite that, as a group black Evansvillians remained stuck in an employ-ment cycle which largely excluded them from the benefits of a thriving indus-trial city. Their poverty and illiteracy also meant that, despite the size of the community, black businesses and professions, which served only blacks, tended to be ephemeral as well as small in scale. In 1909 there were forty-seven black enterprises: seventeen barbershops, five boarding houses, five groceries, two restaurants, two lunch stands, two hairdressing parlors, and two residences which offered furnished rooms. There were also a tailor, a coal dealer, a funeral director, a dressmaker, a shoemaker, a "contracting teamster," a "manufactur-ing dealer," an insurance agent, a saloonkeeper, and a "contracting plasterer." There were no black-owned bakeries, blacksmith shops, carpenter shops, cloth-ing or dry goods stores, house painters, pharmacies, meat markets, or dentist's offices. Only among the city's eighty-five barbershops were blacks overrepresented.[21]

Eleven years later, the city directory revealed similar patterns. There were fifty-one black businesses—ten barbershops, thirteen restaurants or "eat shops," six groceries, four soft-drink stands, three poolrooms, three shoe repair shops,

24. W. A. Gaines, Evansville's first successful black mortician. Special Collections, University of Southern Indiana.

25. W. A. Gaines Funeral Home, 1930s. Special Collections, University of Southern Indiana.

two undertakers, two clothes cleaners, and an assortment of other enterprises, including a real estate agency, a hotel, a junk dealer, and a broom maker. Only a handful of these had existed in 1909, and only a few would survive the decade.[22]

One notable exception was William Henry Bell, who operated a hotel from 1909 to 1911 at 318-320 Upper (South) Water Street, between Main and Locust streets. Bell was also a contracting teamster, conducting his business at that address from 1908 until 1922 (the latter three years as the West End Transfer Company). Bell operated as well a restaurant and saloon at the Water Street building. The restaurant was open until 1929. River-related business was at best risky, especially given the decline of river traffic. Bell's hauling business fell prey to the cost of purchasing trucks as well as the vicissitudes of depending on city government and school corporation contracts, both of which were rewards for political loyalty. The Depression closed his restaurant.[23]

More successful in the hotel business was Henry Black, who established a hotel at 416-420 Walnut Street in 1901. After his death in 1921, his widow ran the small facility until her death in 1923, after which Henry Perkins, a former employee, became the proprietor. The building was razed as part of a slum clearance project in 1933–1934.[24]

Probably the two most prominent black businessmen were Logan H. Stewart and W. A. Gaines. Stewart's life insurance and real estate business, organized at the turn of the century, survived into the mid-twenties. Married to Sallie Wyatt, he also was the guiding hand in the creation of the local chapter of the National Negro Business League, affiliated with Booker T. Washington, which promoted black-owned business and property ownership. Active until World War I, the chapter was prominent in the formation of the Cherry Street YMCA and National Negro Health Week.[25]

Gaines, born in Kentucky in 1865, opened a funeral home in Evansville in 1907. Previous efforts of others to establish such a firm had failed, but Gaines had sufficient capital to succeed, as he had earlier founded similar businesses in Covington and Paducah, Kentucky. During his visit to the city in March 1909 to open a new building, black leaders praised him as the epitome of the Wizard of Tuskegee's strategy for race progress. His firm was initially managed by Marion Harrison of Indianapolis, but eventually Gaines settled in the city and became prominent in civic affairs and Republican politics. By white standards his establishment was small—capitalized at $5,000—but it was the most prosperous black enterprise in the city.[26]

For a time, Gaines had a competitor in the firm of O'Hara and Tidrington. Rudolph O'Hara, a graduate of Clark (1909), who was Gaines's onetime partner, founded a funeral parlor with Ernest Tidrington which lasted from 1920 until 1924. The two then became partners in a law firm which survived until Tidrington died in early 1930.[27]

Other examples of the rare mix of business and professional activities were provided by the Jones brothers—W. E. and J. H.—and Drs. Edward M. Baylor and William F. Dendy. The efforts of the brothers, one a physician and the other a pharmacist, to operate a jointly run business between 1901 and 1903 ended shortly after the 1903 riot. Baylor, a native of South Carolina, was more successful. Arriving in the city in 1923, he opened a medical practice, to which he added a pharmacy. Like Gaines, he became prominent in Republican politics, and his office at 415 Lincoln was a center of political activity. In the fall of 1926, the first black dentist, William F. Dendy, an old friend from South Carolina, opened an office above Baylor's.[28]

More common among Evansville's black businesses were the barber shops, some of which survived several decades. Perhaps the most successful was William Glover's, located at 317 Upper (South) First Street, which was open from 1895 until 1929. Renowned for its attractive furnishings and service, the shop was a favorite among white professionals and businessmen. The shop was closed, after Glover's death, because his son chose to pursue other interests.[29]

Most businesses were smaller in scale. Typical was Julius M. Coleman's shoe repair shop, established in 1908 at 311 Bell Street. A Republican activist, he had been city hall janitor and captain of Hose House No. 9. President of Liberty's Men's Club, he was renowned for his fashionable clothing and his ability to "put on the strut." His small shop remained open until approximately 1928.[30]

A similar business was the American Shoe Shining Parlor, founded about 1920 at 711 1/2 Main Street by Ben Davis and Leemon Waddy. In January 1921, Waddy, who had made a better-than-average income as a waiter, purchased his retiring partner's share for $392, and six months later was sufficiently well-off to join another partner in opening a lunch room and soft drink stand at 601 Oak. Waddy's enterprises survived until the onset of the Depression in 1929, after which he resumed full-time work as a waiter at the McCurdy Hotel.[31]

Given the paucity and marginality of black businesses and the poverty and literacy level of most blacks, it is understandable that efforts to publish a black newspaper were infrequent and unsuccessful. A few "newspapers" appeared between 1880 and 1930, but they were merely ad hoc instruments of Republican politicos. Two longer-lived efforts were a biweekly, *The Transcript*, published for a few months in late 1904 and early 1905, and *The Clarion*, published irregularly in late 1914 and early 1915 by attorney Thomas L. Higgins. Nothing else is known of either of these, however, and no issues, unfortunately, survive.[32]

More opportunities for economic advancement existed in the professions, but there, too, the benefits were meager, as opportunities were limited to black clients. In 1930, as in 1870 and 1900, most of the professionals were pastors and teachers, many of whom served the community for several decades.[33] Few of the other professionals remained long in the city. The longest tenure among black attorneys was held by Rudolph O'Hara, self-educated, who was admitted to the bar in the early twenties and practiced law in the city until shortly after the Second World War. The handful of other lawyers who hung out their shingle left town after a year or two. A somewhat unusual case was that of Ernest

26. William Glover, barber, 1895–
1929. Special Collections, University of
Southern Indiana.

27. The interior of Glover's Barber Shop at 317 Upper (South) First Street.
Special Collections, University of Southern Indiana.

Tidrington, also self-educated, who sought admission to the Vanderburgh County Bar Association in 1919, only to be rejected. Leading the opposition, ironically, was Richard Rosencranz, one of the few white leaders who held what in that era was considered a progressive attitude toward blacks, who asserted that Tidrington was unsuitable and unfit. Observers attributed Rosencranz's position to his staunch support of Mayor Bosse, from whose camp Tidrington had bolted the previous year (see chapter 12). With the support of Republican Judge Phil Gould, Tidrington eventually secured admission to the bar in December 1923, by virtue of an order of the Indiana Supreme Court.[34] In addition to resistance from whites, the small number of clients, poor housing selections, and parochial social life limited the number of attorneys.

These factors also affected black physicians, but fortunately a cadre of doctors remained in the community for many years—Drs. Buckner, Green, Jackson, and Baylor. Three others had promising careers in Evansville cut short by early death—J. H. Jones in 1903, S. S. Dupee in 1913, and Howard R. Thompson, who practiced from 1923 until 1930. Not until 1935, it should be noted, was a black physician—Albert Heard—admitted to the staff of one of the three white hospitals.[35]

Eventually a few dentists opened practices in the city. Dendy, the first, was a graduate of Meharry School of Dentistry and the University of Michigan. He practiced from 1926 until 1972. Shortly thereafter, Raymond King, a native of Lebanon, Indiana, and a graduate of the University of Indianapolis, set up an office near Fifth and Chestnut streets. Dr. Buckner's son, George, also opened a practice in 1930.[36]

As shown on Table 18, the sector of the economy with the greatest potential in this period was lower white-collar clerical, sales, and managerial positions, but it was virtually closed to blacks. In 1930 only twenty-two black men and twelve black women held such posts—about 1 percent of the black work force—as compared with 17.6 percent of white men and 32.5 percent of white women. This indicated a slight degree of progress, as only 0.3 percent had been in such white collar positions in 1900, but one must observe that many of those men holding clerical and sales jobs were lower level clerks in stores (none of them white-owned). There were only four insurance agents or officials, two real estate agents or officials, and two salesmen. There were no bankers, commercial travelers, brokers, accountants, wholesale dealers, auditors, cashiers, stenographers, or typists. Among black women there were five saleswomen, two clerks in businesses, and five unspecified clerks, and no bookkeepers, cashiers, stenographers, or typists.[37]

Neither local nor federal government rendered much assistance in this regard. Blacks had sporadically taken the civil service examinations since the early 1880s, and by the 1890s Frederick Douglass Morton had secured the position of carrier and Ernest W. Clark the post of substitute carrier, but these were apparently the only two successful applicants for carrier positions until Zack Buckner, a Howard University graduate, in 1931. For most, the United States Army was the sole federal agency that would employ them, and even that was undependable, given the limitation of recruitment to several regiments and the occasional surge of antiblack sentiment. Local government hired blacks chiefly as street laborers and custodians. Notable exceptions were Tidrington, who was named special detective in 1915, and Ernest Killibrew, Mayor Bosse's longtime chauffeur. None, however, secured clerical positions in city or county government.[38]

As revealed on Table 18, moreover, even blue collar opportunities were proscribed. The percentage of skilled workers, small to begin with, grew smaller by 1930. That was due in part to the general decline of the skilled trades in the face of the growth of mass production jobs. It also reflected the limited options available to blacks. Although the proportion of semiskilled workers increased slightly, opportunities remained extremely limited. Only twenty men worked, for instance, in the truck or furniture factories, and all of them were custodians or ordinary laborers. Among other things, these patterns made questionable the value of the expanded vocational programs at the high school, as the job market for black carpenters and bricklayers was slim, and not until the early 1940s were young men trained in the newer trades like sheet metal work.[39]

The animosity of white industrialists and labor union members was probably the most important determinant of blue collar opportunities for blacks. A few industrialists—notably Aaron M. Weil of Crown Pottery Company and A. C. Rosencranz and his son Richard of Vulcan Plow Company—encouraged blacks to seek employment at their establishments. Most unions, moreover, excluded Afro-Americans, and union activity among blacks was extremely limited. Perhaps the most durable organization was Local 11 of the Hod Carriers, apparently a racially mixed local of lower level construction workers.[40] That the organization, which by the 1920s was known as the Laborers Union, was an important force in the black community was evident in a news account in September 1904 which indicated that members of the local had agreed to entertain blacks at Lake Park on Labor Day, "and hence save the embarrassment of proscription at Garvin Park," from which blacks had recently been barred.[41] Hod carriers usually marched at the end of the Labor Day parades, after the United Mine Workers.

Some blacks were also members of the UMW, among the most progressive of the members of the American Federation of Labor since its formation in 1890. Although it is safe to assume that racial friction existed, the coal mines were one of the few places in the city where blacks and whites worked side by side. Given their petit bourgeois, accommodationist strategy, black leaders of the era, like the writers of the "Colored Folk" column, said nothing about black coal miners, especially since these leaders loathed the sort of mass action that unions advocated. By 1923, 1.6 percent of the bituminous coal miners in Indiana were black, as compared with 1.4 percent in Pennsylvania and 2.4 percent in Illinois. Evansville's black miners settled near the city's north- and westside coal mines, and even after the demise of coal mining the largest of these black residential clusters persisted—the one just to the west of north Fulton Avenue, near Pigeon Creek.[42]

Blacks were also members of Local No. 5 of the National Brotherhood of Operative Potters, an apparently integrated local listed in city directories from the early 1890s to about 1905. No other records survive. They also belonged to the segregated Tie Carriers Union and a "federal labor union," both of which were listed in directories between 1901 and 1905. Neither survived more than a year or two. The latter, in which Richard Amos and Henry Jackson were officers, was probably one of those locals chartered directly by the American Federation of Labor to avoid race-mixing among the locals of the skilled trades. Precisely what this local fostered is not recorded, but it was undoubtedly weak, like others across the nation, because of the black members' uncertainty of receiving the wage rate established by the craft. Afro-Americans were excluded as well from the railroad unions, but some joined A. Philip Randolph's Brotherhood of Sleeping Car Porters and Maids, organized in 1925. Randolph, brought to the city in 1931 to speak in Washington Avenue Temple's public lecture series, one of the most progressive aspects of river city culture at that time, also addressed a large and enthusiastic crowd at Lincoln the next day. Exactly how the more affluent black leaders received him is unrecorded, but one may safely assume that some distrusted his advocacy of mass organization.[43]

Porters as well as roustabouts attempted to organize, but these efforts were ineffective. On at least two occasions—July 1905 and April 1909—steamboat hands struck for a week or two, as predecessors had done in the 1890s, and in both cases the issue was higher wages. Hostile public opinion and suppression by local police thwarted their efforts. There was at least one attempt, in 1908, to form a "colored saloon porters' union," but it ran afoul of the law after fisticuffs broke out between black proponents and opponents.[44]

In short, opportunities to rise were extremely limited, which were compounded by low wages and poor working conditions. That also helped to explain why such ostensibly menial jobs as custodian or janitor in a public building were prized. Roy S. Perry recalled, however, that such employment depended on unwavering loyalty to a political party. Hired at the city hall on the recommendation of Bosse's chauffeur, he remained until January 1926, when Republican Herbert Males swept out all Bosse-Elmendorf appointments. One of the reasons such a position was attractive was that compensation was higher than most jobs available to blacks; another, and possibly more compelling reason, was that it offered rare access, however limited, to the white power structure, and those blacks granted such trust by whites were considered leaders in the black community.[45]

This economic climate had predictable results. The types of jobs reinforced residential patterns. The coming of mass transit and the automobile and the development of subdivisions on the city's perimeters were of benefit only to whites, and the distance between work and residence increased. Between 1914 and 1929, for instance, the proportion of whites who lived at or within five blocks of their place of employment dropped almost 50 percent. That also applied to those whites with German surnames. Among blacks the proportion actually rose, and in 1929 was almost twice that of whites, whether native or German. Three of ten whites, including those with German surnames, were by 1929 living at least eleven blocks from their place of employment. Among blacks only one in ten was. That reflected white affluence, marked by the growing use of the automobile and access to the new subdivisions on the fringe of the city.[46]

Another obvious effect of all this was that black workers stood little chance of improving their status from one generation to the next. The low rate of residential persistence continued into the twentieth century, illustrated by the fact that only about 13 percent of those Afro-American heads of household listed in the 1909 city directory were also listed in 1920. For those who remained, the prospects for advancement were slim. The 1910 enumeration schedules, moreover, disclose that being born in Indiana did not carry any advantage to being born in, for example, Kentucky. Only a few of those born in Indiana—presumably Evansville or Vanderburgh County—held jobs higher than the semiskilled level, as compared with 8.5 percent of the Kentucky-born and 7.1 percent of those born in other Southern states. The disparity is also evident among those Afro-Americans whose parents had been born in Indiana. None held a position higher than semiskilled. Among whites with a Hoosier father or mother, by contrast, approximately half were employed at least at the level of skilled worker. Among whites with a Kentucky-born father or mother, slightly below four in ten were skilled or white collar workers.[47]

Of those blacks listed in both the 1909 and the 1920 city directories, most (342) experienced no change in occupational level. That high status was not a factor in this regard was evidenced by the fact that 91 percent of those listed in both directories were unemployed or employed at the level of semiskilled worker or below. Only sixty of those who remained rose to a higher occupational level, of these forty-six advanced from having no job to the position of skilled worker or from unskilled to semiskilled employment. Six became proprietors of small businesses. Forty, however, declined in status in this period, mostly from semiskilled to unskilled labor or from unskilled labor to having no job.[48]

Similar patterns prevailed from 1924 to 1929. Among whites listed in both city directories, 18.6 percent enjoyed an improvement in their status and 10.6 percent suffered a decline. Among those with German surnames, the percentages were, in order, 21.7 and 14.1. By contrast, nearly 24 percent of blacks were worse off, as compared with nearly 17 percent who were better off. Of these, most were workers who advanced from unskilled to semiskilled labor.[49]

Put another way, black Evansville from 1900 to 1930 documents the frequency with which hundreds migrating to the north must have considered the city a temporary stop on the trek to a new start, or ignored it altogether. That exodus touched all classes of the black community, but perhaps its saddest legacy was the absence of those who might have formed a stable and sizable mid-

28. These residences in the 600 block of Lincoln Avenue in the 1930s represented one of the most affluent black neighborhoods in the city. They were, from left to right, the homes of Alfred Porter, Thomas Cheeks, Boyd Henderson, William Best, and Raymond King. The block is directly across the street from Lincoln High School. Special Collections, University of Southern Indiana.

dle class. Although the most publicized out-migration occurred in the summer of 1903, the more significant fact was the steady but usually unheralded departure of families or young people who had recently graduated from the high school. The Evansville correspondence column in the *Indianapolis Recorder* of the 1920s reveals the extent, for instance, to which black Indianapolis had been augmented by former Evansvillians. The June 2, 1909, "Colored Folk" column illustrated that poignantly:

> The Butler family, who for years have lived in Evansville on Douglas street, left Monday to take up permanent residence in Washington, D. C. Sam Butler was one of Evansville's best citizens and his moral influence and personal worth will be very much missed.[50]

Because of the high degree of out-migration, only a few families were able to establish themselves as a continuing source of community leadership. Important in this regard were Dr. Buckner and his sons Zack and George. The son of Rev. Rouse, Hugh, became an attorney and educator. The teamster and restaurateur, William Henry Bell, married a daughter of Dr. Green. One of their children, Adrian, rose to prominence in the black community by the 1930s, becoming a post office worker after a stint as a band leader.[51]

Whether examined en masse or individual by individual, the black community, in a word, continued to experience virtually the same limited opportunity as in the late nineteenth century. One implication of this was that few owned their own homes. In 1910 only 10.8 percent of the heads of household did, a rate lower than that of Indianapolis and Terre Haute (14.2 and 26.6 percent, respectively) but higher than that of Cincinnati or Louisville (5.3 and 6.3 percent, respectively). Twenty years later about twice as many owned homes—23.9 percent—one of the lowest rates in Indiana and Kentucky. By comparison, 48.7 percent of the city's native whites owned their homes. In 1930 there were sixteen black Evansvillians for every black-owned home, twice the rate for whites. The median value of black-owned homes in 1930—$2,119—was the twelfth lowest among the eighty-five cities with at least 100,000 residents. Only twelve homes were valued at at least $7,500, and none was worth more than $20,000. Probably the most affluent residential section by 1930 was the block of homes on the side of Lincoln Avenue opposite the school. There resided educators Best and Porter, physician Thompson, dentist King, and businessman Bell.[52]

The results of economic deprivation were evident in other ways, which included the relatively high incidence of lodgers, the ownership of perhaps the most valued status symbol of the era, the radio set, and the persistently high unemployment rate. Taking in lodgers remained an important means of supplementing meager household income (see chapter 11). Only 5.1 percent of black families, moreover, possessed a radio set, as compared with 33.8 percent of all families in Evansville. That was lower than the rate in all but seven of the largest American cities. In addition, unemployment rates remained high. In the early Depression year, 1930, 11 percent of those out of a job, able to work, and looking for work were black. Twenty years earlier, in more prosperous times, 25 percent of the black populace aged thirteen and above had been out of work at some time in the year preceding the 1910 census enumeration, as compared with 14 percent of white workers.[53]

The morass of the post-Civil War years remained, and in some respects the economic condition had worsened. The consolidation of the ghetto and the expansion of various forms of discrimination served as a deterrent to ambitious youth as well as prospective businessmen and professionals. The self-perpetuating culture of poverty existed in a virulent form in Evansville. By 1930 it showed few signs of disappearing.[54]

The Maturation of a Subculture: Black Society in Evansville, 1900–1930

 By the turn of the century black Evansville had spawned many churches, fraternal societies, and clubs. Revealing a number of interests and a rudimentary class structure, they attested to the emergence of a vital subculture which nurtured black Evansvillians in their pursuit of the American dream. Between 1900 and 1930 that subculture matured. As before, few could be considered middle class, and even fewer upper class. According to census data in 1930, for example, only one in ten heads of households owned their own homes, and 3.5 percent of the owners possessed homes valued at $5,000 or more.[1]

Some change occurred in the makeup of the middle and upper classes, due largely to the addition of professionals and businessmen who served an exclusively black clientele. Men like Gaines and Tidrington amassed wealth that was, by black standards, substantial. When Dr. Willis Green died in 1908, he owned several houses and plots in Baptisttown, including the infamous "Green's Alley," and part of Oakdale. After his untimely death in 1930, Tidrington left an estate valued at $50,000. Principal Best earned about $3,000 in the late twenties, an annual salary which placed him near the top among black men in the city.[2]

Slightly below this small group was the black middle class. Dominated by teachers, it also included the owners of small businesses, like William Glover, the barber, and the better-paid pastors.[3] The values and attitudes of the black middle class, like the most affluent, were perhaps best expressed by the "Colored Folk" columns, which held before the black community the virtues of self-help and patience. Although criticizing the excesses of the masses, these writers also warned that men who "dressed well and spoke fine" and did not "exercise diplomacy and good sense" among ordinary persons risked the loss of valuable clients and supporters.[4]

Affluent blacks remained, however, solicitous of white opinion, fearing that all blacks would be likened to the sidewalk society on Fourth, Walnut,

Lincoln, or Green's Alley. As S. S. Dupee naively put it in 1905, whites despised blacks because of their behavior, not their color. When one-quarter of the black population began to pay taxes and have a bank account, he insisted, whites would take better notice of them. Dupee was also critical of the pulpit behavior of many clergymen, whose illiteracy and antics he considered as despicable as that of the patrons of the dives in Baptisttown.[5]

Such persons seemed unable or unwilling to acknowledge that the presence of vice among lower class blacks was symptomatic of deeper problems. Exhortations about good behavior seemed designed, moreover, to improve the image of prosperous blacks in the eyes of whites as much as to provide the wherewithal for racial uplift. By contrast, the typical black resident was concerned with survival on a day-to-day basis. However much he or she may have desired to emulate the more affluent, necessity dictated that attention be focused on simple, immediate goals.[6]

The many organizations formed or developed after 1900 reinforced the semiautonomous character of the black community. Produced by de facto and de jure segregation, they assisted blacks in coping with the vicissitudes of racial discrimination. Many were short-lived, but others had roots in the era of the Civil War. Although they documented the social strata and the variety of interests among black Evansvillians, they also demonstrated that tenuous racial bonds persisted, transcending class interests, due to the common threat that racism posed.[7]

One of the most vivid illustrations of that fragile unity was the reverence expressed for "the old folk" and "the old soldiers" in annual celebrations which extended into the 1930s. That respect allowed the community to maintain a tangible connection with its roots. Annual "old folks" concerts were held, for example, at Liberty from the 1880s onward, a prominent feature of which was the "Broom Drill." Reverence for ex-slaves grew more pronounced as the years passed. As Dupee observed after an interview with Lucy McBride and her sister in 1902, "[i]nvariably their conversation will drift to the sudden and forceful separation of parents and children, relatives and friends, and those who have felt the curse of slavery never cease to yearn for those who have been lost."[8] Ex-slaves like Rev. Rouse were also visible reminders of the distance blacks had traveled since slavery days and of the merits of the "up from the bootstraps" approach.[9]

The "old soldiers"—veterans of the Union Army like Robert Nicholas and Moses Slaughter—were responsible for the annual Decoration Day and Emancipation Day ceremonies. Each year the school board obliged the black community by dismissing students for Emancipation Day, clearly the most important secular holiday on the calendar. In 1904, for example, a thousand gathered at Garvin Park for daylong festivities, the high point of which was a speech by Nicholas, who warned that "the proscriptions against us today are due to our getting too far away from our God, who stood by us from '61 to 65." Nicholas added that he "couldn't see how any negro could force himself upon the Democratic Party when said party had made no overtures nor ever done anything for the welfare of the colored man. . . ."[10]

The passage of the years brought new generations to lead these annual observations. By 1910 educators and other professionals had begun to take leading roles in planning Emancipation Day festivities. The fiftieth anniversary steering committee in 1913, for instance, comprised three teachers, an attorney, and a physician. New generations also brought new concerns and a new tone to the observances. The featured speaker in 1902, white school superintendent W. A. Hester, spoke of the need for industrial education. In 1927 Sallie Stewart raised funds for the Day Nursery Association by organizing races and games for the festivities.[11]

With the consolidation of racial segregation, moreover, about 1910 the line of march changed. Instead of commencing on Main Street and proceeding to Fifth and thence to a local park, it began at Lincoln and Governor and moved thence out Lincoln to Barnett's Grove or Pleasure Park, about the only two parks available to blacks by then. In addition, after 1910 partisan rhetoric was rare. Instead, black speakers stressed racial progress through self-help. With the demise of the old soldiers, by the 1920s it was also common for Lincoln's proclamation of emancipation to be read by a pupil. Regardless of these changes, however, Emancipation Day remained a magnet for hundreds of blacks for miles around, and was the one day each year which was unique to the black community. It was the event that civic leaders, with enthusiastic volunteer assistance, used to mark the development of that community.[12]

Intraracial ties were maintained in other ways. Railroad excursions via the L & N and Illinois Central were frequent occurrences each year between late May and early October, as hundreds departed to visit Kentucky relatives for the day or converged on Evansville from communities as far away as Hopkinsville, Kentucky, or Clarksville, Tennessee, to visit relatives and friends or to participate in special events like the anniversary of a pastor. On Sunday, May 21, 1905, for example, the Illinois Central brought 750 for a day from points along the line in Kentucky. "The visitors spent the day in the city, seeing the sights and mingling with friends," reported one newspaper. "A colored band accompanied the crowd and made things lively with music."[13] On August 7, 1907, 500 Evansvillians boarded a train for a day's outing to Paducah. (The round trip cost $1.50.)[14]

Enterprising black leaders developed special arrangements with the railroad companies to promote these events, and that enhanced their income and prestige. Rev. McIntyre was perhaps the most clever, as he convinced the L & N to allow him to have the exclusive privilege of selling food and drink to the excursionists in return for his enticing hundreds to come to the city as his guests for Sunday church activities and a barbecue at special round-trip fares. McIntyre claimed that he raised hundreds of dollars for McFarland Church in that manner.[15]

Intraracial connections assumed other forms. As the number of blacks leaving the city increased after 1900, the interest in their welfare did as well. The

"Colored Folk" column identified the visitors and the Evansvillians who were in other cities. It also sought to provide information on the progress of blacks in other communities, especially Indianapolis. In 1908, for instance, it reported that Rev. W H. Anderson had traveled to the capital city to preach at a Baptist church which consisted largely of former Evansville residents.[16]

The Indianapolis black newspapers—*The Freeman* and *The Recorder*—were valuable sources of information for Evansville blacks and also enhanced intraracial ties. Each included columns written by correspondents in other cities and towns throughout the nation as well as Indiana. Correspondents were apparently selected due to their ability to sell copies of the papers in their communities. Promotional efforts, such as "the most popular minister in the State of Indiana" in the *Recorder* in 1908-1909 and the "prominent Hoosiers" contest in *The Freeman* in 1920, allowed aggressive salespersons to amass thousands of "votes" with each subscription sold. These competitions, like the columns, strengthened the bonds linking Evansville blacks to those elsewhere.[17]

News about Evansville appeared infrequently in *The Freeman*, perhaps an indication that few copies were sold in the river city. An Evansville column was published regularly, however, in *The Recorder* through most of 1902, irregularly between early 1910 and late 1916, and virtually every week after early 1927. (Extant copies of the paper do not exist for 1917-1924.) Probably the reason that an Evansville column did not often appear between 1903 and 1909 was that during that time the "Colored Folk" column in the Evansville *Journal-News* appeared regularly. Typically *Recorder* columns included details about church and club activities, visitors to the city, and illnesses or deaths of black citizens. As a rule they eschewed social or political commentary.[18]

Given the income and the literacy required to purchase and read newspapers, it is possible that the Evansville column, like "Colored Folk," had a more affluent than average audience. The social activities described in those columns lend credence to that assumption. The wealth of news about ordinary blacks and the sense of racial solidarity conveyed in the columns, however, suggest that the readership was not limited to the middle and upper classes.[19]

Similar tendencies were evident in other rituals. One of the most important events of the year remained the "annual sermon" marking a year's service by a pastor. Interdenominational unity was also present in other special events, such as wedding anniversaries of pastors and their wives, or baptisms in the Ohio River. Also important were "community sings" and concerts given by schoolchildren at Evans Hall or the various churches, all of which drew hundreds. Especially appealing were the occasional appearances of such renowned groups as the Fisk Jubilee Singers.[20]

Athletic competition also became a vital part of the black subculture and transcended class and status considerations. Men's baseball teams had been formed as early as the 1870s, and by the 1890s local groups regularly engaged challengers from Henderson, Mt. Vernon, and Owensboro. Supported by contributions from prominent whites or the more affluent black business and professional men, the teams bore such names as the Delmonicos, the Gold Dollars, and the Dupees. By the late 1920s a formidable team, the "Reichert Giants," was fielded by white contractor Manson Reichert, later mayor of the city. It belonged to the Southern Colored Professional League. As early as 1901, students and young laborers organized football teams to compete with athletes in nearby towns. In October of that year, Ernest Tidrington's eleven defeated all local competition and took on a Louisville college team on Thanksgiving Day. Contributions from parents, teachers, and students themselves also led to the formation of intramural athletic teams at the grade schools and the high school as early as 1904.[21]

Other activities, however, testified to the existence of social stratification. Like their white counterparts, "Colored Folk" columnists paid special attention to the activities of prominent citizens. The wedding of Rev. Rouse's daughter, Sadie, in June 1905 was described, for instance, as one of the biggest society events in years. Similarly, the funeral of longtime resident Daniel Jackson two years later was officiated by the three most eminent black pastors in the city, and Knights and Daughters of Tabor from the city and its environs conducted the burial rites of their departed brother. Great reverence was shown for the city's "first families"—for example, Pleasant Jackson, janitor at city hall, whose daughters had attended Fisk University and married prosperous Indianapolis business and professional men. An increasingly important ritual in black society, as in white, was the reception, often hosted by the wife or daughter of an important civic leader. A clear sense of exclusivity was conveyed in the publication of news of such affairs.[22]

"Society" blacks were acutely conscious of white perception of their behavior. After one gala New Year's party, Dupee wrote in "Colored Folk" that he wished whites could have seen their fine clothing and heard their high quality entertainment. He was especially proud of Peter Moorman, who rose from shoe shiner to owner of a small business, and had "a nice bank account, owns five beautiful houses . . . and has under way of construction . . . four more nice cottages. . . ." This man stood in stark contrast to "[T]he cigarette fiend, the standing collar and boiled shirt culprit, who day after day commit such crimes and deport themselves in such a way as to restrict the liberties of many of our hard-working and honest citizens," but such persons were "rapidly finding their rightful places in our penal institutions and ere long . . . we shall see prejudice and hatred extinguished, and in its stead the white man extending to us a glad hand."[23] In an era of mounting racial bigotry, it was questionable that any of this, however, impressed whites.[24]

Unlike many other cities, Evansville never had a black church which catered to an exclusively middle- or upper-class membership, but in the early twentieth century leaders of the black community belonged, as a rule, to Liberty, Alexander, and McFarland. Records of the election of trustees disclose, on the one hand, that between 1902 and 1905 Liberty's lay leaders included Willis Green and James L. Green. In the 1920s Isaac Coffee was chairman of the board. In 1904 and 1905 Alexander's trustees included G. W. Buckner and John H. Carter. In 1922 teacher M. C. Bryant and barber Willis Rucker were on the board. Ernest Tidrington became a trustee in 1929. In 1903 McFarland's trustees included Pleasant Jackson, the janitor. In the early 1920s John B. Taliaferro and Alex Lauderdale, policemen, and W. F. Cooper, a teacher, were on the board. Prominent citizens were also active in other affairs of these churches. W. E. Best was Sunday School superintendent for many years at Alexander, as was J. D. Cox at Liberty. On the other hand, common laborers and service workers, women as well as men, were trustees of the smaller and newer churches, such as Little Zion Baptist (Oakdale), Little Hope Baptist, and Cleaves CME churches.[25]

By the mid-1920s there were eighteen churches, all but five of which were situated in Baptisttown. That reflected the expansion of residential segregation. Only nine of these had existed prior to 1900. The largest and most influential—Alexander, Liberty, and McFarland—were located on the same sites they had occupied for decades, and among themselves claimed about 2,000 members. One of the newer Baptist congregations was named, somewhat ironically, Little Hope. Situated at 113 Elliott, it traced its origins to High Street. Also among the more recent churches were Cleaves Chapel, established by the Colored Methodist Episcopal Church in 1917, and three holiness or pentecostal churches.[26]

No white Protestant churches had black members, but several Roman Catholic parishes did. Exactly when that began is unclear, but during the First World War Father Francis P. Ryves of Assumption Cathedral—reflecting the growing segregationism of the time—announced that thereafter black families would be served only at his church. A special collection was also taken to establish a separate parish for black Catholics, as "a building for their own race members would encourage the growth of the religion among the colored here."[27] (A separate church was not organized until 1941.) Between 1918 and 1931 blacks sat in a separate section during mass at Assumption, and after 1931 were provided a separate mass as well as "special instructions" for children and adults.[28]

Perhaps as many as twenty other black churches were formed between 1900 and the mid-1920s which did not survive by 1930. Most were small and operated on miniscule budgets. Typical was the fate of St. Paul's Baptist. The cornerstone was laid in September 1901 during an elaborate ceremony led by S. S. Dupee and the United Brothers of Friendship. "The sable sons of Ham with their gay badges displayed and their hands clothed in white gloves, took up the line of march," wrote the *Journal-News*.[29] Four years later the congregation merged with Little Hope with the understanding that the latter would assume the former's debt of $83.[30]

Particularly ephemeral were the pentecostal and holiness churches, which began to appear after 1901, when revival meetings were held at Ninth and Canal streets. By 1908 there were four "missions" run by these groups. To some clergy and lay leaders—solicitous of white approval and eager to display evidences of progress, such as the dedication of a baptistry at Liberty in April 1901, which eliminated the use of the Ohio River for baptisms—such forms of religious expression were abhorrent. Rev. W. H. Anderson was especially critical, because this spontaneous and emotional form of religion, he believed, made blacks appear ludicrous—that is, what whites had said of the behavior of his predecessors in the late 1860s and 1870s. More perceptive was the writer of "Colored News" in January 1908:

> The residents of Baptisttown are being given every opportunity to have their souls saved. . . . The meetings are held almost nightly, and some of them continue there [*sic*] services until the wee hours of the night. Since our leading churches have become so fashionable, there are hundreds of folks, who have good heart-felt religion, who prefer and do attend these missions. The partial disposition to the well dressed is hurting our leading churches.[31]

Such churches grew rapidly among blacks in Northern cities after 1906, threatening established congregations. Extant records of such a group, the Church of the Living at 624 McCormick, confirm the fact that ordinary people—women as much as men, and generally illiterate and at the lowest level of the occupational scale—took leadership roles in such congregations. These Christians depended on charismatic leaders and unwavering agreement on doctrine for their survival. Added to inherent financial limitations, that meant institutional survival was extremely risky. Nevertheless, by 1910 such groups had become an established part of religious life in Evansville.[32]

Since all but a handful of black churches were governed along congregational lines, it might be added, this sort of religious expression threatened the livelihood of pastors at the more traditional churches. Rev. Anderson's critique was understandable, as he was paid twenty-five cents for each Sunday worshipper. L. A. McIntyre, who succeeded Anderson in 1919, was unapologetically parochial. His drive to succeed at a church which had a declining membership and owed $2,600 in back salary to Anderson's widow was boundless. He hired a white attorney to force Mrs. Anderson to settle for about half of what was owed her. He cornered the L & N excursion market to add to his congregation's income, and unabashedly curried the favor of local white leaders. He boasted in particular of a gift of $500 from Klansman Herbert Males, elected mayor in 1925, in return for McIntyre's agreement to support him.[33]

A number of pastors at the city's leading black churches served long and distinguished terms. "Father Rouse" (1854–1929) at Liberty was the most notable in this regard. W. H. Anderson (1848–1913), at McFarland from 1882 until he died, and Frank Long (1872–1926), pastor of Little Hope for the twenty-two years before his death, were also noteworthy. Such longevity, among other things, strengthened the influence of the Colored Ministerial Alliance, which met weekly to discuss theological and social questions. Anderson and Rouse were regularly elected officers of the organization. An Indianapolis church publication referred to Anderson in 1907 as "the dictator and 'Teddy' [Roosevelt] of the ministers' alliance." Two years after his death, Mrs. J. D. Cox recalled that no one ever doubted his integrity or his belief in the value of self-help.[34]

Longevity also meant that Evansville pastors gained substantial influence in regional, state, and national church organizations. Anderson, a member of the executive board of the National Baptist Convention, was a popular preacher at state and national meetings of black Baptists. Rouse was a vice-president of the National Baptist Convention, a longtime member of its Home and Foreign Mission Board, and a frequent delegate to the national convention of the denomination. For fourteen years he was moderator of the Indiana Baptist Association. He also served as an evangelist in Baptist churches throughout the Midwest. In 1900 he was awarded an honorary doctorate from Cadiz (Kentucky) Normal and Theological College. L. A. McIntyre's successes as a fund-raiser and church-builder earned him a call to one of Tennessee's largest black congregations in 1931.[35]

Most important, such leaders helped to create the institutional stability which guaranteed that Evansville's black churches could offer a variety of services to its members and to the community as a whole. In an age in which opportunities for personal development were severely limited, churches were, after the family, the most important social outlet.

Because of its size, Liberty provided the widest range of activities for persons of all ages. The church was also used for the "annual sermons" and other festivities of most fraternal orders, for concerts by schoolchildren, and for meetings of such groups as the Business League and, prior to 1909, the black Republican clubs.[36] A cursory examination of the Evansville column of the *Recorder* reveals an even greater array of activities by the late twenties. In addition to youth and adult programs in May 1927, for example, Liberty hosted the annual memorial service of the Knights of Pythias and "Major Rosencranz Day" to honor the chief white benefactor of black Evansville. Later in the month women's clubs at the church conducted a fund drive for victims of Mississippi River flooding. In December were held the church's annual Fall Festival, a mass rally to raise money for the Cherry Street YMCA, and a Rally Day program in which all the black school principals spoke and the members of all school musical groups performed.[37]

Other churches also supplied a variety of services to the black community which encouraged intraracial contact and cooperation. Particularly important were annual revival meetings, which were interdenominational affairs. A component of Baptist and Methodist rituals since 1865, these were usually held in the fall or early winter and lasted two weeks. Often they featured a preacher from another city, and sometimes these meetings were protracted, as in the instance of R. L. King's services at St. John's in October 1919, in which abbreviated skirts and "wiggles" among young women were the target of his wrath. Citywide church meetings assumed such other forms as Little Zion's entertaining all the members of the Laymen's Union in the city in February 1927.[38]

The larger churches also hosted annual Sunday School conventions as well as regional and state meetings. The Indiana Conference of the AME Church held its annual meetings in 1905 and 1918 at Alexander Chapel. These week-long events concluded with a service of worship at Evans Hall. The Evansville district conference of the AME Zion Church met for four days at Hood Chapel in July 1902, and during the same week Liberty entertained 100 delegates to the state BYPU and Sunday School conventions. The paucity of hotel facilities and the financial condition of most delegates meant that local parishoners had to provide room and board for the visitors.[39]

The center of black subculture, in a word, was the church, an important vehicle for adjusting to and counteracting racial discrimination. And religious life in black Evansville was isolated from that of the larger Christian community. That fact of life, which was reinforced by patterns of residence and occupation, was symbolized before the 1930s by the systematic exclusion of church notices and other news from the weekly church columns of the newspapers. Only rarely was that pattern broken. In September 1918 the state AME conference was held in the city during the same week that delegates from the German Methodist Episcopal churches of the state were assembled. On the last day of the AME conference, the fellow Methodists exchanged greetings at Evans Hall. Beginning in October 1925, members of the white Ministerial Alliance invited black ministers to address their gatherings. It was not until June 1941, however, that black ministers were invited to become members.[40]

The fraternal orders continued to flourish, but unlike the churches they were clearly the province of the more affluent. In 1922 the trustees of McFarland Lodge No. 5 of the Masons, one of the most prestigious groups, included J. D. Cox, W. A. Gaines, and Daniel Dunlap, a janitor. Elected to join them in 1924 was Raymond King, the dentist, and Monroe Talbott, long-time city fireman, was added in 1929.[41]

One of the newest and most active were the Knights of Pythias. An Evansville lodge was established by Ernest Tidrington in 1903. Prospective members, aged nineteen to fifty-five, paid a $3.50 membership fee and were required to be in good health and have good morals. Pythians had four departments: the Subordinate Rank for adult men; the Uniform Rank for young men; the Calanthe Court, a women's auxiliary; and the Endowment, an insurance department funded by Pythians everywhere which supplemented the health and death benefits offered by local societies. State Pythians also established their own savings and loan association in Indianapolis in 1912 at the suggestion of Tidrington, who had risen to the top of the Pythian order in Indiana. Shares cost $5 each, to be paid in twenty-five-cent weekly installments.[42]

It would seem that the development of black insurance companies elsewhere and the creation of a local funeral parlor would have lessened the need for the benefits which these societies afforded, and that the radio, motion picture, and automobile would have met the social needs that secret societies once met.[43] In addition, a number of groups emerged after the First World War to deal with the health and welfare of Evansville blacks. Nevertheless, the fraternal order remained an important part of black Evansville through the twenties. The number of societies rose from twenty-one in 1909 to almost twice that number in the mid-twenties, when there were eight lodges of Odd Fellows, six of the Knights of Pythias, twelve of the UBF, six of the Masons, and one each of the

Elks, Knights of Tabor, Templars, and Fern Leaf Circle.[44] Because of rising segregationism, these orders either owned their own halls or shared quarters with black societies which did. For example, the Odd Fellows, Elks, Pythians, and Taborians convened at Castle Hall, a site on Chestnut between Fourth and Fifth owned by the Pythians (and in which O'Hara and Tidrington and several other professionals had their offices).[45]

The rituals of these groups were probably as attractive as the benefits in the recruitment and retention of members. These affairs were splendid, and each order tried to present the most splendid annual meetings. On May 23, 1909, hundreds of Pythians from Evansville, Boonville, Princeton, Vincennes, Mt. Vernon, and Lyles Station marched behind their band from Cherry and Sixth streets to Evans Hall, where they observed their "annual turnout and services." Women were dressed in "white waists, black skirts, black ties, with a white carnation in their hair," while men wore "black suits, black hats and a white carnation in the lapel of their coat." At the hall, where Chancellor Tidrington presided, Pythians enjoyed solos and band selections and heard addresses from prominent men from Chicago and Indianapolis. After the Sunday afternoon service they marched back to their hall.[46]

Equally important were the funeral rituals for lodge members. Services for Father Rouse, who died in December 1929, were conducted by members of the lodge, McFarland, of which he had been a member for fifty years.[47] When Rufus R. Dodson, "one of Evansville's most popular colored citizens," was buried on June 8, 1903, the "Colored Folk" columnist wrote this:

> The ceremonies [at Alexander Chapel] were held under the auspices of the Knights of Tabor and the Enterprise Lodge of the U. B. F. . . . . [The church] was packed to overflowing and approximately a thousand people stood outside, striving to get in. There were about two hundred and fifty people in line, but none except the grand officers, the Palatine Guards, and the master of the U. B. F. lodge were able to get in. Miss Louella Hutchinson, probably the most accomplished colored musician in the city, presided at the pipe organ. . . . this being followed by a scripture reading by Rev. Dr. J. D. Rouse, a prayer by Rev. S. S. Stone, and then a beautiful public discourse by Rev. Dr. E. A. Johnson. . . . The services were then given over to the hands of the lodges. The ritualistic function of the Taborian order was performed by Mr. Charles W. Walden and Dr. G. W. Buckner. The address of eulogy was delivered by Dr. S. S. Dupee . . . [and] was a source of many laudable comments. It was a fitting tribute brim full of eloquence and showed how thoroughly equipped he was in the work. . . . [T]he community would miss Mr. Dodson first, because he was such a devout Christian. . . . He then referred to Moses, Daniel, Joshua, and the three Hebrew children, saying that they possessed the same key and that any one who has been born of the spirit has it and is able to surmount any of the trials of this life. At the conclusion of his address the U. B. F.'s under the guidance of Mr. James Fry went through their ceremonies and all was over.[48]

Like the churches, the fraternal orders frequently provided interchange with blacks in other communities. The yearly thanksgiving service brought hundreds of lodge members from southern Indiana and western Kentucky by steamboat or train excursions, and similar events elsewhere prompted Evansvillians by the hundreds to join in. State conventions of the Pythians and Taborians, first held in Evansville in 1908 and 1909, respectively, were especially attractive in this respect. Members of the various lodges also participated in each other's celebrations. The local orders were also understandably proud when their members achieved prominence at the state or national levels. Probably the earliest notable was William L. Houston, a native of the city, who was elected to several terms as Grand Master of the 400,000 black Odd Fellows of the United States.[49]

The activities of the secret orders, nevertheless, were intertwined with the aspirations of strong-minded individuals, and in a city the size of Evansvile the rivalries of the lodges were undoubtedly more important than the overarching issues of racial strategy which animated leaders in larger communities. In Evansville this was not a conflict based on theories of racial progress or on rivalries between old versus new elites, as most of the lodges were founded after 1900 and were led by persons whose influence derived from their service to all-black clienteles. All shared a faith in the doctrines of self-help.

The disputes were perhaps best explained as competition among men of similar background and interest for the spotlight in the black community, and in turn for the respect of white leaders. In the summer of 1909, for example, some unidentified members of the Colored Ministerial Association complained about the "Sunday turn-outs," which they contended to be a violation of the Sabbath. That prompted a caustic reply from the writer of "Colored Folk": "The very same fellows . . . for years have caused the negroes of Evansville to grope in the dark and ignorance shrouded by their sins and wrongdoing. . . . No wonder the negroes of Evansville are so far behind."[50] Apparently most clergymen did not press the case, as Sunday afternoon lodge activities continued well into the 1920s.

In the same summer Dupee also attacked leaders of the UBF, notably Buckner and W. W. Townsend, for planning a parade on the day before the Taborians were planning to hold their state meeting in the city and for holding their annual "turn-out" on the same day as the Taborians had. Although Dupee was a Republican activist and Buckner and Townsend active Democrats, and 1909 was a city election year, probably politics were not the only reason for Dupee's outburst, as W. A. Gaines was an eminent member of the UBF and a staunch Republican.[51]

Similarly, a bitter argument erupted in the winter of 1914-1915 between Tidrington and attorney John H. Wilson, whom Tidrington expelled from the Knights of Pythias for allegedly embezzling funds. Wilson was also accused of stealing funds from Dupee's mother after the physician's untimely death. Wilson responded by suing, and after testifying he was assaulted by Tidrington. The Pythian leader was subsequently cleared of all charges, even though Wilson claimed the judge was a crony of Fred Ossenberg, Tidrington's ally. Wilson left town shortly thereafter. That the fraternal order was on shaky footing at the time, for whatever the reason, was evidenced by the sale of its hall in July 1915 to satisfy liens against the order.[52]

That the fraternal societies revolved about the leadership of a few prominent figures was unquestionable. Tidrington became state "grand chancellor" in 1906, at the age of twenty-four, and held the post until his death. He was also elected International Vice President in the 1920s. His rise was made possible by George Stewart, editor of the *Indianapolis Recorder*, and Will H. Porter, also of Indianapolis, who brought the eager young man into prominence to dispel the notion that only capital city Pythians could hold office in the order. Under Tidrington's leadership the tensions between "out-state" and Indianapolis lodges persisted, however, and that led him to reorganize all of the non-Indianapolis lodges under his control, thus checking rival leaders.[53]

Other orders also had strong leaders. The United Brothers of Friendship, the oldest order in the city, were led by attorney James G. Green, elected Indiana Grand Master for the first of several terms in 1904, and W. A. Gaines, who was national Grand Master when he arrived in Evansville. The Knights of Tabor were clearly the work of S. S. Dupee, who served in several prominent positions on the state level. The establishment of the Benevolent and Protective Order of Elks in the early 1920s followed a similar pattern. Shortly after his arrival in the city in 1921, educator Charles Rochelle helped to found a lodge, and soon he headed it, a position he retained for many years.[54]

The fortunes of the secret societies, in short, rose and fell with the presence of tenacious and persuasive individuals. After Dupee's death in 1913, membership in the Knights and Daughters of Tabor dropped sharply, and by the mid-1920s there was only one lodge in the city. The Knights of Pythias remained a strong force in the city until Tidrington's death. Eventually other social programs began to meet the needs that at one time only the lodges could fill. By 1941 there remained only a few evidences of the once-strong fraternal orders— the Masons, the Elks, and the Odd Fellows. Even the UBF no longer existed.[55]

Although the secret societies figured prominently in the black community, there were many other forms of social organization which appealed to a wider range of men and women. At Christmas, as with most whites, blacks formed numerous philanthropic groups.[56] Some were created for social interchange, like the "Manhatten [*sic*] Colored Club" of January 1906, formed for the purpose of "uniting men of the colored race for social purpous [*sic*], thereby in morals and religion improving such people, and providing a decent and respectable place where they can gather and meet for social purposes."[57] The directors of the club included a bartender and a porter. A month later, the "Zelah Club" was established to "provide social amusement and intercourse between black men and women."[58] The directors were a teamster, a driver, and a restaurant keeper, all of whom resided near Lower Water and Third Avenue. In 1908, Thomas J. Mosley, James Lander, and Simon P. Taylor organized the Coachmen's Club to provide for their social needs. A year later, such notables as Isaac Coffee, a janitor, J. Wesley Baker, a clerk, William Glover, S. S. Dupee, and John H. Wilson created the "R-Line Club" for "the social, moral, material, and political betterment" of black Evansvillians and provide club rooms for "social enjoyment." In 1911, a group of janitors and porters established the Progressive Negro Club for similar purposes.[59]

These groups, which lasted at most a year or two, resembled the plethora of clubs formed by whites in that era. They revealed an intermixture of occupational, political, and social interests, and—like white groups—often included alcoholic beverages in their activities. They also signified efforts to create more respectable social outlets than those offered by the many dives or lid clubs in Baptisttown. Such efforts, however, were not without risk. Police raided the Manhatten Social Club on several occasions, and during one election even Dupee was arrested for "illegal saloon keeping."[60]

Other voluntary societies, reflecting the maturation of the subculture and the leadership of farsighted citizens, sought to improve the welfare of the community as a whole. Especially noteworthy in this regard were the Day Nursery Association, the Phyllis Wheatley Association, and the Colored YMCA. Named after the eminent black author of the Revolutionary War era, the PWA was a "residence and job-training center for girls who had come to the city on their own or who were separated from their families for some other reason."[61] The formation of the PWA met no opposition from older black leaders, as the creation of the Wheatley Association in Cleveland did in 1912, due to the integrationist tradition there. The PWA in Evansville originated in the Day Nursery Association, headed by Sallie Wyatt Stewart and Georgia Williams, which in turn had been created in 1916 by Stewart's newly formed City Federation of Colored Women's Clubs. The Nursery Association raised about $3,000 to purchase a dwelling at 906 South Governor Street, Dr. Dupee's former home, and began a day nursery for children of working mothers in early 1919. About thirty attended daily, and their mothers paid fifteen cents per day for the service. Later the group purchased another residence at 410 Southeast Eighth Street as a boarding house and recreational center for young women. The association was not formalized until January 1925, when Stewart and longtime teacher Fannie Snow signed incorporation papers as president and secretary.[62]

By October 1925 the association sponsored a variety of activities—a girls' baseball team, for example, and classes in homemaking and sewing. A matron, Mary Belcher, administered the programs, although it is not clear whether she was paid for her efforts. The decline of employment in the Depression, especially in domestic service, led to the eventual closing of the day nursery, and the girls' program was moved to the house on South Governor. By the early 1930s about 400 girls a week participated in activities or boarded at the house, and ten girls' clubs met there regularly. The name "Phyllis Wheatley Association" was adopted by 1930, although the incorporated name, the Day Nursery Association, was never formally changed.[63]

The paucity of historical records makes unclear the precise role that white women played in the development and the maintenance of the DNA and the

PWA. In Cleveland white philanthropy was amply evident, and as a price for receiving it black women acceded to allowing whites to select leaders of the PWA. Neither minutes of the Evansville YWCA nor the sparse newspaper accounts of the era offer evidence of that in Evansville, but one might safely assume that whites contributed to fund drives. In April 1918, Mrs. Bacon spoke at the Cherry Street Library on the need for a child welfare organization, and it is likely that she was involved in the formation of the DNA. Leadership in the frequent DNA fund drives was provided, though, by blacks—notably the indefatigable Sallie Stewart—and black women provided the volunteer labor to keep the facility open. The organization's attempts to be included in the Community Chest drive were rejected on the grounds that it did not conduct public fund drives annually.[64]

The Colored YMCA, on the other hand, was clearly identified with white philanthropy and control. An initial effort in February 1905 to begin such a branch met with financial failure.[65] In November 1907 several prominent Indianapolis blacks, including George Knox, editor of *The Freeman*, attended a state convention at the Evansville YMCA, and in the course of their visit spoke at black churches on the need for a YMCA. Two months later such a branch was organized. Some clergymen were involved, and meetings were initially held at Hood Chapel on Sunday afternoons, but most of the leadership came from businessmen and other professionals, particularly J. D. Cox, P. T. Miller, Moses Davis and G. W. Buckner. In addition, supporters of the white branch helped to raise money, and soon the black branch opened a facility on the second floor at 427 Walnut Street which was used for reading and meeting rooms.[66]

The black community's enthusiasm for the project so impressed white plow maker A. C. Rosencranz that he donated $6,000 to purchase a larger building. He lent another $1,500 for renovations at no interest, with the understanding that the black community would raise $1,500 by February 1, 1910. Teams of black leaders were formed which raised the required amount in an enthusiastic campaign. The new two-story building—a vacant saloon and store measuring seventy by twenty feet, located at Seventh and Cherry streets—was dedicated June 19. The facility provided space for a gym, dressing and locker rooms, sleeping quarters, and several meeting rooms.[67]

The Cherry Street YMCA soon became the center of social and recreational activity in black Evansville. Various community organizations met there, and many new groups—for example, a troop of the Boy Scouts, formed in early 1917—came into existence because of the facility. Nonetheless, the organization perennially suffered from financial difficulties. Title to the building, moreover, was held by the white YMCA, which supervised Cherry Street's operations and influenced the selection of its directors and programs. On three occasions the branch closed due to money problems, but in 1923 the solution seemed to have been found, when the Cherry Street YMCA began receiving funds from the Community Chest. The only black agency in the unified drive, it received $3,800 in 1923 (out of a total budget of $140,000). In January 1928, however, the Central YMCA discontinued the operation of Cherry

29. A Bible class at the Cherry Street YMCA, mid–1920s. Standing are the teachers, George Jackson and P. T. Miller. Special collections, University of Southern Indiana.

Street because of the cessation of the Community Chest. That, in turn (see chapter 9), led to the organization of the Inter-Racial Council and the Community Association.[68]

Although the community's limited financial resources contributed to the demise of Cherry Street, they did not deter other efforts at social improvement. A Civic Improvement Society was formed in April 1909, because of "the undeveloped condition of this section of the city."[69] Also short-lived were the Mutual Cooperative Home Business Association of 1906, which was organized to assist in the purchase of homes, and in the same year a "DuBois Society" among youth, an indication of some dissatisfaction with the accommodationist strategy urged by most leaders. No records of those groups survive.[70]

Of longer duration was the Colored Federation of Women's Clubs, established about 1916 by Sallie Stewart. This society may have been the offspring of one formed in March 1914 by several other women whose occupations or those of their husbands marked them as more affluent than most. These women incorporated the "Colored Association of Charities" to assist the Pigeon Township Trustee in investigating applications for relief, to effect cooperation among charitable organizations, to seek employment for the "deserving poor," to provide a municipal lodging house, and to encourage thrift by forming "a penny provident savings bank."[71] Among other things, the CFWC sewed clothing for the needy and distributed it through the township trustee. Such member groups as the "Outlook Mothers Unit" raised funds and donations of food and clothing for black soldiers during the war. The Federation was the mainstay of the Day Nursery Association and the force behind the formation of "Colored Girls Week" in the fall of 1925 to promote home economics, physical education and music appreciation among school-age girls. A related group was the Colored WCTU, headed by Mrs. Buckner, which was created about 1916 and survived into the 1920s.[72]

TABLE 24:   Family Headship, by Percent, 1910 and 1930

Type of Head/Year	All	Black	White	Native White/ Foreign Born Parents	Foreign-Born
1. Couple					
1910	80.3	65.0	81.2	79.9	78.4
1930	85.0	74.0	86.3	79.2	77.6
2. Single-Parent					
Female-Headed					
1910	12.6	21.5	12.5	14.7	14.7
1930	15.0	26.0	13.7	20.8	22.4
Male-Headed					
1910	6.2	11.0	5.6	4.3	4.9
1930	—	—	—	—	—
3. Single-Member					
1910	0.9	3.1	0.7	1.0	2.0
1930	—	—	—	—	—
Total					
1910	100.0	100.0	100.0	100.0	100.0
1930	100.0	100.0	100.0	100.0	100.0
Number					
1,910	1,914	164	1,556	394	102
1930	25,716	1,720	23,002	5,355	990

Sources: Thirteenth Census, Population Schedules for Vanderburgh County, 1910; Fifteenth Census, 1930, *Population*, volume VI: *Families* (Washington, D.C. 1933), 407. The data for 1930 distinguished only between female-headed families and all other families. In column three the statistics for 1910 apply to all whites, but in 1930 only to native whites. Hence all male-headed families are counted in the category couple-headed. Column four applies to those with a foreign-born father. The 1910 data is derived from a systematic sample, but the 1930 data constitute the total population.

Established in the mid-twenties was the Elvira Roach Home for the Aged. Located in Baptisttown, its trustees were such notables as Tidrington and William H. Fauntleroy, a post office employee. The home survived at least through the decade via occasional fund-raising events, such as a concert held "in the colored school buildings" in November 1924.[73] Created in the same period was the Otis Stone Post of the American Legion. Charles Rochelle assumed the position of commander, a post he would continue to hold for many years, and Dr. Dendy was finance officer. In addition, a committee led by Drs. Buckner and Jackson, Revs. Frank Long and W. H. Ferguson, and William Glover raised funds for a swimming pool, named the Booker T. Washington Pool, which was opened shortly after the end of the war. Located at Governor and Mulberry streets, its operations were apparently subsidized by city funds in the 1920s. A city-run playground was also opened across the street from the pool in 1931 on the site of the former Governor Street School.[74]

Regardless of social strata, however, the family remained, as before, the center of Afro-American society. In 1910 (Table 24) two-thirds of Evansville's blacks lived in couple-headed families, a slightly smaller proportion than ten years earlier. Three-quarters resided in households in which there was a male head who was the principal breadwinner. These proportions, as in the late nineteenth century, were high, but not as high as those of white families.[75]

Examined by region, marital status, age, and occupational level, these figures disclose the same patterns that had existed prior to 1900. Female-headed black families were most prevalent in Ward 3, a region with many hotels, restaurants, private homes, and steamboats—the region most likely to attract single, divorced, or widowed women due to the number of service positions. The highest proportion of couple-headed families resided in Ward 4, where there were many black miners. The microcosm of the black community was Ward 7, in which 65 percent of its families were couple-headed.[76]

Widows headed slightly over two-fifths of the female-headed black families, as compared with one-fifth among white and three-tenths among second-generation German-Americans. Where the female head was German-born, 60 percent were widows. When the ages of the female heads are considered, a clearer understanding of the sources of female headship emerges. As in the years 1870-1900, Afro-American widows were younger than all white widows. There were more widows among German-born female heads because the German-born were older than the population as a whole. That also accounts for the relatively large proportion of female-headed families where the head was born in Germany.[77]

The vagaries of opportunity in the urban setting, in short, seemed once more to be the most important determinant of family headship in the black community. In 1910, as earlier, the more affluent the family, the more likely it was that it was couple-headed. The odds were over three times greater that a professional or proprietor would head a family with a husband and a wife than one with a single parent. Job opportunities in service attracted rural females who were widowed, divorced, or single, and death, desertion, and divorce took their toll on families living in the city. Particularly important in that regard was the fact that at all age levels the death rate was higher in the black community than in the white. Nevertheless, the male or couple-headed family, in that era the symbol of social stability, was the mainstay of black Evansville. About four in five families in 1910 and three in four in 1930 fell into that category.[78]

It must be noted that the percentage of female-headed black families in Evansville increased every census year after 1870. (See also chapter 5.) That suggested the long-term effects of city life and discrimination on black families were increasingly negative. The differences between black and white families in this respect created by the time of the Depression yet further evidence of the fact that two societies coexisted in the river city.

TABLE 25:   Family Composition, by Percent, 1910

Type	Black	White	Native White/ Foreign-Born Parents	Foreign- Born
Nuclear	35.6	60.6	59.4	54.9
Extended	21.5	19.0	24.1	29.4
Augmented				
with boarders	28.8	9.9	6.3	3.9
with servants	5.5	5.7	6.6	6.9
Single Member	2.5	0.7	1.0	2.0
Other	6.1	4.0	2.5	2.9
Total	100.0	100.0	100.0	100.0
Number	164	1,744	394	102

Source: Thirteenth Census, Population Schedules for Vanderburgh County, 1910.

Differences between blacks and whites were more pronounced in family organization. As shown on Table 25, although the nuclear family was the center of black society, a significant share of black families added relatives and boarders, lodgers, and/or servants. Like the employment of women and children, this reflected the meagerness of family income. One in three families which rented their homes had boarders or lodgers, twice the rate of those which owned their homes. The lower the occupational level of the head of the household, the more frequently such arrangements occurred. About 30 percent of the families in which the head was a semiskilled, service, or unskilled worker had boarders or lodgers, nearly twice the proportion of those in which the head was a professional or proprietor. All of the families augmented by servants, however, were headed by persons with higher status. The taking in of relatives was also more likely at the lower end of the occupational spectrum, as one in four at the lowest two occupational levels did so, as compared with less than one in ten among the top two. That suggested that relatives supplemented family income. Family extension and augmentation were more likely to exist in those enumeration districts, moreover, in which the percentage of lower-level occupations was greatest—that is, districts 99 (Ward 2), 143, 144, and 145 (Ward 7). [79]

In 1910, in a word, the greatest differences between white and black families continued to be the harsher socioeconomic conditions faced by Afro-Amer-

icans. Proportionally more black families had a female head and were augmented by boarders or lodgers. These patterns persisted through the 1920s. As
demonstrated by Table 24, nearly twice as many black families in 1930 had a
female head as did those of native whites. The proportion was slightly higher
than those headed by whites with one or two foreign-born parents or those
with foreign-born heads. Given the lack of data regarding the age and marital
status of the female heads, one must infer that the factors contributing to these
differences were the same as in 1910. Lower status and female headship were
more clearly correlated, however, as black women headed 22 percent of families
in which the home was owned, as compared with 27 percent in which the
home was rented. City residence also continued to be a factor: among all rural
black families in Indiana, 12 percent had a female head, less than one-half the
rate among urban families in the state.[80]

Census data also reveal that the incidence of augmentation among black
families remained high. Among native white families in the city, 10.4 percent
took in boarders and lodgers, as did 9.4 percent of those in which the head was
foreign-born. In the black community, however, 29.3 percent—8 percentage
points above the level for urban blacks in Indiana—were so augmented. Owner
families were also less likely to have boarders and lodgers (22.9 percent) than
were renters (31 percent). It should also be noted that 57.3 percent of the
1,720 black families in 1930 contained no children under age twenty-one. (The
percentages for native whites with native parents and for native whites with
foreign-born parents were, by contrast, 40.8 and 36.9.) That suggested another
dimension to the low economic level of the black family: the inability to support children as well as the encouragement for black youth to find employment
outside the family.[81]

As with churches, fraternal organizations, clubs, and other voluntary
associations, family life reflected class and status distinctions. Lower-class families tended to be augmented and have both husband and wife at work. They
were also less likely to be couple-headed. Middle- and upper-class families, like
that of Logan Stewart, afforded women the leisure time and the resources to
engage in club activities, and the schedules of professionals like Dupee were
flexible enough to permit civic activities. For most blacks the family was, however, the chief means of coping with the vicissitudes of city life, a shelter for
relatives and boarders as well as members of the immediate family, and of nur-
turing what few opportunities for advancement existed. Beyond it, the most
important institution to the black masses was the church and, on occasion, the
club. Recreational activities also became more important by the 1920s.

Despite limited progress and the rich variety of social organizations that
the community generated on its own in an increasingly segregated city, many
blacks continued to exist marginally. On the one hand, the rise of the black
ghetto had given rise to a small middle class and even smaller upper class and to
a number of self-help societies. On the other, the consolidation of racial discrimination prior to the 1930s posed a continuing dilemma for black leaders.
While ghetto life was harsh, it was less harsh than that of the rural South, and

some opportunities for mobility existed. In the context of the ghetto, a modicum of power could be secured, and a sense of common destiny could be fostered.[82]

That sort of progress was inherently ambiguous, as it required that blacks defer to whites. The idea of racial autonomy was somewhat illusory, as some important voluntary associations—notably the Community Association—depended upon white philanthropy or direction. Election time was the most vivid illustration of that.

TWELVE

Black Leaders and the Black Vote,
1900–1930

 Because of the high degree of racial exclusion in Evansville after 1865, the accommodationist approach urged by Booker T. Washington generally confirmed existing patterns of behavior instead of initiating new ones.[1] There were, however, disagreements over the implementation of that strategy, especially regarding the voting activities of the black masses.

Because of their reliance on white philanthropy, their obsession with white perception of black behavior, and their emphasis on economic security, some clergymen and educators, including ones who had once been vocal, urged the masses to eschew partisan politics and focus instead on material and moral improvement. This group included older leaders like J. D. Rouse, who once championed Republican loyalty, and also younger men like Principal Best, whose position in an era of intense racial bigotry depended on full support of this form of accommodation.[2] Others like W. W. Townsend of Little Hope Baptist Church, hotelkeeper Henry Black, and Principal J. D. Cox joined Dr. Buckner in urging blacks to switch to the Democratic party. Still others like Dr. Jackson, Stewart, and Gaines urged allegiance, as old soldiers like Robert Nicholas had stressed, to the GOP. To them the party of Lincoln was the only guarantor of race progress. Within this group, however, some younger leaders expressed restlessness regarding the lack of reward for black voter loyalty. It might be added that the size and the cultural setting of Evansville's black community worked against the appearance of both the "New Negro" as well as Garveyism.[3]

White leaders also realized that this issue was vital, but for a different reason: The black vote was, as both parties freely admitted, the difference between victory and defeat in a city whose white voters were otherwise evenly divided. The battle for the black vote between 1900 and 1930 was waged with ferocity and with little regard for electoral niceties. The economic and cultural plight of most blacks encouraged and reinforced that situation, as well as the fact that political rewards, until the emergence of politico Ernest Tidrington, were scanty.[4]

Handsome and light-skinned, Tidrington was especially close to Fred Ossenberg, who had risen in Republican ranks because of his ability to deliver Baptisttown votes. A quick learner, Tidrington increased his political strength through his alliance with the young Ossenberg, and in 1903 became a sheriff's deputy—the same year he established a lodge of the Knights of Pythias. As Adrian Bell recalled, Tidrington was admired by many black youth because of his ability to succeed through wit and charm in a world in which success for blacks was extremely limited. To Bessie King, he was "The Boss"—one whose word could make or break any black citizen.[5]

"[T]he colored vote is indispensable to republican [sic] success," wrote a *Courier* reporter in 1901. "In fact no republican candidate for Congress since 1864 [sic] has been elected from this district without the colored vote."[6] Democrats responded to that by courting as well as manipulating the black vote, not by eliminating it. This took several means. One was the sporadic publication of a column for "colored folks" in the Democratic daily, usually at election time, to compete with a similar column in the Republican daily, which boasted of 1,916 black readers in 1903.[7]

Another was the black political club. Most at first were Republican, and until approximately 1910, three or four clubs had contingents in election-eve parades. In the elections of 1901, 1905, and 1908, however, other political organizations also appeared. They were headed by such men as J. D. Cox, who at Emancipation Day ceremonies in 1904 warned blacks that their support was being exploited by cynical Republican bosses. As in Louisville, die-hard Republicans like Nicholas warned that splitting the black vote would guarantee Democratic hegemony and encourage racial discrimination.[8]

The fact remained that political rewards were meager, whatever party blacks supported. Physicians fared better than most. In 1913, for instance, Dupee received $106 for services rendered during the three months prior to his death.[9] Some leaders responded to this and growing antiblack sentiment by urging blacks to shun politics and organized opposition to discrimination. The most prominent spokesman for this position was Rouse, whose remarks to a group of white pastors in January 1902 were prominently featured in the *Journal-News*. The pastor of the largest black church in the city insisted that blacks should be given a chance to prove themselves in the economic arena, in return for which they would eschew politics and the unseemly behavior which accompanied it. "I ask you," he implored," to assist us in this a second emancipation of the race from that condition that deprives us of the right to earn a living. . . . [W]e ask your friendship in the endeavor to become self-sustaining and self-reliant."[10]

This stance was appealing to members of the Colored Ministerial Association. "A minister who gives his time and study to God and His church," argued one observer in 1905, "can never find time to devote to politics and other worldly things."[11] Whether a convenient excuse for avoiding the unpleasant race relations of the day or an extension of the conservative theology prevalent among black clergymen, that position was staunchly defended in meetings of the pastors' association devoted to the subject prior to mid-1909. Thereafter, most black clergymen ceased being associated with partisan political causes and addressed public issues only in blatant instances of racial injustice, such as the Von Behren case of 1913.[12]

A variation of this theme was raised by Rev. W. H. Anderson, the former critic of Jim Crow, who also turned against politics. Anderson caused a stir in the black community beginning in the fall of 1905 when he refused to officiate at funerals in which a black undertaker who had recently established a business was not utilized. Dupee criticized Anderson (and Rouse, who also refused to officiate when Anderson declined to do so) for "the intelligent element of our race are disgusted and tired of these 'nigger' preachers continually holding up our people for ridicule and arousing prejudice against the whole race. . . ." He added, "we beg you white people who employ colored domestics to teach them that it is foolish of them to give one cent of their money for the support of such scalawags."[13]

Anderson refused to relent. "[T]he negro undertaker should have the preference among his own people. If negroes refuse to patronize their own professional men and business enterprises, how are they to succceed?" Evansville had fewer black businesses in proportion to its black population than any city in America, he insisted, due to "the lack of race pride and public spirited men."[14] At an observance of the centennial of Lincoln's birth two years later, he described such actions as necessary because a new day had dawned. The Confederate flag now signified "an interchange of pleasantry." Blacks were no longer wards of the nation but were expected "to contribute our quota of moral force necessary to good citizenship. To do this we must set a high premium upon good citizenship and virtue and a ban upon vice and immorality."[15]

Although they did not disagree with the notion of self-help, others— mostly non-clergymen—urged continued support of the Republican party. Dupee was the most outspoken spokesman for this view. He did not quibble with the notion that blacks had to prove their worth by better habits, but he insisted that one of the reasons that progress had not occurred was that such black militant editors as Monroe Trotter provided wrongheaded advice to the masses about how to cope with race prejudice. Black clergymen compounded the problem by instructing parishioners to prepare for the life heareafter instead of urging them to save money and buy homes. He extended the criticism to their lack of concern for public health, as evidenced by the men and women "among the congregations of the various churches assembled, coughing and expectorating great mouthfuls of spit, loaded with germs of this affection [*sic*]."[16] Such men, he chided, seemed to be more concerned about the evils of Sunday "turn-outs" than the advancement of the race.[17]

Electoral records for 1901 through 1909 reveal that perhaps both Rouse and Dupee were whistling in the dark. It was more convenient for whites that blacks remain ignorant and pliable and that elections be run with scant regard for law or justice. Blacks responded by demonstrating their willingness to sell their vote to the highest bidder. A prime beneficiary of this was Tidrington, a new sort of black leader. Election officials "helped" the hundreds of illiterate voters, and partisans offered a few dollars for the vote—a great deal of money to those accustomed to earning several dollars a week. Zealots found a variety of ingenious ways to guarantee that the payoff was legitimate—drilling peepholes through the ceiling above the voting booth, for instance, or using hand signals to political workers outside the polling place to indicate whether the voter deserved a reward. As before, voting occurred in private homes and saloons, which also encouraged election irregularities.In addition, the pervasiveness of vice made changes in the electoral process inconvenient. Madams, gamblers, and operators of dives generated financial contributions and voters for one party or the other, thus perpetuating the selective administration of city ordinances.[18]

Changes in the composition of the county commission and the city council also brought frequent shifting of polling places and the redistricting of precincts and wards. Democrats complained in 1904, for example, that Republicans had redrawn precinct lines so that three precincts would be predominantly black and presumably Republican. Heavily white Democratic regions were made twice the size, thus making for crowded polling places. That made voting Democratic difficult, especially since Republicans allegedly imported illegal black voters into these districts, had them get to the front of the line before the polls opened, and forced election officials to challenge their credentials, thus clogging up the voting process.[19]

In the seven elections between 1901 and 1909 Republicans usually took most if not all of the predominantly black precincts. The total cast for the GOP in these regions ranged from 61 to 77 percent. Democrats fared better in these sections in the city elections of 1901, 1905, and 1909, when most patronage jobs were available and ideology had little bearing on the campaigns, than they did in presidential or congressional races in even years.[20]

The 1905 municipal election vividly illustrated the sordidness of city elections. The GOP charged Democrats with importing a Baptist minister from Kentucky to deceive blacks and having scores of fictitious voters registered in the Lower Water Street region. On election day they reported "many instances of slugging, browbeating and intimidation in various parts of the city. . . ."[21] Democrats accused Republicans of having shipped in 235 blacks and hidden them in the saloons, restaurants, and warehouses of the riverfront region. Two days before the November 7 election the *Courier* alleged that so many "idle Negroes" had been paid to vote Republican that steamboat captains could not round up sufficient numbers of roustabouts to depart the city. On election day it asserted that city firemen were paying off loyal blacks at the polls by giving them slips of paper stamped with the name of Mayor Charles Covert's cigar factory, where they could be redeemed for cash.[22]

Precisely how many blacks supported the victorious Democrat, John W. Boehne, is unclear. The conservative Lutheran lay leader, however, posed a curious challenge to the black community. On the one hand, rewards for black Democrats were thin: a few fire department, custodial, and public works positions. No blacks had been named to the police force since the time of Mayor Bridwell in the 1880s. Not only did Boehne continue that practice, but—as noted earlier—his safety board also attempted to eliminate the all-black fire company. His works board also proposed to build through streets in Baptisttown and to raze a number of black residences there.[23]

On the other hand, Boehne's campaign against vice earned him the support of a number of black leaders. The Colored Ministerial Association praised his enforcement of an ordinance closing saloons after 11:00 p.m. and all day Sunday.[24] One effect of this, as the newly created progressive daily, the *Evansville Press*, observed in the fall of 1906, was that about 500 drifters had left the city and were "scattered all along the river between Henderson and Paducah." A "certain class of colored people" would not "remain in the city where they cannot have all-night access to the saloons."[25] In an era in which leaders of both parties spoke contemptuously of "the worthless Negro element" and *The Clansman* was popular in city theatres, Boehne's toughness on vice was perceived as a boon to those blacks who believed that the chief reason for racism was the misbehavior of poor blacks.[26]

It was in this context that the number of spokespersons for greater voter sophistication began to grow. Among these was Dr. Dupee, who in February 1908 developed more fully a theme he had suggested the year before. Elected Republican precinct committeeman in precinct 29 that month, he insisted "this vote selling is causing untold prejudice and we will welcome the day when neither the Republicans nor the Democrats will cater to the whims of such degenerate and debased citizens. . . ."[27]

Like insurgents in Louisville, Dupee had come of age in an era in which the GOP was turning against its commitments to blacks. The attainment of a modest amount of political power gave him the opportunity to call for more intelligent voter behavior and to underscore the importance of the black vote. The significance of that was obvious: Better political rewards were possible. In March 1908, for instance, he urged support in the primary for certain Republicans—the coroner, who had given business to Gaines, and the county assessor, who had appointed three blacks as assistants. "The boys are getting above the beer keg politics and believe our articles are bearing good fruit," he averred.[28]

Dupee was a loyal supporter of the GOP in the fall elections of 1908, which the Republicans swept. The *Courier* attributed the party's victory to the Baptisttown vote. Accordingly, in February 1909, the Democratic city council retaliated by redistricting precincts and eliminating Dupee's. Only two heavily black precincts remained. It also announced plans to raze homes in Baptisttown. Dupee criticized the city administration for inferring that the reason for the cleanup of that portion of the city was the irresponsibility of black residents. The real villains, he asserted, were absentee landlords, "who for the sake of personal profit damn the moral, civil, and sanitary welfare of the tenants."[29] Pleading with the administration to enforce the law in order that blacks might be better protected, he noted that blacks in these two precincts constituted a third of the city's black vote.[30] An essential force in local politics, they

> have risen to that point of intelligence to know that county and municipal affairs are not to be confused with state and national affairs and are very outspoken along the line. Let's support the man (regardless of his politics) who intends to do something for the colored man. Four colored policemen in Baptisttown would be appreciated.[31]

Acknowledging that John J. Nolan (who became Evansville's first Roman Catholic mayor after Boehne was elected to Congress in 1908) was a decent man whose candidacy in 1909 was being supported by a number of black leaders, Dupee warned Republicans not to take blacks for granted. During the municipal campaign of 1909, moreover, the number of independent or Democratic organizations in Baptisttown was greater than ever.[32]

Possibly related to this was W. E. B. DuBois's appearance in the city in June of that year. Probably it was school board chairman A. C. Rosencranz who was instrumental—with undoubtedly the support of such teachers as the Davises—in inviting DuBois to speak at the Clark High School graduation. Touring the Midwest in the late spring, the arch-enemy of accommodationism spoke to a large crowd at Evans Hall on the evening of June 16. His remarks were reported in the regular columns of the *Journal-News* the next day, not in "Colored Folk," which had insisted the day before that the only sure means to race progress was via practical education, not the "talented tenth." DuBois reportedly argued that "negroes have advanced too far now to go backward." Students should be urged to go to college and learn a trade, but not to become too specialized, he added, as the college-educated youth were the chief guarantors that 100 years of progress would not be ended. The audience, according to the news report, "loudly applauded throughout his address."[33]

There is, unfortunately, little documentation of the long-term effect of DuBois's visit on black Evansville. The extent to which reaction to his address reflected disapproval of the self-help strategy is unclear. Some were unwilling to accept racial discrimination passively, as the Davises' assault on residential restrictions later that sumer demonstrated. Approximately half of Clark's graduates in that era, moreover, went on to college after graduation. The outcry over the appearance of *The Clansman* and the ephemeral efforts to form a chapter of the NAACP also indicated that support for accommodationism was not unanimous. The vast majority of those who took a public position on race matters, however, eschewed protest.[34]

The level on which most blacks and whites dealt with the race question, however, remained considerably lower than that urged by Dupee or the handful of supporters of DuBois. Control of the city's saloons seemed to be the major issue in the 1909 campaign, as the Democratic city council during the previous year had forced all saloons in the city to apply for licenses, which those run by Republican activists like Ossenberg were denied. On election day the

30.   Cartoonist Karl Kae Knecht's commentary on the character of Evansville elections. *Evansville Courier*, November 5, 1910.

worst fears of the Democrats were realized, as Charles Heilman and his slate won a solid victory. For example, Republican leader of the sixth precinct, Matthew Foster, led ninety black voters through the voting machines in the first hour after the polls were opened, and rules about having no more than three persons within the ropes setting off the voting machines were flouted everywhere. There was no doubt, stated the *Press*, that Heilman won due to the black voters that Republican henchmen had been able to gather, and that "beer-keg" politicians ruled the city.[35]

Over the next twelve years the pervasiveness of vice, factional struggles in the national and local Republican party, and the pliability of the black vote combined to effect unprecedented political upheaval, and the focal point was invariably Baptisttown. "Strange Negroes" were a part of every election, and leaders of both parties courted the black vote with impunity. Investigations of vote fraud became commonplace.

The 1910 election was typical of those that followed. Since the election of Mayor Heilman, vice in the city had reputedly been permitted to run rampant. Immediately before the fall election, each major party accused the other of padding poll books with imported voters. Rev. Townsend described Dupee as the "old snake" and "the pampered Negro of the courthouse ring who is drawing $500 a year as charity doctor and being supplied with protection for his 'lid' club [the R-Line Club?]. . . ."[36] Charles Covert, Republican postmaster and customs collector and former mayor, admitted that he had threatened blacks who worked for local government with the loss of their jobs if they followed men like Townsend, who organized, according to the *Press*, the "better class of colored men" to resist GOP chicanery. Townsend and Buckner, for example, discovered 200 black men camped out north of the city limits and charged that the Republicans were planning to vote all of them. Despite an election day marred by numerous reports of fisticuffs and of vote-buying in black precincts, these efforts seemed to reap rewards. The appeal of Congressman Boehne was also a factor. According to the *Press*, Boehne was reelected in part because the largest number of blacks voted Democratic in the city's history. Although the heavily black precincts voted Republican, Democrats took 37 percent of the vote in them.[37]

Another factor in this era was growing Republican factionalism. Some blacks may have been troubled by President William Howard Taft's weak leadership on racial matters and attracted to insurgent Republican leaders. On the local level a rift developed between the Heilman and Ossenberg wings of the Republican party over patronage and spoils—not whether Taft or Roosevelt had a better approach to leadership. That redounded to the benefit of the Democracy. By 1912, for example, Dupee, a Heilman man, was reportedly working for Woodrow Wilson, but that may have been more a reaction against the Ossenberg faction than an endorsement of the progressive Democrat.[38]

The Democratic party's gains in the heavily black precincts were marked in 1912, as two of the four heavily black precincts cast their votes for Woodrow Wilson, and the Republican total in these four dropped below 60 percent. The chief reason the GOP did not lose more was that Tidrington, precinct number 28 committeeman, delivered most of his votes for Taft and others on the regular GOP ticket. According to the *Press*, the four-way contest for president was a boon to the increasingly independent black community. In no hurry to vote, most demanded $3 from party officials who desired their support.[39]

Tidrington's growing importance was evident the next spring, when his mentor, Fred Ossenberg, made a deal with Benjamin Bosse, Democratic candidate for mayor. The untimely death of Dupee in late March following an appendectomy meant that the more cynical sort of political leadership in the Seventh Ward was now virtually unchallenged. Heilman had refused to accede to Ossenberg's demands for total control over black patronage and saloon interests. Ossenberg, Republican party county chairman, quietly cast his support to Bosse in the primary, and the two secured control over the appointment of election officers in each precinct. Bosse eked out a four-vote victory in the primary over John J. Nolan, thanks in part to Ward 7 support.[40]

In the fall Bosse faced Heilman in the race for control of the city. It was well known that Bosse had Ossenberg's support. That was evident, for example, by the incumbent's establishing a private campaign headquarters because he lacked confidence in the leadership of Herbert Males, city chairman, an Ossenberg crony. Bosse campaigned in Baptisttown, ironically, for an end to brothels, gambling, and "lid clubs," and Congressman Boehne also spoke in the Seventh Ward, attacking the spread of vice during the Heilman years. Rev. Townsend chided Republicans for saying all the Democrats ever did for blacks was to send Dr. Buckner to Liberia. (President Wilson had appointed him minister to Liberia earlier that year, but because of illness contracted in that African country Buckner's tenure was less than a year, and the physician returned to the city.) The Independent Voters' League, headed by Isaac Coffee and former GOP stalwart Julius Coleman, also waged a vigorous campaign. On election day Seventh Ward voters cast 995 votes for Bosse, just 100 fewer than those cast for Heilman and the highest ever for a Democrat. Republicans managed to obtain only 47 percent of the vote in the four largest black precincts. Bosse and the entire Democratic slate won the city by about 800 votes.[41]

The assistance of black leaders like Coleman undoubtedly contributed to the Democratic victory in November 1913, but the most important force was provided by Ossenberg and Tidrington. Some observers insisted that as many as 2,000 black votes were purchased in that election. For the following five years many Evansville blacks supported Democrats in local elections while retaining their loyalty to the GOP on the national level. That was due to Tidrington's influence and to the patronage available in city and county government. (Hugh Rouse, for instance, was made city hall janitor.) Perhaps the most significant decision was Bosse's appointment of Ossenberg to the safety board, an act which prompted all three editors to criticize him for, as the *Press* put it, placing the city in the hands of a political tyrant.[42] The political value of the black vote may have been behind Bosse's change of heart regarding black aptitudes, which he had questioned while president of the safety board. By the fall election of 1914, the *Journal-News*, like the *Courier* of old, inquired: "shall the negroes of Baptisttown decide every election in Evansville and Vanderburgh County?"[43]

The "Democratic-Bull Moose" alliance worked well on election day, controlling election officials in every precinct. Voting machines in the Seventh Ward were placed in public places so that officials could signal party workers to pay off those who voted correctly. Democrats took over half the vote in black Republican precincts and won the Congressional race as well as all county contests. Democrats captured races in the 28th precinct, on the average, by 358–249. Particularly crucial had been the race for sheriff, as Heilman—by now a bitter foe of Fred Ossenberg—was the Republican candidate. For the first time since the early 1880s, Democrats simultaneously controlled city and county government.[44]

Following the election, the Bosse administration assigned four plainclothesmen to work Baptisttown and also proposed—as noted in chapter 8—some improvements in Baptisttown housing and streets. Delay in implementation may have been in part due to the opposition of Ossenberg, who had begun in early 1915 to hint that he might be ready to make peace with the GOP in return for his naming the candidates for sheriff and prosecutor. For that he could "deliver 2,000 purchasable votes."[45] That may have been the reason that the mayor, in June 1915, named Tidrington to the police force—the first black in twenty-five years. The appointment of this "special officer" sparked the same sort of protest as had Ossenberg's, but the mayor stood firm.[46]

The mayor's alliance with Ossenberg and Tidrington was clearly a marriage of convenience. In the 1916 primary, for example, the Seventh Ward leaders again sought to regain control of the Republican party by securing Males's nomination for sheriff, but white and black party regulars in the Seventh, including W. A. Gaines and his young assistant, Rudolph O'Hara, prevented that, and Heilman won the nomination. (Shortly thereafter, Bosse named Males to the safety board.) Following the election, Gaines also defeated Tidrington in the county convention election for delegates to the state convention. Tidrington vowed revenge. Several weeks later Democratic county officials brought charges of fraudulent use of trustee funds against Gaines and O'Hara (namely, burying the dead without coffins), but those charges were not sustained in the trial that followed. Similar charges were made in the fall and also proved baseless.[47]

Ossenberg-Tidrington forces once more worked for the Democratic slate. A GOP-aided evangelistic campaign, coinciding with the fall election, portrayed the city as a modern Sodom, and Republicans charged that Bosse's cronies, Ossenberg and Tidrington, were making thousands from political appointments and Baptisttown vice. Some of that was not simply campaign rhetoric, as the noted independent Isaac Coffee urged blacks to support Gaines and the GOP as a means of cleaning up Baptisttown. On election day anti-Tidrington forces increased the Republican vote in the largely black precincts to 58 percent and took the four most heavily black precincts, but Democrats took the county on November 7.[48]

Alleged corruption in that election was so widespread that in February 1917 federal marshals arrested 122 whites and blacks—including Bosse's chief of police, the GOP county chairman, as well as Coffee, O'Hara, and Tidrington. (Similar investigations were launched simultaneously in Terre Haute.) Forty-five pleaded guilty—all but one of them black—and testified against those higher up. In the trial in federal court in Indianapolis the defense based its argument on the limited mental capacity of the witnesses. All but three of those arrested—eighty-two Republicans and thirty-seven Democrats—were found guilty on May 24, but they were never sentenced because of legal technicalities.[49]

America's entrance into the European war in April also helped divert attention from the scandal. The mayor projected himself as a highly patriotic leader of a "100 percent American" city, and given the fact that 1917 was an election year, such an image was highly beneficial. Bosse's reelection, nevertheless, depended on Baptisttown support. "Lid clubs" and other forms of vice were major issues in the campaign, especially given the legislature's support of prohibition. Even John Boehne expressed disgust, pointing to the presence of the notorious Blue Goose Saloon, site of the origin of the 1903 riot, as a case in point. Boehne criticized Democratic leaders for blunting the efforts of blacks and whites who wished to clean up inner Lincoln Avenue. Like other white reformers of the times, he was annoyed because the area was an eyesore to commuters who resided in the newly developing subdivisions along outer Lincoln. Some black leaders like Jeremiah Jackson were also outspoken, but for different reasons: Since blacks were restricted to a few regions of the city, they ought to have the opportunity to live in respectable neighborhoods. Bosse responded at a preelection rally at the UBF hall that he had treated all citizens, black or white, fairly, and that his first priority after the election would be the building of a swimming pool for blacks.[50]

The mayor undoubtedly benefited from citizen anxiety resulting from the war as well as labor strikes in the city in October. Socialist Frank LaMonte, who campaigned for mayor on the grounds that involvement in the European war was improper, probably also indirectly assisted Bosse's candidacy. (LaMonte, a lawyer, was disbarred prior to the election for such allegedly unpatriotic behavior, but nevertheless won 17.3 percent of the vote.) On the morning of the election the Democratic newspaper released the news that an Evansvillian, James Bethel Gresham, had been the first American killed in France. The effect of that announcement on Bosse's campaign was unclear. Bosse was reelected with 52.2 percent of the vote. The five heavily black precincts cast their vote for the incumbent, and in those regions the GOP took only 36 percent of the total vote. The Ossenberg-Tidrington machine was credited with the victory.[51]

For several reasons, however, the uneasy alliance was broken during the following year. First, the mayor was preoccupied with "100 percent Americanism," and that included heavy-handed efforts to curb German influence in Evansville and a campaign to bring a college to the city. That meant that promises to the black community tended to be forgotten. More significant was Ossenberg's announcement in April 1918 that he was returning to the Republican fold. Following that, Males resigned, as did Tidrington, who was replaced on the police force by another black. That was possibly occasioned by Bosse's statement that, as Democratic county chairman, he had to support Wilson and the entire Democratic ticket, and that he could not serve two masters. It is also probable that the astute Ossenberg sensed the likelihood of a Republican victory in the fall. One clue was that he mustered enough votes to win Males's nomination for sheriff and secured a seat in the county delegation to the state convention (as did three blacks). Tidrington was subsequently named assistant custodian and engineer of state property in Indianapolis by Governor James P. Goodrich.[52]

Ossenberg's shift led Heilman, his old nemesis, to announce his support for the Democratic party and to claim that the origin of the bitter rivalry had been his refusal to allow Ossenberg to dictate his appointments and to secure a monopoly on gambling, prostitution, and saloon interests. That announcement was less important, though, than control of the black vote, and a concerted administration effort to register black voters took place. The effort was not helped by the announcement of the "law enforcement committee" of the Colored Ministerial Association: "Hundreds of the colored people voted for you, because you promised a more moral Evansville, but the conditions at this time are the worst we have seen during our pastorship."[53]

Whether Republicans were behind that is unknown, but the GOP sought to exploit it. They also warned—like Democrats of old—of hundreds of "floaters" imported by Bosse's party and alleged that scores of federal agents were in the city to prevent a repetition of the 1916 election. Democrats responded, ironically, by portraying Republicans as the tools of Fred Ossenberg, whose Seventh Ward voters contributed heavily to a GOP sweep of Vanderburgh County in the fall election. In the process, the opportunistic Ossenberg machine secured control of the key law enforcement posts of sheriff and prosecutor.[54]

The coming of prohibition added an explosive element to postwar Evansville. The culture of the region, shaped by settlers from the Upper South and southern Germany and by the free-wheeling qualities of life along a major waterway, contributed to an insatiable demand for alcoholic beverages. The "Red Scare" of 1919 and 1920, fueled in Evansville by wartime anti-German hysteria and postwar labor unrest among pottery and furniture workers, also contributed to a demand for law and order, as citizens believed that existing institutions could not be trusted. A foretaste was provided in January, 1919, when a mob, members of which included civic leaders and veterans of the AEF, descended on the Courthouse to demand the resignation of a county commissioner and the county attorney, his son. The successful effort, which the political dailies likened to the Boston Tea Party, resulted from the allegation that the two had been "pro-German" in the recent war.[55]

31.   Ernest G. Tidrington, civic and
political leader. *Souvenir History of the
Evansville Police Department*, 1918.

Doubts about the qualities of local government were invigorated in May
1920, when seventy-six citizens from both parties, including the Democratic
chief of police, the Republican sheriff, and Fred Ossenberg were arrested by
federal agents for violation of the liquor law. All but a few were white.
Although most were acquitted, the police chief and Fred Ossenberg were sent
to federal prison. Ossenberg's imprisonment was delayed until May 1922, and
eventually he served only six months. To the editor of the *Press*, F. R. Peters,
the incident was the final proof that the faction which had dominated Evansville since the Heilman era, profiting from trading votes in return for unre-
strained vice, had to be put out of existence.[56]

The desire for "normalcy," combined with local interest in law and order,
led to a Republican landslide in November 1920. The predominantly black precincts voted solidly Republican, giving 65.8 percent of their vote to the GOP.
In precinct 2 of Ward 7, where Tidrington was election clerk, Republicans
received an average of 840 votes to the Democrats' 270. (The increased number
of voters resulted from the implementation of the Nineteenth Amendment.)[57]

Back from his post in Indianapolis and having persuaded Rudolph O'
Hara to join him in business and politics, the forty-four year-old Tidrington
was able to amass enormous influence. His significance to the Ossenberg-
Males-Gould faction of the GOP was unquestioned, and after Ossenberg's
death shortly after returning from prison, he was considered even more vital to
the Seventh Ward.[58]

The vulnerability of the black voter and the resourcefulness of Tidrington
were the keys to the ascendancy of the most powerful black leader in the city's

history to that point. His rise was abetted by the silence of most clergymen and teachers on partisan matters. Openly critical of the "hat in hand Negro" who accepted crumbs from white leaders, he developed unparalleled power on his own, and perhaps that—even more than his disloyalty to Bosse—was the underlying reason that white leaders opposed him. For years whites had designated a black leader or two to speak for the black community, whether on Baptisttown cleanup in 1916 or the improvement in interracial relations in 1928. Racial discrimination had not only encouraged the formation of a rich subculture but also provided a powerful tool to clever politicos.[59]

One cost of this was the perpetuation of vice, and in the 1920s that was especially evident in the high incidence of violation of the liquor law. Police and coroners' records reveal that between 1920 and 1929 police and sheriff's deputies made 1,758 arrests for such violations and confiscated over 50,000 gallons of alcoholic beverages. Eighteen deaths were due to alcoholism. Because of the unevenness of law enforcement, it is probable that these figures represent the tip of the iceberg. The epicenter of this turbulent decade was the "Bloody Seventh," the scene of numerous election-day fights, especially at the Blue Goose and Hot Dog saloons, where voters were "likkered up" by bootleggers, black and white, who prospered because of their ability to deliver the vote as well as income to the authorities.[60]

The administration of Mayor Bosse thus entered the election year of 1921 with a number of liabilities—charges of complicity in the liquor ring scandal and lax enforcement of prohibition, and opposition from the Ossenberg faction. A recruiter for the Ku Klux Klan, Joe Huffington, arrived in the summer, declaring that his organization was "not an outgrowth of the old, pillaging, night-riding, lawless bands ... [but] a clean organization, standing for the uplift and protection of untainted Americanism."[61] Despite objections from Catholic and Jewish leaders and the mayor himself, the Klan held a rally at the Coliseum in September, at which Caleb Ridley, a national leader of the Hooded Order, asserted that the chief dangers to the Republic were "non-Christians and colored people."[62] The Klan played no discernible role, however, in the fall election.

During the campaign the independent *Press* criticized Bosse for allowing the city to be dominated by the National City Bank and the public utility holding company, for opposing city manager government, and for relying on unsavory means of securing reelection. The mayor—who also built parks, paved many streets, motorized the police force, and opened a baseball stadium—was portrayed as offering "gladiator battles to soothe the citizens he outraged."[63] His own party daily implicated him in the liquor scandal, to which he responded by purchasing the paper and replacing the entire staff. Regarding the black community, Bosse dismissed the charges of Jim Crowism from Tidrington, who had criticized his plan to build a separate park for blacks, and added that blacks were "the plaything of scheming political dictators."[64] Voting Republican, he asserted, would increase the power of the Ossenberg faction and not aid the black community.[65]

Bosse and his slate won by the slim margin of about 900 votes out of 33,000 cast. A number of blacks supported him—including reportedly W. A. Gaines, longtime enemy of Tidrington—but the Republicans fared much better in heavily black precincts than they had in 1917. Bosse lost the second precinct in the Seventh (Tidrington's) by 548 to 414 and the entire ward by about 250 votes. Businessman Logan Stewart was the Republican city council candidate from the Seventh Ward, the first major party candidate who happened to be Afro-American since Nicholas in 1897 (and the last until Charles Decker's race for the state legislature in 1946). In each of the five precincts in that ward Stewart's Democratic opponent received more votes than Mayor Bosse, probably a reaction to Stewart's color. Interestingly enough, the second precinct voted 496–423 against Stewart. Tidrington may have engaged in an act of revenge on a longtime rival and ally of his factional opponent, Gaines.[66]

The narrowness of Bosse's victory led Circuit Court Judge Phil Gould, an Ossenberg Republican, to call for a grand jury investigation, and that predictably led to indictments against Democratic election officials, white and black. All the losers filed suit, but the suits were dropped after the controversial mayor died unexpectedly in early April. Allegations of election fraud persisted, however, as did charges that Bosse's successor, William Elmendorf, was soft on gambling and liquor law violations. "Law and order" candidates won in the May 3 primary, and a week later, the KKK held its first public demonstration. "Indiana Klan Number 1" claimed 500 members.[67]

The interrelationship of the Klan, the black community, and Mayor Bosse form a confused backdrop for understanding the politics of the 1920s. Evidence is, unfortunately, sketchy and conflicting. That some whites felt Bosse was too friendly with blacks was made obvious in early 1922, when a local meat market owner (who later admitted that he was one of the first Klansmen), circulated a petition asking for the removal of blacks from the police force because one had allegedly fraternized with a white woman while on duty. Shortly before his death, Bosse did remove the offender after an investigation, but refused to comply with the remainder of the request. The use of black policemen, he insisted, was logical where there were large numbers of blacks, and he added that he would not violate the pledges he had made to the black community.[68]

Yet the fact remained that the mayor needed to shore up his control of the black vote. On the one hand, in the flurry of revelations following the imprisonment of Indiana's Grand Dragon, D. C. Stephenson, in the mid-twenties, the former Evansville resident asserted that Bosse had been the first to point out to him the potential of the Klan, and that the mayor perceived the order might be useful as a means of keeping blacks in line. Before the mayor's death, in fact, Stephenson had filed as a Democratic candidate for Congress, but after Bosse died he left the city to organize the Klan in Indianapolis. Within a year he had built a state organization second to none in the United States. Using effective salesmanship and the obscure "Horse Thief Detective Law," which permitted the organization of voluntary constabularies, "Steve" became a powerful factor in state politics and a close ally of a number of Republican leaders. In 1927 Attorney General Arthur L. Gilliom of Indiana, a Republican, reiterated this story about Stephenson's roots. Bosse, he said, had used Stephenson to further his campaign for governor.[69]

On the other hand, Stephenson's long-time rival, Joe Huffington, head of the Evansville Klavern, told a different story. The head of the only Indiana Klavern which did not secede from the Atlanta organization in 1924, Huffington argued that Bosse had had nothing to do with the Klan's origins. He stated that he had been asked to come to Evansville to organize a Klavern, and that Stephenson—a failure in a series of business efforts—had later joined. The two had a falling out over who was in control, and Atlanta officials gave Huffington Evansville and Stephenson the choice of Indianapolis or California.[70]

The intense rivalry between Huffington and Stephenson and the absence of Bosse's testimony weaken both stories. There is no doubt, however, that membership in the Evansville and Indiana Klan rose rapidly after the summer of 1922, and that the candidates it supported in the fall were victorious. A year later it claimed a local membership of 4,000. Huffington's perceived effectiveness led him into an alliance with Males, Gould, Tidrington, and Fred Ossenberg's brother, Al, and by the 1924 primary that faction of the party had unquestioned control of the Republican party, a position it did not lose until the spring of 1929. Most Republicans found Klan support convenient, but some—notably Males—went further and joined the hooded order.[71]

Although the rise of the Klan in some American cities, like Indianapolis, was rooted in white fears of a rapidly growing black populace, its success in Evansville had different origins. The many Roman Catholics of German descent, virtually all of whom were Democrats, were prime targets in an era charged with anti-German and anti-bootlegger fervor, especially among those young men of Upland South roots who longed for the sort of camaraderie that the KKK provided. The anti-Catholic, anti-bootlegger theme was evident from the beginning. Despite Mayor Elmendorf's complaint in his annual message of January 1, 1923, that law enforcement officers had their hands full, handling twice as many cases in 1922 as in 1921, because "the demand for white mule whisky is greater than the supply," critics argued that city officials were far too lenient.[72]

The black community, smaller in size than in 1900 and constrained by a variety of forms of racial discrimination, was not a prime target for the Klan. That the Klan was antiblack was indisputable, as the petition on black policemen illustrated. Antiblack rhetoric, moreover, may have contributed to Mayor Elmendorf's removing the remaining black policemen by the end of his term. But it is fairer to portray the Klan as reinforcing existing patterns of race relations, not authoring segregation. The Evansville Klan engaged in no recorded acts of terrorism against blacks. Instead, it formed patrols to raid bootleggers and to frighten couples parked on country roads. It also became an adjunct of the Republican party. Although misguided and naive, Klan members were on the whole sincere in their beliefs, but unfortunately their leaders utilized the

32. Election day in Baptisttown, 1920s. Photograph files, *Evansville Courier*.

hooded order for personal aggrandizement, and it was those revelations that contributed to the organization's eventual downfall.[73]

Ironically, because the Seventh Ward political machine was responsible for the rise of Herbert Males, black politicos—especially Tidrington and O'Hara—contributed heavily to the success of the Klan-dominated politics in the 1920s, a period of unparalleled corruption in the city's history. Even W. A. Gaines came to support Males, as did Drs. Jackson and Thompson (precinct judge and clerk, respectively, in the second precinct of Ward 7), because the Republican offered greater rewards to black Evansvillians than any of his predecessors. Rev. L. A. McIntyre was also a vocal supporter, and speaking at McFarland Baptist Church was obligatory for any Republican candidate.[74]

The Seventh Ward vote, and especially in its second precinct, where Tidrington was election inspector, was solidly Republican in the 1920s. As a rule three-fifths or more of the votes in heavily black precincts were GOP. Even in 1922, when the popular Democratic county clerk, William Wilson, was elected to Congress and about half the voters in predominantly black precincts voted for him, the second precinct of Ward 7 cast 70 percent of its vote for the Republican. Candidates who wished to win had to appear at Castle Hall, the Pythians' meeting place, and be introduced by Ernest Tidrington.[75]

Baptisttown's importance was especially evident in the city election of 1925. Males, who ran on an anti-Catholic platform which promised stricter law enforcement, overwhelmed his opponent in the primary, in part due to Tidrington's vocal support. Increasingly active was O'Hara, by now a member of the Vanderburgh County Republican Central Committee, due to Tidrington's responsibilities with the state and national GOP. Amidst a circuit court grand jury investigation of fraudulently cast votes in the primary, election-eve raids by deputies (under a Klan-supported sheriff) on dens run by black Democrats, fisticuffs in the Seventh on election day, and a Klan-inspired campaign against papal influence in Evansville, Males and the entire Republican ticket were swept into office on election day with nearly 60 percent of the vote, the largest margin in the history of municipal elections to that time. Several thousand absentee ballots—the newest vehicle for election fraud—were cast, many of them in Baptisttown, on Males's behalf. Despite postelection grand jury investigations, including one of Tidrington's son, whom Males named captain of Hose House No. 9, the results were upheld.[76]

The promise of political reward was a major determinant of black voting behavior. Males was treated kindly by such influential black observers as the *Indianapolis Recorder*, which in early 1926 pointed out that Males had appointed 100 blacks—eighty more than his predecessors—to city jobs. Six were named to the police force and eight to the fire department, twice the previous total. The remainder were named to labor and custodial posts in every department. More important, for the first time these appointments had been recommended by "race men"—Tidrington and O'Hara. The two demonstrated the vitality of black Republicanism by forming the Henry Lincoln Johnson Club in mid-January in honor of the World War I hero, and 200 joined. Tidrington's strength was underscored by his being nominated for the federal post of Register of the Treasury by his friend, Senator James E. Watson, in 1925— for which he was still in contention at the time of his death—and his being named head of the Colored Bureau of the Indiana Republican party in the summer of 1926. President Calvin Coolidge appointed him to a six-member committee to study "Negro conditions" in the United States. He was also selected as a member of the executive committee of the National Colored Republican League. Thus more of his Evansville duties were carried out by his law partner.[77]

Klan-dominated government, in a word, provided more political reward and gave black leaders more autonomy than ever. It was also responsible for the school board which proceeded with plans to build a new black school, as noted earlier. Speaking to the City Council in January 1929, Mayor Males pointed with great pride to Lincoln as a symbol of community progress.[78]

A baser benefit of Males's leadership was selective administration of the law, particularly regarding prohibition. The incidence of vice was as great, if not greater, than that of his predecessor. The mayor resorted to the same argument as Elmendorf—that the demand for liquor was too great for the police to cope with. In addition, members of his administration were linked with aiding and abetting gamblers, madams, and bootleggers, engaging in vote fraud, and using public office for personal gain.[79]

Because of the prevalence of vice, anti-Tidrington blacks in both parties tried unsuccessfully to unseat "the Baptisttown dictator" in the primary of

1926, and in the summer a grand jury attempted to bring indictments against black and white politicians for liquor law violations. The three newspapers carried stories of impending investigations of city government on virtually a daily basis by the fall. D. C. Stephenson's testimony in Marion County helped to spur local interest in rooting out corruption in government. Efforts to effect change, however—including passage of a city manager government ordinance—were unavailing.[80]

Between the fall of 1927 and the spring of 1929, each day brought new revelations of misconduct in city government. Nevertheless, the vast majority of black voters, led by the Tidrington organization, remained loyal to the mayor. The key black precincts voted for Republican candidates in the fall of 1926 and in the presidential election of 1928. Tidrington's influence was so great that the city council agreed to rename Gordon Avenue in Baptisttown after him. But the aggregate effects of dubious leadership eventually caught up with these Republicans. By June 1929, virtually every member of the Males administration, including the mayor, had been indicted for graft, embezzlement, or vote fraud. Tidrington was indicted on the latter charge, but he, like most of the others, escaped punishment because, among other reasons, vital evidence was missing from city records. Some were not so fortunate. Huffington and his chief assistant were imprisoned for running an auto theft ring, and Congressman Harry Rowbottom, who had been elected in 1924, was sentenced to a year in prison for accepting bribes in return for post office contracts.[81]

In the primary of 1929, Republican "good government" forces, led by John Stuart Hopkins, defeated the mayor. The Seventh Ward was the major battleground. Supporting Males to the end, Tidrington's forces used every device they could—illiterate voters' affidavits, absentee ballots, payoffs, and intimidation—and delivered the ward to the incumbent. That was not enough, though, and Hopkins's slate was elected. The challenger also won enough precinct committee races to oust Males as party chairman.[82]

Blacks had contributed to the rise of Klan-dominated government, but the degree of opposition is, unfortunately, poorly documented. The Inter-Racial Commission, for instance, was a response to the closing of the Cherry Street YMCA and not racial bigotry. Rouse and Best, the two most respected leaders, made no public statements on the Klan. The number of blacks who became Democrats because of KKK excesses—as in the case of the editor of the Indianapolis *Freeman*—is not known. As election records demonstrate, however, at least a third of the voters in the Seventh Ward did not vote Republican, despite Tidrington's power. Yet the vast majority did. The "Southern Strategy" of the party of Lincoln and the migration of blacks to Northern cities had begun to create a shift in political loyalties. Although Evansville blacks had shown their independence much earlier, in the 1920s most remained Republican.[83]

In the election of 1929, several weeks after the Great Crash, four of the five heavily black precincts, however, voted Democratic, and Frank Griese and his slate received slightly over half of votes cast in the five. A major reason was Tidrington's decision to work for Griese. That was because Tidrington's loyalties lay with Males, as the incumbent was opposed to Hopkins. Seventh Ward votes contributed a major share of the Democrats' margin of victory. As in 1913 through 1917, black voters were delivered to the Democratic party because of factional disputes within the GOP, not because of an ideological shift. One must note, however, that in 1930 Democrats took half of the votes cast in these precincts, as well as three of the precincts, and in 1932 Franklin D. Roosevelt captured two-thirds of the vote and all of the precincts. That pattern would prevail for the rest of the decade.[84]

Whether that shift would have occurred under Tidrington's leadership will never be known. On the evening of January 22, 1930, as he sat at the wheel of his parked limousine at Lincoln and Governor, he was shot to death by Luther Bell, a poolroom operator. His wife, Hallie, was slightly injured in the shooting. Bell claimed that Tidrington had been harassing him since the election, when Bell supported Hopkins. He stated that "the boss" had told him to leave town. When Griese took office, police raided Bell's pool hall, ordered him to close, and refused to grant him a license to reopen. Earlier on the twenty-second, moreover, Bell was arrested on what he alleged was a framed charge of drawing a deadly weapon.[85]

Tidrington's body lay in state at his home on Linwood Avenue until the morning of the twenty-fifth, when it was moved to McFarland Chapel, as the AME church, where he had been a trustee, was too small. According to the *Recorder*, 10,000 paid honor to the fallen leader before the services, in which the city's leading black pastors were in charge. Tributes were delivered by Pythian officials from across the nation. Following that, he was buried in Oak Hill cemetery.[86]

Tidrington was as controversial in death as in life. The defense of his killer was anticipated in late January, when the *Journal-News* quoted extensively from anonymous opponents who described Tidrington as an unmerciful and vengeful bully whose killing by Bell had been justifiable. In the trial in April, Bell's attorney claimed his client had been temporarily insane, and portrayed Tidrington as "the black beast of Baptisttown" and "the despoiler and betrayer of his people." Declared the *Recorder*, "from the major portion of testimony given . . . the slain man and not the slayer was on trial." The jury of twelve white men agreed. Following the verdict the special judge appointed a commission of three physicians to determine Bell's mental state, and they judged him sane. Bell was a free man.[87]

That Tidrington had attained unparalleled influence was unquestionable, and the outpouring of grief in the black community, even from black pastors, revealed the degree of respect in which he was held. Tidrington had obtained substantial influence, but his efforts were also directed at the improvement of the entire community. His death also demonstrated the constraints under which even he had to operate. No white leaders were listed in the newspapers as being present at his funeral, and none paid any sort of public tribute to him. The fate of Luther Bell led many in the black community to believe that Tidrington had been assassinated and that the defense had been financed by those assassins. Tidrington's followers were shown that "The Boss" had overreached himself and that his power ultimately depended upon white approval. No black machine, as Congressman Oscar Depriest of Chicago learned in the 1920s, could exist independently of a white machine for long.[88]

Although O'Hara, Tidrington's understudy, became prominent in state as well as local Republican politics, he never attained the clout of his former partner. He and W. A. Gaines wrestled for control of the Seventh Ward throughout the thirties. Other black leaders, moreover, sought to rid themselves of the image that they were bossed by anyone. That was advantageous to both parties, which learned from the experience of Tidrington's independence and attempted to regain control of Baptisttown by selecting the blacks who would speak for the black community and offering them limited benefits for the privilege. New Deal welfare programs, which diminished the importance of the precinct worker and the township trustee, also contributed to the demise of machine politics. The New Deal also permanently weakened the GOP in Baptisttown.[89]

The political developments of the 1920s, and especially the enterprising approach advocated by Tidrington and his understudy, belied a more fundamental change which was occurring. The years of physical and social separation, as in other Northern cities, had produced "a sense of unique goals and needs" which "helped unify the black community and provided the practical basis for the future struggle against racism in all its manifestations."[90] This battle would become manifest during the days of the Great Depression and the Second World War.

PART IV

Toward a New Era,
1930–1945

Change and Continuity in the Age of the Great Depression and the Second World War, 1930–1945

 Because of the disadvantages that black Americans had at the onset of the Depression, their experiences between 1929 and 1941 were especially severe. About one-third of the black families in Evansville were on relief by 1934. Yet this would also be a time of renewal and change, as out of the 1930s would emerge new leaders, a host of new approaches to improving the welfare of the black community, and a revival of racial pride. The misery that blacks and whites shared was one factor. As Helen Best recalled, blacks and whites did not wait in separate lines for relief at the courthouse. The assistance provided by the federal government was a major influence, as it circumvented a number of the traditional obstacles to betterment in black Evansville. The arrival of a Plymouth assembly plant in the mid-thirties, followed by the establishment of Local No. 705 of the United Auto Workers (CIO), was also important, as was the quality of local leadership, black and white, which surfaced in the decade.[1]

Federal involvement in community relief and recovery during the Depression contributed to the improvement of black Evansville. Most of that, however, did little to disturb patterns of race relations. The Civilian Conservation Corps, for instance, had a separate unit for blacks at Wadesville, about twenty miles west of the city. The Works Progress Administration not only became the largest employer of blacks in the city, but also provided a wealth of services aimed at community improvement. Although most projects were segregated—in May 1940 there were separate WPA banquets commemorating progress under the agency, for example—they proved to be of enormous benefit. The WPA provided nursery school at McFarland Chapel, adult literacy and education classes, including religious education, an employment bureau, and—through its National Youth Administration—vocational training and school lunch programs. Charles Rochelle became state National Youth Administration advisor in December 1939.[2]

33.   An all-black crew at work on a WPA street resurfacing project on Wabash Avenue in April 1936. Photograph files, *Evansville Courier*.

34.   Evansville's WPA Police, 1936. There were two black men (fourth row, right) on the force. Photograph files, *Evansville Courier*.

The Public Works Administration also had substantial influence on the life of the community. Through its public housing programs, Baptisttown renewal became a reality. In the spring of 1930 the city building commissioner reported that at least 125 dwellings in the heart of black Evansville were in poor condition. That, combined with the absence of through streets in the area, prompted Mayor Frank Griese to propose a $200,000 "Baptisttown Park." Backed by the Inter-Racial Commission and the Board of Realtors, he insisted that the major obstacle to change was the slum landlord. Ninety percent of the homes in the region, he declared, paid 27 percent of their property valuation in one year. The proposal was initially approved by the City Council, but the Seventh Ward council member opposed it. William Best and Sallie Stewart were strongly for it, but many black leaders voiced their opposition. One criticism from Republicans—a familiar one—was that this was a ploy to cut the number of black voters. Significantly, Rudolph O'Hara, attempting to revive the local chapter of the NAACP, argued that the plan sought to confine blacks to segregated park facilities and that the black community had not been involved in preparing the plan. Others were concerned that it did not provide alternative housing for those driven out of the area. Combined with lobbying from landlords and arguments that the city did not have the funds for the project, these criticisms led to the shelving of the proposal.[3]

In 1933 Principal Best asked the mayor to revive efforts to clean up Baptisttown, and Griese responded by appointing a committee of fifteen eminent blacks to prepare a plan. Aided by Rosencranz and two other white leaders— Jerome Salm, a Jewish store owner, and A. E. Harper, president of Evansville College—in April 1934 they introduced a proposal for public housing funded by the PWA. Within eighteen months bids were being taken to demolish an area affecting 160 families, and two blacks—Mrs. L. A. George and Dr. Raymond King, prominent Democrats—were appointed by the newly elected mayor, Democrat William B. Dress, to facilitate the families' move. In December 1935 the PWA approved plans for the building of 200 units in the thirteen-acre region, and work was commenced the following summer. Indiana's second public housing project was opened in July 1938, amidst great fanfare in the black community. Dr. King was named manager of the facility, named Lincoln Gardens, which aside from decent, low-cost housing provided black Evansville meeting rooms and modest recreational space and an object of pride.[4]

Also important was the opening of a Plymouth assembly plant in the fall of 1935. Chrysler Corporation soon was reputed to be the most liberal local employer, although virtually all black employees worked as custodians and helpers. Its workers were organized by the UAW-CIO, one of the most racially progressive unions. Although rank-and-file members of Local No. 705, many of whom were Kentuckians, were generally hostile to blacks, its local officers— a few of whom were black—spoke out against racial discrimination in Evansville.[5]

Local white and black leaders also provided a force for change. The IRC provided a forum for inter-racial communication and championed improve-

35.   Baptisttown's center in 1938, after homes had been razed to make way for Lincoln Gardens. Canal Street is in the upper center, Governor Street is on the far left, and Lincoln Avenue is in the foreground. Tidrington, on the right, was merged into the extension of Garvin Street to make a north-south thoroughfare. Photograph files, *Evansville Courier*.

36.   Lincoln Gardens shortly after its opening in July 1938. Photograph files, *Evansville Courier*.

ment in the living conditions of black Evansvillians. In February 1935 it sponsored an unprecedented meeting at McFarland Chapel to discuss the contributions of the black community to the life of the city. Newly appointed school superintendent Ralph Irons, who became a vocal supporter of the betterment of black Evansville, was one of those who addressed a crowd of 300. (This event may have been the basis for the establishment, in the mid-thirties, of Negro History Week in Evansville.) The IRC's primary concern, however, was the financial stability for the Community Center, and when the center began receiving funds from the revived Community Chest, it became moribund. It was revived in 1940 in conjunction with defense preparedness issues.[6]

Whether associated with the IRC or not, a small but outspoken group of white Evansvillians advocated a fairer deal for the black community: Jack Skirball, rabbi of the Reformed Washington Avenue Temple; Don Scism, editor of the *Evansville Courier*; John Soucie, business agent of the Laborers' Union, which employed black and white construction helpers; Joseph Moore, rector of St. Paul's Episcopal Church; businessmen Richard E. Meier and Samuel Weil; and attorney Milford Miller. Skirball, for example, strongly criticized the YWCA for firing a staff member in 1932 who had held classes for young black women in the building and attempted to organize them for the purpose of securing higher wages as domestics and tobacco factory operatives. By the late thirties, moreover, the *Courier* regularly carried stories about the accomplishments of blacks. Evansville College admitted a black student in 1934. Missouri Synod Lutherans established a parish for blacks (Grace) in 1938, and three years later St. John's parish was created for black Catholics. White clergymen in June 1941 invited black pastors to join the Evansville Ministerial Association. In the same year the Chamber of Commerce opened its membership to black businesses.[7]

As vital as the support from sympathetic whites was, even more significant was the growing assertiveness of black leaders. The internal dynamics of the black community was largely responsible for this. "Large numbers of ex-slaves and their descendants," as August Meier has observed, "were becoming proud of their race and self-dependent, and yet were assimilating to American middle-class standards and were anxious to partake of all the rights of American citizens." The "New Negro's" racial outlook was rooted "in the social and intellectual movements of the age of [B. T.] Washington"—that is, the urbanization of blacks as well as the development of businessmen and professionals committed to the notion of solidarity, self-help, and race pride.[8]

In May 1931, for example, the local chapter of the National Negro Business League was revived by businessman James Roberts, whose chief concern was that Lincoln graduates find jobs "among members of their own race."[9] At approximately the same time O'Hara revitalized the local NAACP, much to the chagrin of the IRC, which thought protest against segregation untimely. At first some like Best withheld their support because they believed a more patient strategy was preferable, but a variety of issues eventually attracted most black leaders and some whites to the organization. The higher educational level

37. The congregation of Grace Lutheran Church, Missouri Synod, late 1930s. Unique for its time, it was established by a white congregation and had a white pastor. Special Collections, University of Southern Indiana.

attained by younger black leaders, as demonstrated by the formation of the "University Men's Club" in 1935, was undoubtedly an important factor in this regard. Officially reorganized in 1934, the NAACP chapter was rechartered in 1938, and by May 1939 it claimed 175 members—among them educators Robert Anglin, Best, and Rochelle, clergymen L. S. Smith and M. R. Dixon, Dr. Baylor, and others like Zack Buckner and Adrian Bell.[10]

Initially led by Smith and O'Hara, the understudies of the previous generation's most prominent leaders (Rouse and Tidrington), the resurgent NAACP signified the emergence of an anti-Jim Crow strategy in which the church was the focal point of social protest. The most important issue to galvanize the organization was the trial of a young illiterate man for the murder of a white grocer in late 1937. The chapter rallied to his defense, noting that the all-white jury and the white judge had given him a death sentence and his alleged white accomplice life imprisonment. At rallies at several black churches, it raised money for a review of his sentence. Although their efforts ultimately proved unavailing, his execution was delayed until the summer of 1939. The NAACP also implemented—through its youth branch—a successful boycott of Lincoln Avenue stores which did not employ blacks. In 1939 and 1940, moreover, it protested—unsuccessfully—against discrimination in the use of publicly funded facilities, chiefly the public libraries and the new Mechanic Arts School, a vocational high school opened in the fall of 1938. The UAW-CIO joined the

NAACP in the fight to desegregate Mechanic Arts. To both, opportunity for employment in defense-related work was meaningless if proper manual training was not available to black and white alike. (Ironically, the governor had appointed Rochelle to the state vocational education board, and his signature appeared on Mechanic Arts's accreditation certificate.)[11]

Other successful protests strengthened community self-confidence. The Griese administration in 1931 dismissed four policemen for lying about an incident in which a white policeman shot a black vagrant, who they claimed had attacked the white officer. (The inquiry which followed revealed that the white officer, parked on a lonely road with a woman, had shot the drifter for sport.) Three years later, a sheriff's deputy shot and killed a black businessman who owned a taxi company in what the deputy called self-defense. A crowd of 200 blacks nearly killed the officer before he was taken to jail. In what was perhaps the first ruling of its kind, the court sentenced the deputy to prison for involuntary manslaughter—not murder, as the crowd insisted, but at least the white was not set free, as so many had been before.[12]

Community self-confidence and resourcefulness were evident in oher ways. Lincoln's Lions, which by the early 1930s regularly fielded strong teams in most sports, won the National Negro High School Championship in basketball in 1940. Sallie Stewart was elected president of the National Association of Colored Women in the fall of 1930, and her prominence was further reinforced by her being invited to a White House conference on children. Her accomplishments, like those of such men as Rochelle and O'Hara, were infectious. Alfred Porter remembered what might seem to some a minor incident in the late thirties, when the organizer of a downtown parade asked his Lincoln band members to "just fall in" at the end of the line of march, as they had done for many years. Porter refused to comply, and as a result lots were drawn to determine marching order. (Later, alphabetical order was used.). Equally if not more dramatic was the establishment of the *Evansville Argus* in June 1938. Published and edited by Julius Holder, the weekly was a strong advocate of the NAACP. Aside from its publicizing the assaults on segregation and promoting black business development, one of its most novel contributions was the "Mayor of Bronzeville" campaign, whereby blacks would elect their own unofficial spokesman to represent them in the white community. The first such "mayor" was Dr. Baylor.[13]

Much evidence of the past, however, survived. Nearly 90 percent of black workers in 1940 were unskilled or in service. About 40 percent of the work force was female. Unemployment was also high, as 17.6 percent were seeking work, and another 21 percent were on WPA rolls. Most black housing remained substandard, crowded, and relatively expensive: Less than a fifth of black household heads owned their homes; less than a fifth (as compared with 60 percent of the whites) had mechanical refrigeration; three-fifths cooked with coal (as compared with nearly 90 percent of the whites, who used gas). Restrictive covenants remained. In addition, racial stereotypes abounded in the newspapers, as headlines identified blacks by race, not name, and "negro" was always

38. Sallie White Stewart, educator and civic leader. She was president of the National Association of Colored Women in the 1930s. Evansville Museum of Arts and Sciences.

attached to the name in the body of the story, which more often than not dealt with alleged criminal behavior. Separate obituary sections for blacks continued to be used, and racial preferences were specified in classified advertisements. Public facilities remained segregated, often with great irony. The "Sepia Stars" from Harlem were featured at a popular night spot among whites, Dreamland, in the spring of 1934, and its promoters announced that for this occasion a section had been "reserved for colored people." Whites who were interested in the improvement of black Evansville did not as a rule advocate desegregation, and opportunities which had existed for many years for whites—such as a fully equipped school library, which Lincoln received only in 1935—came slowly and begrudgingly.[14]

Perhaps the greatest sign of the persistence of tradition was in the political arena. On the one hand, blacks as a rule supported Democratic candidates in the 1930s, in large part because of the New Deal and the leadership of black Democrats like Dr. King. The movement of blacks to the party of FDR—75 percent in 1936 in Evansville as well as the entire state—was epitomized by the creation of the Indiana Negro Democratic Central Committee in 1935, and King was a member of its first rules committee. On the Republican side, Rudolph O'Hara acquired great stature in his party, and in the fall of 1936 was named to the black advisory committee of the Republican National Committee. He also worked successfully to bring the "Colored Bureau" in Indianapolis into the same building as the state Republican organization and proclaimed that he wished to end the use of separate departments for blacks altogether.[15]

39. Page one of the first issue of the *Evansville Argus*. June 25, 1938.

On the other hand, vote-buying remained an essential part of Evansville elections, and rewards for faithful support were meager. Black leaders continued to rue the fact that the masses inquired how much they were to be paid at election time. They were, nonetheless, hopeful. In April 1940, Holder wrote—probably unaware of what persons like Dupee had said forty years earlier—that "candidates of all parties now realize that the members of our race can swing an election the way that we so choose. . . ."[16]

The coming of world war provided an even greater opportunity to effect change. Beginning in 1940, Evansville attracted a number of defense contracts—enough to rank it among the top six cities in Indiana. These stimuli boosted the population of Vanderburgh County to 144,000 in mid-1943. The longterm effect was evident in the census of 1950, which revealed that since 1940 the city's population had increased about 33 percent.[17]

Black leaders were confident that black citizens would do their duty and that they would be repaid with a greater measure of justice. The fact that the governor had appointed Charles Rochelle to the twelve-person county draft board in 1940 seemed to signal substantial changes. The editor of the *Evansville Argus* announced on December 20, 1941, "This Is Our War!" In the same issue George Washington Buckner, the elder statesman of Indiana blacks, recalled that his mother's three brothers had run away from their master to join the Union army, and that Evansville blacks had been enthusiastic supporters of war in 1898 and 1917.[18]

Rochelle and others made it clear, however, that it was not enough to wage war against the Axis. Commander of the black post of the American Legion, he told his fellow Legionnaires in early 1942 that the black had to wage "two battles: he will fight against the Axis powers and also for his rights of citizenship in this country. These fights he will wage until the end."[19] Like the editor of the *Indianapolis Recorder*, Julius W. Holder of the *Argus* announced a wartime platform which included securing skilled training, abolishing discrimination in defense plants, curbing juvenile delinquency, and improving housing and recreational facilities. Such men acknowledged that achieving these goals would be difficult, given the century-old tradition of racial exclusion and the poverty and disorganization of most black Evansvillians.[20]

After defense contracts began to inundate the city, blacks assumed that their lot would improve. One sign of that was an increase of approximately 2,000 black residents by mid-1943. This placed great pressure on housing stock which was inferior in quality as well as quantity. The strain was relieved somewhat in the summer of 1943, when the local housing authority purchased fifty trailers for black families with federal funds. In 1944, 150 permanent units were opened in Mill Terrace, a segregated site on the north edge of town, near Blankenburg. That many war workers stayed on was evident in the 1950 census, which showed a 25 percent increase in the number of black Evansvillians during the decade. The chief reason for this was jobs. By early 1944, business and labor leaders estimated that 10 percent of the local work force was black.[21]

The larger question was whether Afro-Americans were being hired by a wider range of employers and at higher levels than before the war. In general, progress on these fronts was slight. In the spring of 1941, black organizations had sponsored Negro Defense Week to declare their willingness to do their part in the defense effort. Some whites offered their support. The editor of the *Evansville Courier*, Don Scism, wrote that blacks needed a chance to work in defense plants because they could stand the heat and the strain as well if not better than whites. "They are often surprisingly capable of operating precision machinery," he added, "because they have good muscle coordination and sense of rhythm."[22]

Despite those arguments and President Roosevelt's executive order in 1941 curbing discrimination, the status of Evansville blacks remained unchanged by the end of 1941. Efforts to desegregate Mechanic Arts School were unsuccessful, even though the local CIO Industrial Union Council continued to support the NAACP in that struggle. The school board responded by funding a complete foundry facility at Lincoln. In early 1942, a state WPA official visited the city and warned blacks not to surrender racial gains in the name of patriotism.[23]

In February 1942 the editor of the black newspaper organized the Council of Clubs, a confederation of twenty-three organizations. The new body petitioned Democratic Congressman John W. Boehne, Jr., regarding Mechanic Arts and sent a representative to the Industrial Labor Council to seek assistance. It also arranged the local "Double V Mobilization Day" on March 8, 1942. Thirteen captains arranged for the canvassing of all black citizens to gain support for the goals which the *Argus* and the Council of Clubs had endorsed.[24]

In addition, in conjunction with J. Chester Allen, a black state legislator from South Bend who had been appointed coordinator of Negro activities for the Indiana State Defense Council, a local Negro Defense Council was created in the spring of 1942. The council's task was to survey the black labor market and educate blacks about job opportunities and the need to develop good work habits. Allen urged blacks to take advantage of wartime job opportunities to avoid being "doomed to relegation to the status of virtual vassals and peons in our own country."[25] Several weeks later, Allen returned to announce the creation of the Indiana Plan for Bi-Racial Cooperation, and urged local implementation of the plan.[26]

By the fall of 1942 Holder and others, however, observed that blacks had not yet been allowed to join fully in the war effort. Complaining to visiting War Manpower Commission officials, they noted that the local bureau of the United States Employment Service (USES), for example, refused to refer qualified blacks to most defense plants. Local factories would hire them only as helpers, not journeymen. They were also denied admission to most job training programs. Holder declared that a heavy veil of futility hung over the black community.[27] In June of the following year, regional WMC and NYA personnel, officers of the local NAACP, and J. Chester Allen spoke at a rally at Liberty on

40. The "Fighters," a softball team organized by black war workers at the Chrysler plant during the Second World War. Special Collections, University of Southern Indiana.

the need to improve the quality as well as quantity of wartime employment, and the next day UAW-CIO officials echoed similar concerns at a meeting at the UAW hall.[28]

Various factors contributed to that. Although the first recognition by a state agency that a race problem existed, the Bi-Racial Plan was a weak substitute for the state's failure to adopt a fair employment practices bill. The plan assumed that "idle hands cannot be tolerated. . . . Negroes who use the present emergency to apply pressure for unwarranted advancement will find their new status imperilled when the emergency which supports it has passed."[29]

Related to this was the weakness of the Fair Employment Practices Commission, which Evansville's Southern setting exposed. FEPC officials received few complaints about the city, and when they investigated, employers explained that the reason for their failure to hire blacks was that there were no qualified blacks. The small number of complaints reflected the practice of local USES officials' referring blacks only to a few factories, notably Chrysler and Sunbeam, which were deemed sympathetic to minority hiring. Management at these two factories also upgraded black men and women, but somewhat timidly. When Briggs promoted two black women to semiclerical work in the fall of 1944, for example, the backlash was so great that the plan was scrapped. For the most part, blacks held unskilled, semiskilled, and service positions even in the most progressive defense plants. The most explosive situation was at the LST shipyard, where some blacks were hired as welders. Navy Department officials estimated that because of racial unrest it took twice as many workers (11,000) and over twice the cost ($9,000,000) to produce four barges a month at Evansville as it did to produce five in the same period at Jeffersonville, Indiana, 120 miles upriver. The weakness of the FEPC prompted Republican Congressman Charles LaFollette, an Evansville attorney elected in 1942 with the support of the local CIO and many blacks, to become one of the leading advocates of a permanent and more powerful FEPC.[30]

Local unions were generally, however, an obstacle to progress. Leaders of the AFL in the city opposed hiring as well as upgrading. In early 1944 a prominent AFL official warned that blacks ought not to be "overtrained" for local jobs, as "overtraining can cause trouble."[31] By contrast, the Hod Carriers, Building and Common Laborers' Union was sympathetic. Its business agent, John Soucie, encouraged blacks to come to Evansville for construction jobs. Blacks figured prominently in the construction of the LST shipyard and the Republic Aviation plant. Equally sympathetic was the leadership of the CIO's Industrial Union Council, which had supported the desegregation of Mechanic Arts and the Double V campaign.[32]

Even the CIO's efforts were uneven. Interracial solidarity, as in Detroit, tended to dissipate at the lower levels. Management and union officials at Chrysler, with the apparent support of blacks, agreed early in the war that blacks would be segregated in three departments in order to avoid agitating Southern-born war workers. Pay rates would be the same, regardless of race, for equal work performed. The system threatened to fall apart from time to time, as in the fall of 1943 when management transferred fourteen black women to a department with fifty-two white men. About 2,000 white workers walked out, returning when the transfer plan was scrapped. At the Briggs auto body plant, where only fifty of the 2,500 workers were nonwhite, UAW leadership and management favored upgrading, as only a few black men were skilled workers, and black women were matrons, but white rank-and-file prevented a change in practices there.[33]

Still another reason for the minor advances in occupational justice was the Congress's termination of the WPA and NYA in June 1943. These two agencies had figured largely in the black community for eight years. In 1942, for instance, the NYA helped to build training facilities for skilled employment at Lincoln. In the fall of that year, it began to train black women as machine operators at its West Iowa Street facility. The elimination of these agencies also removed important sources of racial advocacy.[34]

A final obstacle was the limited and sporadic training that blacks received. The drive to desegregate Mechanic Arts waned by mid-1942, and thereafter black leaders concentrated on achieving better equipment and instruction at Lincoln. The school board granted $9,000 for foundry classes in February 1942 (on the same day it appropriated $200,000 for Mechanic Arts). The head of the local USES—which took applications for training at the Lincoln and NYA facilities—complained that blacks were not taking such courses as blueprint reading and aircraft sheet-metal layout. Principal William Best replied that the problem was that the hours of the classes—1 to 6 each afternoon—were unsuitable for workers, and subsequently the hours were changed to 6 to 11 at night.[35]

Better equipment and hours, and the use of instructors from Mechanic Arts, increased enrollments at Lincoln by the fall of 1942. A lengthy waiting list also appeared. Black students were assured that their equipment and instruction were similar in quality to that of Mechanic Arts, and that they could find employment locally with their new skills. Limited facilities and hours of instruction persisted, nonetheless, and it was estimated that blacks took twice as long as whites to finish a skilled trades course.[36]

Pressure from the War Manpower Commission and the shortage of labor made the employment of blacks more acceptable. Federal officials estimated in August 1942 that 45,000 war workers would be needed by the end of 1943, as compared with the 19,000 currently employed. Chrysler, for instance, began to train black machine operators in October 1942, and at about the same time the city of Evansville hired blacks as security guards at its reservoir. As a confidential Federal Security Agency report a year later noted, however, by the time factory operators came to consider using black workers, military service had cut sharply into the pool of available male employees. Hence black women were increasingly called upon as war workers. A garment manufacturer began a training program for black women in the spring of 1943, for example, and the Chicago and Eastern Illinois Railroad boasted of the hiring of twelve women to wash engines, load coal, and clean passenger cars at its roundhouse.[37]

That the attainment of these positions was considered racial progress reveals much about the level of employment experienced by the vast majority of Evansville blacks. The Federal Security Agency reported in September 1943 that blacks continued to work in segregated conditions. The newsletter of Republic Aviation revealed that as late as the summer of 1945 only nine blacks were employed by the manufacturer of P-47 aircraft—six as maintenance workers and three as truck drivers. Thomas Cheeks, Lincoln's eminent coach, commented at an integrated public meeting late in the war that "jobs offered Negroes here are still decidedly limited. . . . Negroes are employed neither as guards or office workers in local war plants." The black resident wanted "the opportunity to advance according to his ability, and not according to the color of his skin."[38]

Wartime also stimulated the growth of black social organizations because of the influx of war workers, the building of Camp Breckinridge thirty miles to the south (which housed 2,000 black soldiers as well as thousands of whites), and the continued reality of segregation. Black soldiers on leave from the nearby camp were denied access to virtually all public accommodations in Evansville, including the USO. Sleeping and recreational facilities were scarce. Only the Red Cross canteen at the L & N depot served a racially mixed clientele. Evansville blacks were forced to rely on their own initiative and resources to meet the needs of the hundreds of soldiers who visited the city on weekend leave. Wrangling among white officials as to the site and management of a black USO prompted a committee of black women to establish a center for soldiers at Lincoln Gardens, which they ran with donations and volunteer labor. By the spring of 1943 the center, known as the Lincoln USO, had a paid director and sponsored a wide range of activities at several sites.[39]

Beginning with Negro Defense Week in March 1941, black organizations responded enthusiastically and generously in other ways. Groups raised funds for the Red Cross Canteen and the day rooms at Camp Breckinridge. In November 1942, Sallie Stewart organized a Colored Women's War Work Committee to sell war bonds and stamps. Students at Lincoln consistently led the city's high schools in per capita war stamp purchases and scrap metal drives. The Community Association served as a recreational, informational, and job placement center.[40]

Wartime social stress, revealed especially in juvenile delinquency, underscored the need for better recreational facilities. The desire for a better community center had been expressed for a number of years before the war, and in 1941 a group of white leaders joined blacks in supporting the idea. Nothing came of the proposal, but black leaders did not let the idea die, especially because of the coming of black soldiers on weekends. Black teachers and parents developed after-school and evening programs. A major step forward occurred in January 1945, when a coalition of organizations, spurred by the success of the Lincoln USO, formed the Carver Community Organization, whose purpose was to create a year-round recreational center. Such a facility, however, was not established until the war was over.[41]

Wartime needs led to other changes. The county probate judge appointed the first black probation officers in the fall of 1942. In response to labor shortages in mid-1943, white officials decided—in the face of the scarcity of housing—to encourage local women to seek factory work rather than to recruit more male workers. That led to the opening of day nurseries supported by federal grants, donations, and fees, and Lincoln and Third Avenue schools were included in the program. Wartime conditions also expanded the educational program of the black auxiliary of the county tuberculosis association, which led by 1944 to the first decline in the tuberculosis rate in the black community's history. Because of the number of soldiers on weekend leave, vice remained a problem. Several black women's groups attempted to address this by developing "stay at home camps" for teenage girls, but inadequate recreational space was a major obstacle to their success.[42]

Evansville's blacks also responded to the call for servicemen. Predictably—as in 1898 and 1917—there were hindrances. Black volunteers were belatedly accepted by army recruiters in the summer of 1940, and segregation of the armed forces created problems for the local draft board in regularly meeting racial quotas. The two dailies and the Sunday newspaper rarely publicized the activities of black men and women in the service. Unlike previous wars, however, a black served on the draft board, and blacks had more choices as to service opportunities and secured higher ranks of leadership than ever before.[43]

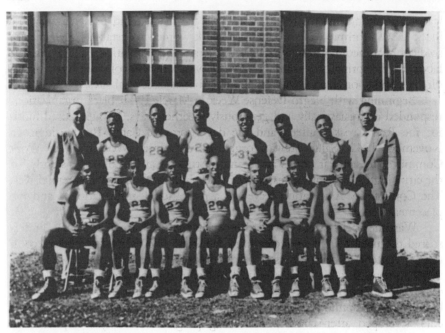

41. Lincoln High School basketball team, mid-1940s. The coach, Thomas Cheeks, whose Lions had always been a powerhouse in state, regional, and national competition among black high schools, is standing on the far left. Special Collections, University of Southern Indiana.

Wartime proved somewhat beneficial in improving race relations and fighting racial discrimination. With regard to the former, there was much continuity with the prewar era. That was evident in the exclusion of blacks from most war plants and in opposition to occupational upgrading. A dual system of justice prevailed, and racial stereotypes persisted in the newspapers. Public accommodations and schools remained segregated, and blacks were excluded from important decision-making bodies like the Office of Civilian Defense.[44]

The arrival of black and white war workers from the South also produced racial strife, although not on a scale of that in Detroit. The race-baiting Senator Theodore Bilbo charged in the *Congressional Record* that the streets of Evansville had been taken over by "uppity blacks." There was clearly some racial tension in the city, although court records indicate that with few exceptions blacks committed crimes against other blacks. Late-night clashes between white soldiers and black youths were a problem, and the apogee of this was in late June and early July 1943, when white paratroopers and black zoot-suiters engaged in late-night brawling.[45]

One immediate result of the summer conflicts of 1943 was the reactivation of the Inter-Racial Commission—"level-headed citizens . . . who might be ready to work toward the preventing of trouble between the two groups and to be useful in the event that an occasion should arise."[46] This was symbolic of the modest gains achieved in most aspects of interracial relations in the war. Athletics were somewhat more advanced. Lincoln High School was admitted to the Indiana High School Athletic Association in 1942, and within a year was competing with local white schools in track and basketball. Local Golden Gloves contests were by 1943 interracial, due largely to the influx of black and white soldiers from Camp Breckinridge.[47]

The larger question—progress in the battle against discrimination—is harder to answer. On the one hand, prewar efforts by the NAACP to end discrimination in education, employment, and public accommodations were continued into the Double V campaign in the spring of 1942. By mid-1943, however, the chief concerns of the chapter were the sale of war bonds and the raising of funds for the Lincoln USO. Similarly, the *Argus* ceased most of its campaigns, including the Mayor of Bronzeville contest, after the summer of 1942. The *Argus*, in fact, unceremoniously ended publication in October 1943. The Inter-Racial Commission was not directed at desegregation so much as maintaining white control. The IRC's study of "Negro conditions" in 1942, for example, included a recommendation that black administration of the community center was inefficient, and that better service would be provided by the elimination of the Community Assocation and the addition of whites to the board of the center. Segregation remained a pervasive fact of life in Evansville in September, 1945.[48]

On the other hand, some advances had been made. In addition to the limited progress on the occupational front, a handful of prominent whites spoke more boldly against discrimination. Pointing to the sacrifices being made by black Evansvillians, educators Best, Cheeks, and Rochelle also publicly called for racial justice in speeches before white church and civic groups.[49]

That whites would invite blacks into their churches and clubs to talk on racial matters, and that local newspapers would carry their remarks about injustice were signs of progress. So was the admission of black churches to the Evansville Council of Churches in the summer of 1943. Perhaps the most valuable sign was the calling of a regional conference on race in Evansville in late February 1944. The product of efforts by the Inter-Racial Commission, the white YMCA and YWCA, and the editor of the *Courier*, the conference was the first of its kind in the city's history. The three-day event attracted 300 delegates from the city and several midwestern states. Speeches on discrimination in housing, health care, employment, and education were delivered by nationally prominent religious and academic leaders. Delegates then met in small groups to discuss means of addressing their concerns.[50]

Although the conference adjourned without adopting any formal resolutions, leaders of both races agreed that it was essential that interracial communication needed to be improved. In that sense the meeting was successful. That the *Courier* gave it particularly prominent coverage and included the candid comments of local black participants on the problems that Evansville blacks faced was also an important step forward. The meeting also laid the basis for several subsequent community discussions on racial discrimination. The Inter-

Racial Commission continued to meet through the remainder of the war and was well enough off by 1945 to hire an executive director. This was the foundation for Mayor William Dress's establishment of the Human Relations Commission in 1948.[51]

When Mary McLeod Bethune spoke at Lincoln High School during Negro History and Brotherhood Week in February 1945, a sense of hope seemed to pervade the black community—fueled by advancements during the previous four years—that the war was the crucible out of which postwar racial progress would flow.[52] Measured by the standards of later years, these achievements were slight. Put against the history of the city's blacks from the Civil War to 1941, however, they were the most significant in the city's history. Perhaps the most important achievement of all was the degree of initiative and cooperation in the black community, for it was out of those cooperative efforts that the various needs of wartime Evansville were met, and that self-confidence and pride were instilled—two vital ingredients for the postwar struggle for racial justice.

Epilogue

 In the immediate postwar era, there was some reason to hope that century-old racial patterns were coming to a end. Charles Rochelle, the first black to receive a doctorate in education from the University of California, Berkley, was named by the governor to the Indiana Board of Education. A year later, in 1946, Charles "Dusty" Decker, a Republican CIO official, was elected to a term in the Indiana House of Representatives—the first (and last) black from southern Indiana to achieve that honor. In addition to Mayor Dress's commitment to a city-wide Human Relations Commission, perhaps the most important public policy decision was the Indiana General Assembly's 1949 law ending the erection or establishment of segregrated schools in the state.[1]

Progress, however, would be slow. School desegregation proceeded slowly in Evansville until the 1960s. Despite the expansion of the World War II era, moreover, the 8,895 blacks in the 1950 census represented only 6.5 percent of the total population. Some improvement occurred in occupational patterns. The proportion of those in unskilled labor and service dropped to 87.5 percent, while that of professionals and small proprietors rose slightly, to 8.5 percent. The amount of change was more marked when analyzed by the sector of the economy in which blacks worked: In 1930, one in ten worked in manufacturing, as compared with 14 percent in 1950; during the same period, the percentage of black workers in commerce increased from 5.9 to 16.5, but the share in transportation and public service dropped from 10.1 and 20.1, respectively, to 3.9 and 8.1. This was, however, deceptive, as the level at which blacks were employed was as a rule menial.[2]

Residential segregation—the product of urban renewal, discrimination, and changing occupational patterns, such as the decline of coal mining—increased, however, in this period. Black households in 1950 were located on only 174 of the 1,850 city blocks (9.4 percent). Most of these were near Lincoln and Governor. Fifty-three of these blocks were 75 percent or more black, and 60 percent of black Evansville resided in them. Only about a fifth of the

Distribution of the Black Population in Evansville, Indiana, in 1950

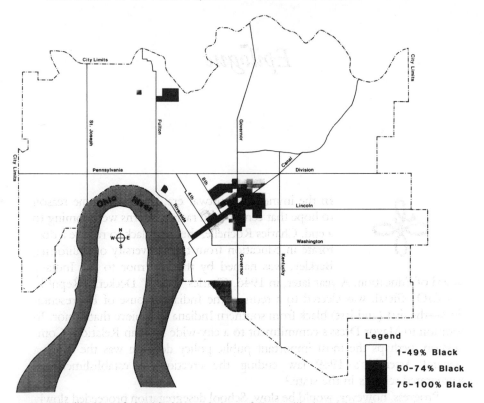

Legend

☐ 1-49% Black
▨ 50-74% Black
■ 75-100% Black

6. Distribution of the black population of Evansville in 1950. The map, based on the first block housing statistics accumulated by federal census takers in the city's history, shows how few (less than 10 percent) of the city's nearly 1,850 blocks had any black residents. It also discloses the degree of segregation in those black-occupied regions. Larry Ordner prepared this map, which is based on the Seventeenth Census, *1950 Housing Report*, volume V, part 62, *Block Housing Statistics, Evansville, Indiana* (Washington, D.C., 1953), pp. 4–22.

city's blacks lived in neighborhoods which were less than 50 percent black. Not surprisingly, the index of dissimilarity had risen to 72. Census officials also reported that about 30 percent of these households lacked indoor plumbing and/or running water.[3]

Nevertheless, despite the absence of marked outward improvement, certain preconditions for racial progress, as Harvard Sitkoff has observed, had been established. The need for laborers and the affluence secured during the war permitted blacks to improve their condition somewhat without appearing to do so at the expense of whites. In the fight against totalitarianism during and after the Second World War, moreover, the blatant racism of the past seemed increasingly anachronistic. The three branches of the federal government, supported by business, educational, and labor leaders, also had begun to weaken the hold that Jim Crow had had on the nation for fifty years. Perhaps most of all, blacks had been encouraged to wage a frontal assault on the proscriptions which had bound them for decades, and that did not as a rule deepen the divisions between blacks and whites.[4]

In Evansville, however, demography, culture, and geography posed a serious threat to substantial alteration of traditional patterns of race relations and of the status of the black community, and the small size and the economic condition of the black community were also liabilities. The words of Robert Nicholas in 1875—"We ask only a fair trial"—remained a melancholy reminder in 1945 that progress in the struggle for freedom and equality in the river city had barely begun.

NOTES

Abbreviations Frequently Used in the Notes

EA	*Evansville Argus*
EC	*Evansville Courier*
ECD	*Evansville City Directory*
EDJ	*Evansville Daily Journal*
EJN	*Evansville Journal-News*
EP	*Evansville Press*
IR	*Indianapolis Recorder*
IRC	*Inter-Racial Commission Survey, 1942*
OH, USI	Oral History Collection, Special Collections, University of Southern Indiana Library
School Board	Minutes of the Evansville School Board
SCJ	*Sunday Courier and Journal*
SCP	*Sunday Courier and Press*
VCA	Vanderburgh County Archives

PREFACE

1. The treatment of blacks in the histories of Evansville is generally meager. The pattern was established in the Vanderburgh County Historical Society Minute Book for 1879–1884, in which early settlers recollected the first several decades of Evansville's development. There are no references to black people. One *relatively* exceptional work is Brant and Fuller, *History of Vanderburgh County, Indiana* (Madison, Wisc., 1889), which appears to have conscientiously sought to record the histories of black veterans, churches, and clubs. Frank M. Gilbert, *A History of the City of Evansville and Vanderburg [sic] County, Indiana* (Chicago, 1910), provides an extensive but negative treatment of the black presence in Evansville. Kenneth P. McCutchan's anecdotal *At the Bend of the River* (Woodland Hills, Calif., 1982), comments briefly on the Underground Railroad, the 1903 riot, and Ernest Tidrington. Mildred Ann Clift, " A History of the Negro in Vanderburgh, Posey, and Gibson Counties in Indiana" (M. A. thesis, Indiana University, 1940), is dated and superficial, and Dallas Sprinkles, *The History of Evansville Blacks* (Evansville, 1974) contains some valuable information, but it is brief and deficient in historical analysis and organization. Emma Lou Thornbrough, *The Negro in Indiana before 1900: The Study of a Minority* (Indianapolis, 1957), and *Since Emancipation: A Short History of Indiana Negroes, 1863–1963* (Indianapolis, n.d.) provide a valuable introduction to the subject on a statewide scale.

2. A number of studies of the Afro-American urban experience have appeared in the past two decades. The earliest ones stressed the tragic sameness of life—notably Gilbert Osofsky, *Harlem: The Making of a Negro Ghetto* (Second edition, New York, 1971); Allan H. Spear, *Black Chicago: The Making of a Negro Ghetto, 1890–1920* (Chicago, 1967); and David M. Katzman, *Before the Ghetto: Black Detroit in the Nineteenth Century* (Urbana, Ill., 1973). More recent works have emphasized the making of community and the rich variety of textures in it. In this regard Kenneth L. Kusmer, *A Ghetto Takes Shape: Black Cleveland, 1870–1930* (Urbana, Ill., 1976), is outstanding. See also John W. Blassingame, *Black New Orleans, 1860–1880* (New York, 1973); Douglas Henry Daniels, *Pioneer Urbanites: A Social and Cultural History of Black San Francisco* (Philadelphia, 1980); and George C. Wright, *Life Behind a Veil: Blacks in Louisville, Kentucky, 1865–1930* (Baton Rouge, La., 1985). Joe William Trotter, Jr., *Black Milwaukee: The Making of an Industrial Proletariat*, 1915–1945 (Urbana, Ill., 1985) develops a unique approach—"proletarianization"—to the subject. Thomas C. Cox, *Blacks in Topeka, Kansas, 1865–1915: A Social History* (Baton Rouge, 1982), and James E. DeVries, *Race and Kinship in a Midwestern Town: The Black Experience in Monroe, Michigan, 1900–1915* (Urbana, Ill., 1984), deal with much smaller communities. Howard N. Rabinowitz, *Race Relations in the Urban South, 1865–1890* (New York, 1978), is insightful.

3. All of the oral histories done by the author and his students are on file in the Special Collections Department of the University of Southern Indiana Library.

ONE

1. Vanderburgh County Recorder, Deed Record Book A, p. 367; City of Evansville, *Charter and Ordinances* (Evansville, 1859), appendix. David M. Katzman, *Before the Ghetto*, pp. 3–50, and Kenneth L. Kusmer, *A Ghetto Takes Shape*, pp. 3–31, treat the pre-1865 period.

2. U. S. Fourth Census, Population Schedules of Vanderburgh County, 1820, National Archives Microfilm Publications No. M33, Roll 14, Indiana, pp. 179–183; U. S. Fifth Census, Population Schedules of Vanderburgh County, 1830, National Archives Microfilm Publications No. M19, Roll 32, Indiana, pp. 386–422; U. S. Sixth Census, Population Schedules of Vanderburgh County, 1840, National Archives Microfilm Publications No. M704, Roll 96, Indiana, pp. 321–60; U. S. Seventh Census, Population Schedules of Vanderburgh County, 1850, National Archives Microfilm Publications No. M432, Roll 176, Indiana, pp. 727–1008; U. S. Eighth Census, Population Schedules of Vanderburgh County, 1860, National Archives Microfilm Publications No. M653, Roll 302, Indiana, pp. 399–926. See also Darrel E. Bigham, "The New History and Forgotten Hoosiers: A Case Study of Blacks in Vanderburgh County, 1850–1880," *Indiana Academy of the Social Sciences Proceedings, 1977*, Third Series, XII (1978), 89–91. Data for 1820–1900 is based on lists of every black enumerated in the county. The total population size forced the author to rely on a sample of the 1910 census (note 17, chapter 7).

3. Frederick J. Blue, *The Free Soilers: Third Party Politics, 1848–54* (Urbana, Ill., 1973), pp. 178 and 203–4. Also see Don E. Fehrenbacher, *The Dred Scott Case: Its Significance in American Law and Politics* (New York, 1978), 160–62.

4. See especially Emma Lou Thornbrough, *The Negro in Indiana*, pp. 21–22, and *Indiana in the Civil War Era, 1850–1880* (Indianapolis, 1965) p. 13.

5. Charles Kettleborough, *Constitution Making in Indiana*, volume I (Indiana Historical Collections, volume I; Indianapolis, 1916), 360–63.

6. Thornbrough, *The Negro in Indiana*, pp. 45–47.

7. Kettleborough, *Constitution Making in Indiana*, volume II (Indianapolis, 1916), pp. 617–18; *Evansville Daily Journal*, August 11, 1851. The newspaper was

known by this title in much of the nineteenth century and by *Journal-News* from 1901 until its end in 1936. The name *Journal* will be used in the text for the sake of clarity and simplicity.

8. Population Schedules, Vanderburgh County, 1820–1860; *Evansville Courier*, April 3, 1910; Deed Record Book A, p. 367.

9. Seventh Census, Population Schedules for Vanderburgh County, 1850; Darrel E. Bigham, "Work, Residence, and the Emergence of the Black Ghetto in Evansville, 1865–1900," *Indiana Magazine of History*, LXXVI (December, 1980), 289.

10. Fourth Census, Population Schedules for Vanderburgh County, 1820; Fifth Census, Population Schedules for Vanderburgh County, 1830; Sixth Census, Population Schedules for Vanderburgh County, 1840; Seventh Census, Population Schedules for Vanderburgh County, 1850; Population Schedules for Vanderburgh County, 1860; City of Evansville, *Charter and Ordinances* (1859), 207.

11. Population Schedules, 1850–1860; Williams, *Evansville City Directory for 1860–61* (Evansville, 1860), passim.

12. W. H. Chandler, *Directory of the City of Evansville for 1858* (Evansville, 1858), pp. 23, 29; Williams, *Evansville Directory for 1863* (Evansville, 1863), pp. 4, 12, 18–19; Williams, *Evansville Directory for 1865* (Evansville, 1865), p. 22. See also Vanderburgh County Recorder, Deed Record Book T, p. 480, for records of the first rural church. (See note 26 for further discussion.)

13. Thornbrough, *The Negro in Indiana*, pp. 13–30. Several cases are recorded in the Vanderburgh County Recorder's office in which owners brought their slaves to this county and freed them. See especially Miscellaneous Record Book K, p. 169, and Miscellaneous Record Book V, p. 158.

14. Population Schedules, Vanderburgh County, 1850–1860, passim; *ECD, 1858*, *ECD, 1863*, and *ECD, 1865*, passim.

15. Population Schedules, Vanderburgh County, 1850–1860, passim.

16. Ibid., 1840–1860, passim.

17. Ibid.

18. Ibid.

19. Ibid., 1830–1860, passim. Lyles is spelled Liles in the population schedules prior to 1870. No blacks were enumerated in Union Township in 1860.

20. Ibid.

21. Ibid., and Vanderburgh County, Early Marriage Book, 1818–1838, comp. Mr. and Mrs. J. Phillips, and Marriage Records of Vanderburgh County, Indiana, 1835–1846, comp. Doris Kolb and Kay Lant, both of which are housed in the genealogical collection of Willard Library. A summary of recent scholarship on the black family in this period can be found in Mary Frances Berry and John W. Blassingame, *Long Memory: The Black Experience in America* (New York, 1982), pp. 70–94, 429–32.

22. Emma Lou Thornbrough, *The Negro in Indiana*, p. 15; Session Minutes of the Evansville Presbyterian Church, Willard Library, Reel 1, April 28, 1858. Frank Gilbert, *History of the City of Evansville*, I:177, described "Old Aunty" as a loyal member of "one of our best churches."

23. Thornbrough, *The Negro in Indiana*, p. 54–56.

24. Vanderburgh County Recorder, Miscellaneous Record Book K, p. 473; Brant and Fuller, Vanderburgh County, Indiana, p. 284. Cf. Thornbrough, *The Negro in Indiana*, p. 56.

25. *ECD, 1858*, p. 23; *ECD, 1863*, p. 22; Population Schedules for Vanderburgh County, 1860, passim; Brant and Fuller, Vanderburgh County, p. 284; and *EDJ*, September 28, 1858, which refers to services at the AME Church. Abram Hill is identified as a circuit rider. Services were held on Sunday morning, Sunday evening, and Wednesday evening. This was perhaps the first newspaper reference to the presence of the church. See also Miscellaneous Record Book A, pp. 141, 230, and 267, for records of the election of trustees.

26. Vanderburgh County Recorder, Deed Record Book T, p. 480. Only Gillespie and Jackson can be found in population schedules of 1850. The former was a huckster living in Evansville. With property valued at $600.00, he was relatively well off. Jackson was a confectioner. Both were natives of Tennessee. See Population Schedules for Vanderburgh County, 1850.

27. Thornbrough, *The Negro in Indiana*, pp. 166–67.

28. Population Schedules for Vanderburgh County, 1850–1860, passim; *EDJ*, February 20, 1856, November 29, 1860, July 10, 1861, and March 16, 1863.

29. August Meier and Elliott Rudwick, *From Plantation to Ghetto* (Third edition, New York, 1976), pp. 174–75; Katzman, *Before the Ghetto*, p. 23; *EDJ*, November 3, 1863, December 14, 1863, January 19, 1864, and March 29, 1864.

30. Thornbrough, *The Negro in Indiana*, pp. 39–44; *Evansville Gazette*, May 4, 1822.

31. *Evansville Gazette*, February 19 and April 9, 1823; *EDJ*, November 4, 1850, and September 10, 1857; George P. Rawick, ed., *The American Slave: A Composite Autobiography*, series 1, volume 6: *Alabama and Indiana Narratives* (Westport, Ct., 1976), 117; John E. Iglehart, ed., *An Account of Vanderburgh County*, volume 3 of Logan Esarey, *History of Indiana from Its Exploration to 1922* (Dayton, Ohio, 1922), 148–51; Vanderburgh County Recorder, Deed Record Book K, pp. 69–71, and Deed Record Book V, p. 158. Between 1848 and 1860, Vanderburgh County's election returns suggested a fairly even distribution of Democratic and non-Democratic voters. In 1848 it voted by a narrow margin for Zachary Taylor, the Whig, and in 1852 it endorsed—also narrowly—Franklin Pierce, the Democrat. In 1854 it elected a Whig to Congress and Democrats for sheriff and superintendent of public instruction. In 1858 it supported an independent for Congress, and in 1860 threw its support, by a close vote, to Abraham Lincoln. See *EDJ*, November 11, 1841; October 18, 1852; October 13, 1854; October 14–15, 1858; and November 9, 1860.

32. William M. Cockrum, *History of the Underground Railroad* (Oakland City, Indiana, 1916), pp. 17–19; *EC*, December 5, 1915; Iglehart, *Vanderburgh County*, pp. 116–17, 128–30, and 148–51; and Thornbrough, *The Negro in Indiana*, pp. 39–44.

33. Cockrum, *Underground Railroad*, pp. 117–19; Iglehart, *Vanderburgh County*, pp. 116–17; Reswick, *The American Slave*, V: 240–41; *Brown's Three Years in the Kentucky Prisons from May 30, 1854 to May 18, 1857* (Indianapolis, 1857); Gilbert, *History of the City of Evansville*, I:176, identifies A. L. Robinson as "the greatest abolitionist here." His discussion of "Old Tom" is found on pp. 164–77. McCutchan, *At the Bend of the River*, pp. 34–5, lists James G. Jones and Robert Barnes as agents of the Underground Railroad. He credits Justice of the Peace Samuel McCutchan, moreover, with assisting runaways. He does not, unfortunately, document any of this. Similar problems exist in Sprinkles, *The History of Evansville Blacks* (Evansville, 1974), p. 1. According to local tradition, a "safe haven" was the Old North Methodist Church on Stringtown Road, north of the city in Center Township. The story of Willard Carpenter's involvement was not told until after his death by an associate, Thomas E. Garvin, and that was not published until 1915, after Garvin had died. See *Willard Library: Statement of the Trustees* (Evansville, 1915), p. 11. Local legends about stations on that line abound, and and by the 1980s virtually every antebellum dwelling in the city and county has apparently been included. See, for example, *Evansville Press*, July 2, 1985. No local historian has considered that free blacks were the chief allies of the runaway, as Larry Gara pointed out in *The Liberty Line: The Legend of the Underground Railroad* (Lexington, Kentucky, 1961).

34. *EDJ*, September 9, 1852, and October 11, 1852; Gilbert, *A History of the City of Evansville*, I:164–77.

35. Ibid., April 15, 1853, and August 19, 1857.

36. Ibid., April 15, 1854, and May 15, 1854.

37. Ibid., July 22, 1857. For an account of anti-black riots elsewhere, see, for example, Katzman, *Before the Ghetto*, pp. 8 and 45–47.

38. Ibid., July 23 and 24, 1857. According to the census enumeration of the township in 1850, John Lyles was 25 and Weston [Wesley] 21.

39. Ibid., July 27, 1857.

40. Ibid., July 28 and 29, 1857 (cf. Thornbrough, *The Negro in Indiana*, pp. 130–31). Daniel Lyles apparently purchased land in Gibson County between 1847 and 1853 (Thornbrough, *The Negro in Indiana*, p. 134), and apparently moved there in the early to mid-1850s, leaving the Vanderburgh County holdings in the hands of John Lyles. See also Vanderburgh County Recorder, Deed Record Book 5, p. 180, and Record of Leases Book I, pp. 19–20, 48–49. The Lyles family apparently acquired a substantial amount of land, including the Henry Beatty farm, and between 1857 and sometime shortly after the Civil War leased most or all of it to whites. The federal census enumeration of 1870 showed Daniel Lyles and most of his family back in Union Township; in that year Lyles had land valued at $15,000.00, an enormous sum by the standards of the day, white as well as black.

41. Ibid., July 30 and 31, 1857, and August 1, 1857.

42. Ibid., August 7 and 10, 1857.

43. Ibid., August 19 and 25, 1857. News accounts on the August 19 reported all the blacks had gone after either selling or leasing their land. Apparently the charges against the older Lyles brothers were dropped.

44. Ibid., December 2, 1859, pictured John Brown as the author of a "harebrained" scheme. In the presidential election of 1860, Vanderburgh County voters cast 1,867 votes for Abraham Lincoln to 1,542 for Stephen Douglas. They also gave John Bell 302 votes and John Breckinridge 183. Lincoln's strength lay in upper Pigeon (i. e., not Lamasco), Center, Scott, and Union townships (*EDJ*, November 9, 1860).

45. Ibid., January 5, 1864.

46. Ibid., November 11, 1864. George McClellan who received 1,230 votes to Lincoln's 1,870 in Pigeon Township, carried Armstrong, German, and Knight townships.

47. Ibid., September 30 to October 24, 1864; May 17, 1865. Clement Vallandigham of Ohio, a Congressman from 1856 to 1863, was the most notable "Copperhead" Democrat.

48. Ibid., August 6, 1864. See also ibid., January 8 and 17, 1863, June 10, 1863, October 15, 1863, February 17, 1864, March 3, 1864, May 11, 1864, November 29, 1864, and December 10, 1864.

49. Ibid., July 18, 1862.

50. Ibid., March 3, 11, and 23, 1863, April 10, 1863, August 1 and 4, 1863, January 9, 1864. Thornbrough, *The Negro in Indiana*, pp. 197–98, states that Indiana's blacks served initially in the 28th Regiment, U.S. Colored Troops. Later they also served in the 8th, 13th, 14th, 17th, 23rd, and 65th regiments of infantry and the 4th Heavy Artillery Regiment. See also Thornbrough, *Indiana in the Civil War Era*, pp. 137–39. Unlike white units which were formed locally, blacks were sent to Indianapolis, where units were created.

51. Ibid., August 10, 1864.

52. Ibid., August 16, 1864.

53. *EC*, December 5, 1915; *EDJ*, August 19 and 23, 1864. The use of the term "Ethiopian" was commonplace in the Republican newspaper between the early 1860s and the early 1880s.

54. *EDJ*, January 19, 1865; see also September 16, 1864, October 5, 1864, March 29, 1864, March 12, 1865.

55. Brant and Fuller, *Vanderburgh County*, pp. 542–43. Among local historians only Brant and Fuller discuss the fact that Evansville blacks served in the war.

56. *EC*, December 5, 1915; *Evansville Courier and Journal*, May 26, 1935. In 1886, thirty blacks in the county (or their widows or orphans)—half of them from Pigeon Township—registered with county officials as veterans entitled to a pension. Of those whose units can be identified, fifteen were veterans of Kentucky regiments. William H. Anderson, an eminent Baptist clergyman, was a veteran of the 13th Indiana. See Enrollment of the Late Soldiers, Their Widows and Orphans, of the Late Armies of the United States Residing in the State of Indiana, 1886, Vanderburgh County Archives, Willard Library. Sixty-seven veterans or their widows or orphans registered four years later. Half were clearly veterans of Kentucky units, chiefly the 118th and the 125th. See Enrollment . . . 1890, VCA. The references to the organizations established during the Civil War appear in Williams, *ECD, 1877*, p. 19, and Williams, *ECD, 1878*, p. 24.

57. *EDJ*, April 6, 1863.

58. *EDJ*, November 9, 1863.

TWO

1. Vanderburgh County Recorder, Miscellaneous Record Book A, p. 251. Brant and Fuller, *Vanderburgh County*, pp. 291–92, aver that the first pastor was a Colonel Woods, a white man. That may have been Miles Woods, a Methodist minister in Lamasco (*ECD, 1866*, p. 241). For a discussion of the importance of the church and the school to newly emancipated blacks, see especially Leon F. Litwack, *Been in the Storm So Long: The Aftermath of Slavery* (New York, 1979), pp. 450–501.

2. Ninth Census, Population Schedules for Vanderburgh County, Indiana, National Archives Microfilm Publications No. M-593, Roll 364, pp. 89–515a. The population of Indiana blacks doubled in the 1860s to 24,560 (Thornbrough, *The Negro in Indiana*, pp. 206–7). See also Clift, "A History of the Negro," pp. 4–6. The Afro-American population of Gibson County increased from 274 to 437 in the 1860s, and by 1880 it was 1,027. The increase in Posey was from 127 in 1860 to 564 in 1870 and to 955 in 1880.

3. Rawick, *Slave Narratives*, VI: 176.

4. Ibid., p. 198.

5. Ninth Census, Population Schedules for Vanderburgh County, 1870; Brant and Fuller, *Vanderburgh County*, pp. 542–44.

6. Kusmer, *A Ghetto Takes Shape*, pp. 35–36.

7. An introduction to recent literature on the development of the Northern ghetto is found in ibid., pp. 12–14, including fn. 13–15, and Trotter, *Black Milwaukee*, pp. 264–82.

8. Darrel E. Bigham, *Reflections on a Heritage: The German Americans in Southwestern Indiana* (Evansville, 1980), pp. 3–4.

9. Ninth Census, Population Schedules for Vanderburgh County, 1870; Tenth Census, Population Schedules for Vanderburgh County, 1880, National Archives Microfilms Publications No. T9, Rolls 316–17, pp. 82–542; Twelfth Census, Population Schedules for Vanderburgh County, 1900, National Archives Microfilm Publications No. T623, Rolls 239–4. The black population in rural parts of the county was 722 in 1870, or about 34 percent of the total county population; in 1880 it was 1,168, or about 30 percent. Twenty years later, it was 531, about 7 percent of the total.

10. Ibid. See also *EJN*, July 3, 18, and 19, 1902; *The Freeman*, May-September, 1894, passim. Also see Kusmer, *A Ghetto Takes Shape*, pp. 40–41. Native-born blacks in Cleveland were 35.7 percent of the population, as compared with 19.3 percent of the black population in Chicago, 32.2 percent in Detroit, 28.4 percent in Cincinnati, and 29.4 percent in New York City.

11. Kusmer, *A Ghetto Takes Shape*, pp. 38–39.

12. Population Schedules for Vanderburgh County, 1870, 1880, and 1900. The ratio of foreign-born whites in Cleveland in 1890 and 1900 was, respectively, 1.13 and 1.05 (Kusmer, *A Ghetto Takes Shape*, p. 39).

13. Tenth Census, Population Schedules for Vanderburgh County, 1880; Kusmer, *A Ghetto Takes Shape*, p. 39; Census Office, Department of the Interior, *Report on the Population of the United States at the Eleventh Census*, part I (Washington, D.C., 1895), 529, 742, 795.

14. Ninth Census, Population Schedules for Vanderburgh County, 1870. Boundaries for the wards are provided in Williams, *Evansville Directory for 1870–1871*, (Evansville, 1870), 34–35. They remained the same until the late 1890s. Cf. Bennett, *Evansville City Directory* for 1900 (Evansville, 1900), passim. See also Rabinowitz, *Race Relations in the Urban South*, pp. 97–98 (cf. Spear, *Black Chicago*, pp. 11–14).

15. Bigham, "Work, Residence, and the Emergence of the Black Ghetto In Evansville," pp. 302–4, and Kusmer, *A Ghetto Takes Shape*, p. 41, especially fn. 7.

16. Bigham, "Work, Residence, and the Emergence of the Black Ghetto," pp. 304–5.

17. Ibid., fn. 24 and 25, and *Evansville City Directory* for 1891 (Evansville, 1891), passim. The 1890 federal population schedules were destroyed by fire.

18. Population Schedules for Vanderburgh County, 1880 and 1900; see also Bigham, "Work, Residence, and the Emergence of the Ghetto," pp. 305–6. The street numbers and names are those used prior to the changes in street names and numbers adopted by the Evansville City Council in 1929. Sprinkles, *The History of Evansville Blacks*, p. 113, and Adrian Bell, interview with Darrel E. Bigham, July 10, 1973, Oral History Collection, Special Collections Department, University of Southern Indiana (hereafter OH, USI).

19. Population Schedules for Vanderburgh County, 1880 and 1900. Cf. Kusmer, *A Ghetto Takes Shape*, pp. 42–43. Cleveland had no all-black street in 1900. Katzman, *Before The Ghetto*, pp. 67–68, which indicates a greater degree of segregation existed in Detroit than in Cleveland.

20. Population Schedules for Vanderburgh County, 1880 and 1900; Rabinowitz, *Race Relations in the Urban South*, pp. 97–98, 124; Spear, Black Chicago, pp. 11, 14, 20–21; Wright, *Life Behind a Veil*, pp. 102–22; Trotter, *Black Milwaukee*, pp. 23–24. For discussion of the index of dissimilarity, see Karl Taeuber and Alma Taeuber, *Negroes in Cities: Residential Segregation and Neighborhood Change* (New York, 1972). 235–38. See also Kusmer, *A Ghetto Takes Shape*, pp. 43–44. The author used data for the enumeration district rather than the block, as data for the latter were not available. The index of dissimilarity (D) is derived via the following formula: $D = 1/2 \ (N[1]/N - W[1]/W)$. N[1] is the number of black households in the district and N the total number in the city; W[1] is the number of white households in the district and W the total in the city. Kusmer, p. 43, notes that the index for blacks in Cleveland as opposed to native whites was 61.

21. See Kusmer, *A Ghetto Takes Shape*, p. 44, and population schedules for Vanderburgh County, 1880 and 1900. Kusmer, p. 43, fn. 11, discusses an index of dissimilarity for Cleveland, but given the fact that few foreign-born Evansvillians were non-German, such an elaborate format seems unnecessary for Evansville. In 1890 there were 7,148 foreign-born persons in the city, of whom 5,639 were German-born. After the Germans, the next highest number was English, with 552. See Eleventh Census, 1890, *Population*, I:670–71.

22. Kusmer, *A Ghetto Takes Shape*, p. 45; Spear, Black Chicago, p. 26.

23. Eleventh Census, 1890, *Population*, I:xcii, clxii, 409–10; Population Schedules for Vanderburgh County, 1880 and 1900.

24. Rabinowitz, Race Relations in the Urban South, pp. 97–98; Spear, Black Chicago, pp. 23–27.

25. *EDJ*, August 15, 1867.

26.   Ibid., and Thornbrough, *The Negro in Indiana*, pp. 209–10. Cf. Rabinowitz, *Race Relations in the Urban South*, pp. 97–98.

27.   Robert C. Weaver, *The Negro Ghetto* (New York, 1948), p. 21, cited in Kusmer, *A Ghetto Takes Shape*, p. 47. See also Rabinowitz, *Race Relations in the Urban South*, pp. 97–98; Spear, *Black Chicago*, pp. 23–27.

28.   Tenth Census, Population Schedules for Vanderburgh County, 1880.

29.   *EDJ*, April 25, 1897. In 1900, the most densely black census district was 126, which had 847 residents, of whom 678 were black. See Twelfth Census, Population Schedules for Vanderburgh County, 1900. Also see Rabinowitz, *Race Relations in the Urban South*, pp. 122–24. Gilbert, *A History of the City of Evansville*, I:178–79, notes that blacks were originally scattered throughout Evansville in ramshackle structures, but by the turn of the century most lived in Ward 7.

30.   Kusmer, *A Ghetto Takes Shape*, p. 48.

31.   *EDJ*, March 25, 1867.

32.   Ibid., May 19, 1870.

33.   See, for example, ibid., June 13 and August 17, 1870, July 1, 1872, December 1, 1874. The issue was still being discussed in Mayor John W. Boehne's administration in 1908. See ibid., May 21, 1908.

34.   Ibid., December 5, 1874, October 5, November 12, 14, and 20, 1897, and April 12, 1898. In 1893, for instance, police arrested 3,026 persons, of whom 833 were black; 535 of the blacks were charged with drunkenness, ibid., April 8, 1894.

35.   Kusmer, *A Ghetto Takes Shape*, p. 49.

36.   Ibid., p. 48, and *EDJ*, May 21, 1899. The brief life of the cleanup effort is documented in *EDJ*, May 21, 1908.

37.   Kusmer, *A Ghetto Takes Shape*, pp. 50–52; Wright, *Life Behind a Veil*, pp. 110–11; Rabinowitz, *Race Relations in the Urban South*, pp. 97–98.

THREE

1.   Meier and Rudwick, *From Plantation to Ghetto*, p. 194.

2.   See especially Rayford W. Logan, *The Betrayal of the Negro: From Rutherford B. Hayes to Woodrow Wilson* (New York, 1965), chapters 6, 9–13. See also Louis R. Harlan, *Booker T. Washington*, volume I: *The Making of a Black Leader, 1856–1901* (New York, 1972), chapter 11; Berry and Blassingame, *Long Memory*, chapters 4, 7, and 8; Rabinowitz, *Race Relations in the Urban South*, pp. 29–49, 182–96, 224–25, 329–39.

3.   Kusmer, *A Ghetto Takes Shape*, p. 54.

4.   Ibid.

5.   Ibid., p. 55, esp. fn. 3., and p. 56; Rabinowitz, *Race Relations in the Urban South*, pp. 29–49.

6.   Thornbrough, *Since Emancipation*, pp. 4–5, 6–7; Thornbrough, *The Negro in Indiana*, pp. 259–60, 266–70, 270–87, 310–20. Several efforts to repeal the anti-miscegenation statute before 1900 failed. The penalty was a maximum of three years in prison and a $5000.00 fine.

7.   Rabinowitz, *Race Relations in the Urban South*, pp. 29–49.

8.   *EDJ*, June 30, 1865.

9.   Ibid., July 31 and August 1, 1865. See also Conrad Baker to Oliver P. Morton, D.C., August 9, 1865, in the Conrad Baker Papers, Indiana Historical Society Library.

10.   James G. Jones to Morton, August 2, 1865, Baker Papers.

11.   *EDJ*, September 18 and 19, 1868, and April 27, 1871; Thornbrough, *The Negro in Indiana*, pp. 273–74; *Indianapolis Journal*, April 29 and May 2, 1871; *EDJ*, August 25 and 27, 1870.

12.   *EDJ.*, July 6 and 7, 1866, and February 17, 1868.

13. Ibid., January 1, 1875, and October 27, 1878; Tenth Census, Population Schedules of Vanderburgh County, 1880. See also *ECD, 1891* and *ECD, 1900*, passim.

14. Minutes of the Evansville City Council, 1865, pp. 127, 141. Cf. Clift, "A History of the Negro," pp. 21–24, which relies heavily on oral tradition.

15. Minutes of the Evansville City Council, 1865, pp. 349, 351, 412, 482.

16. *EDJ*, April 4, 1866.

17. Minutes of the Evansville Presbyterian Church, January 3, 1867, Reel 1, Willard Library.

18. *EDJ*, August 15, 1867 and September 23, 1868; City of Evansville, Assessment Rolls for 1869, VCA, p. 59. Cf. Sprinkles, *The History of Evansville Blacks* p. 7, which repeats the erroneous material in Clift, and McCutchan, *At the Bend of the River*, p. 50, which identifies the first school as being opened in 1867 at Fifth and Chestnut.

19. Thornbrough, *The Negro in Indiana*, pp. 323–31, and Since Emancipation, pp. 49–50.

20. Cited in Robert Anglin, "The Development of Education in Evansville, Indiana, from 1819 to 1900" (M.S. thesis, Indiana University, 1948), p. 63.

21. Ibid. Minutes of school board actions prior to 1871, unfortunately, have not survived.

22. Berry and Blassingame, *Long Memory*, p. 263.

23. *EDJ*, April 28, 1870, and February 23, 1872; *ECD* for 1870–71, p. 23. See also Anglin, "The Development of Education," p. 86, and *EDJ*, August 5, 1873. Townsend, born in Gallipolis, Ohio, in 1841 to devout members of the AME Church, started preaching while in his teens. He served in the 54th Massachusetts in the Civil War, after which he attended Oberlin for two years. Then he came to Evansville, where he taught school and served as AME pastor for four years. He continued his studies at Wilberforce and subsequently held pastorates in Richmond, Terre Haute, and Indianapolis. In 1883 he received the honorary degree of Doctor of Divinity from Wilberforce. In 1884 he was elected to the Indiana General Assembly, the first black to be so honored, where he served as a Republican member for one term. In 1889 President Benjamin Harrison named him Recorder of Deeds in the General Land Office in Washington. Preferring the ministry, he returned to Richmond, Indiana, where he served—with the exception of a brief tenure at Quinn Chapel in Chicago—until his death in 1913 (Thornbrough, *The Negro in Indiana*, p. 301). The Freedmen's Bureau connection is made in Board of Trade, *The Industries of Evansville* (Evansville, 1880), p. 46.

24. Minutes of the Evansville School Board (hereafter cited as School Board), September 2, 1871, May 9, 1873 to May 26, 1874, and August 10 and 28, 1874; *EDJ*, May 27 and October 1, 1874.

25. School Board, September 3, 1874, August 3, 1875, April 30, 1877, and April 28, 1897.

26. Ibid., September 25, 1876, October 12, 1876, August 6, 1877, January 28, 1878, September 17, 1878, and September 15, 1880; *EDJ*, June 15, 1882, and September 3, 1899.

27. School Board, September 15, 1880, and July 6, 1896; Anglin, "The Development of Education," p 9; *EDJ*, August 26, 1900.

28. School Board, May 27, 1887, June 29, 1887, March 23, 1889, July 6, 1896, June 14, 1897, September 7, 1897, and August 27 to November 21, 1898; Clift, "A History of the Negro," pp. 1–24; *EDJ*, June 11, 1888. Also see Thornbrough, *The Negro in Indiana*, pp. 342–43.

29. Anglin, "The Development of Education," pp. 78, 91, and 97; Twelfth Census, volume II, Part 2: *Population* (Washington, D.C., 1902), cxviii and 440; School Board, September 15, 1880, and August 9, 1901.

30. Anglin, "The Development of Education," pp. 66–77; *EDJ* June 16, 1899, and February 27, 1900; School Board, September 15, 1880, and August 9, 1901.

31. Anglin, "The Development of Education," p 72; School Board, July 28, 1884, June 29, 1887, September 19, 1898, June 26, 1899, August 9, 1901; *EDJ*, September 3, 1899. Edwin F. Horn and his parents had moved from Tennessee to the city in the early 1870s. An able student, he was selected to speak at the dedication ceremony for the Governor School in January 1875. Shortly thereafter Horn, a mulatto, was selected as a teacher at St. John's. He was sixteen. Five years later he left the city for Indianapolis, and later moved to Chattanooga, Tennessee, where he became a prominent business and civic leader. He was the grandfather of Lena Horne. See *EDJ*, January 25, 1875, and Gail Lumet Buckley, *The Hornes: An American Family* (New York, 1986), pp. 35–36.

32. Twelfth Census, volume II, part 2: *Population*, cxx, 162–64, 386.

33. *EDJ*, June 15, 1899.

34. Ibid., June 11, 1888 and June 15, 1900; School Board, November 25, 1901.

35. Evansville City Council Minutes, 1865, p. 351; *EDJ*, April 12, 1895, and June 16, 1899 (see also February 27, 1900).

36. Cited in Anglin, "The Development of Education," p 98. See also School Board, November 18, 1890, October 29, 1891, October 16, 1893, and October 14, 1898. On the value of schools in the urban South, see Rabinowitz, p. 179.

37. *EDJ*, February 23, 1872; School Board, January 14, 1878, June 15, 1896, February 8, 1897, and September 7, 1897; *EJN*, April 2, 1899.

38. *EDJ*, June 13, 1882, June 11, 1888, June 16, 1897, and June 15, 1900.

39. See, for example, School Board, August 23, 1886, January 6, 1898, and February 19, 1900; *EDJ*, January 6, 1898. For Horn's speech, see *EDJ*, January 25, 1875.

40. School Board, November 10, 1884, August 5, 1885, April 8, 1889 to June 29, 1889, January 27, 1890, and May 14, 1900. Five black teachers were charged with misconduct between 1884 and 1901. Only one case of misconduct involving a white teacher was found in the same period. See also Berry and Blassingame, *Long Memory*, pp. 270–71.

41. Population Schedules for Vanderburgh County, 1880 and 1900, passim; *ECD, 1891*, pp. 29–592, passim; School Board, Books 1–3, passim; *EDJ*, June 16, 1899 and August 26, 1900; Sprinkles, *The History of Evansville Blacks*, pp. 11–12.

42. Burch and Polk, *Evansville Directory for 1871–1872* (Evansville, 1871), pp. 366–70; Williams, *Evansville City Directory* for 1880 (Evansville, 1880), pp. 11–12, 15–17, 20–23. In 1880 there were six black churches, three lodges of the *UBF*, two of the Odd Fellows, and one of the Masons. There was also a benevolent aid society.

43. *EDJ*, May 9, 1894; *EC*, February 29, 1913, and April 28, 1940. In the population schedules for 1880, black and white orphans were enumerated in the same dwelling. Rabinowitz, *Race Relations in the Urban South*, pp. 182, 189.

44. *EDJ*, June 13, 1865, September 23, 1868, September 23, 1869, June 13, 1870, September 7, 1870, and September 23, 1897; Rabinowitz, *Race Relations in the Urban South*, pp. 29–49, 182, 189. Will Lavender's recollections are found in two unpublished, undated manuscripts at Willard Library: *The Mixing Bowl* and *An Autobiography of Pleasant Memories of a Hoosier Boy's Home*.

45. See, for example, *EDJ*, September 23, 1868, July 6, 1870, December 5, 1874, January 1, 1875, July 5, 1976, April 7, 1892, and September 4, 1900.

46. Ibid., May 19, 1870, December 5, 1874, October 5, 1879, November 16 and 23, 1894, and August 30 and October 16, 1899. See also Population Schedules for Vanderburgh County, 1850 and 1900, passim.

47. *The Freeman*, February 6, 1892; Population Schedules for Vanderburgh County, 1900, passim; *EDJ*, May 21 and October 12, 1899.

48. *EDJ*, October 2, 1874, September 25, 1894, and January 17, April 2, and May 13, 1899.

49. Population Schedules for Vanderburgh County, 1870, 1880, and 1900, passim; *ECD, 1891*, pp. 22–51; *EDJ*, July 12, 1908 and March 31, 1913.

50. Interment Records, Oak Hill and Locust Hill Cemeteries, Books 1 and 2, Vanderburgh County Archives (hereafter VCA), passim; "Colored Folk" column, *EDJ*, 1899–1900, passim; Twelfth Census, volume III, part 1: *Vital Statistics*, lxxix, lxxv, 330–31; Indiana State Board of Health, *Annual Report . . . for 1883* (Indianapolis, 1884), pp. 264, 285; Bigham, "Work, Residence, and the Emergence of the Black Ghetto," pp. 312–13, fn. 36.

51. *EDJ*, October 13, 1869; Mayor's Docket, October 17, 1882, VCA; *EDJ*, October 14, 1869, July 12, 1870, and December 7, 1875.

52. Ibid., October 22, 1878.

53. Justice of the Peace Records, June 11, 1882, VCA.

54. *EDJ*, April 6, 1899.

55. For an overview of this, see Berry and Blassingame, *Long Memory*, chapter 7; Thornbrough, *The Negro in Indiana*, pp. 270–87, and *Since Emancipation*, pp. 6–7. One effect of the rash of lynchings was to encourage blacks to think that few if any blacks were guilty and whites to believe that they were above the law (Berry and Blassingame, p. 234). *EDJ*, September 24, 1868, September 8, 1874, October 13–19, 1878, and April 25, 1899. *The Freeman* (e.g., January 16, 1897) provided an annual list of lynchings for its readers.

56. *EDJ*, September 7, 1870, July 1, 1872, October 6, 1873, November 3, 1874, and April 8, 1894; Superintendent's Report to the Police Commissioners, 1883–1897, VCA, passim; Evansville Police Department, Record of Arrests, 1893–1897, VCA, passim; City of Evansville, Prison Docket, 1882–1885, VCA, passim; Superintendent's Report to the Police Commissioners, 1883–1897, VCA, passim. Because of the unevenness and incompleteness of recordkeeping, the author examined the records of the month of November during 1883–1892.

57. Prison Docket, passim; Vanderburgh County, Jail Register, 1893–1894, VCA, passim; Rabinowitz, Race Relations in the Urban South, p. 43.

58. *EDJ*, May 3, 1870, September 17 and December 12, 1885, March 4, 1886, June 11, 1888, December 4, 1892, November 16 and 23, 1894, December 1, 1894, and November 14, 1897. See also Berry and Blassingame, *Long Memory*, pp. 232–39.

59. *EDJ*, October 17, 1870, and May 3, 1894. As in 1894, the *Courier* story on September 12, 1946, stated that this was the first all-black jury in the county's history. Note as well *EDJ*, March 18–25, 1892.

60. *EDJ*, April 22, 1894, September 29, 1895, and September 13, 1896. The September 29, 1895, issue also carried an article on "Negro Characteristics" written by a correspondent in Memphis. Blacks were supposedly happy-go-lucky and inordinately fond of being devious. Mulattoes were inclined to moodiness. The race also was prone to prevarication and irrational behavior, with tendencies toward the extremes of brutality and jolliness. The author mused about what would happen if blacks were removed from the influences of both heredity and environment—a curious suggestion indeed— and concluded that the future of the race in America was bleak. See also Rabinowitz, *Race Relations in the Urban South*, p. 43.

61. *EDJ*, June 11, 1888, September 25, December 1 and 4, 1894, May 8, 1896, September 27, 1897, and April 25, 1899.

62. Ibid., June 28, 1895, and November 14, 1897. For other illustrations, consult ibid., September 5 and 10, 1898, and City Council Minutes, 1884–1885, p. 404.

63. *EDJ*, December 31, 1899.

64. *EDJ*, September 15, 1879, August 15, 1880, July 5, 1895, and November 14, 1897; *ECD, 1891*, passim. For examples of the "Colored Folk" columns, see *EDJ*, November 11, 1894, and *EC*, March 2, 1897. The column subsequently was variously titled "Colored Folks," "Colored News," and "About Colored People." Prior to 1894, the *Journal* sporadically selected a person in the black community to write on matters

affecting local blacks. Usually the news appeared without the title "Colored News" and with a reference to the fact that the material had been "communicated." Edwin F. Horn apparently had that role in the late 1870s. See Buckley, *An American Family*, p. 38. He may have been the author of the derisive piece on black revival services in *EDJ*, December 6, 1875. Needless to say, the task required the correspondent to write as the white editor desired. The growth of racism in the late nineteenth century is discussed in Logan, *Betrayal of the Negro*, pp. 165–241, and Rabinowitz, *Race Relations in the Urban South*, pp. 29–49, 333–39.

65. Kusmer, *A Ghetto Takes Shape*, pp. 53–65, and Rabinowitz, *Race Relations in the Urban South*, pp. 195–96.

FOUR

1. For an overview of economic trends in this period of Evansville and Indiana history, see Thornbrough, The Negro in Indiana, pp. 347–59, and J. W. Milliman and W. G. Pinnell, "Economic Redevelopment for Evansville, Indiana: A Case Study of a Depressed City," *Community Economic Development Efforts: Five Case Studies*, Committee for Economic Development, Supplementary Paper No. 18 (New York, 1964), pp. 242–43. An introduction to the concepts of class, status, and mobility can be found in Richard Beringer, *Historical Analysis: Contemporary Approaches to Clio's Craft* (New York, 1978), pp. 177–91.

2. Theodore Dreiser, *Dawn* (New York, 1930), p. 120. Rawick, *The American Slave*, V: 29–30; *EDJ*, September 30, 1863, December 10, 1864, March 29, 1865; Ninth Census, Population Schedules for Vanderburgh County, 1870.

3. Ninth Census, Population Schedules for Vanderburgh County, 1870. Most service positions have been combined with semiskilled ones in this analysis, but laundress, washwoman, bootblack, gardener, fisherman, and hostler were placed in the unskilled labor category. Because of the importance which being a porter had in the black community, that position was counted as semiskilled.

4. Given the absence of data in the 1890 federal census regarding Evansville occupations, the author used the Evansville city directory for 1891. See also Population Schedules for Vanderburgh County, 1870, 1880, and 1900.

5. Population Schedules for Vanderburgh County, 1870, 1880, and 1900. The decrease in the number of persons identified only as laborer between 1870 and 1900 is largely due to the increasing specificity of occupational identification—e.g., as laborer on a steamboat.

6. Ibid.

7. Ibid. Lacunae in census records after 1900 make impossible a similar study in the twentieth century.

8. Ninth Census, Population Schedules for Vanderburgh County, 1870.

9. Tenth Census, Population Schedules for Vanderburgh County, 1880.

10. Ibid.

11. *ECD, 1891*, 59–592; Twelfth Census, Population Schedules for Vanderburgh County, 1900.

12. Twelfth Census, Population Schedules for Vanderburgh County, 1900.

13. Twelfth Census, volume VIII: *Manufactures* (Washington, D.C., 1902), 204–17, 994–95. See also Kusmer, *A Ghetto Takes Shape*, pp. 66–76; Wright, *Life Behind a Veil*, pp. 77–101; Trotter, *Black Milwaukee*, pp. 3–38; Spear, *Black Chicago*, pp. 29–41; Rabinowitz, *Race Relations in the Urban South*, pp. 61–96; St. Clair Drake and Horace Cayton, *Black Metropolis: A Study of Negro Life in a Northern City*, I (New York, 1945), 287–311; and Sterling D. Spero and Abram L. Harris, *The Black Worker: The Negro and the Labor Movement* (New York, 1972), pp. 149–81.

14. Kusmer, *A Ghetto Takes Shape*, p. 67; Twelfth Census, Population Schedules for Vanderburgh County, 1900.

15. Kusmer, *A Ghetto Takes Shape*, pp. 67–68.

16. Ibid., p. 68; *ECD, 1900*, p. 53; Vanderburgh County Recorder, Miscellaneous Record Book C, pp. 257, 402, 457, and Book D, pp. 415, 569; Thornbrough, *The Negro in Indiana*, pp. 349–52; *EDJ*, April 7, 1892, and September 4, 1900. No blacks were listed in the Miscellaneous Record Books as trustees or officers of these unions— the cigarworkers, the bricklayers, or the carpenters. For an introduction to black-white union relations, see Nick Salvatore, *Eugene V. Debs: Citizen and Socialist* (Urbana, Illinois, 1982), esp. ch. 4–6, and Trotter, *Black Milwaukee*, pp. 109–10, 228–38.

17. Kusmer, *A Ghetto Takes Shape*, p. 69.

18. *EC*, May 2, 1899.

19. Kusmer, *A Ghetto Takes Shape*, p. 69. Also note Trotter, *Black Milwaukee*, pp. 29–49.

20. *EDJ*, October 7, 1897.

21. Ibid., April 2, 1899, and June 4, 1899.

22. Ibid., April 30 and May 1, 1899; September 16, 1897.

23. Kusmer, *A Ghetto Takes Shape*, p. 70.

24. Population Schedules for Vanderburgh County, 1870, 1880, 1900; Kusmer, *A Ghetto Takes Shape*, pp. 73, 75, fn. 10.

25. Bureau of the Census, *Department of Commerce and Labor, Special Reports: Occupations at the Twelfth Census* (Washington, D.C., 1904), pp. 556–59; Kusmer, *A Ghetto Takes Shape*, pp. 73–75. Also see, passim, the city directories for 1880–1900. Kusmer, p. 75, fn. 10, notes three factors for the slower decline of the skilled trades in some cities: a tradition of racial liberalism; smaller size and consequently less advanced state of industrialization and industrial specialization; and a smaller immigrant population. He argues that in medium-sized Midwestern cities, despite a high degree of racial discrimination, the skilled trades may have been less adversely affected among blacks because of the second and third factors.

26. Twelfth Census, Population Schedules for Vanderburgh County, 1900; Twelfth Census, Special Reports: Occupations, pp. 556–59; Kusmer, *A Ghetto Takes Shape*, pp. 75–77, and especially p. 77, fn. 12, for data on barbers in various cities.

27. Kusmer, *A Ghetto Takes Shape*, pp. 78–79.

28. Twelfth Census, *Special Reports: Occupations*, pp. 556–69; Kusmer, *A Ghetto Takes Shape*, pp. 78–79; *EJN*, June 7, 1909.

29. Kusmer, *A Ghetto Takes Shape*, pp. 79–80.

30. Population Schedules for 1870, 1880, 1900; *ECD, 1900*, passim. See also *EJN, Christmas Art Supplement*, 1903 (n. d., n. p.), and *Indianapolis Recorder*, January 6, 1930.

31. Population Schedules for Vanderburgh County, 1870, 1880, 1900; *ECD, 1891*, passim; Clerk of the Vanderburgh County Circuit Court, Physicians' Certificates, 1885–1897, p. 27; Adrian Bell, OH, USI; Sprinkles, *The History of Evansville Blacks*, pp. 55, 58–59; *ECD, 1900*, pp. 65–753, passim; Thornbrough, *The Negro in Indiana*, p. 364.

32. Population Schedules for Vanderburgh County, 1870, 1880, 1900; *ECD, 1891, and ECD, 1900*, passim. Lott, a native of Illinois, was at one time city attorney of Paxton, Illinois. The successful lawyer was the subject of a biographical sketch in *The Freeman* of December 25, 1915. He is probably the "J. H. Scott" described in Thornbrough, *The Negro in Indiana*, p. 366.

33. Population Schedules for Vanderburgh County, 1870, 1880, and 1900. See also Eighth Census, Population Schedules for Vanderburgh County, 1860, and Bennett and Co., *Evansville City Directory for 1920* (Evansville, 1920), p. 162. Bennett's *Evansville City Directory for 1909* (Evansville, 1909), pp. 758–97, lists seventy-eight barbershops. Also note Kusmer, *A Ghetto Takes Shape*, pp. 82–84. William Glover's father was an ex-

slave who upon arriving in Evansville became a houseman; he died in July 1900 (Charlotte Glover Moody, interview with Darrel E. Bigham, July 12, 1973, OH, USI).

34. *The Freeman*, February 6 and October 15, 1892; Twelfth Census, Population Schedules for Vanderburgh County, 1900; *EDJ*, June 19, 1899, June 23, 1901, March 1, 1903, July 5, 1905, and July 12, 1908; *ECD, 1909*, pp. 758–97. Black's Hotel is referred to in *EDJ* as early as June 30, 1902.

35. Population Schedules for Vanderburgh County, 1870, 1880, and 1900, and Kusmer, *A Ghetto Takes Shape*, p. 84. Evansville's growth rate was much slower than that of Cleveland, where there were black newspapers, plumbers, and bankers by 1900.

36. Bigham, "Work, Residence, and the Emergence of the Black Ghetto in Evansville," p. 297, and Population Schedules for Vanderburgh County, 1870, 1880, and 1900; *EC*, September 13, 1905. See as well Twelfth Census, *Population*, II: 217, 386, an Bureau of the Census, Department of Commerce, *Negro Population, 1740–1915* (Washington, D.C., 1918), 410. Kusmer, *A Ghetto Takes Shape*, pp. 88–89, observes that all ages of black women were represented in the work force, as compared with the tendency of working white women to be concentrated in the younger age brackets.

37. Twelfth Census, *Special Reports: Occupations*, pp. 556–59. The occupational index is discussed in Kusmer, *A Ghetto Takes Shape*, pp. 279–80. Evansville's smaller size meant that statistics for occupations were not provided prior to 1900. The author's occupational index uses a scale of 100 (high) to 700 (low), as does Kusmer, *A Ghetto Takes Shape*, but a somewhat different list of categories—the combining of service and semiskilled workers and the use of a semiprofessional category—is included. Cleveland's black males declined from 510 to 568 between 1870 and 1910; females slightly improved their status, going from 618 to 609. *All* male workers improved their status slightly (422 to 412), and females went from 617 to 447 (Kusmer, *A Ghetto Takes Shape*, pp. 85–88).

38. Douglas Lander, interview with Darrel E. Bigham, October 15, 1982, OH, USI. A good job in 1920 was being a porter, which paid $6.00 weekly.

39. Twelfth Census, *Special Reports: Occupations*, pp. 556–59.

40. Ibid., pp. 558–59.

41. Bigham, "Work, Residence, and the Emergence of the Black Ghetto," p. 299.

42. Ibid., p. 299, fn. 17. See also *ECD, 1891* and Twelfth Census, Population Schedules for 1900, passim.

43. Ibid., p. 300, fn. 18. High transiency rates were not limited to those at the bottom of the socioeconomic scale. Of the seventeen heads of household who were employed in skilled, professional, or proprietary positions in 1870, only five were in the city ten years later.

44. City of Evansville, Assessment Rolls, 1869, pp. 71–550. The set for this year is one of the few extant tax records for the city in the nineteenth century. Also see Population Schedules for Vanderburgh County, 1870; Census Office, Department of the Interior, Ninth Census, volume III: *The Statistics of the Wealth and Industry of the United States . . . 1870* (Washington, D.C., 1870), 28.

45. Census Office, Department of the Interior, *Report on Farms and Homes: Proprietorship and Indebtedness in the United States at the Eleventh Census, 1890* (Washington, D.C., 1890), pp. 38, 184, 367; Twelfth Census, *Population*, volume II, part 2, clvii-clxxxvi, cxciv-cc, 662–63, 703, 714–15. The federal enumeration schedules prior to 1900 do not provide information on home ownership; those after 1870 do not supply data on the value of real or personal property. Kusmer, *A Ghetto Takes Shape*, pp. 89–90, notes that in 1910 about 11 percent of the blacks in that city were homeowners—about one-third the proportion of whites.

46. Kusmer, *A Ghetto Takes Shape*, p. 90.

FIVE

1. For example, *EDJ*, March 28, 1892.
2. W. E. B. Du Bois, *The Philadelphia Negro: A Social Study* (Philadelphia, 1899), 309–10. See also Katzman, *Before the Ghetto*, pp. 135–74; St. Clair Drake and Horace R. Cayton, *Black Metropolis*, passim; Wright, *Life Behind a Veil*, pp. 123–55.
3. Kusmer, *A Ghetto Takes Shape*, p. 90.
4. Ibid.
5. Ibid., p. 91.
6. See, for instance, Darrel E. Bigham, "The Black Family in Evansville and Vanderburgh County, Indiana, in 1880," *Indiana Magazine of History*, LXXV (June, 1979), 117–46, and "The Black Family in Evansville and Vanderburgh County, Indiana: A 1900 Postscript," ibid., LXXVIII (June, 1982), 154–69, and Berry and Blassingame, *Long Memory*, pp. 70–91.
7. Bigham, "The Black Family in Evansville and Vanderburgh County, Indiana: A 1900 Postscript," pp. 155–60. For a comparison between Afro-American and German families, see Bigham, "Family Structure of Germans and Blacks in Evansville and Vanderburgh County, Indiana, in 1880: A Comparative Perspective," *The Old Northwest*, 7(Fall, 1981), 255–75.
8. Bigham, "The Black Family . . . 1880," p. 133, and "The Black Family . . . A 1900 Postscript," pp. 160–61. See also Population Schedules for Vanderburgh County, 1880 and 1900, and Bigham, "Work, Residence, and the Emergence of the Black Ghetto," p. 158, Table II.
9. Population Schedules for Vanderburgh County, 1880 and 1900.
10. Quoted in Kusmer, *A Ghetto Takes Shape*, p. 92. See also Berry and Blassingame, *Long Memory*, pp. 94–113; Rabinowitz, *Race Relations in the Urban South*, pp. 224–25; and Wright, *Life Behind a Veil*, pp. 125–31.
11. *EDJ*, August 14, 1896.
12. *ECD, 1865*, p. 95; *ECD, 1870–71, p. 24; ECD, 1871–72*, p. 371; *ECD, 1874*, p. 16; *ECD, 1876*, p. 16; Brant and Fuller, *Vanderburgh County*, pp. 291–92; *EDJ*, April 2, 1874.
13. *ECD, 1870–71*, p. 24; *ECD, 1883*, p. 17; Brant and Fuller, *Vanderburgh County*, pp. 291–92; *EDJ*, September 11–12, 1882; Vanderburgh County Recorder, Miscellaneous Record Book A, p. 251; Sprinkles, *The History of Evansville Blacks*, p, 77.
14. *ECD, 1875*, pp. 15–16; *ECD, 1876*, p. 15; *EDJ*, September 12, 1882; Brant and Fuller, *Vanderburgh County*, pp. 284, 291–92; *ECD, 1880*, pp. 15–17; *ECD, 1882*, pp. 17–18; Miscellaneous Record Book C, p. 555; *ECD, 1900*, pp. 20–63. Also see Brant and Fuller, *Vanderburgh County*, p. 291.
15. Brant and Fuller, *Vanderburgh County*, pp. 284–292; Kusmer, *A Ghetto Takes Shape*, p. 95.
16. Quoted in Kusmer, *A Ghetto Takes Shape*, p. 95.
17. *EDJ*, January 29, 1894, and April 30, 1899.
18. Kusmer, *A Ghetto Takes Shape*, p. 95.
19. *EDJ*, December 6, 1875, and April 7, 1892.
20. *EDJ*, April 14, 1895 and September 4, 1890; *ECD, 1878*, p. 24; *ECD, 1880*, p. 27; *ECD, 1881*, p. 18; *ECD, 1882*, pp. 22–30.
21. Miscellaneous Record Book A, p. 376, and Book C, pp. 180 and 506; *ECD, 1891*, passim. Most churches and civic organizations reported their elections in a desultory fashion. Liberty, Alexander, and McFarland were exceptions.
22. Miscellaneous Record Book B, pp. 536–37, and Book C, pp. 21, 160, and 296; *ECD, 1891*, passim.

23. See, for example, *EDJ*, November 11, 1894, and March 10, 1895; *The Free-man*, January 6 and August 4, 1894, and October 30, 1898.

24. *EDJ*, November 13, 1869, and May 31 and June 8, 1894.

25. *ECD, 1900*, pp. 20–63; Kusmer, *A Ghetto Takes Shape*, pp. 96–97. Also note Rowland Berthoff, *An Unsettled People: Social Order and Disorder in American History* (New York, 1971), pp. 270–74.

26. Kusmer, *A Ghetto Takes Shape*, p. 97; *ECD, 1900*, pp. 20–63; *EDJ*, September 23, 1869. Oral tradition dates the establishment of the first UBF lodge in 1864 or 1865, but the first record in the County Recorder's Office was entered in July 1872 (Miscellaneous Record Book B, p. 480). The city directory of 1877 lists Asbury Lodge as having been formed in January 1864, and Brant and Fuller, *Vanderburgh County*, p. 396, say it was established in 1865. The first mention of the Masons in city directories is in the *ECD, 1871–'72*, p. 370. Olive Branch Lodge No. 23 lasted for a brief time and was cited in *ECD, 1872–'73*, p. 19, but *ECD, 1877* records a newly reorganized McFarland Lodge No. 5. For a discussion of secret societies and fraternal orders elsewhere, consult Rabinowitz, *Race Relations in the Urban South*, pp. 241–45, and Wright, *Life Behind a Veil*, pp. 131–36.

27. Miscellaneous Record Book D, pp. 135–36.

28. Miscellaneous Record Book A, p. 480; Brant and Fuller, *Vanderburgh County*, p. 396; *EDJ*, May 28, 1867.

29. *EDJ*, October 7, 1873, March 1, 1896, and September 23, 1897; *The Free-man*, April 14, 1894; Population Schedules for Vanderburgh County, 1870; Rabinowitz, *Race Relations in the Urban South*, p. 241.

30. Brant and Fuller, *Vanderburgh County*, p. 396; Population Schedules for Vanderburgh County, 1870; Miscellaneous Record Book A, p. 480; *ECD, 1871–'72*, passim; Miscellaneous Record Book D, pp. 135–36; *ECD, 1891*, passim.

31. *EDJ*, July 6, 1870, June 2, 1875; Brant and Fuller, *Vanderburgh County*, pp. 384–85; Population Schedules for Vanderburgh County, 1880; *ECD, 1891*, passim; Miscellaneous Record Book B, pp. 381, 481, and Book C, pp. 180, 285.

32. *The Freeman*, August 5, 1893; *EDJ*, January 8, 1876; *ECD, 1880*, pp. 21–23; *EDJ*, March 6, 1893, March 1 and September 23, 1896.

33. Miscellaneous Record Book B, p. 499, and Book C, pp. 28 and 472.

34. Kusmer, *A Ghetto Takes Shape*, pp. 97–98; Recorder, August 2, 1899; Brant and Fuller, *Vanderburgh County*, p. 396; Miscellaneous Record Book D, pp. 107, 205; *ECD, 1896*, passim; *EDJ*, October 9, 1875, April 30 and May 26, 1899.

35. Kusmer, *A Ghetto Takes Shape*, p. 98. For definitions of classes among blacks, see ibid., pp. 93–94, fn. 4, and pp. 98–99, fn. 13, and Wright, *Life Behind a Veil*, pp. 135–36, fn. 26. These terms, which reflect occupation and income, do not have equivalents in white society but (Kusmer, p. 94) are used for "analytical convenience."

36. *EDJ*, October 17, 1870 and June 4, 1874; Kusmer, *A Ghetto Takes Shape*, p. 98; Population Schedules for Vanderburgh County, 1860–1880.

37. Population Schedules for Vanderburgh County, 1870–1880; *EDJ*, July 10, 1908, and *Evansville Press*, July 21, 1908 (hereafter cited as *EP*).

38. Kusmer, *A Ghetto Takes Shape*, pp. 99–103; Wright, *Life Behind a Veil*, pp. 135–36; and Rabinowitz, *Race Relations in the Urban South*, pp. 241–45; Tenth Census, Population Schedules for Vanderburgh County, 1880; *EDJ*, *Christmas Art Supplement*, 1903.

39. *ECD, 1891*, passim; Population Schedules for Vanderburgh County, 1880 and 1900; School Board, Book 3, p. 162; *EDJ*, July 9 and November 2, 1907; Kusmer, *A Ghetto Takes Shape*, pp. 103–4, fn. 20; Katzman, *Before the Ghetto*, pp. 164–66; Trotter, *Black Milwaukee*, p. 80; Spear, *Black Chicago*, pp. 71–90; and Wright, *Life Behind a Veil*, pp. 156–75.

40. Kusmer, *A Ghetto Takes Shape*, pp. 104–5; *EC*, August 29, 1910; *EDJ*, *Christmas Art Supplement*, 1903; *EDJ*, June 15, 1899.

41. Cited in *EDJ, Christmas Art Supplement*, 1903.

42. Twelfth Census, Population Schedules for Vanderburgh County, 1900. Kusmer, *A Ghetto Takes Shape*, p. 105, states that the middle class in Cleveland was larger—20 percent—than the approximately 4 percent who represented the upper class. In Evansville there were at best 300 persons (out of 3,611) whose occupations clearly put them in the middle class. See also School Board, Book 3, pp. 162, 175.

43. Kusmer, *A Ghetto Takes Shape*, pp. 105–6; *EC*, June 15, 1899; *EDJ*, August 28, 1901.

44. *EDJ*, September 20, 1869, August 4, 1887, and April 30, 1899; *EC*, May 26, 1899; *The Freeman*, October 27, 1894, and July 24, 1897.

45. *EJN*, June 10 and 13, 1900.

46. Ibid.

47. Kusmer, *A Ghetto Takes Shape*, p. 107.

48. *The Freeman*, December 25, 1897.

49. *EDJ*, April 30, 1899.

50. Ibid., December 18, 1901.

51. Ibid., April 4, 1902.

52. Kusmer, *A Ghetto Takes Shape*, p. 108.

53. Population Schedules for Vanderburgh County, 1900; Kusmer, *A Ghetto Takes Shape*, pp. 108–9, fn. 27; Douglas Lander, OH, USI; Thirteenth Census, *Abstract* (Washington, D.C., 1910), pp. 706–7.

54. Kusmer, *A Ghetto Takes Shape*, p. 109; Twelfth Census, Population Schedules for Vanderburgh County, 1900; Douglas Lander, OH, USI.

55. Kusmer, *A Ghetto Takes Shape*, p. 111. For a fuller discussion of this lifestyle, see chapter 4. The correspondence from Evansville in *The Freeman* and the *Indianapolis Recorder* illustrate this.

56. Kusmer, *A Ghetto Takes Shape*, p. 111; Katzman, *Before the Ghetto*, pp. 169–71; Population Schedules for Vanderburgh County, 1900; *EDJ*, June 5–6, August 30, October 16, 1899. Also consult chapter 4.

57. Rabinowitz, *Race Relations in the Urban South*, pp. 253–54, and Trotter, *Black Milwaukee*, pp. 109–10.

SIX

1. *EDJ*, May 23, 1899.

2. Cf. Kusmer, *A Ghetto Takes Shape*, pp. 116–36, for a discussion of the integrationist tradition in Cleveland. See also Thornbrough, *The Negro in Indiana*, pp. 288–316, for a review of Indiana politics in this period. For an overview of Afro-American thinking in this era, consult August Meier, *Negro Thought in America, 1880–1915* (Ann Arbor, 1966), pp. 19–120. A rare glimpse into black politics in urban America is found in Wright, *Life Behind a Veil*, pp. 171–93.

3. *EDJ*, September 23, 1868; August 9, 1870; and August 1 and 8, 1872.

4. Ibid., January 1, 1875.

5. Ibid.

6. Ibid., March 15, 1875, and Buckley, *An American Family*, pp. 37–38. The Civil Rights Act of 1875 was emasculated by the Supreme Court in 1883. The county voted Democratic in the October election of that year, 3,327 to 3,273. See *EDJ*, March 9 and October 13, 1868. Niblack served the First District from 1857 to 1861 and from 1865 to 1875 (Congressional Quarterly, *Members of Congress since 1789* [Washington, D.C., 1977], p. 102).

7. *EDJ*, September 22 and October 9, 1866, and September 6, 1869.

8. Ibid., August 1, 1872.

9. Ibid. One dissenter was Charles H. Sheldon, who was a prominent saloon-keeper. He and several others spoke on behalf of Horace Greeley.

10. Ibid. Newspaper records as to whether blacks continued to elect "their" representative to the Republican Central Committee are at best murky, and no reference to the practice appears after the early 1890s. A review of *ECD, 1872–'73*, passim, allows one to identify the first officers of the black political organization as leaders of the inchoate black elite.

11. Ibid., June 8, 1867.

12. Thornbrough, *The Negro in Indiana*, pp. 294–95.

13. *EDJ*, October 14 and 15, 1870.

14. Ibid., and April 28 to May 2, 1871.

15. Ibid., October 6, 1876.

16. Ibid., October 6 and 7, 1876.

17. Ibid., November 3, 1876.

18. Ibid., November 8, 1876.

19. Ibid., September 12, 1886. See ibid., October 7, 1878, for a typical appeal—this time by J. S. Nance—to the black voters. *EC*, November 4, 1884, and *EDJ*, March 14 and September 12, 1886.

20. *EDJ*, August 12, 1872; June 4, 1874; April 5, 1895; and April 6, 1897. Aside from Nicholas, the policemen were Eli Jackson, Bryant Goin, and Daniel Banks. Also note *Evansville Argus*, July 23, 1940. The first black convention delegate may have been Blis Jackson (*EDJ*, August 28, 1878).

21. *EDJ*, October 12, 1872, October 16, 1874, October 2 and 13, 1876, and October 11, 1878.

22. *EDJ*, October 12–16, 1872; October 12–16, 1874; October 2 and 13, 1876; November 11, 1882; November 8, 1884; November 8, 1888; and November 8, 1890. After 1880, state and county elections were held on the same day as federal elections—on the first Tuesday after the first Monday in November.

23. Ibid., October 3, 1876, October 11, 1880, and October 22, 1884.

24. Ibid., August 3 and October 26 and 27, 1888. Also note ibid., April 5, 1886, November 10, 1882, November 8, 1884, November 6, 1886, November 8, 1888, and November 8, 1890.

25. Thornbrough, *The Negro in Indiana*, pp. 303–18; *EDJ*, October 27, 1888. Election news in that year showed an increase in the number of Democratic clubs in the black community. Similar developments were occurring in the urban South, according to Rabinowitz, pp. 282–304.

26. Quoted in Thornbrough, *The Negro in Indiana*, p. 307.

27. Minutes of the Evansville City Council, 1890–1900, passim; Rabinowitz, *Race Relations in the Urban South*, p. 124.

28. *EDJ*, November 18, 1894.

29. Ibid.; *The Freeman*, December 29, 1894.

30. *EDJ*, October 6, 1888, and September 27, 1895; Bobby L. Lovett and Karen Coffee, "George Washington Buckner: Politician and Diplomat," *Black History News and Notes*, no. 17 (May, 1984), 5; School Board, November 4, 1901, p. 437.

31. *EC*, March 9, 25 and 26, April 5–7, and 20, 1897. George Williams became captain of the black fire company and Tom Hathaway custodian at city hall. See ibid., March 25 and 28, 1899, and *EDJ*, April 2–4, 1899.

32. *The Freeman*, March 19, 1892, April 4, 1893, March 20, 1895, and March 10, 1897. Ward delegates elected the council candidates in ward meetings, and the convention elected the mayoral and at-large council candidates. *EDJ*, May 30, 1894, and May 21, 1898.

33. *EC*, April 3, 1897, and November 1, 1901; *EDJ*, August 19, 1900.

34. *EDJ*, November 13, 1897, and August 19, 1900; Wright, *Life Behind a Veil*, p. 171.

35. Note, for instance, *EDJ*, August 19, 1900.

36. Ibid., April 8 and 9, 1891; April 2 and 3, 1899. New voting procedures were introduced in the decade which lent themselves easily to voting irregularities. Ballots had the party symbol on them, and to vote a straight-party ticket, the voter had to cross out the symbol properly. Otherwise the ticket was voided. Also see Rabinowitz, *Race Relations in the Urban South*, pp. 243–5.

37. *EDJ*, April 1–4, 1899, and November 6 and 7, 1900.

38. For example, consult ibid., March 7 and September 7, 1900; and *EC*, March 10, 1897. Useful in this respect are Spear, *Black Chicago*, p. 125; Meier, *Negro Thought in America*, pp. 26–41; and Rabinowitz, *Race Relations in the Urban South*, pp. 282–304.

39. *EDJ*, April 7, 1891, April 5 and November 9, 1892, May 30 and November 8, 1894, April 3, 1895, October 31 and November 8, 1896, February 11, 1897, November 10, 1898, April 5, 1899, and November 8, 1900. Precincts were reorganized in 1897, and precincts 52–61 in that ward were heavily black.

40. The first newspaper reference to Tidrington appeared in ibid., September 16, 1897. The fifteen-year-old youth apparently was the leader of a group of black workers at a canning factory who protested working conditions and became engaged in a fracas with fellow white workers.

41. *The Freeman*, November 4 and December 2, 9, and 30, 1893, and January 13 and May 5, 1894; Meier and Rudwick, *From Plantation to Ghetto*, p. 249; Louis Harlan, *Booker T. Washington*, I:227, 293; John Hope Franklin, *From Slavery to Freedom: A History of Negro Americans* (Fifth ed., New York, 1980), pp. 222, 238, 246; Berry and Blassingame, *Long Memory* p. 379. See also *EDJ*, June 10, October 19, 1901, and January 2 and 29, 1894; and *ECD, 1894*, p. 634.

42. *The Freeman*, May 5, 1894.

43. Ibid., July 2, 1892; *EDJ*, January 29, April 9, June 5 and 8, and August 4, 1894. Wright, *Life Behind a Veil*, pp. 63–64, also discusses the separate coach law and Anderson's role in testing it.

44. *EDJ*, May 31, 1894, and March 20 and April 1, 1895; *The Freeman*, December 25, 1915; Meier, *Negro Thought in America*, p. 71; Wright, *Life Behind a Veil*, pp. 171–93. Meier states that Turner's assembly ended the Negro Convention Movement which had begun in 1830.

45. Cf. Kusmer, *A Ghetto Takes Shape*, pp. 116–40, who discusses the split between conservative integrationists and accommodationists in that city. The paucity of historical records makes a review of the thinking of black leaders in Evansville extremely difficult, but those that exist do suggest varying degrees of accommodationism. Also see *EDJ*, May 31, 1894; March 20, 1895.

46. *EDJ*, June 6, 1897. See Harlan, *Booker T. Washington*, I: 204–28, and Meier, *Negro Thought in America*, pp. 85–120, for a discussion of the development and appeal of the accommodationist approach.

47. *EDJ*, June 6 and November 13, 1897.

48. Ibid., June 10, 1901.

49. Ibid., October 24, 1901; *Journal Christmas Art Supplement*, 1903; *EDJ*, February 14 and September 2, 1905.

50. *EDJ*, October 24, 1901. Kusmer, *A Ghetto Takes Shape*, pp. 141–48, points out that the self-help philosophy led Cleveland blacks to seek white customers. Evansville blacks could not do that, given their poverty, their small middle class, and the exclusion tradition. Rabinowitz, *Race Relations in the Urban South*, pp.195–96, 221–25, and Wright, *Life Behind a Veil*, p. 173 deal with the same issue.

51. Kusmer, *A Ghetto Takes Shape*, pp. 152–53.

52. Ibid., pp. 153–54.

53. *EDJ*, April 2, 1899.

SEVEN

1. *Indianapolis Recorder*, June 27, 1903. (Hereafter cited as *IR*.)
2. Ibid.
3. See population data provided in Table 14.
4. *EC*, February 15 and 20, 1903, February 26 to March 10, 1903, April 26, 1903; *EJN*, July 3, 1903; George Fredrickson, *The Black Image in the White Mind: The Debate on Afro-American Character and Destiny, 1817–1914* (New York, 1971), 256–82.
5. *EC* and *EJN*, July 4, 1903. See also Coroner's Inquest No. 73, July 9, 1903, VCA. The witnesses were Al Ossenberg and three black men. A reading of the transcript encourages one to doubt that the inquest was impartial—for example, Brown (Lee) was portrayed as a troublemaker who was sober at the time of the shooting.
6. *EC* and *EJN*, July 5–10, 1903. A law passed in 1899 allowed the governor to call the militia in such cases. Thornbrough, Negro, pp. 270–87. For a discussion of race riots in the South in the decade, see Joel Williamson, *The Crucible of Race: Black-White Relations in the American South since Emancipation* (New York, 1984), pp. 111–40.
7. Ibid., and *IR*, August 15, 1903. In an interview with the author on January 25, 1986, the late Susan Hopkins Ingle, granddaughter of Thomas Garvin, related that during the height of the crisis a number of blacks took refuge in his fashionable home. Armed with a shotgun, Garvin stood guard at his doorway to protect his charges.
8. *EC*, July 7, 1903, and November 1, 1901; *EJN*, July 10, 11, 14, and 15, 1903.
9. *EJN*, July 18, 1903; Minutes of the City Council 1903–1905, pp. 75, 83, 84, 85–86, 108–11. In July, 1904, the Safety Board disallowed the firing of pistols, guns, and revolvers, with or without blanks, within city limits (*EJN*, July 2, 1904).
10. *EJN*, July 6 to 31, 1903; *EC*, January 2 and July 2, 1903.
11. *EJN*, July 17 and August 21, 1903. Black Baptists meeting in Indianapolis attributed the riot to the behavior of lower class blacks and whites (*IR*, July 18, 1903).
12. *EJN*, July 18, 1903.
13. Ibid., August 6, September 20–21, and October 29, 1903.
14. Ibid., June 11, July 2, August 27, and September 4, 1904, May 26, 1905, April 29, May 27, and August 27, 1906, and July 1 and November 1, 1909.
15. For an overview of demographic changes in this period, see Meier and Rudwick, *From Plantation to Ghetto*, pp. 232–70.
16. Bureau of the Census, Department of Commerce and Labor, *Thirteenth Census of the United States Taken in the Year 1910: Abstract of the Census with Supplement for Indiana* (Washington, D.C., 1913), pp. 95–96, 598–615; Bureau of the Census, Department of Commerce, *Negro Population, 1790–1915* (Washington, D.C., 1918), pp. 598–615, 720–21, 782, 768–91. The largest number of Evansville blacks came from these western Kentucky counties—Henderson, Daviess, Union, McLean, Hopkins, and Muhlenberg. Most of the blacks there were engaged in farming. In Henderson in 1910, 469 were in agriculture, of whom 293 were sharecroppers; 300 farmed less than twenty acres. All of these counties experienced population declines between 1900 and 1910. Louisville's black population remained at approximately 20,000 from 1900 to 1920 and increased slightly in the twenties (Wright, *Life Behind a Veil*, p. 46).
17. *Negro Population, 1790–1915*, p. 74; U.S. Bureau of the Census, Department of Commerce, Thirteenth Census of the Population of the United States, 1910, Microfilm Rolls 263–264, T624, 382–83, Volumes 122–125 (hereafter cited as Thirteenth Census, Population Schedules of Vanderburgh County, 1910). The data, derived from a systematic sample of the entire county census, was coded and analyzed via the Statistical Package for the Social Sciences. The reliability of the sample (2.5 percent of

the total) is suggested, among other things, in its yielding the same percentage of blacks and whites and men and women as the printed census.

18. Thirteenth Census, Population Schedules for Vanderburgh County, 1910. Ward boundaries were essentially the same—especially Ward 7—as in 1900.

19. Ibid. The thirteen districts were numbers 99, 100, 103, 112, 114, 139, 141–145, 147, and 155.

20. Ibid. and *ECD, 1911*, pp. 875–1038.

21. Population Schedules for Vanderburgh County, 1900 and 1910; Thirteenth Census, Abstract, p. 623; Kusmer, *A Ghetto Takes Shape*, pp. 43–44.

22. Population Schedules for Vanderburgh County, 1900 and 1910. Early references to Oakdale appeared in *EJN*, "Colored Folk" on April 20, 1901, and October 24, 1902; to Jimtown on January 14, 1902, June 30, 1902, July 3, 1902, October 24, 1902, December 19, 1902, and January 12, 1906; and to Newtonville on September 3, 1901, September 5, 1901, and April 18, 1902.

23. Thirteenth Census, Population Schedules for Vanderburgh County, 1910, and *Negro Population, 1790–1915*, pp. 471–73.

24. *EJN*, June 10, 1904, December 6, 1908, January 24 and February 15, 1909, June 2, 1912, and April 29 and May 7, 1913.

25. *Evansville Press*, February 28 and March 17, 1914 (hereafter *EP*); *EJN*, July 18, 20, and 29, 1914; Robert G. Barrows, "The Homes of Indiana: Albion Fellows Bacon and Housing Reform Legislation, 1907–1914," *Indiana Magazine of History*, LXXXI (December, 1985), 309–50. Barrows, pp. 312–13, states that Indiana housing reform began with an Evansville convention of the Indiana Conference of Charities and Correction in October 1907, at which Mrs. Bacon gave a paper. The paper appeared, with photographs of Evansville housing conditions, in *Charities and the Commons* on December 5, 1908.

26. Albion Fellows Bacon, *Beauty for Ashes* (New York, 1914), pp. 53, 232–34; Rabinowitz, *Race Relations in the Urban South*, p. 124.

27. *EJN*, February 9 and May 2–3, 1915; *EP*, August 4, September 28, and December 28, 1915. On September 28 the building commissioner reported that there were thirty-two rooms with no outside air opening, thirty-six dwellings in which three or more families used one privy vault, and fifty-seven in which three or more families used a common cistern. On December 28 he declared that the city had the best record for housing improvement among cities under 250,000, as the city had razed eighty-three dwellings that year, as compared with twenty-eight in the previous year. There were also 271 building corrections in 1915, up from 202 in 1914.

28. *EJN*, May 2, 9, 10, 1915, and February 10, 1916; *EC*, March 26, 1916; *EP*, May 27, 1916; Barrows, "The Homes of Indiana," pp. 347–48.

29. *EC*, April 27, 1918; *EJN*, February 15, 1909, and July 25, 1914; Douglas Lander OH, USI; Sprinkles, *The History of Evansville Blacks*, p. 4; Barrows, "The Homes of Indiana," pp. 348–49.

30. *EJN*, June 21, August 1, 29–30, 1907; *EP*, August 28 and 29, 1907. See also Kusmer, *A Ghetto Takes Shape*, pp. 46–52.

31. *EJN*, August 28–30, September 7, 1907; *ECD, 1908*, passim.

32. Alfred Porter, interview with Darrel E. Bigham, June 12, 1974, OH, USI; Deed Records, volume 96, pp. 433–34; Kusmer, *A Ghetto Takes Shape*, pp. 46–48.

33. Bureau of the Census, Department of Commerce, *Negroes in the United States, 1920–1932* (Washington, D.C., 1935), p. 86; *Fourteenth Census of the United States Taken in the Year 1920*, volume III: *Population* 1920 (Washington, D.C., 1922), 305.

34. *Negroes in the United States, 1920–1932*, pp. 26, 184, 276, 723; *Fifteenth Census of the United States*, 1930, volume III, part 1, *Population* (Washington, D.C., 1932), 700, 744; *Negro Population, 1790–1915*, p. 279. There is much evidence of continued migration from Evansville to urban places farther north. This, it must be added,

was characteristic of Indiana's black population as a whole. In 1930 the state ranked second among the five East North Central states in the percentage of its native blacks residing in other states (32.6) and was at the bottom in the percentage of native-born blacks (67.8) living in the state. The state's net gain through interstate migration between 1900 and 1930 was consistently low. In the 1920s, for example, it was 57,805—less than half of Michigan, a third of Ohio, and a fourth of Illinois.

35. *Sunday Courier and Journal*, November 2, 1930.

36. Bennett and Co., *Evansville City Directory* for 1914 (Evansville, 1914), pp. 62–803; *Evansville City Directory for 1919* (Evansville, 1919), pp. 60–800; *Evansville City Directory for 1924* (Evansville, 1924), pp. 52–607; *Evansville City Directory for 1929* (Evansville, 1929), pp. 101–783. The author systematically sampled the directories, entering every fiftieth name for SPSS analysis. The number yielded for the sample ranged from about 750 in 1914 to 865 in 1929. He used surnames to determine German and non-German ethnicity.

37. *ECD, 1929*, passim.

38. School Board, September 14, 1925; ibid.; *EP*, February 22, 1982.

39. *ECD, 1924*, passim.

40. *ECD, 1929*, passim.

41. Kusmer, *A Ghetto Takes Shape*, pp. 171–73; *Negroes in the United States, 1920–1932*, pp. 278, 280, 281, 283; Fifteenth Census, *Population*, volume VI: *Families* (Washington, D.C., 1933), 399, 400; Moody, OH, USI; *EJN*, May 9, 1930, May 24, 1931, November 4, 1933; *EP*, April 25, 1935, January 1, 1935.

42. Kusmer, *A Ghetto Takes Shape*, p. 171. See chapter 9 for further discussion of the school relocation issue. In Evansville the easiest route for the expansion of the black ghetto was via marginal housing tracts to the immediate northeast and east of Baptisttown. By 1930 the northern, eastern, and southern limits of the black community were, approximately, Division, Kentucky, and Bellemeade.

43. See, for example, Bigham, *Reflections on a Heritage*, pp. 12–13; Spear, *Black Chicago*, pp. 20–26; Fifteenth Census, volume III, part 1: *Population*, 696–98.

44. Kusmer, *A Ghetto Takes Shape*, p. 173; *IR*, June 27, 1903. Also note Kenneth Kusmer's essay in *The State of Afro-American History: Past, Present, and Future*, ed. Darlene Clark Hine (Baton Rouge, La., 1986). Cf. Spear, *Black Chicago*, p. 49.

EIGHT

1. Russell Baker, *Growing Up* (New York, 1982), pp. 203–206.

2. *Journal-News, Christmas Art Supplement*, 1903.

3. Franklin, *From Slavery to Freedom*, p. 313. See also pp. 308–17 for a survey of the lynchings common to this era, and *EJN*, June 3, 14, and 20, August 29, October 2, 1901, and November 19, 1915; *EP*, October 16, 1916.

4. *EJN*, September 9 and 17, 1901, September 2, 1906, and June 8, 1907.

5. Ibid., January 8, 9, 13, 14, 24, February 28, and March 16, 1906; *IR*, February 10, 1906.

6. Franklin, *From Slavery to Freedom*, p. 325; Meier and Rudwick, *From Plantation to Ghetto*, p. 210.

7. *EJN*, November 28, 1906; *IR*, December 1, 1906. Harlan, *Booker T. Washington: The Wizard of Tuskegee, 1901–1915* (New York, 1983), pp. 39–40, and Meier and Rudwick, *From Plantation to Ghetto*, pp. 212, 223–24, describe the Afro-American Council as a protest organization formed in 1890 which died ca. 1908. From 1900 to 1907 it was under the control of Washington supporters.

8. *EJN*, June 3 and July 5, 1910.

9. Ibid., August 14, 1915; *EP*, August 14, 1915.

10. *EJN*, August 15, 1915.

11. *EC*, December 7, 1915; *EP*, December 1 and 6, 1915; *EJN*, December 5, 1915. Thomas R. Cripps, *Slow Fade to Black: The Negro in American Film, 1900–1942* (New York, 1977), pp. 41–69, sees this episode as an early effort of the NAACP to mold public opinion. Some mayors heeded their concerns regarding *The Nigger*, but *Birth of a Nation* was shown almost everywhere. Until World War II the NAACP used the movie as the litmus test of white racism. Solomon Stevenson, interview with Darrel E. Bigham, October 19, 1984, and Sprinkles, *The History of Evansville Blacks*, p. 71, supplement newspaper coverage of the early NAACP chapter.

12. *EP*, December 6, 1915; cf. *EJN*, December 7, 1915. When the film was shown a second time (*EP*, May 24, 1918), there was no black protest.

13. Stevenson interview, October, 1984; Cripps, *Slow Fade to Black*, pp. 41–69.

14. *EC*, November 14, 1907, and *EJN*, November 14–16, 1907. On the appeal of Tillman, see Joel Williamson, *The Crucible of Race*, chapter 6.

15. *EC*, November 16–17, 1907, and Gilbert, *A History of The City of Evansville*, I:177–82.

16. *EJN*, July 24, 28–29, August 2, 1914.

17. *EP*, May 28, 1932; *EJN*, November 4, 6, 1907, February 1, 1908; *IR*, October 30, 1909; Evansville YWCA board minutes, 1911–1920, passim; cf. Kusmer, *A Ghetto Takes Shape*, p. 149.

18. *EJN*, August 30, 1902, and December 18, 1909; Mabel Hart, interview with Daniel A. Miller, January 23, 1986.

19. *EP*, April 9, 1918, and *EJN*, November 1, 1909.

20. *EP*, April 10 and 16, 1918 (cf. the sparse reference in *EJN*, April 11, 1918, and *EC*, April 9, 1918); School Board, April 15, 1918.

21. *EJN*, June 11, 1904. See also ibid., September 2, 1902, and February 17, 1905. *ECD, 1905* designated a building for the black Masons at 13 Main Street, between Water and First.

22. *EJN*, July 1, 1909.

23. Ibid., September 17, 1901, and May 31, 1910; *EP*, January 23, 1919; Heiman Blatt, *Sons of Men* (Evansville, 1920), p. 314.

24. School Board, September 8 and 13, 1902.

25. Ibid., October 5, 1903, and November 4, 1901. See also *EJN*, May 14, 1907, and *EP*, June 4, 1919, and School Board, February 28, 1910.

26. School Board, April 7, July 23, and August 29, 1902.

27. Ibid., September 12, 1904, May 25, 1908, September 12, 1910, January 22, 1912; *EJN*, January 29 and September 21, 1904.

28. *EJN*, June 14 and September 18, 1901, July 31, 1902, August 8, 1903, June 16 to 19, 1909; *IR*, June 5, 1909; School Board, May 3, 1909. Also see Helen Best, interview with Darrel E. Bigham, July 6, 1973, OH, USI, and Bell OH, USI.

29. *EJN*, March 11, 1916.

30. Ibid., June 10–11, 1916, and Sprinkles, *The History of Evansville Blacks, pp. 3–6.*

31. *IR*, November 18, 1916.

32. School Board, November 5, 1917, and July 26, 1920.

33. Ibid., April 24 and October 16, 1911, January 3, 1916, April 14, 1919; *EP*, June 4, 1919; *EJN*, July 4, 1911 and September 22, 1919.

34. School Board, May 19, 1913, August 3, 1915, January 8, 1917, and June 9, 1919. The total value of black school buildings in July 1906 was $29,300, as compared with $359,000 for the entire school system.

35. Ibid., August 9, 1901, November 2, 1914, June 3, 1918, and March 12, 1920. Figures for the white high schools apply to department heads. No such positions existed at black schools. In March 1920, nondepartment heads were to get a maximum of $2000 (women) and $2100 (men). There was also evidence of the recent formation of a white teachers' federation, which asked for substantial salary increases on January

19, 1920. On June 21, 1920, the black teachers also requested increases. The functional relationship between the groups is undocumented.

36.   Ibid., December 4, 1905, November 18, 1907, November 12, 1917, and April 26, 1920. See also *EJN*, May 10, 1901, June 15 and September 13, 1905, and December 3, 1907. The board reported in September 1905 that black children tended to return to school later than whites because of the number who had summer jobs. That, combined with night school enrollments, suggests blacks had a different approach to education than that published in *EJN* August 31, 1907. Regarding the story of a fire at Governor School, the paper reported that "the little pickanninies stood around the street clapping their hands in joy as they saw the school going up in a conflagration."

37.   School Board, June 1, 1903, July 30, 1906, March 25, 1907, February 10, 1913, April 4, 1919, and May 10, 1920; Best, OH, USI.

38.   *EJN*, March 27, 1909, and November 24, 1918.

39.   See DeVries, *Race and Kinship*, esp. pp. 47–102, which is based largely on Frederickson, *The Black Image in the White Mind*, pp. 256–282. One Evansville example is John A. Ellert, *Souvenir History of the Evansville Police Department* (Evansville, 1918), pp. 85, 87, which portrays blacks as having a fondness for pilfered chicken.

40.   For example, *EJN*, July 17, 1903, and July 17, 1907.

41.   Ibid., September 27, 1920.

42.   For example, *EP*, November 2, 1913, printed a story about a minstrel show at the Wells-Bijou. Reports about lynchings can be found in *EJN*, August 26, 1901, and June 8, 1907.

43.   *EC*, June 27, 1903, January 25, 1904, January 6, 1906, and September 11, 1912.

44.   *EJN*, April 29, 1901, August 24, 1904, and March 23, 1908.

45.   Ibid., October 5, 1903, January 21, 1906, May 29, 1904, and September 11, 1912.

46.   Ibid., July 23, 1907, and May 21, 1908.

47.   Ibid., January 29 and February 14, 1904.

48.   Ibid., January 29, 1904.

49.   Ibid., February 1 and March 24, 1915, and *EP*, September 16, 1907.

50.   *EJN*, July 15 and 25, and October 21, 1902, February 15 and October 11, 1903, May 20, 1905, May 6, 1906, July 21, September 29, and October 4, 1908, and December 29, 1913.

51.   Ibid., August 26, 1901, February 15, June 8 and 14, 1903.

52.   Ibid., June 8, 1903.

53.   Ibid., October 11, 1903. See also April 20, 24, and May 20, 1906.

54.   Ibid., August 30, 1907.

55.   Ibid.

56.   Ibid., August 15, 1906.

57.   Ibid., May 28 and August 27, 1906, October 14, 1907, July 21, 1908.

58.   Ibid., August 20, 1908, December 29, 1913; *EP*, October 30, 1909; Police Court Record Book, 1908–1912, and Criminal Record Book, 1915–1918, VCA.

59.   Police Court Record Book, 1908–1912, VCA.

60.   Criminal Record Book 1900–1912, and 1915–1918, passim. In 1906 Marion County jailed 4,342 persons, of whom 38 percent were black. Statewide, 12.3 percent of those 31,632 jailed in 1906 were black, as were 11.8 percent of the 29,432 jailed in 1905 (*IR*, May 4, 1907).

61.   Ibid. and *EDJ*, January 23 and 24, 1905.

62.   *EJN*, April 28, 1901, September 22, 1903, September 8 and December 31, 1906, January 7, 1907, September 29 and October 4, 1908, and September 10, 1918; Criminal Record Book, 1915–1918.

63.   *EJN*, February 8, 1913.

64. *EJN* and *EC*, February 8 to June 13, 1913; *EP*, May 14, 1913.
65. *EJN*, *EC*, and *EP*, May 14, 1913.
66. *EJN*, February 20–21, 1913, and February 28, 1914.
67. Ibid., May 16 and June 25, 1913, and February 18, 1914.

NINE

1. Information on local response to the War of 1898 can be found in *EDJ*, April 27, September 2, and October 30, 1898, January 4, 1899. A number of Evansvillians served in the two Indiana companies of black volunteers. It is interesting to note, however, that a group of black volunteers refused to drill at Gaines's establishment in the spring of 1914 after the Tampico incident. The bitter legacy of the Brownsville episode was still very much with them. Gaines said his men had "no intention of coming to the aid of a country whose customs divided white and black races. . . ." (*EJN*, April 26, 1914).

2. *EJN*, April 1, 7, 8, 10, 13–14, 20, 22, May 1, 6, 23, June 3, 13–14, 22, 26, July 10, 20, September 22–23, and October 18, 1917, April 18, 1918; *EP*, September 24, 1917; *The Freeman*, September 22, October 13, and December 8, 1917. The local draft board remained confused as to what to do with blacks, because if they were not called up, white draftees would be overcommitted (*EP*, September 24 and October 10, 1917, and April 10, 1918). See also Allen R. Millett and Peter Maslowski, *For the Common Defense: A Military History of the United States* (New York, 1984), p. 349.

3. *EJN*, July 10 and September 17, 1917, March 26, April 18, May 16, 24, and 28, August 20, 1918, and November 1, 1918; *EP*, May 25, 1918. Leaders of the Colored Division of the Patriot Fund were Jeremiah Jackson, Logan and Sallie Stewart, Ernest Tidrington, W. A. Gaines, and Hugh Rouse.

4. *IR*, January 11, 1930; also see *EC*, November 19, 1943, which noted that a room of the segregated USO had been named for a local war hero, Captain Matthew Payne, who commanded the first black company of the Indiana National Guard. See as well *EP*, January 22–23 and May 28, 1919; Blatt, *Sons of Men*, pp. 312, 314, and 199–238, passim; and Iglehart, *History of Vanderburgh County*, pp. 224–26, 275–560, passim.

5. Kusmer, *A Ghetto Takes Shape*, p. 186; Scott Ellsworth, *Death in a Promised Land: The Tulsa Race Riot of 1921* (Baton Rouge, 1982); Elliott M. Rudwick, *Race Riot at East St. Louis, July 2, 1917* (Carbondale, Illinois, 1964); and William M. Tuttle, *Race Riot: Chicago in the Red Summer of 1919* (New York, 1970).

6. Cf. Kusmer, *A Ghetto Takes Shape*, pp. 186–87, and Tuttle, *Race Riot*, p. 103. Vanderburgh County Recorder, Discharge Record 2, pp. 6–454, passim, lists at least twenty-one black veterans born elsewhere who settled in Evansville after the war.

7. William E. Wilson, "Long, Hot Summer in Indiana," *American Heritage*, XVI (August, 1965), 61; Kusmer, *A Ghetto Takes Shape*, pp. 187–9, and C. Vann Woodward, *Strange Career of Jim Crow* (Second revised edition, New York, 1966), pp. 111–18. A review of Klan-dominated Indiana can be found in David M. Chalmers, *Hooded Americanism: The First Century of the Ku Klux Klan* (Garden City, 1965); Kenneth T. Jackson, *The Ku Klux Klan in the City, 1915–1930* (New York, 1967), especially chapter 10, which deals with Indianapolis; and Emma Lou Thornbrough, "Segregation in Indiana During the Klan Era of the 1920s," in Meier and Rudwick, *The Making of Black America*, volume II (New York, 1969), 184–203. Indiana history in the 1920s is examined in James H. Madison, *Indiana through Tradition and Change: A History of the Hoosier State and Its People, 1920–1945* (Indianapolis, 1982), pp. 26–75.

8. Thornbrough, "Segregation in Indiana," pp. 184–87; *EP*, May 11 to June 19, 1920, and *EJN*, April 19, August 29, and October 24, 1922.

9. *EP*, November 17, 1924, and April 10, 1926; *EC*, May 4, 1921. Thornbrough, in "Segregation in Indiana," p. 203, argues that the Klan and segregation were not causally related.

10. *EP*, August 8, 1923, October 25, 1924, and August 4, 1933.

11. City Court Order Books, 31 and 32, September 1921–November 1923; Arrest Record Book, 1925–1926; Police Department Identification Record Book 3, VCA; *Evansville Argus*, October 18, 1940.

12. Charles Rochelle, interview with Darrel E. Bigham, October 5, 1972, OH, USI; Bell, OH, USI; Pauline Thompson, interview with Darrel E. Bigham, June 26, 1973, OH, USI; *EC*, March 21 and April 21, 1918; *SCJ*, April 28, 1929.

13. *EC*, June 28, July 25, and September 6, 1928; *EJN*, October 11 and November 6, 1902, July 5, 1903, March 21, 1915, and November 22, 1927; *EP*, October 23 and November 11 and 22, 1928; Rochelle, Bell, and Thompson, OH, USI.

14. *IR*, April 30, 1927; Thornbrough, "Segregation in Indiana," pp. 191–94.

15. School Board, December 29, 1924, and May 4, 1925.

16. *EP*, July 24, 1925; School Board, May 18, 25, June 8, August 3, and September 14, 1925; Porter, OH, USI.

17. School Board, September 14, 1925.

18. Ibid., and *EP*, September 15, 1925.

19. School Board, January 4 and 11, April 19, May 3 and 10, 1926; *EC*, May 4, 1926.

20. *EP*, November 1, 1927; School Board, August 2, 1926, October 31, November 28, and December 19, 1927, and January 30 and February 23, 1928; *EC*, April 13, 1928.

21. *SCJ*, September 9, 1928; EJ, October 6, 1928; *Annual Report of the City of Evansville . . . 1928* (Evansville, 1929), p. 41.

22. School Board, March 19, 1928; Board of Education, *Directory of the Evansville Public Schools, 1929–1930* (Evansville, 1930), p. 30. The only other black school kept open was Third Avenue, located at Third Avenue and Iowa, which served the Blankenburg community until 1957. Enrollments were always small (130 in 1929–1930), and only grades one through four were offered. J. D. Cox was principal there until his retirement in 1943. The black children who did not live close to Lincoln and who were not eligible for grades one to four at Third Avenue were bussed to Lincoln (School Board, April 7, 1930, and August 31, 1931.) The board contracted a private bus service—as it previously had with owners of horse-drawn vehicles—toward that end.

23. *Public School Directory, 1929–1930*, p. 26; School Board, November 18, 1929. The latter indicated that there were 247 high school and 869 elementary school students in the black schools that term. See also *EP*, September 23, 1928; *EJN*, May 8, 1929; School Board, May 2, 1928, and May 6, 1929; and Helen Best, interview with Darrel E. Bigham, July 6, 1973, OH, USI.

24. School Board, January 14 and December 2, 1929, May 23, 1932; *EJN*, March 29 and December 11, 1921, and October 24, 1924; *SCJ*, September 9, and October 7 and 21, 1923. A different perspective was provided in the Inter-Racial Commission Survey, a study of educational, social, and economic conditions printed in mimeograph form in 1942 (pp. C7–8). Students in the white schools consistently outscored black students in intelligence and aptitude tests, and curriculum and physical facilities at the white schools were of much higher quality. Lincoln students, asserted the whites who made the report, were poorly prepared for college as well as the vocations.

25. *EJN*, November 22, 1920, March 29, 1921, and October 24, 1924; *SCJ*, September 9, 1923; *EP*, October 1, 1922; School Board, December 10, 1923, and March 17, 1924.

26. *SCJ*, March 21, 1926, March 28, 1928, and May 5, 1929; *EC*, June 13 and July 16, 1928; *EJN*, September 16, 1924, and May 9 and June 13, 1930; *EP*, September 17 and 23, 1928. Beginning in the 1927–1928 year, the board hired an athletic

director at Douglass—E. C. Niles—at $170 per month (School Board, September 26, 1927). The next spring it decided to pay Rochelle and Porter an additional $100 per year to serve as, respectively, athletic business manager and instrumental music director (School Board, May 2, 1928).

27. Porter, OH, USI.

28. School Board, May 2, 1928, May 4, 1931; Porter, OH, USI; *EJN*, September 14, 1924.

29. School Board, February 2, 3, and 6, 1928.

30. *EJN*, March 29, April 3 and 10, and June 5, 1921; *SCJ*, September 9 and October 7, 1923, and August 25, 1935; *EC*, June 13 and July 16, 1928; *EP*, October 24, 1924, March 21, 1926, March 3, September 23, and October 7, 1928, and May 5, 1929. The football team initially played at Bosse Field, but after 1928 it used Lincoln Field.

31. *IR*, December 9, 1933; EJ, October 23, 1929, May 1, 1930, and September 20, 1931.

32. *Inter-Racial Commission Survey* (Evansville, 1942), p. B42. A similar organization in Louisville is described in Wright, *Life Behind a Veil*, pp. 262–82.

33. *IRC*, p. B42.

34. *EP*, January 25, 1928; *EJN*, October 9, 1928, and June 2, 1930; *IRC*, pp. B18–32. The IRC recommended that the Community Association be abolished, given its "inefficiency," especially that of its director, Neely. In 1941 three movie theatres were open to blacks—all via balcony sections (*EC*, March 27, 1941, and *IRC*, pp. B18–20).

35. *IRC*, pp. B42–3; *EJN*, October 9, 1928.

36. *IRC*, pp. A 5 and B43; *EC*, May 21, 1931 and February 12, 1935; *IR*, April 11 and 25, 1931, July 2, 1932, and July 14, 1934; Kusmer, *A Ghetto Takes Shape*, pp. 188–89. The white birth rate was consistently higher—in 1918, 17.1 per 1,000, as compared with 12.5; in 1923, 18.5 to 12.4; in 1928, 17.6 to 14.0. The death rate was higher among blacks—twice that of whites in 1932, and 50 percent higher than the average among blacks in the United States. The IRC study (pp. A4–5) attributed that to the prevalence of vice among Afro-Americans.

TEN

1. Meier and Rudwick, *From Plantation to Ghetto*, pp. 232–42; David Graham Nielson, *Black Ethos: Northern Urban Negro Life and Thought, 1890–1930* (Westport, Connecticut, 1977); Florette Henri, *Black Migration: Movement North, 1900–1920* (Garden City, New York, 1975); Trotter, *Black Milwaukee*, pp. 39–74.

2. Bureau of the Census, Department of Commerce and Labor, *Thirteenth Census of the United States Taken in the Year 1910: Abstract of the Census with Supplement for Indiana* (Washington, D.C., 1913), pp. 697–8, 706–7; Fifteenth Census, 1930, volume III: 1, *Population*, 730, and volume IV: *Occupations* (Washington, D.C., 1933),495–8; Milliman and Pinnell, "Economic Revelopment for Evansville, Indiana," pp. 242–43.

3. Determination of the type of proprietorship evident in the printed census is difficult. Based on external information—namely, newspapers—it is probable that there were no more than five higher level businessmen in the 1920s, of whom Logan Stewart and W. A. Gaines were the most notable. Comparisons with other black communities can be found in Trotter, *Black Milwaukee*, pp. 39–79, and Wright, *Life Behind a Veil*, pp. 213–28.

4. Occupational data for 1930 did not differ markedly from that of 1920, even though the former represented the early months of the Great Depression.

5. The degree of detail in the printed census for Evansville is low prior to 1930, when it passed the 100,000 population level. Similarly, 1940 data is quite thin

because the population dropped below 100,000 in the 1930s. Given that, and the absence of the federal population schedules, it is extremely difficult to trace occupational patterns which compare, for example, native whites with native parents and native whites with foreign-born parents, because such specialized tables are not provided. Data derived from city directories help to fill that gap, but must be used cautiously.

6. *ECD, 1914*, and *ECD, 1924*, passim; *EP*, March 8, 1922.

7. The shift in the percentage of laborers is undoubtedly due to the fact that workers were given more specific identification—that is, some were listed in service, others in commerce, and still others in transportation—even though the level of their work was still menial.

8. See also Wright, *Life Behind a Veil*, pp. 213–28. Even though racial identification ceased after 1926, one can determine race in the 1929 directory by comparing names with those in the 1926 directory.

9. Fifteenth Census, 1930, IV: *Occupations*, 495–98. Trotter, *Black Milwaukee*, pp. 229–30, observes that urban black workers exhibited great differences in the degree of "proletarianization."

10. Fifteenth Census, 1930, IV: *Occupations*, 495–98.

11. Ibid.

12. Ibid., and Fourteenth Census, 1920, IV: *Population*, 264.

13. Ibid. See also Kusmer, *A Ghetto Takes Shape*, pp. 199–203. Discussion of the occupational index is provided on pp. 279–80. As noted in chapter 4, the author gave servants the number 6 (along with semiskilled workers) and laborers the number 7. He also included the category of semiprofessional. Hence semiskilled is given a number 6, not a 5, as in Kusmer's study. The occupational index is determined by the following formula: $100 \times (1a + 2b + 3c + 4d + 5e + 6f + 7g / a + b + c + d + e + f + g)$. A is the percentage of professionals, b the percentage of high–level proprietors, managers, and officials, etc.

14. Kusmer, *A Ghetto Takes Shape*, p. 203.

15. See, for example, Spero and Harris, *The Black Worker*, and William Harris, *The Harder We Run: Black Workers Since the Civil War* (New York, 1982), passim.

16. *EJN*, May 27, 1917; Fifteenth Census, IV: *Population*, 495–8.

17. Thirteenth Census, Population Schedules for Vanderburgh County, 1910; Bigham, "Work, Residence, and the Emergence of the Black Ghetto," p. 297; *Negroes in the United States*, 1920–1932, pp. 298, 301. The percentage of black women at work, 40.4, was slightly lower than that in Chicago, Cincinnati, and Indianapolis. In Southern cities the rate was substantially higher: 54.3 in Louisville, for example.

18. Thirteenth Census, Population Schedules for Vanderburgh County, 1910; *CD, 1924* and *CD, 1929*, passim; Fifteenth Census, 1930, IV: *Occupations*, 81–82, and VI: *Families*, 409. The rate in Chicago in 1930 was 44.4. It was 40.6 in Indianapolis, 40 in St. Louis, 40.4 in Cincinnati, 31.3 in Des Moines, 32.3 in Albany, and 30.4 in Ft. Wayne. Evansville's size—which meant, among other things, that there were fewer hotels and affluent whites who hired domestics—and the relative absence of mass production work evidently influenced the rate of female employment.

19. Fifteenth Census, 1930, VI: *Families*, p. 409. Perhaps the most notable shift was the demise of the black washwoman and laundress, which meant that proportionally more worked outside the home. How that affected black family life, and especially the rate of juvenile delinquency, is not known. See *Negroes in the United States*, 1920–1932, p. 284.

20. Thirteenth Census, 1910, *Abstract*, p. 706; *Negroes in the United States*, 1920–1932, pp. 298, 301; Fourteenth Census, 1920, IV: *Population*, 677; Fifteenth Census, 1930, IV: *Occupations*, 495, 497, 519–21. The rate of employment among blacks aged ten to fifteen was about twice that of Chicago and Indianapolis and three times that of Detroit. It was slightly lower than that of Louisville and St. Louis and substantially lower than that of Southern cities.

21. *ECD, 1909*, pp. 758–95.

22. *ECD, 1920*, pp. 441–89.

23. *ECD, 1908*, p. 101; *ECD, 1909*, p. 104; *ECD, 1910*, p. 80; *ECD, 1916*, p. 93; *ECD, 1919*, p. 71; *ECD, 1922*, p. 121; *ECD, 1929*, p. 131.

24. *ECD, 1901*, p. 116; *ECD, 1918*, p. 99; *ECD, 1922*, p. 76; *ECD, 1932*, p. 99; *EP*, January 1, 1935.

25. *EJN*, June 16, 1899, June 23, 1901, January 2, 1902, October 10, 1904, May 5, 1914, May 4, 1921, October 16, 1926. See also *ECD, 1920*, p. 383. On the Business League, see ibid., May 23 and July 5, 1905, January 31, February 1 and 18, and July 5, 1906, February 13 and March 24, 1908, May 30 and June 30, 1909, and March 21, April 1, and August 15, 1915. For an overview of the League, see Harlan, *Booker T. Washington*, volume II: 98, 101, 229, and 235–36. The group was moribund from the First World War until 1931 (*EC*, May 18, 1931, and *IR*, May 30, 1931). Stewart was declared insane in Probate Court in 1926 and placed in the Indiana State Hospital.

26. *EJN*, July 19 and November 20, 1907, February 18, March 13 and 19, 1909, April 22 and 26, 1914, December 19, 1921; Vanderburgh County Recorder, Articles of Association, Book 2, pp. 28–29. Gaines, his wife, and Rudolph O'Hara were listed as the incorporators on March 18, 1918. References to earlier efforts can be found in *EJN*, August 1, 1903, and May 18 and September 2, 1905. Also see *Evansville Argus*, August 23, 1940.

27. *ECD, 1920*, p. 301; *ECD, 1924*, p. 418; *EJN*, June 17, 1909; *EP*, October 9, 1922; *IR*, July 17, 1926.

28. Sprinkles, *The History of Evansville Blacks*, pp. 55–56; *EJN*, April 9, 1901, July 2, 1902, July 10, 1903; *ECD, 1924*, p. 77; *ECD, 1927*, p. 82; *ECD, 1930*, p. 125; *ECD, 1945*, p. 51; *ECD, 1955*, p. 34.

29. *ECD, 1895*, p. 257; *ECD, 1920*, p. 162; *ECD, 1928*, p. 239; Charlotte Glover Moody, OH, USI.

30. *ECD, 1909*, pp. 758–97; *ECD, 1920*, p. 97. See also *EJN*, August 4, 1903, June 7, 1909; *IR*, May 4, 1908; *ECD, 1928*, p. 153.

31. Vanderburgh County Recorder, Miscellaneous Records, Book 1, pp. 346, 350–51; *ECD, 1910*, p. 730; *ECD, 1915*, p. 769; *ECD, 1920*, p. 407; *ECD, 1927*, p. 539; *ECD, 1930*, p. 646.

32. *EJN*, January 23, 1905, and December 26, 1914.

33. *EJN*, June 10, 1901, November 8, 1913, October 8, 1922, November 4, 1930, and December 12, 1934; *IR*, March 18, 1913, March 27, 1915, December 9, 1916, January 4 and March 8, 1930, and March 9 and 16, April 27, and May 11, 1935; *EP*, October 23, 1942.

34. *EJN*, June 30, 1901, January 2, September 4–5, and October 31, 1902, July 1 to 10, 1903, June 29, 1907, December 26, 1914, January 2–4, 10, and 25, March 11–14, 1915, and October 10, 1923; *ECD, 1924*, p. 418; *EP*, December 28, 1923, and January 31, 1924; Minutes of the Evansville Bar Association, File 2, December 19, 1919, and December 31, 1923, Special Collections Department, USI; *The Freeman*, March 6, 1920.

35. *EJN*, April 9, 1901, July 2, 1902, July 10 and December 28, 1903; *IR*, October 11, 1913. For details on Willis Green, see *EJN*, July 10 and December 13, 1908; for Buckner, see *EC*, August 29, 1913, and *EA*, February 20, 1943; for Jackson, see *EC*, June 15, 1899, and September 18, 1901. Also note Pauline Thompson, OH, USI.

36. Sprinkles, *The History of Evansville Blacks*, pp. 55–57; *EA*, July 5, 1938; *EC*, June 20, 1940; Bessie King, interview with Darrel E. Bigham, June 27, 1973, OH, USI.

37. Fifteenth Census, 1930, IV: *Occupations*, pp. 495–98.

38. *EJN*, July 19, 1902, March 18, 1908, June 22, July 9, and October 13, 1909, February 20, 1910, July 27, 1913; *EC*, December 6, 1970; Adrian Bell, OH, USI.

39. Fifteenth Census, 1930, IV: *Occupations*, 495–98.

40. Spero and Harris, *Black Worker*, pp. 149–318, passim; Kusmer, *A Ghetto Takes Shape*, pp. 196–99; *ECD, 1920*, pp. 337, 416; Vanderburgh County Recorder, Miscellaneous Records, Book E, pp. 32, 230; *EJN*, December 21, 1902, July 2, 1903. One perspective on the treatment of black workers is afforded in *EJN*, September 17, 1918. The Evansville Manufacturers' Association denied employment cards, required by the federal government, to those firms which employed blacks, because blacks were considered unreliable. Allegedly blacks would work no more than a half day and stop working any time they wished.

41. *EJN*, September 2, 1904; Roy S. Perry, interview with Darrel E. Bigham, June 20, 1973, OH, USI.

42. *EJN*, March 21, 1909; Fifteenth Census, 1930, IV: *Occupations*, 495; Spero and Harris, *Black Worker*, pp. 206–45, 352–82, and especially pp. 208, 245, 366, and 373–74.

43. *IR*, December 12, 1931; Franklin, *From Slavery to Freedom*, p. 358; Spero and Harris, *Black Worker*, pp. 95–96, 264–315, 435; *EJN*, April 14, 1901, August 30, 1906, and July 15, 1907; *ECD, 1903*, p. 56; *ECD, 1905*, pp. 54–56.

44. *EJN*, July 11 and 14, and September 2, 1907, October 8, 1908, and April 15, 1909.

45. *Ibid.*, July 19, 1902, August 4, 1903, and March 17, 1908; Douglas Lander, OH, USI; Roy S. Perry, OH, USI; Fourteenth Census, 1920, IX: *Manufactures* (Washington, D.C., 1923), 397.

46. *ECD, 1914*, and *ECD, 1929*, passim.

47. Thirteenth Census, Population Schedules for Vanderburgh County, 1910; *ECD, 1909*, pp. 69–757, and *ECD, 1920*, pp. 33–439.

48. *ECD, 1909*, pp. 69–757, and *ECD, 1920*, pp. 33–439.

49. *ECD, 1929*, pp. 101–783.

50. *EJN*, June 2, 1909.

51. Clift, "A History of the Negro," pp. 26–31; *EC*, September 20, 1943, and August 8 and December 6, 1970; Adrian Bell, OH, USI.

52. *Negro Population, 1790–1915*, pp. 471–73; *Negroes In the United States, 1920–1932*, pp. 278, 280, 283; Kusmer, *A Ghetto Takes Shape*, p. 211.

53. *Negro Population, 1920–1932*, pp. 252, 278, 280, 281, 283, 285, and 286; Fifteenth Census, 1930, VI: *Families*, pp. 399–400, and VII: *Unemployment*, pp. 326, 327; Thirteenth Census, Population Schedules for Vanderburgh County, 1910.

54. Cf. Kusmer, *A Ghetto Takes Shape*, pp. 210–34.

ELEVEN

1. *Negro Population, 1920–1932*, pp. 252, 278, 280, 281, 283, 285, and 286; Fifteenth Census, 1930, VI: *Families*, pp. 399–400; Clift, "A History of the Negro," pp. 32–41. For other cities, note Wright, *Life Behind a Veil*, pp. 123–55; Spear, *Black Chicago*, pp. 51–110; Kusmer, *A Ghetto Takes Shape*, pp. 103, 106; and Trotter, *Black Milwaukee*, pp. 80, 109–10.

2. *EP*, July 21, 1908, and February 8, 1930; *EJN*, July 10, 1908; *IR*, February 15, 1930.

3. *EJN*, February 11, 1905; cf. Kusmer, *A Ghetto Takes Shape*, p.106. Also note the mimeographed commemorative, "Historicity of the McFarland Baptist Community Center, 1919–1945" (Evansville, 1945), pp. 5–6.

4. *EJN*, May 19, 1905, and November 11, 1907.

5. See, for example, *EJN*, August 6, 1903, October 18, 1904, and October 10, 1905.

6. For more details, refer to chapter 10.

7. Cox, *Black Topeka*, pp. 196–97, and Trotter, *Black Milwaukee*, pp. 109–10.

8. *EJN*, April 18 and September 21, 1902, May 28 and November 28, 1903, May 23, 1904, June 11 and November 28, 1907, and January 27 and September 5, 1908.

9. *EA*, February 20, 1943.

10. See the September 22 and 23 editions of *EJN*, 1900–1930.

11. Ibid., September 23, 1900, June 7 and 9, 1901, June 30, 1902, June 27, 1903, August 24, 1913, September 22, 1922; *EP*, September 14, 1915; *IR*, May 10, 1902, and January 5 and 19, 1935.

12. *EJN*, September 22, 1922, September 20, 1924, and September 27, 1927.

13. Ibid., May 22 and June 14, 1905, and July 26, August 2 and 8, 1907.

14. Ibid., July 3, 12, 26, and August 8, 1907.

15. "Historicity . . . of McFarland . . . ", p. 9.

16. *EJN*, July 3, 1902, October 2, 1903, July 3 and 26, 1907, and July 12, 1908; *IR*, December 23, 1907, and January 2 and March 14, 1908.

17. *The Freeman*, September 25, 1920; *IR*, January 9, 1909, and January 14, 1933. No Evansvillian won any of these contests until Sallie Stewart in 1935 (*IR*, May 11, 1935).

18. *The Freeman*, June 16, 1915; *IR*, March 8, 15, and 29, April 26, May 10 and 17, November 8 and 11, 1902, June 27, 1903, January 8, 1910, November 23 and 30, 1912, June 21, 1913, January 10, 1914, October 28, November 4, 11, 18, and 25, and December 2, 9, 16, 23, and 30, 1916. Edith Hite edited the column from 1927 through the 1930s.

19. *IR*, November 11, 1905.

20. *EJN*, June 4, 1901, October 21 and 24, and December 5, 1902, July 2, 1904, May 28, 1906; *EP*, November 4, 1910, December 18, 1918, and January 24, 1919.

21. Ibid., May 26, 1899, May 15 , June 7, and October 15, 1901, May 26–27 and July 2, 1904, April 20, 1906, November 1, 1907, March 28, 1909, March 29, 1915, October 29, 1922, September 30, 1927, and October 31, 1934; *IR*, May 25, 1929.

22. *EJN*, April 2, 1902, January 2 and February 13, 1903, June 30, 1905, April 30, 1906, July 26 and August 28, 1907, and January 27, February 29, and June 9, 1908; *IR*, January 10, 1914, and November 11 and 18, 1916.

23. *EJN*, July 10 and 17, 1903, October 10, 1905, and January 2, 1908.

24. For example, see ibid., July 22, 1908.

25. Vanderburgh County Recorder, Miscellaneous Records, Book E, pp. 116, 158, 320, and 458, and Book F, pp. 250 and 318; Articles of Association, Book 3, pp. 34, 35, 116, 124, and 199, Book 4, pp. 58, 172, 417, and 489, and Book 5, pp. 128, 247, 296, and 369; *ECD, 1905, ECD, 1920*, and *ECD, 1926*, passim.

26. *ECD, 1900*, pp. 20–63; *ECD, 1924*, p. 45; John Caldwell, interview with Darrel E. Bigham, July 11, 1973, OH, USI; Sprinkles, *The History of Evansville Blacks*, pp. 77–95. Little Hope, which began in the High Street area in the late 1800s, was eventually renamed New Hope. The AME Zion Church was renamed Hood Temple. Trustee records of Oakdale Baptist are found in Vanderburgh County Recorder, Miscellaneous Records, Book E, p. 421 (1908). Sydney E. Ahlstrom, *A Religious History of the American People* (New Haven, 1972), pp. 708–9, indicates that the black branch of the Southern Methodist Episcopal Church was known as the Colored Methodist Episcopal Church (CME). Northern Methodists formed a separate conference for blacks later known as the Central Jurisdiction.

27. *EJN*, November 18, 1918.

28. *IR*, October 2, 1937; *EA*, June 27, 1941.

29. *EJN*, September 23, 1901.

30. Ibid., June 20, 1901, January 14, March 15, and April 4 and 15, 1902, and July 3, 1905.

31. *EJN*, April 20, 1901, March 14 and October 23, 1902, February 10 and August 4, 1903, and January 10, 1908.

32. Vanderburgh County Recorder, Articles of Association, Book 3, p. 443, and Book 4, p. 228; Ahlstrom, pp. 1058–63.

33. "Historicity . . . of McFarland . . .," pp. 3–19; *EJN*, April 9, 1925; *EP*, 1925, passim.

34. *IR*, March 27, 1915, October 30, 1926, and January 4, 1930; *EJN*, June 30, 1902, June 11, 1903, June 19, November 6 and 12, and December 31, 1907, March 17, 1908, May 30, 1909, and November 8, 1913.

35. *EJN*, June 10 and 16, and September 18, 1901, July 19 and December 5, 1902, and September 23 and October 22 and 24, 1907; *EC*, September 20, 1931; *IR*, December 20, 1902, and September 16, 1911.

36. *EJN*, April 16, 1901, July 21, 1902, April 20, 1907, July 31, 1907, and February 13, 1908.

37. *IR*, April 30, May 14 and 28, and December 3 and 10, 1927.

38. *EJN*, March 17 and April 17 and 21, 1901, March 15 and October 7, 1902, February 10, 1903, December 23, 1907, April 17, 1909, and October 7, 1919; *IR*, March 20 and December 4, 1926, February 5 and December 3, 1927, and December 7 and 14, 1929.

39. *EJN*, July 19 and 21, 1902, September 13, 1905, April 24, 1909, and September 15, 1918; *The Freeman*, September 14, 1918; *IR*, November 18, 1916, and April 24, 1926.

40. *The Freeman*, September 21, 1918; *EJN*, October 8, 1925; IRC Study, 1942, pp. B13–15.

41. Vanderburgh County Recorder, Articles of Association, Book 3, p. 43, Book 4, p. 280, and Book 5, p. 101.

42. *IR*, February 18, 1905, February 24, March 28, and July 13, 1912, July 2, 1913, and September 23, 1916; *EJN*, July 3 and 25, 1903.

43. See, for example, Kusmer, *A Ghetto Takes Shape*, pp. 206–7.

44. *ECD, 1905*, pp. 33–40; *ECD, 1909*, pp. 22–68; *ECD*, 1924, pp. 49–50; *ECD, 1926*, pp. 14–23; *IR*, October 17, 1905. If the average membership in a lodge or its women's auxiliary was twenty-five, then about 900 Evansville blacks belonged to these societies in 1924. Also note *EJN* October 29, 1922; *EP*, July 23, 1924.

45. *ECD, 1924*, pp. 49–50; *EJN*, July 3, 1907.

46. *EJN*, May 16, June 13 and 22, 1903, May 15, 1907, and May 19, 1909.

47. *IR*, January 4, 1930.

48. *EJN.*, June 9, 1903.

49. Ibid., July 28 and 31, 1908 , May 22, 1903, September 22 and December 19, 1905, August 2–7, 1909, and May 31, 1910; *EP*, July 23, 1924.

50. *EJN*, June 2, 1909, and October 29, 1922.

51. Ibid., May 16, 1903, December 9, 1905, and July 4–6, 1909. See also Harlan, *Booker T. Washington*, II: 97–98.

52. Ibid., December 26, 1914, January 2–4, 10, and 26, March 11, 12, and 16, and July 23, 1915; *EP*, June 21, 1915.

53. *EJN*, July 25, 1903, December 30, 1905, and April 17, 1909; *IR*, "Victory-Progress" edition, undated, 1945.

54. *EJN*, April 19, June 17, and July 10, 1901, June 30, 1902, June 22, 24 and July 3, 1903, October 4, 1904, May 18 and September 22, 1905, July 17 and November 2 and 28, 1907, and January 18, 1908; *ECD, 1924*, p. 50.

55. *ECD, 1924*, p. 50; *EP*, July 23, 1924; IRC Study, 1942, pp. B17–18.

56. *EJN*, December 19, 1905.
57. Articles of Incorporation File, January 24, 1906, VCA.
58. Ibid., February 16, 1906. See also *ECD, 1906,* passim.
59. Ibid., December 15, 1909. See also *ECD, 1909,* passim.; Vanderburgh County Recorder, Miscellaneous Records, Book F, pp. 390.
60. *EP*, November 4, 1910.
61. Franklin, *From Slavery to Freedom*, pp. 105–6, 109; Kusmer, *A Ghetto Takes Shape*, pp. 149–51, 251, 257–59.
62. *IRC*, pp. B15–16; Vanderburgh County Recorder, Articles of Association, Book 4, pp. 226–27; *IR*, December 9 and 16, 1916; *EA*, November 11, 1940.
63. *SCJ*, October 25, 1925; *EC*, May 20, 1928; *IR*, December 10, 1927; IRC, pp. B15–16.
64. Kusmer, *A Ghetto Takes Shape*, p. 151; *EJN*, April 21, 1918, and January 15, 1919; IRC, pp. B15–16; School Board, December 12, 1932.
65. *EJN*, February 17, 21, and 25, March 1, and December 18, 1905; Kusmer, *A Ghetto Takes Shape*, pp. 265–66.
66. *EJN*, November 4, 6, and 9, 1907, February 1, and December 8 and 18, 1908.
67. Ibid., February 14, 1909, January 9, 10, and 15, February 2, June 15, and July 3, 1910; *IR*, October 30, 1909. Rosencranz died in April 1920 (*EJN*, April 20, 1920).
68. *IR*, December 2, 16, and 30, 1916; *EJN*, October 29, 31, and November 2, 4, 8, 9, 10, 13, and 22, 1922, September 16, 1925, and June 2, 1930; IRC, pp. B21–32; *EP*, January 25, 1928.
69. *EJN*, April 17–18, 1901, April 18, 1902, July 2 and August 8, 1903, and April 14, 16, and May 27, 1909.
70. Ibid., February 1, April 4, and July 5, 1906.
71. Vanderburgh County Recorder, Articles of Association, Book 1, pp. 75–77.
72. *EP*, September 28, 1917; *IR*, November 18 and December 2, 1916; *EJN*, December 8, 1918; *SCJ*, October 25, 1925.
73. *EJN*, March 25, 1916; School Board, November 17, 1924; Vanderburgh County Recorder, Articles of Association, Book 3, p. 40; *IR*, May 28, 1927.
74. *IRC*, pp. A17–18; *ECD*, 1926, pp. 22–3; *IR*, December 1, 1934; *SCJ*, October 25, 1925, and October 20, 1935; *EC*, April 15, 1915; *EP*, August 24, 1925; *EJN*, June 11 and October 8, 1930.
75. Thirteenth Census, Population Schedules for Vanderburgh County, 1910.
76. Ibid.
77. Ibid.
78. See chapter 5 for further discussion, and also ibid. and Fifteenth Census, 1930, VI: *Families*, 407.
79. Thirteenth Census, Population Schedules for Vanderburgh County, 1910.
80. Ibid., and Fifteenth Census, 1930, VI: *Families*, 407.
81. Fifteenth Census, 1930, VI: *Families*, 396, 399, 400, 403, 406, and 409.
82. Kusmer, *A Ghetto Takes Shape*, pp. 233–34.

TWELVE

1. Kusmer, *A Ghetto Takes Shape*, pp. 235–36, 252, and 274.
2. *EJN*, January 14, 1902.
3. *EJN* and *EC*, October 1908, and October 1912. Also note Meier, *Negro Thought in America*, pp. 166–255.
4. For example, note *EC*, October-November, 1901, passim; Trotter, *Black Milwaukee*, p. 228; and Martin Kilson, "Political Change in the Negro Ghetto, 1900–

1940's," *Key Issues in the Afro-American Experience*, ed. Nathan I. Huggins, et al., volume II (New York, 1971), 167–92. Socialists were an important factor in Evansville politics from 1900 to 1917. In the city election of 1917, for example, they drew one-sixth of the vote for mayor. There is no evidence of their attempting to court blacks, however, and that was due in large part to demography and geography: They were strongest among railroad workers in Howell and had some support among German American workers.

5. Bessie King, OH, USI; Adrian Bell, OH, USI.

6. *EC*, November 1, 1901.

7. *EC*, March 1 to April 9, 1899; *EJN*, December 19, 1901, July 11, 1902, and January 1, 1903.

8. *EJN*, April 17, May 16–17, September 5, and October 19, 1901, November 1, 1902, September 23 and October 4, 1904, January 4, 1906, July 4, 1907, January 18 and 25, 1908, January 21, 1914, and January 19, 1919; Wright, *Life Behind a Veil*, pp. 246–47.

9. Cf. *EJN*, November 7, 1900, and March 24, 1901.

10. *EJN*, January 14 and March 5, 1902.

11. Ibid., January 23, 1905.

12. Ibid., October 29, 1903, and May 30, 1909; Trotter, *Black Milwaukee*, pp. 138–39.

13. *EJN*, April 17 and September 2–3, 1905, and November 29, 1907.

14. Ibid.

15. Ibid., February 14, 1909.

16. Ibid., March 17, 1908. See also October 29, 1903, April 17 and May 20, 1905, and January 27 and February 22, 1908.

17. Ibid., June 2, 1909. Also note February 14 and March 9, 11, 1908, February 27, October 29, and November 23, 1907, as well as Harlan, *Booker T. Washington*, II: 202–5, 236–37.

18. *EC*, October 30, 1904.

19. *EJN*, November 7, 1901, April 15 to October 28, and November 1 and 4, 1902, and March 1 to 10, 1909.

20. Ibid., April 2, 1901, May 24, 1904, and February 26, 1909. The election returns of 1901-1909 are found in ibid., April 2, 1901; *EC*, November 5, 1902; *EJN*, November 6, 1904 and November 8, 1905; *Sunday Journal-News*, November 11, 1906; *EC*, November 5, 1908; and *EJN*, November 3, 1909.

21. *EC*, November 8, 1908, and *EJN*, November 7, 1905.

22. *EJN*, October 29 to November 7, 1905, and October 25 to 28, 1906.

23. Ibid., November 8, 1905. See also April 22, 1901, December 6, 1905, January 3, 5, 19, May 28, and August 27, 1906, August 22, 1907, and February 4, 1909. Three of the four heavily black precincts voted Republican, and the Republicans captured 64.3 percent of the total in the four. Boehne carried the city with 56.1 percent of the vote.

24. City Council Minutes, 1905–1907, esp. September 4 and 22, 1906, and January 7, 1907; *EJN*, December 6, 1907.

25. *EP*, October 17, 1906.

26. *EJN*, September 2, 1906, June 8, 1907, and February 27, 1909.

27. Ibid., January 27, February 14 and 22, March 11 and 27, 1908.

28. Ibid., February 5 and March 9, 1908, and February 27, 1909; Wright, *Life Behind a Veil*, pp. 246–47.

29. *EC*, November 4, 1908, and *EJN*, November 23, 1907, and February 26–27, 1909.

30. *EJN*, February 27, 1909.

31. Ibid., March 26, 1909.

32. Ibid., November 3, 1909; *EP*, July 22 and 24, and November 4, 1908, October 30, and November 1–3, 1909; *EC*, October 31, 1908.

33. School Board, May 3, 1909; *ECD, 1909*, p. 50; *EJN*, June 16–18, 1909; *IR*, June 5, 1909.

34. Harlan, *Booker T. Washington*, II: 238–44, discusses Washington's private efforts to subvert the excesses of Jim Crow. Undoubtedly some of that occurred in Evansville on the part of men like Buckner and Dupee.

35. *EP*, October 30 and November 3, 1909; *EJN*, September 22, 1906, July 21, 1908, and January 19, 1909.

36. *EP*, October 22, 26, and November 4, 1910.

37. Ibid., November 4–9, 1910. Voting patterns for 1910–1921 can be found in *EJN*, November 9, 1910, and *EC*, November 7, 1912, November 4, 1914, November 8, 1916, November 7, 1917, November 8, 1918, November 4, 1920, and November 9, 1921. The black precincts identified in the study were numbers 6, 16, 18, and 29 for 1910–1916, and Ward 2, precincts 3 and 4, and Ward 7, precincts 1–3, for 1917–1921.

38. Harlan, *Booker T. Washington*, II: 338, 405–9; *EC*, November 9, 1910.

39. *EC*, November 6, 1912, and November 5, 1918; *EP*, November 5, 1912; *EJN*, November 6, 1912.

40. *EJN*, March 1, 2, 14, and 31, April 8, 19, and 24, May 5–6, 13, and 15, 1913; *EC*, March 31, 1913; *EP*, March 31 and May 1 to 15, 1913. Hugh Rouse ran as an at-large candidate for City Council in the Republican primary—the first black to run for that post—and came in fifth because voters reportedly thought his name was German. He supported Bosse in the fall, and as a reward was named city hall custodian.

41. *EJN* and *EP*, September 1 to November 6, 1913.

42. *EJN*, October 21, 26, 1913, January 5, February 15, October 4, and November 3, 1914; *EP*, November 18, 1913, March 14, 1914; *EC*, November 13, 14, and 17, 1913.

43. *EJN*, January 7, February 15 and 22, April 26, and October 4, 15, and 30, 1914; *EP*, April 6, October 28, and November 3, 1914.

44. *EJN*, October 4, 15, 28, 1914, and January 1, 1915.

45. Ibid., November 20, December 9–12, 1914, and February 3, 1915.

46. Ibid., June 16, 1915.

47. Ibid., March 2–8, May 19, 1916; *EP*, May 20–21, 1916.

48. Ibid., September 17 to November 8, 1916; *EP*, September 16 to November 8, 1916.

49. *EP*, February 14–15, 20, March 21–22, April 3–4, 25, 28, May 17, 23–24, 1917.

50. Ibid., April 24 and July 5, 1917.

51. *EC* and *EP*, October 3 to November 7, 1917.

52. Ibid., April 1 to 30, 1918; *EJN*, February 6 and May 11, 1918; *EP*, April 11, 17, 1918. See *EJN*, August 16, 1918 and January 23, 1930, for illustrations of the rewards of political service.

53. *EJN*, August 16, September 1, 17, 19, October 13–14, 30, and November 5–6, 1918.

54. Ibid., November 4–6, 1918; *EC*, November 5–6, 1918.

55. *EJN*, January 9, 1919.

56. *EJN*, April 21, 28, May 5, 11, 17, and June 18, 20, 1920; *EP*, May 12 to June 19, 1920.

57. *EP*, November 3, 1920; *EJN*, October 5, 14, and November 4, 1920.

58. Evansville Bar Association, File 2, USI Special Collections; *EP*, January 3, 8, 1920, December 28, 1923, and January 26, 1925; *EJN*, October 10, 1923; *IR*, January 30 and September 18, 1926.

59. Solomon Stevenson, interview with Darrel E. Bigham, November 30, 1972, OH, USI; Roy S. Perry, OH, USI.

60. *EP*, January 16 and 24, 1930, and April 19, 1931.

61. Ibid., June 24, 1921.
62. Ibid., September 19–22, 28, and 30, 1921.
63. Ibid., June 1, 1921.
64. *EC*, September 17, 1921.
65. *EP*, October 28, 1921; *EC*, October 1 to November 9, 1921.
66. *EP*, November 9, 1921, and *EJN*, November 9, 1921. In Ward 7, precinct 1, Hopkins received 543 votes to Bosse's 190. In 7:2, 7:3, 7:4, and 7:5, the records were, respectively, 548–414, 247–272, 329–321, and 329–541. In the race between Stewart and his opponent, the returns in precincts 1 to 5 were, in order, 537–197, 423–496, 195–320, 260–371, and 238–613.
67. *EJN*, November 12, 14, and 18, 1921, and April 9, 1922; *EP*, January 16 and 20, and March 27, 1922; *EC*, April 4–10 and May 12, 1922.
68. *EP*, January 18 and 28, 1922.
69. Louis Francis Budenz, "There's Mud on Indiana's White Robes," *The Nation*, CXXV (July 27, 1927), 81–82; Jackson, *The KKK in the City*, pp. 144–60, 235–49; *EJN*, June 10, 1922; *EP*, May 12 and June 9–10, 1922, October 19 to 30, 1926; *EC*, March 23, 1922. An intriguing variation was provided by John Moore (*EP*, October 4, 1927), who said that he had been acting head of the Klan in early 1922, and that upon the advice of physician W. E. French, he sent to Atlanta for a Klan recruiter, who turned out to be Huffington. He and Huffington recruited Stephenson, whose talents as an organizer soon became apparent. Bosse, he declared, had nothing to do with the rise of the Klan. He also claimed that he was the only member of the order in Evansville before Bosse's death.
70. *EP*, October 4, 1927.
71. Ibid., June 10, 1922, and June 24, 1924; *ECD, 1920*, p. 382, lists Stephenson as a resident of the city.
72. *EP*, October 1 to November 10, 1922, August 7–8, 1923, October-November, 1924, October 19, 1926; *EC*, July 25, 1923.
73. *EP*, November 6–7, 1922, October 4, 1927; Wilson, "Long, Hot Summer in Indiana," pp. 62–63; *Annual Report of the City of Evansville, 1922* (Evansville, 1923), p. 15; Madison, *Indiana through Tradition and Change*, esp. pp. 45–55.
74. *EJN*, November 3, 1922, May 24, 1925, October 14, 1925; *EP*, March 7, 1925.
75. *EJN*, April 2 and 29, May 6, and November 6, 1922, and September 17 and October 27, 1924. In January 1928, precinct 2, of Ward 7 became precinct 3.
76. Ibid., April 29 and October 7 to November 4, 1925; *EP*, May 2, July 16 and 19, August 20, and November 4, 1925, and March 4, 1926. Grand jury investigations were consistently hampered by the disappearance of witnesses and of absentee ballots. See also *IR*, January 26, August 7, September 18, October 2 and 23, 1926, and January 25, 1930. Election records for 1921–1930 are found in *EC*, November 9, 1922, November 8, 1928, and November 6, 1929, and *EJN*, November 5, 1924, November 4, 1925, November 3, 1926, and November 5, 1930.
77. *EP*, January 6, 1926, and January 23, 1930; *IR*, January 16 and 23, March 13, August 7, September 18 and 25, and October 2 and 23, 1926; *EA*, July 26, 1940.
78. *Annual Report of the City of Evansville, 1928* (Evansville, 1929), pp. 40–42; Thornbrough, "Segregation in Indiana," pp. 201–3; Alfred Porter, OH, USI.
79. *Annual Report . . . 1925* (Evansville, 1926), p. 21, and *ECD, 1926* (Evansville, 1927), pp. 24, 33; cf. *ECD, 1923* (Evansville, 1924), p. 15, and *ECD, 1924* (Evansville, 1925), pp. 11–12.
80. *EJN*, May 4, 1926; *EC*, May 4 and November 3, 1926; *EP*, May 5 and 18, September 20 to October 30, November 1–3, 1926.
81. *EP*, August 27, September 3 and 13, October 21 to 31, November 4, 7, and 9, and December 5, 1927, January 4, February 13, 16, 21, and 27, March 24, May 5, 8, and 12, September 13, 1928, February 13, 16, and 19, March 8 and 26, April 27, May

5 and 12, July 1 to 29, and September 9 to 19, 1929, January 30–31, February 1 and 18, and December 9, 1930, February 13 and April 16, 1931.

82. Ibid., April 29 to May 15, 1929.

83. *IR*, September 22 and 29, 1928; Thornbrough, "Segregation in Indiana," pp. 201–2; Ellis W. Hawley, *The Great War and the Search for a Modern Order: A History of the American People and Their Institutions, 1917–1933* (New York, 1979), pp. 180, 188.

84. *EP*, October 16 to November 11, 1929; cf. *EJN*, October 20 to November 7, 1929.

85. Cf. *EP*, *EC*, and *EJN*, January 23, 1930. The most elaborate coverage can be found in *IR*, January 25 and February 1, 1930. For election returns, 1932–1934, see *EJN*, November 9, 1932, and *EC*, November 8, 1934.

86. *EJN*, January 25–26, 1930; *IR*, February 1, 1930; *SCJ*, January 26, 1930.

87. *EJN*, January 23, 1930; *EP*, February 28, 1930; *IR*, February 15 and May 3, 1930; *EC*, April 27, 1930.

88. *IR*, February 1, 1930; *SCJ*, January 26, 1930; Solomon Stevenson, Roy S. Perry, and Adrian Bell, Oral History, USI; Berry and Blassingame, *Long Memory*, pp. 169–71.

89. *EP*, January 24, 1930; *EA*, July 23, 1938, July 26, 1940, and May 9, 1941; IRC Study, 1942, p. B18; *EC*, May 18 and 21, 1931; *IR*, May 30, 1931, July 2, 1932, August 5, 1933, July 14, 1934; Franklin, *From Slavery to Freedom*, pp. 386–401; Solomon Stevenson, OH, USI.

90. Kusmer, *A Ghetto Takes Shape*, p. 274.

THIRTEEN

1. *EC*, September 30, 1931; *EA*, 1939–1940, passim; *IR*, March 1, 1934; Helen Best, OH, USI.

Secondary literature on the era includes Richard Dalfiume, "The Forgotten Years' of the Negro Revolution," *Journal of American History*, 55 (1968), 90–106; Harvard Sitkoff, "The Detroit Race Riot of 1943," *Michigan History*, 53(1969), 183–206, and *A New Deal for Blacks: The Emergence of Civil Rights as a National Issue*, volume I: *The Depression Decade* (New York, 1978); Russell Buchanan, *Black Americans in World War II* (Santa Barbara, Calif., 1977); John Morton Blum, *V Was for Victory: Politics and American Culture During World War II* (New York, 1976), pp. 182–220; Richard Polenberg, *War and Society: The United States, 1941–1945* (Philadelphia, 1972), pp. 99–130, 270–71; August Meier and Elliott Rudwick, *Black Detroit and the Rise of the UAW* (New York, 1979).

2. *IR*, November 23, 1935, March 21 and 28, 1936, and January 2 and 22, 1927; *EA*, July 2, 1938, January 14, April 29, May 6, October 8, and December 9, 1939, and April 12 and 19, 1940; *EC*, May 20, 1940.

3. *EJN*, May 9, 1930, July 7, and September 16 and 19, 1931; *EP*, April 25, 1931; *EC*, May 26, 1931.

4. *EJN*, November 4, 1933, and October 22, 1935; *EP*, April 28, 1934, January 3 and December 9, 1935, and July 14, 1937; *EA*, July 2, 1938.

5. *EJN*, October 23, 1935. For a review of the UAW and black Americans, see Meier and Rudwick, *Black Detroit*. Cf. Trotter, *Black Milwaukee*, p. 139, who argues that "proletarianization" increased tensions among black classes. In Evansville the CIO and the black middle class seem to have had harmonious relations.

6. *IRC*, passim; *EC*, February 12, 1935.

7. For example, see Samuel McBride, interview with Darrel E. Bigham, June 26, 1974, and John Caldwell, interview with Darrel E. Bigham, July 13, 1973, OH, USI; Helen Best OH, USI; *EP*, May 28, 1932, and May 7, 1984; *EJN*, June 16, 1936;

IRC, pp. B1–8, 12–14, and 43–44. The desegregation of the Methodist-affiliated Evansville College resulted in part from a campaign led by Rev. David Jordan, pastor of St. John's Methodist Episcopal Church, who petitioned the Methodist bishop about the matter and authored a pamphlet, *The Forward Evansville Movement* (Evansville, 1932).

8. Meier, *Negro Thought in America*, p. 259.

9. *EC*, May 18, 1931; *IR*, May 20, 1931.

10. *IR*, July 2, 1932, July 14, 1934, April 20, 1935; Best OH, USI. Cf. Trotter, *Black Milwaukee*, p. 215. In Evansville many of the NAACP's leaders came from the older elite.

11. *EC*, February 26, 1940; *EA*, July 26, 1938, to July 1, 1939; *IR*, February 18, April 15, June 24, and July 1, 1939; *EP*, December 9, 1937; *IRC*, p. B18.

12. *IR*, April 14, May 12 and 19, and June 4 and 23, 1934; *EP*, September 20, 1931; Meier, *Negro Thought in America*, p. 259.

13. *EA*, July 2, 1938; *IR*, March 3, 1940; Porter OH, USI; and Darrel E. Bigham, "The *Evansville Argus* and Black Evansville, 1938–1943," *Black History News and Notes*, no. 24 (February, 1986), 4–8. The community's resourcefulness was also evident during the devastating flood of late January and early February, 1937. Baptisttown was hit hard by the flood, but its residents had to rely largely on their own resources. Charles Rochelle was named director of the segregated Red Cross Unit No. 10, whose nearly 300 members included WPA and CCC workers, as well as Boy Scouts and members of the Otis Stone Post. Lincoln was the unit's base of operations. Volunteers served 1,000 meals daily at the school and gave 4,200 typhoid inoculations. Lincoln also housed 180 flood refugees from flood waters (*EC*, February 1–7, 1937).

14. Bureau of the Census, Department of Commerce, *Sixteenth Census of the United States: 1940, Population*, volume II: *Characteristics of the Population*, part 2: *Florida-Iowa* (Washington, D.C., 1943), 794, 916, and 918; *EP*, October 17, 1931; *EJN*, May 18, 1934; *SCJ*, September 1, 1935.

15. *EP*, November 4, 1930, November 8, 1932, and November 7, 1934; *IR*, July 28 and September 15, 1934, November 23, 1935, and November 7, 1936.

16. *EA*, April 26 and July 26, 1940.

17. *EC*, Pearl Harbor Commemorative Edition, December 7, 1981, passim; *EP*, January 20, 1942; Madison, *Indiana through Tradition and Change*, pp. 377–96; Max Parvin Cavnes, *The Hoosier Community at War* (Bloomington, Indiana, 1961), pp. 225–65; and *Sunday Courier and Press*, October 31, 1943 (hereafter *SCP*). See also Sixteenth Census, 1940, *Population*, volume II: *Characteristics of the Population*, part 2 (Washington, D.C., 1943), 705, 784, and volume III: *The Labor Force*, part 2 (Washington, D.C., 1943), 794; U.S., Bureau of the Census, Department of Commerce, *Census of Population: 1950*, volume II: *Characteristics of the Population*, part 14, *Indiana* (Washington, D.C., 1952), 53, 265.

In January 1942, for example, the Chrysler assembly and Briggs body plants received contracts to produce shell casings and cartridges, and employment soon increased from 4,000 to 15,000. Chrysler also received a subsequent contract to outfit tanks.

18. *EA*, December 20, 1941. See also ibid., January 2, 1942, and *IR*, December 13 and 20, 1941, and September 5, 1942.

19. *EA*, January 2, 1942.

20. Ibid., January 31, 1942, February 28, 1942, and May 9, 1942.

21. *IR*, July 7, 1945; *EA*, October 17, 1942, June 18, 1943, July 30, 1943, September 3, 1943; *EC*, August 29 and November 17, 1943, and January 22, February 29, and August 10, 1944; *SCP*, January 16, 1944. In July, 1945, 60 percent of the housing units inhabited by Evansville blacks were judged poor or bad.

22. *EA*, September 17, 1938, April 9, 1939, October 18, 1940, and January 31, March 14, April 11, and May 23 and 30, 1941; *SCP*, March 29, 1941; *EC*, March 23, 1941.

23. *EA*, July 11 and 18, 1941, December 6, 13, and 20, 1941, January 2, 10, and 17, 1942; *EC*, June 20, 1940.

24. *EA*, February 14, 1942, March 7, 1942; *EC*, February 26, 1942.

25. *EA*, March 7, 1942, and Madison, *Indiana Through Tradition and Change*, pp. 385–87.

26. *EA*, March 7, 1942, April 10, 1942.

27. Ibid., April 25, and August 15, 1942.

28. Ibid., August 22 and September 26, 1942, and June 11, 1943; *SCP*, June 13, 1943.

29. Quoted in Madison, *Indiana Through Tradition and Change*, pp. 386, 387; *IR*, March 10, 1945. A weak FEPC bill passed the Indiana General Assembly in March, 1945.

30. Cavnes, *The Hoosier Community at War*, pp. 125–27; Darrel E. Bigham, "The Other LaFollette: Charles M. LaFollette and Liberal Republicanism, 1942–1951," in *Their Infinite Variety: Essays on Indiana Politicians* (Indianapolis, 1981), pp. 409–50; *SCP*, January 14, 1945; *EA*, April 4 and May 16, 1942; *EC*, February 29, 1942; *IR*, May 23, 1942. At Chrysler, most blacks worked in the salvage and custodial departments.

31. Cavnes, *The Hoosier Community at War*, p. 127; *EC*, February 29, 1944.

32. Nelson Lichtenstein, *Labor's War at Home: The CIO in World War II* (Ithaca, New York, 1982), pp. 124–26; *EA*, December 13, 1941, January 10, 1942, and July 2 and 23, and September 17, 1943; *IR*, November 21, 1942.

33. Lichtenstein, *Labor's War at Home*, pp. 124–26; Cavnes, *The Hoosier Community at War*, pp. 126–27; *EA*, October 1, 1943.

34. *EA*, January 2, May 30, August 8, and October 10, 1942, and June 11, 1943; *IR*, May 2, 1942.

35. *EA*, February 7, 1942; *IR*, May 2, 1942; *EC*, July 31 and August 8, 1942.

36. *EA*, August 1 and 8, and October 10, 1942; *IR*, September 12, 1942; *SCP*, January 16, 1944; Cavnes, *The Hoosier Community at War*, p. 147. Prospective black welders at the shipyards spent four to six weeks in instruction at Lincoln and then several weeks, eight hours daily, in classes at the yards. The highest ranking clerical worker in the city was Mrs. Bertha Washington, a Fisk graduate, who was the only black interviewer at the USES office (*EA*, November 21, 1942).

37. Office of Defense Health and Welfare Services, Region VI, Chicago, with the Cooperation of National Resources Planning Board, Region IV, Indianapolis, *Report on Evansville War Production Area* (n.p., August 20, 1942), pp. 3–4; *EA*, August 15, September 26, and October 3, 1942, April 23, May 21 and 28, and June 11, 1943; *EC*, September 3, 1943; Federal Security Agency, Office of Community War Services, Region VI, *Report on Evansville, Indiana* (n.p., September, 1943), p. 8.

38. *EC*, February 29, 1944; *EA*, August 10, 1943; FSA, *Report on Evansville*, p. 8; *Republic Aviation News-Indiana Division*, IX (January 19, February 2, and March 9, 1945).

39. *EA*, July 18, September 5 and 25, October 21, November 14, and December 1 and 9, 1942, and March 19, April 2, and June 18, 1943; *SCP*, July 18 and November 19, 1943; *EC*, September 2, 1942, February 5, 1943, and April 4, 1944. Newspaper publicity of activities available for visiting soldiers eventually included the Lincoln USO.

40. *EC*, April 5, 1942; *SCP*, May 3, 1942, July 21, 1943, November 23, 1943, January 22, 1944; *EA*, September 26 and November 21, 1942; *IR*, May 23, 1942.

41. *EA*, February 21, 1941, January 10, 1942; *EC*, March 27, April 10 and 19, and May 17, 1941, November 9, 1943, January 20, February 26, and May 10, 1944, and January 15, June 5, 1945, and October 30 and 31, 1945; Cavnes, *The Hoosier Community At War*, pp. 76, 234–35, 243–44, 248–49, 257, and 265. A group of Lincoln students met with Mayor Manson Reichert in the fall of 1943 to request a community

center, but he did nothing on their petition. At the same time, he was leading a drive to establish a center for white youth. After the war that project materialized.

42. *EA*, October 8, 1942, February 27, 1943, June 23, 1943, and September 3, 1943; *EC*, June 2, 1943, January 25, 1944, February 17, 1944, June 14, 1944, August 5, 1944, and February 9, 1945; Cavnes, *The Hoosier Community at War*, pp. 225–7. The annual tuberculosis rate for blacks during 1939–1944 was three times that for whites.

43. *EC*, August 1, 1940, January 8, 1941, May 28, 1941, May 7 and 9, 1942, October 8, 1942, February 11, 1943, and March 31, 1944; *EA*, February 21, 1941, July 25, 1941, June 6, 1942, September 5, 1942, and August 13, 1943; *SCP*, January 16, 1944; *IR*, November 27, 1943, and March 25, 1944.

44. Cavnes, *The Hoosier Community At War*, p. 149; *EC*, February 22, 1942; *EC*, December 10, 1942, January 30, 1943, October 11 and 21, 1943.

45. Bigham, "The Other LaFollette," p. 427; *EA*, February 27, March 19, April 30, July 2, August 20, and September 17, 1943; *EP*, June 28, 1943; *IR*, July 3, 1943.

46. *EA*, July 30, 1943; Articles of Incorporation, March 19, 1941, VCA. The FSA report on Evansville in September 1943 (pp. 9–10) portrayed the 1942 *IR* study of racial attitudes as optimistic, noting that it overlooked the views of lower-class whites, most of whom were antiblack.

47. Cavnes, *The Hoosier Community at War*, p. 148; *EA*, June 27, 1941, August 8, 1942; *EC*, January 19, 1944, February 25, 1944.

48. *EA*, March 8, 1940, December 5, 1942, June-October, 1943, passim; *EC*, February 7, 1941. Membership in the NAACP was about 350 in mid-1943, according to the *Argus*. Why the *Argus* ceased publication is somewhat of a mystery. No internal clues, other than the fact that the number of pages and advertisements decreased, and the issues appeared irregularly after early 1943. The scarcity of newsprint may have been a factor, but the difficulty of sustaining such a paper with ads from marginal businesses like taprooms—the main sort of black business—was much more important. Holder left Evansville for Los Angeles shortly thereafter. Whether he departed for greener pastures or due to financial problems with the paper, or both, is unclear (Bigham, "The *Evansville Argus*, p. 7). For examples of the historical debate over the impact of the war on the civil rights movement, cf. Franklin, *From Slavery to Freedom*, p. 444, and Sitkoff, *The Struggle for Black Equality, 1954–1980* (New York, 1981), pp. 12–13, with Madison, *Indiana Through Tradition and Change*, pp. 385–88.

49. *EA*, June 20, 1942, March 26, 1943; *EC*, December 7, 1943, October 9, 1944.

50. *EA*, June 11, 1943; *EC*, January 14, 1944, February 28–March 2, 1944; *SCP*, February 27, 1944. The immediate backdrop of the conference was the creation of a governor's commission on race in Illinois, and representatives from Illinois assisted Evansvillians in planning their meeting.

51. *EC*, April 5 and 21, 1944, and February 19 and October 24, 1945; *IR*, May 22 and June 23, 1945; *EP*, November 1–10, 1946. The Roman Catholic Memorial High School opened its doors to blacks in the fall term of 1944, probably the result of the Diocese's having created a black parish three years earlier.

52. *EC*, February 19, 1945.

EPILOGUE

1. Emma Lou Thornbrough, *Since Emancipation: A Short History of Indiana Negroes, 1863–1963* (Indianapolis, 1963), pp. 39, 41, and 60.

2. Ibid., pp. 60–63, and Seventeenth Census, 1950, volume II, part 14, *Indiana*, pp. 59 and 237–39. Trotter, *Black Milwaukee*, p. 147, notes overall improvement of work opportunities for blacks during the war.

3.   Seventeenth Census, *1950 Housing Report*, volume V, part 62, *Block Housing Statistics, Evansville, Indiana* (Washington, D.C., 1953), pp. 4–22.

4.   Sitkoff, *The Struggle for Black Equality*, pp. 10–18. Cf. Trotter, *Black Milwaukee*, who argues the NAACP and other civil rights activities deepened black-white divisions.

INDEX